FATAL TRADEOFFS

FATAL TRADEOFFS

Public and Private
Responsibilities for Risk

W. KIP VISCUSI

New York Oxford
OXFORD UNIVERSITY PRESS

Oxford University Press

Oxford   New York   Toronto
Delhi   Bombay   Calcutta   Madras   Karachi
Kuala Lumpur   Singapore   Hong Kong   Tokyo
Nairobi   Dar es Salaam   Cape Town
Melbourne   Auckland

and associated companies in
Berlin   Ibadan

Copyright © 1992 by Oxford University Press, Inc.

Published by Oxford University Press, Inc.,
198 Madison Avenue, New York, New York 10016-4314

First issued as an Oxford University Press paperback, 1995

Oxford is a registered trademark of Oxford University Press

Library of Congress Cataloging-in-Publication Data
Viscusi, W. Kip.
Fatal tradeoffs :
public and private responsibilities for risk /
by W. Kip Viscusi.
p.   cm.   Includes bibliographical references and index.
ISBN 0-19-507278-2
ISBN 0-19-510293-2 (Pbk.)
1. Risk.   2. Decision-making.   3. Life—Economic aspects.
4. Safety regulations—Economic aspects.   I. Title.
HB615.V57   1992   363.1—dc20   91-36121

9 8 7 6 5 4 3 2

Printed in the United States of America
on acid-free paper

To the Memory of
Evelyn Martin Viscusi

Preface

Recognition of limits has never been a popular undertaking. Politicians who advocate higher taxes are routinely rebuffed at the polls. Similarly, economists who indicate that our resources are constrained and that we cannot achieve absolute levels of health and safety are often viewed as immoral purveyors of the dismal science. Although ideally it would be desirable if we could all adopt a high-minded commitment to a risk-free existence, unfortunately such an objective is beyond our reach.

Tradeoffs inevitably must and will be made in our pursuit of health and safety. The intent of this book is to ascertain how we currently make these tradeoffs and how we should be making them. The focus is on both individual decisions as well as societal choices in the form of regulatory policy. The overall theme of this effort is not that we are engaged in a quest for safety that is being continually thwarted by budgetary constraints; rather, the emphasis is more constructive. We have a number of available opportunities for promoting health and safety. The task we must set out for ourselves is how to best utilize our resources to promote health and safety.

The substantive issues considered within the context of these risk tradeoffs are divided into three categories. Part I of the book addresses individual risk-dollar tradeoffs and the guidelines they provide for setting government policy. Part II assesses the degree to which our responses to risk are rational. Are we making the correct tradeoffs, or are there systematic inadequacies at work that call for government intervention? Part III addresses principles for risk regulation. These concerns are not independent of the risk valuation estimates in Part I, since it is the risk-dollar tradeoffs of individuals in society that establish the price the government should be willing to pay for greater safety. In a democratic society the government should respect citizens' preferences and foster health and safety in a manner that reflects these interests.

This book is a hybrid between a collected-papers volume and an original book manuscript. Some of the material presented here is new, whereas other chapters represent reworked versions of earlier papers. With the exception of Chapter 9, no paper appears in exactly the same form as when originally published. All of the chapters have been rewritten to eliminate overlapping material and to bring the contents of the chapter as up-to-date as possible. The emphasis guiding my selection of these chapters and the writing of them was to focus on my policy-oriented work in the risk area. The implications of research with a more methodological orientation are consequently discussed in a less technical fashion so as to make the book more broadly accessible to students and policymakers.

A READER'S GUIDE

Chapter 1 introduces the substantive themes of the book and indicates the fundamental role that risk tradeoffs necessarily must play not only in our own decisions but also in the government policies that are enacted.

Chapter 2 introduces the conceptual and policy issues that will be the focus of Part I of the book, which deals with risk valuation. What do we mean by the value of life, and what are the concerns raised for society at large with respect to these valuations? The exploration of these issues in Chapter 2 is based in part on material presented in my article of the same title, which appeared in Richard Zeckhauser, ed., *The Strategy of Choice* (Cambridge: MIT Press, 1991). This volume was prepared in honor of Thomas Schelling, an influential early contributor to the value-of-life debate.

Chapter 3 introduces the reader to the principal source of empirical evidence regarding the value of life—labor market analyses of wage-risk tradeoffs. This chapter focuses on two case studies. The first is based on my article "Labor Market Valuations of Life and Limb: Empirical Evidence and Policy Implications," *Public Policy*, Vol. 26 (1978), pp. 359–386. This article presented the first empirical estimates of the value of life that took into account workers' subjective perceptions of the risks as well as potential compensation for other risks of the job, such as nonfatal injury risks. A principal theme of these results is that there is substantial heterogeneity in the value of life. The role of this heterogeneity is explored in detail, drawing on results from my article "Occupational Safety and Health Regulation: Its Impact and Policy Alternatives," in J. Crecine, ed., *Research in Public Policy Analysis and Management: Proceedings of 1979 APPAM Conference*, Vol. 2 (Greenwich: JAI Press, 1981), pp. 281–299. These estimates represent the first findings in the literature pertaining to the heterogeneity of the value of life, which turns out to be quite substantial. Although these studies are more than a decade old, they characterize the general methodology that continues to be used in this literature.

In an effort to provide an update on the value-of-life literature, Chapter 4 provides a comprehensive empirical survey of the entire set of studies in this area. In particular, it includes a new summary of the findings of labor market studies of the value of life, labor market studies of the value of injuries, studies of the value of life from other market contexts, survey studies of the value of life, and survey studies of the value of other health impacts. All these studies have a common focus—assessing the pertinent risk-dollar tradeoff. The market contexts and the methodologies differ, as Chapter 4 indicates.

An important distinction is whether the value-of-life concept in question pertains to prevention of accidents or compensation of accident victims and their survivors after the event. Chapter 5 contrasts the differing theoretical underpinnings of these two different concepts as well as the different empirical magnitudes implied by them. In addition, it explores how market tradeoffs in response to workers' compensation can be used to assess the adequacy of social insurance efforts. I originally presented much of the material in this chapter as the inaugural Risk Economics

Lecture sponsored by the Geneva Association for the Study of the Economics of Insurance. The lecture was originally published under the same title in the *Geneva Papers on Risk and Insurance Theory*, Vol. 15 (1990), pp. 115–139.

If all market decisions were rational, there would be little need for government intervention for risks traded in the market, such as those pertaining to jobs and products. However, a substantial literature has documented the inadequacies in the way in which individuals perceive and respond to risk. These are the issues that are the focus of Part II of the book.

Chapter 6 begins an exploration of these topics, focusing particularly on the implications of biases in risk perception for models of rational learning, notably the Bayesian decision theory model. Although a small portion of the material in this chapter is based on my article "A Bayesian Perspective on Biases in Risk Perception," *Economic Letters*, Vol. 17 (1985), pp. 59–62, considerable other research results not in that paper also appear in Chapter 6.

Chapter 7 presents the results of my model of choice under uncertainty that I developed to account for the anomalous behavior that has been observed. In particular, how must we amend the assumptions of the standard Bayesian expected utility theory model in light of the empirically observed biases in risk perception and inconsistencies in individual decisions? The prospective reference theory model described in Chapter 7 has the advantage over a variety of competing alternative frameworks in that it *predicts* a broad range of aberrational behavior, such as the Allais paradox and the overvaluation of risk changes that achieve complete elimination of the risk. Moreover, this theoretical model can be viewed as a Bayesian extension of a standard expected utility model so that it does less violence to the usual rationality assumptions than other alternative frameworks that have been proposed. An earlier version of this paper appeared as "Prospective Reference Theory: Toward an Explanation of the Paradoxes," *Journal of Risk and Uncertainty*, Vol. 2 (1989), pp. 235–264.

This framework is then applied to various inconsistencies in risk-taking behavior, which are the subject of Chapter 8. An earlier, less extensive version of this paper appeared under the same title in the *American Economic Review*, Vol. 80 (1990), pp. 257–261.

Part III of the book addresses a variety of aspects of risk regulation, where the main task here is for government regulators to establish their own risk-dollar trade-off that is pertinent for government policy. Chapter 9 introduces the broad sets of policy issues once we move to the regulatory policy context. This chapter originally appeared under the same title in *Science*, Vol. 248 (1990), pp. 559–564. This paper was coauthored with Richard J. Zeckhauser, with whom I have had the privilege of collaborating not only on this paper but also on a variety of other endeavors in the risk policy field in the past two decades.

One of the most controversial regulations ever issued was the OSHA cotton dust standard. This regulation was the object of a major political battle, and even more importantly, it is the only regulation that has been given a detailed *ex post* assessment so that we can determine the degree to which the *ex ante* regulatory analysis provided an accurate indication of the benefits and costs actually derived from this measure. The material in Chapter 10 is drawn primarily from two papers: my article "Cotton Dust Regulation: An OSHA Success Story?" *Journal of Policy Analysis and Management*, Vol. 4 (1985), pp. 325–343; and "Uncertainty in Regulatory Analysis: A Retrospective Assessment of the OSHA Cotton Dust Standard," with Paul Kolp, in V. Kerry Smith, ed., *Advances in Applied Microeconomics*, Vol. 4 (Greenwich: JAI Press, 1986), pp. 105–130. Because of the more detailed information we have about the performance of the cotton dust standard, it is also possible to obtain a more precise assessment of the actual impact it has had than we can by simply observing aggregate injury statistics.

Chapter 11, which focuses on the 1972–1975 period, provides a broader overview of the impact of occupational safety and health regulation at the industry level. An earlier version of this chapter appeared as "The Impact of Occupational Safety and Health Regulation," *Bell Journal of Economics*, Vol. 10 (1979), pp. 117–140. In addition to assessing the impact of OSHA on safety in the early 1970s, this chapter also includes a detailed exposition of the econometric framework used to test the effect of OSHA. Moreover, the appendix in this chapter provides a model of the accident-generating process that considers both the role of technological inputs by the firm and safety precautions by workers. An important result of this chapter, which relates in turn to the findings in Chapter 13, is that in situations where government policies are not too stringent one will never observe a counterproductive effect of safety regulations. If there is an offsetting effect on safety of decreased worker precautions in response to the technological requirements of the regulation, the overall net effect will still be favorable except in unusual circumstances.

Chapter 12 provides an update on the assessment of OSHA from 1973 to 1983, and it also provides a current update on the literature. The econometric estimates included in Chapter 12 originally appeared in an article under the same title in *Rand Journal of Economics*, Vol. 17 (1986), pp. 567–580.

Chapter 13 extends these concerns to the product safety context, and in particular provides an illuminating case study of the role of safety precautions for pharmaceutical products. In this case the data on the specific aspects of the precautions, such as whether consumers leave safety caps off bottles, provide a detailed perspective on the behavioral mechanisms that generate the decrease in precautions resulting from government regulations. The material in this chapter is based in large part on my two papers: "The Lulling Effect: The Impact of Child-Resistant Packaging on Aspirin and Analgesic Ingestions," *American Economic Review*, Vol. 74 (1984), pp. 324–327; and "Consumer Behavior and the Safety Effects of Product Safety Regulation," *Journal of Law and Economics*, Vol. 28 (1985), pp. 527–554.

The final chapter provides a comprehensive assessment of the performance of all major health, safety, and environmental regulations in the 1980's, which was a decade of substantial regulatory reform. A modified version of this chapter is scheduled to appear in Martin Feldstein, ed., *American Economic Policy in the 1980's* (Chicago: University of Chicago Press).

The synthesis and rewriting of these chapters and the writing of the original material constituted a substantial task. I am indebted to Dorothy Armento for much of the word processing. Lisa Feinstein handled both the computer work and supporting library research work. I would also like to thank Herbert J. Addison and Mary Sutherland at Oxford University Press, whose advice and enthusiasm have been of immeasurable help. Much of the readability of the manuscript is attributable to the copyediting of Susan Ecklund.

Durham, N.C. W.K.V.
October 1991

Contents

FATAL TRADEOFFS

1

The Fundamental Role of Risk Tradeoffs

THE INEVITABILITY OF TRADEOFFS

Risk is an inherent part of almost every facet of our lives. We encounter risks in our food, transportation, employment, and recreation. These risks are seldom certain prospects. Usually there is some probability less than 1 that we will incur some adverse health outcome. In the case of extremely undesirable consequences, such as severe injury or death, the odds of occurrence are usually quite slim.

On a typical day in the United States, for example, there will be 133 people killed in motor vehicle accidents, 30 workers killed on the job, 98 workers killed off the job, and 56 individuals killed at home.[1] When averaged over the entire population, the odds of an adverse event are often relatively small. Unfortunately, these small probabilities are coupled with catastrophic consequences so that these risks should not be ignored. The task for the individual as well as for society at large is to choose which of these risks we will incur. Nobody intentionally puts his or her life in danger unless there is a strong reason for doing so. In fact, there must be some tradeoff—some offsetting advantage of the risky activity—that leads one to choose to engage in an activity despite its risks.

These tradeoffs are inevitable since we cannot eliminate risk from our lives. The difficulty of reaching a zero-risk society is universal. The United States is roughly in the middle of developed nations in terms of its accident performance. Countries such as England, The Netherlands, West Germany, Sweden, and Australia have lower accidental death rates than does the United States. Other nations, including New Zealand, Poland, Switzerland, and France, have higher accidental death rates.[2] The relatively safer performance of some countries is not always the result of a greater concern with safety but rather a different mix of activities and a different set of opportunities for promoting safety. Countries where automobile transportation is not prevalent, for example, tend to have lower accidental death rates than those that place greater reliance on cars.

The task of selecting the appropriate rate of tradeoff is epitomized by the choice of the size of one's car. The elementary laws of physics imply that small cars will be more hazardous to drive than large cars because they offer less protective bulk to surround the passenger and to resist the impact by another vehicle. The U.S. Department of Transportation estimates that 1,300 lives are lost per year because of the switch from larger cars to the smaller, more fuel-efficient vehicles.[3] The principal drawback of the small cars is that they impose a higher probability of death on their passengers. The main advantage that they offer is a lower fuel bill. Whenever we choose to purchase a smaller car to conserve energy costs, in effect we are making an explicit tradeoff between the expected health impact and greater fuel economy.

The fact that we are making such a decision does not imply that we are irrational or shortsighted. Indeed, it is exactly this kind of thought process one should engage in when making decisions involving risk. If we were to purchase a car that was risk-free, inevitably we would be restricted to driving vehicles that closely resembled tanks. These risk-free cars would be slow and expensive to operate. Clearly, we do not want to go to these extremes. Indeed, when individuals have been offered the opportunity to purchase greater car safety at a substantial cost, they have often foregone the opportunity to do so. Some cars offer air bags, and in some cases air bags for both the passenger as well as the driver, but automobile dealers have not been overwhelmed with a surge in consumer demand for these safer cars. Antilock brakes are another beneficial safety feature that many consumers have found attractive to purchase, but the great majority have not.

We cannot say in the abstract whether these decisions are sound. If individuals were fully informed of the consequences of their decisions and made rational choices, then in a democratic society we should respect these choices. However, it is not clear that consumers always understand the implications of the various safety devices that are available. We know that consumers should value safety to some extent and that an absolute level of safety cannot be achieved. What is less clear-cut is where we should stop in terms of the optimal level of safety. In effect, what we are searching for is the appropriate rate of tradeoff that we should strike between added safety and greater cost. The quest for this appropriate tradeoff rate is the fundamental task not only of those who make risky decisions but also of risk-regulation agencies that expend society's resources to promote health and safety.

The overall theme of this book focuses on a series of related questions pertaining to these tradeoffs. At the level of the individual, we want to know what tradeoffs people make when they address these safety and health risk decisions. These tradeoffs in effect set the price that people are willing to pay for greater safety. Individuals' willingness to bear risk also establishes the price firms must pay for marketing hazardous products.

The second class of issues that will be explored is the errors in the tradeoffs that people make with respect to risk. To what extent are there systematic biases in decisions involving risk? If there are such biases, they will frequently provide a rationale for government intervention either to provide information or to regulate the risk directly.

The third set of issues pertains to the design of regulatory policy. Even if we agree upon the importance of government involvement in promoting safety, we must also select the stringency of the government's promotion of safety. For example, in the case of enhancing automobile safety, the government could potentially require that all cars have air bags, antilock brakes, and every other technologically feasible safety device. The fact that the government can mandate all of these safety improvements does not mean that it should. The key issue is whether the merits of doing so would be in society's best interests. Our search for pertinent reference points will inevitably take us back to market contexts where individuals have decided the terms of trade that they believe are appropriate.

The need for some limits is an inevitable consequence of our budget constraints. Suppose that it were possible to make expenditures to eliminate all of the 94,500 accidental deaths that occur in the United States every year.[4] If we were to devote the entire U.S. gross national product to eliminating these deaths, we would be able to spend an average of only $55 million per death prevented.[5] Let us assume that we spent no money on anything else, including food, health care, housing, or any of the other current components of our consumer expenditures. Suppose we also neglect all other health outcomes and attempt to avert only fatalities. Even though we could afford to spend an average of $55 million per life, there would still be 9 million disabling injuries per year as well as millions of health-related illnesses. The finite nature of our resources requires that we make the difficult decisions of rationing our expenditures across the health and safety opportunities.

The size of the risk alone does not govern these decisions. Scientists estimate that our risk of death from asteroid impact is 1/6,000.[6] This risk level from a "doomsday rock" dwarfs many of the risks that are major objects of individual and public concern. For example, the average fatality risk faced by an American worker is 1/10,000. The greater threat from an asteroid's impact than the average job risk does not imply that we should ignore risks on the job as being too trivial to merit our attention. The real issue is whether steps can be taken to reduce these risks. If so, will these measures produce sufficient risk benefits to justify taking such actions? We may be able to do very little at the present time to reduce the death risks from asteroids, but we can make substantial progress in altering the health and safety risks of jobs. The fundamental issue is not the level of the risk but whether we can decrease the risks and whether the cost of these efforts is warranted by the risk reduction.

These tradeoffs do not always involve money. An unusual case that developed in 1991 involved a potential cancer cure, the drug Taxol. Some scientists viewed this drug as the most promising cure for cancer that had been identified in at least a decade. Although the drug was still undergoing clinical testing, the available evidence indicated the striking success of Taxol in combating several forms of cancer.[7]

Unfortunately, it will not be possible to synthesize Taxol artificially for several more years. To produce this drug presently, one must utilize the bark of a type of tree from the Pacific Northwest United States known as the Pacific yew tree. To produce enough Taxol to treat one cancer patient requires up to six, 100-year-old Pacific yew trees of a diameter of ten inches or larger, and in order to be able to harvest these trees, many other surrounding trees are removed in the process. The conflict here is not saving lives versus money but rather environmental preservation over potential lifesaving benefits. In this situation a variety of established environmental groups have thrown their support to the trees rather than the cancer patients, and a group known as the Native Yew Conservation Council has formed a lobby on behalf of the trees.

The policy question that has emerged is the extent to which lives should be sacrificed to preserve trees that most Americans did not know existed. Moreover, since it takes 100 years for these trees to be large enough to produce Taxol, even if we decide to produce the drug we must also determine how fast we will deplete our stock of these trees. Should we cut down the trees now or defer such action until the properties of the drug produced from the Pacific yews are better known? Although confronting such issues is not a task that government risk regulators can readily resolve, these are the kinds of fundamental questions that they must address daily and that society at large must be prepared to think about in a systematic manner.

Our resources are constrained, and we cannot eliminate all risks. But we can approach these risks sensibly so as to ensure reasonable levels of safety given the justifiable importance that we should attach to health and safety outcomes as well as the limits imposed by our available resources.

THE CHARACTER OF INDIVIDUAL TRADEOFFS

The basic elements of this economic approach to risk were formulated over two centuries ago by Adam Smith, who observed that workers will demand extra compensation for their jobs if they are required to face added risk. This relationship is no secret to the fire fighters sent to quell the fires in the oil fields of Kuwait in 1991; these workers earned $500,000 per year for their hazardous employment.[8] Chapter 2 outlines the essential elements of this methodology, from the standpoint of both individual and societal valuations of safety. Perhaps the most striking aspect of our economic valuation of health and safety is that the value of risk reduction is quite substantial and will lead to aggressive efforts to control risk. Our concern here is with statistical lives rather than specific identified lives at risk.

When we talk about establishing valuations of risk, we are not limiting our concerns to the monetary consequences alone. The value of improved automobile safety is not simply the earnings loss that will be prevented by greater safety, although that will obviously be an important safety benefit. Rather, what we want is an overall assessment of the merits of improved safety relative to other product attributes such as higher cost.[9]

Moreover, when we are assessing these tradeoff values, what we want to determine are the valuations reflected in an individual's decision rather than what some external observer believes these tradeoffs should be. A critical component of this process is that we are dealing with risk-dollar tradeoffs for risks that are of small magnitude, not certain health effects. Our willingness to pay for small reductions in risk will be quite different than the amount we would pay to avoid certain death. This attitude toward incremental reductions in risk is what is pertinent from the standpoint of the choices we make as well as the policies that government agencies must adopt.

Choosing how far we will go either as individuals or as a society toward reducing these expected adverse health outcomes is an inevitable consequence of our limited resources. We could choose not to talk about these issues because of their sensitivity. Indeed, some analysts have proposed that government agencies make these tradeoffs but do not publicly discuss them because of their controversial nature. This back-room approach to lifesaving issues is reminiscent of the comment

Economist editor Walter Bagehot made with regard to British royalty: "Above all things our royalty is to be reverenced, and if you begin to poke about it you cannot reverence it."

In the view of some, analyzing lifesaving issues turns something that should be reverenced into an economic commodity. We should, of course, recognize the inherent sensitivities involved in this area, but that should not be an absolute barrier to critical thought. Consideration of risk decisions need not devalue the lives at risk. Indeed, confronting such choices is an inescapable component of our lives. Risk-protection decisions will be made daily, even if we choose not to analyze their consequences. In all likelihood, the price we will pay in terms of lives lost and injuries that could have been prevented by undertaking a sound economic analysis of the merits of alternative policies outweighs the degree of discomfort that we might experience because of the inherently controversial nature of this decision process.

Risk-dollar tradeoffs reflect individual preferences that will differ across individuals, just as do tastes and preferences for other economic goods. The search for the risk-dollar tradeoff, which in the case of fatality risks comes under the terminology "value of life," is not an elusive quest for some natural constant such as "e" or "π." Rather, we should be concerned with ascertaining the distribution of values that are pertinent to the preferences of the individuals whose lives are at risk.

The value that will be placed on greater safety will differ across individuals and across countries. One important relationship of this type is the positive relationship between individual wealth and the value one places on health status. Indeed, it may be largely because of this greater wealth that there has been a dramatic surge of interest in health and safety regulation issues in the latter part of the twentieth century, even though the overall level of our safety has been steadily improving throughout this century.[10]

The role of societal wealth often has fundamental implications for the stringency of risk-regulation policies. If the evaluation of risks increases with one's wealth, then we should require higher levels of safety for products targeted at higher-income consumers. Safety standards similarly should be tighter for the developed countries than for the developing nations. Recognition of the role of societal wealth and the increases in wealth that will occur over time also should make our policies forward-looking. If we want to leave future generations with an efficient level of safety and environmental quality, then we should place a greater value on the benefits to these generations than we would on our current welfare because of the increased value of health and environmental benefits that these future beneficiaries of today's policies will have. We must, of course, discount these future values to reflect their temporal remoteness, but the benefit values being discounted will be greater than our current valuations.

Although thinking about risk-dollar tradeoffs is often an instructive exercise, ultimately we must grapple with what the tradeoff amounts are and what they should be for society at large. The principal approach that has been adopted by economists who examine the risky choices that people actually make is to infer the rates of tradeoff based on risky decisions. Chapter 3 of the book presents the results of two empirical studies to illustrate the methodology that typifies this approach. The object of the analysis is to ascertain the wage compensation workers require to accept added risks posed by their jobs.

In some cases this hazard compensation is readily apparent. Elephant handlers at the Philadelphia Zoo receive an extra $1,000 compensation annually because elephants are said to pose a risk to handlers they do not like. Fire fighters in Kuwait, stuntmen, and professional football players also receive substantial compensation in return for the risks they face. In a more typical case, the risks are not as extreme and the compensation is less apparent. However, with the aid of statistical analysis of wage patterns for workers, labor economists have been able to isolate the wage premium for unit risk.

The amount of compensation received per statistical death is known as the value of life. These amounts run in the millions of dollars per statistical death—amounts far in excess of an individual's lifetime earnings. Moreover, the estimates of these risk-dollar tradeoffs vary in predictable fashion with the character of the workers and their jobs. Workers who gravitate to higher-risk jobs, for example, exhibit a greater willingness to bear risk than workers who are attracted to the safer positions. In particular, the estimated values of life that these workers on risky jobs have is substantial—on the order of roughly $1 million in current prices—but it is far less than workers in safer forms of employment.

The empirical estimates discussed in Chapter 3 constitute but a small segment of what has become a substantial literature on the valuation of risks to life and health. Chapter 4 provides a comprehensive survey of the literature on the valuation of risks of death, injury, and illness. The studies performed include analyses of the attitudes toward risks not only in the United States, but also in countries such as the United Kingdom, Canada, Australia, and Japan.

Evidence on the value of life comes primarily from a variety of market sources. Although the great majority of studies are based on the labor market, because of the availability of extensive employment data, other contexts have been analyzed as well. In particular, economists have assessed the risk-dollar tradeoffs reflected in automobile speed choice, seat belt use, smoke detector purchase, property values, and cigarette smoking decisions. Moreover, even in the job case, there has been an attempt to consider more than risks to life, as there has also been a series of studies that have assessed the value of nonfatal job injuries as well.

Ultimately, there is a limit to the ability of market data to address the valuations of different kinds of risks. In the case of some job risks, particularly those involving illness and disease, we lack the extensive data needed to make the link between the risk and the wage compensation. Other classes of risk are not the object of market transactions. We would like to determine the valuation of health outcomes such as cancer, chronic bronchitis, or even the common cold. However, to do so, we must utilize data other than market information. The approach that analysts have selected is to construct surveys that attempt to replicate the choices individuals would make in a market context if there were a market process involving these health impacts. These surveys are intended to present individuals with choices that will elicit the risk-dollar tradeoffs they are willing to make with respect to these other classes of health outcomes, thus extending the breadth of our knowledge concerning the health risk tradeoffs. Chapter 4 surveys this literature as well.

These tradeoff values serve as a measure of our *ex ante* valuation of risk. In other contexts we are interested in the appropriate amount of *ex post* compensation that we would choose to provide after a fatality or a serious injury. Chapter 5 analyzes the distinction between these two approaches to valuing risks. Obtaining an understanding of the differences between these measures illustrates the critical role of the context of the decision process in the valuation process. In particular, the valuation of risks to life and health will be different in situations in which we are preventing the adverse outcome as opposed to compensating victims.

Ascertaining the appropriate amount of *ex post* compensation requires some knowledge of the structure of utility functions. The empirical evidence reviewed in Chapter 5 suggests that serious injuries not only lower one's welfare but also affect one's ability to derive benefit from consumption expenditures. In particular, severe job injuries reduce one's marginal utility of income, whereas less serious consumer injuries can be treated as monetary loss equivalents. This distinction affects not only the optimal amount of insurance one would choose to provide but also influences our understanding of the preference mechanisms that underlie the risk-dollar tradeoffs from the standpoint of deterrence.

The estimation process that determines the shape of utility functions requires that one observe more than one point on any given individual's constant expected utility locus. Otherwise, we could not determine the underlying character of individual preferences, since all we would know is the local risk-dollar tradeoffs. The availability of survey data on individual valuations of different levels of risks enables us to confront more refined issues such as this so that surveys not only increase the range of health outcomes one can analyze but also expand the subtlety of the economic questions one can ask.

ARE TRADEOFFS RATIONAL?

In some instances, individuals may make the wrong tradeoff because of either a misunderstanding of the risk or a failure to act in a rational manner. The most well-documented biases in these decisions stem from misassessment of probabilities. Fortunately, these biases tend to be systematic, so that we have some knowledge of the types of errors people usually make. For example, there is a pronounced tendency to overestimate low-probability events and to underestimate larger risks that we face. As indicated in Chapter 4, one can demonstrate how such biases influence our understanding of the observed risk-dollar tradeoffs in the marketplace. Perceptional errors affect how individuals make choices under uncertainty as well as the degree to which government intervention is warranted to address these errors. Biases could be in either direction, some of which imply overreaction to risk and others that suggest inattention to risk. Before we can embark on a strategy to control risk, we should know the direction of error as well as its extent.

Chapters 6, 7, and 8 are devoted to these various kinds of risk-perception errors.

Biases of this type are not only possible but would be predicted as part of a rational but imperfect learning process. Moreover, they help explain a variety of widely observed phenomena. We overreact to some risks, such as newly discovered carcinogens, and underreact to others. Individuals fail to use seat belts to the degree that is warranted based on the benefits and costs of these protective devices.[11] This inattention to risk is a consequence of the character of individual risk perceptions and can be traced to the role of imperfect risk information. Individuals need not be "irrational" to err in this manner, as we will show in Chapter 6. The fact that such behavior may be reasonable does not, however, imply that they are correct in making these errors. Systematic inattention to risk will lead to excessive societal risk levels.

These inadequacies in choices provide a fundamental rationale for government intervention, as does the character of many health, safety, and environmental risks. Many of these hazards take the form of externalities that are not the object of any explicit market transaction but instead are imposed involuntarily. The fact that market processes fail, however, does not imply that society should necessarily eliminate all of these risks. The reference point that is appropriate from an efficiency standpoint is to replicate what would have occurred had markets functioned fully efficiently.

SOCIAL REGULATION OF RISK

Chapter 9 introduces the societal choice issues and provides an overall perspective on the choices that must be made. The task for society is to formulate a reasonable risk policy given the limitations of individual choice. Unfortunately, these same inadequacies in our behavior toward risk also contribute to the political pressures for government action in a democratic society. Many of the same biases in individual decisions are mirrored in the government policies targeted at risks. Individuals' propensities to overestimate low-probability events and to overreact to newly discovered hazards create pressures for similar biases in government efforts, which frequently veer from the extremes of excessive complacency to inordinate attention to the newly publicized risks.

The overriding principle that should provide the basis for government policy is that we must strike an appropriate and reasonable balance between risks and the costs to reduce them. The best starting point for such an assessment is the valuation that individuals who benefit from these policies place on the risk reductions. Thus, there is a critical link between the individual valuation findings in the first portion of the volume and the guidelines for government policy that constitute the latter part of the book.

Chapter 10 presents a case study of a particularly controversial job safety regulation, the cotton dust standards of the Occupational Safety and Health Administration (OSHA). This regulation was the object of a U.S. Supreme Court decision as well as an extensive political debate before its adoption. It has also been the object of the most thorough *ex post* analysis of what actually occurred as a result of the regulation, which makes it a valuable case study in regulatory economics.

The purpose of this regulation was to reduce the cotton dust exposure of textile workers who suffered a lung disease known as byssinosis as a result of these exposures. Much of the controversy of this regulation stemmed from the magnitude of the price paid for better health. Examination of the costs of the standard indicate that the price for these health benefits was substantial indeed—on the order of several hundred thousand dollars per temporary disability prevented.

This regulation embodied other kinds of tradeoffs as well. In particular, achieving the mandated reduction in cotton dust exposures required that firms adopt new technologies. However, these new and unfamiliar technological improvements led to a temporary increase in accident rates as workers had to become accustomed to the new technologies introduced in the textile mills. Job accidents rose temporarily after the new safety standards took effect. There was, however, the expected improvement in health risks resulting from the regulation, as cotton dust exposures dropped substantially and worker turnover, much of which was health-related, diminished as well.

Perhaps in part because of the political saliency of this particular regulation, we have observed fairly dramatic effects from it. The norm for U.S. job safety regulation does not reflect such pronounced impacts. Firms face a tradeoff when they consider how they will respond to a regulation. Firms will not choose to comply with the regulation unless the expected costs associated with noncompliance exceed the expected costs of meeting the regulatory standard. The initial wave of U.S. job safety regulation imposed considerable burdens on firms but created few financial incentives for firms to take action. When faced with the prospect of revamping workplace technologies or being exposed to a negligible risk of government sanctions, the overwhelming majority of firms chose to flout the regulations.

The evidence in Chapter 11 documents the small effect of the initial wave of the Occupational Safety and Health Administration regulations. In the early 1970s there is no evidence of any statistically significant effect of these regulations either on job safety or on firms' investments in safety.

The absence of such an influence is not unexpected, and it reflects a quite rational tradeoff on the part of the affected firms. The chance that any firm would see an OSHA inspector, which is the key step before any sanctions could ever be levied, was comparable to the chance that one would view Halley's comet in any given year. If one were unlucky enough to encounter an OSHA inspector, the result would be fines that were dwarfed by the cost of introducing the mandated safety devices. When averaged across the entire United States, the average OSHA penalty per establishment in the United States was only $1.52 per year.

Whereas government regulation imposed negligible fines—on the order of less than $10 million per year—the safety incentives created by the market and by social insurance were considerably greater. The wage compensation U.S. workers receive for risks now costs firms over $100 billion per year—a price tag that provides powerful incentives for firms to improve their safety performance and reduce their wage costs. Similarly, the mandated social insurance compensation for workers under the U.S. workers' compensation system imposes insurance premium costs on firms in excess of $30 billion per year. Especially for large firms, these premiums are linked to the firms' safety performance, providing incentives for safety improvements. Indeed, estimates of the effect of workers' compensation on death risks indicates that workplace fatality risks would be 20 to 30 percent higher in the absence of the workers' compensation incentives.[12]

Financial incentives do matter, and even from a regulatory standpoint they are a driving force in their promotion of safety. It is for that reason that some economists have suggested that regulatory agencies adopt an injury tax approach to promoting safety rather than relying on the command-and-control regulatory mechanisms.[13] In the same vein, there has been increased enthusiasm in the environmental context for various pollution-permit schemes and pollution-penalty approaches.

The inadequacy of the financial incentives and the need for increases in the expected costs of noncompliance have been recognized by government officials as well. In the late 1970s and early 1980s, OSHA increased the targeting of its inspections at the high-risk enterprises and undertook a more vigorous enforcement effort. The result is that there is now evidence of a significant impact of these regulations on safety, although the magnitude of these effects is not great. Overall, workers' compensation has roughly ten times the effect on worker safety as do OSHA regulations.

Ultimately, it is the financial incentives created for safety that will affect the tradeoffs that firms make in the promotion of safety. Whether regulatory standards or financial penalty schemes are more effective in creating these incentives depends in large part on the magnitude of the incentives being generated. Regulatory standards are only absolute to the extent that they will be enforced absolutely. To date, they have not.

Chapter 13 reviews the performance of consumer product safety regulation. Analysis of the performance of these regulations is particularly instructive in illuminating the mechanisms by which regulations will have their influence. Government regulations do not mandate outcomes; they generally provide incentives for firms to alter the technological inputs to safety. The overall safety performance of the economy will be a consequence of the interaction of the characteristics of the product with the decisions of the individuals who use it. If product users alter their behavior in response to the changes mandated by product safety regulations, then the goals of the regulation may be undercut.

The example explored in Chapter 13 is consumers' response to the introduction of safety caps for medicines and other products. Consumers also must make a risk tradeoff. How much safety precaution should we exercise? Should, for example, all medicines be kept in a locked cabinet, or is a more casual approach warranted by the level of the risk?

The results of the safety cap regulations are consistent with what I term the "lulling effect." These caps are frequently and, somewhat optimistically, referred to as being "childproof." There is evidence that individuals may have been lulled into a false sense of security by these caps, leading to diminished safety precautions. The reduction in the perceived efficacy of the caps has altered the risk-effort tradeoff so that consumers are more lax in taking precautions.

In addition, the effort component of this tradeoff is often quite high. The caps are difficult for consumers to conquer, particularly elderly consumers and those with arthritis. Individuals who have found the caps difficult to use have left the caps off the bottles, leading to a rash of open-bottle poisonings.

The net result has been that there is no demonstrable effect of these regulations on the products that have been targeted for the safety caps. Indeed, there is some evidence of an adverse spillover effect of the safety cap regulations on related products, for which consumers also appear to have reduced their precautionary behavior. The presence of such effects does not imply that one should abandon all product safety regulations, only that we should understand all of the diverse mechanisms at work and ensure that we incorporate this understanding in the policies that we formulate.

The lessons that we can derive from our experiences with the social regulation efforts go beyond these particular case studies. In Chapter 14 I provide an overview of the entire set of risk and environmental regulations that have been in place for the past two decades. The chief issue that has been involved in all of these regulations has been that of striking the appropriate regulatory tradeoff. The legislative mandates of the regulatory agencies have typically been highly restrictive, dictating that the agency not balance benefits and costs. In some extreme cases the agency is prohibited from considering costs at all. The result is that the tradeoffs we are making often differ widely across agencies, leading to opportunities for promoting greater safety at less cost by reallocating our priorities across different safety efforts.

The major task of the regulatory reform efforts instituted by the White House over the past two decades has been to foster greater balance in these risk-regulation policies. The character of these reform efforts has evolved substantially over that period. Under the Nixon and Ford administrations, the main effort was to simply require regulatory agencies to assess the costs and benefits of their efforts so that we knew what the effects were on the economy. The next wave of reform took place under the Carter administration, where there was an attempt to require that regulations be cost-effective. We should not pursue one regulatory strategy if an alternative policy could achieve the same risk reduction benefits with less cost. Under the Reagan and Bush administrations, there has been an effort to achieve a greater balancing of benefits and costs and to impose a benefit-cost test.

Unfortunately, some of the policies that were pursued under the guise of regulatory reform are not those that efficiency-oriented economists would embrace. Much remains to be done to put our regulations on a sounder footing in order to achieve all that we should with our regulatory expenditures.

Comparison of the efficacy of various agencies' regulatory efforts suggests the widely divergent tradeoffs involved. In its efforts to improve airline safety, the Federal Aviation Administration has promulgated a series of regulations, each of which saves lives at less than $1 million per life. In contrast, agencies such as OSHA and the Environmental Protection Agency (EPA) have mandated many regulations with price tags far in excess of $100 million per life. Indeed, the current leader in profligacy is a regulation of formaldehyde exposures with a price tag of $72 billion per statistical life. Recall that even if we expended our entire GNP on averting accidents, the upper limit of what we could spend would be $55 million per life. The cost-per-expected-life-saved numbers are quite sobering, particularly as these agencies identify more opportunities for regulation.

The most optimistic development is that the same kinds of risk-dollar tradeoffs reflected in individuals' risk-taking decisions have now been embodied in the benefit assessments of regulatory agencies. Government agencies no longer equate the value of saving an expected human life with the value of earnings one would have had. Instead, the kinds of risk-dollar tradeoffs that we explore throughout this book now provide the basis for benefit assessment.

There has also been growing enthusiasm for adopting market-oriented policies that will promote risk-dollar tradeoffs on a decentralized basis. Schemes that will establish price mechanisms for environmental pollution are chief among these. One example where such an approach has been used has involved the trading of pollution rights for airborne lead emissions. It is also noteworthy that, as Chapter 14 documents, the improvements in lead pollution have been among the most dramatic of any class of pollutants. The reduction of lead pollution represents a remarkable success story in terms of the real achievements of environmental regulation in enhancing individual health.

Our quest for determining the appropriate tradeoff between risks and costs will continue so long as our concerns with health and safety remain. By always establishing a balance between how much we value these benefits and the costs they impose on society, we will be fostering the policies that will promote the best interests of those whom we are trying to protect.

NOTES

1. National Safety Council (1988), p. 11.
2. National Safety Council (1990), p. 21.
3. *Product Safety & Liability Reporter*, Vol. 18, No. 38 (September 21, 1990), pp. 1054–1055.
4. National Safety Council (1990), p. 1.
5. Council of Economic Advisors (1991), p. 286. All figures are for 1989 to ensure comparability with the risk data.
6. See the *New York Times*, June 18, 1991, p. B5.
7. See the *New York Times*, May 13, 1991, p. A1.
8. See the *Wall Street Journal*, March 27, 1991, p. A1.
9. This valuation should reflect other nonpecuniary influences as well.
10. National Safety Council (1990), pp. 26–27.
11. See Arnould and Grabowski (1981).
12. See Moore and Viscusi (1990a).
13. See, for example, Robert S. Smith (1976).

PART I

**Risk Valuation:
Concepts and Estimates**

2

Strategic and Ethical Issues in the Valuation of Life

2.1 VALUATION METHODOLOGY

Traditionally, issues pertaining to the valuation of human life had been treated as strictly moral concepts, not matters to be degraded through economic analysis of choices and tradeoffs. However, as Schelling (1968) observed, substantial insight can be obtained by assessing the benefits of risk reduction in the same manner as we value other economic effects. In general, the appropriate benefit measure for risk reductions is the willingness to pay to produce the particular outcome.[1] Similarly, the selling price for changes in risk establishes the value for risk increases.

In the usual risk policy decision—for example, determining what safety characteristics to provide in automobiles—the policy result to be assessed is an incremental risk reduction rather than a shift involving the certainty of life or death. This need to think in terms of statistical lives as opposed to certain lives defines the main character of our choice problem. In particular, the matter of interest is individuals' valuation of lotteries involving life and death.

Addressing value-of-life issues by focusing on our attitudes toward lotteries involving small risks of death provides a methodology for formulating these issues in a sound economic manner. This approach also avoids the more difficult task of confronting the valuation of lives at risk of certain death, which understandably raises a different class of ethical issues. Nevertheless, even when only small risks are involved, the concerns involved remain inherently sensitive, and we should not be cavalier in making these judgments.

Because of the central role of individual preferences, individual values of life may differ considerably, just as do other tastes. A central concern is who is valuing the life and for what reason. A particular life may have one value to the individual, another to his or her family, and still another to society at large.

As the willingness-to-pay methodology has become better understood, the controversy surrounding the entire line of research on the value of life has diminished. Much of the early opposition to the economic valuation of life stemmed from the reliance on value-of-life concepts that had been developed to inform decisions on compensating survivors rather than on reducing risks to life. Initial efforts consequently sought to value life using the human capital approach. In particular, analysts such as Rice and Cooper (1967) and Mishan (1971) estimated values of life based on various measures of earnings. This technique, which continues to be used throughout the United States court system to assess damages for personal injury, addresses only the financial losses involved. The death of a family member, for example, would impose a financial loss on survivors, which would be measured as the present value of the income the deceased would have earned net of taxes and his or her consumption. Similarly, the present value of taxes the deceased would have paid represents the financial loss to the rest of society.[2]

Value-of-life issues raise a series of questions for research. The first is how we should think about these issues methodologically. The second class of issues involves estimating the risk-dollar tradeoffs that, in effect, represent the value of life. Third, how can individuals make sound decisions regarding the risks they face? Finally, what approach should guide choices when society is making protective decisions?

Although the role of altruism complicates all policy valuations, the final class of questions becomes most problematic when we depart substantially from the private market analogy. When the government is providing risk reductions to a group with similar preferences and similar risks, then matters are relatively straightforward. However, if preferences differ because of wealth, if individuals cannot make fully rational decisions with respect to a risk, or if the parties affected are not currently alive, the choice process involves a greater leap because we become less confident of how hypothetical markets would function if they were perfect.

This chapter will explore the development of the value-of-life methodology and its broader ramifications. I begin with a brief introduction to the procedure by which we derive a value of life, which will be explored in detail in subsequent chapters. Although private values of life are an important matter of interest, in practice value-of-life discussions arise principally in the context of public decision making, which is the focus of the following section.

A continuing theme in the value-of-life literature has been the role of ethical and strategic issues in decision making. Although we can analyze decisions involving the value of life as we would any other economic choice, many of the more intriguing aspects of the topic are related to the distinctive and highly sensitive concerns that may arise. One such set of concerns has to do with rationality and self-control. In particular, if individuals do not make sound decisions on their own behalf, what role should society play in influencing these decisions? Moreover, if we are going to intervene when there is an apparent lack of self-control, how do we identify the "authentic self"?[3] I extend the domain of these considerations from the individual and his or her alter ego to the mother and her unborn child. If we do not fully trust the decisions individuals make on their own behalf, to what extent should we allow mothers to make decisions on behalf of the fetus, especially if these decisions pose a risk to the unborn child?

The recognition of disparities in wealth poses particularly controversial issues for valuation of life. The ramifications of individual wealth depend on the context—for example, are we talking about rich and poor groups who are alive today, or future generations that may differ in wealth from our own? I conclude this chapter with observations about the appropriate role of economics in framing value-of-life decisions.

2.2 THE VALUE OF STATISTICAL LIVES

The ultimate purpose of the value-of-life literature is to provide some basis for sensitive social decisions. Before investigating how society should make decisions involving the saving of lives, we will first assess whether we can establish an empirical reference point for making tradeoffs involving life and health. In the absence of such empirical information, there will be few operational contexts in which economic analysis of value-of-life decisions is instructive. Some sense of the order of magnitude of the value-of-life estimates will also assuage many of the concerns expressed about the morality of this line of work. If the appropriate economic value of life is over $1 million, resistance to this methodology will probably be much less than if the estimate is, say, $200,000. Chapters 3 and 4 will provide a more complete examination of this literature.

The basic approach to establishing a value of risk reduction parallels the technique for benefit assessment for other contexts. If, for example, one were attempting to assign benefits to the building of a new public parking garage, the appropriate benefit measure would be the sum of the willingness to pay of all the residents for this new facility. In a similar manner, when assessing the benefits of risk reduction, the pertinent value is the willingness to pay for the risk reduction. What we are purchasing with our tax dollars is not the certainty of survival. Rather, it is the incremental reduction in the probability of an adverse outcome that might otherwise have affected some random member of our community. What is at stake is consequently statistical lives, not certain identified lives.

In the case of risks that we must bear, the concern shifts from our willingness to pay for added safety to the amount that we require to bear the risk, which is usually termed our willingness-to-accept amount. For sufficiently small changes in risk, the willingness-to-pay and willingness-to-accept amounts should be approximately equal, but in practice they are not. As is explored in Chapters 7 through 9, there is often an alarmist reaction to increases in risk above the accustomed level so that willingness-to-accept amounts may dwarf the willingness-to-pay amounts if we respond irrationally to the risks.

In each case, the underlying concern is with a lottery involving a small probability of an adverse outcome. Our attitude toward this lottery defines the terms of trade that we believe are appropriate, where these terms of trade represent our risk-dollar tradeoff.

Broome (1978) suggests, however, that if lives have an infinite value, then use of value-of-life lotteries cannot provide us with a solution to this intractable problem. This observation does not indicate a flaw in our methodology. An infinite value of life would be mirrored in an infinite value for a lottery involving a risk of death. The fact that we make a myriad of decisions involving life and death—including choosing the animal fats we ingest and the risky but fuel-efficient cars that we drive—indicates that we are willing to trade off small risks of death for other valued objectives. The approach I will take here will adopt the value-of-life lottery methodology recognizing that this formulation structures the difficult choices but does not eliminate them.

Consider a specific example. Suppose that our municipality could relocate its landfill to decrease the fatality risk from our drinking water by 1/100,000. Suppose that you were willing to pay $20 for a risk reduction of this magnitude. The summary manner in which economists have characterized the terms of trade reflected in this tradeoff is the following. Suppose that there are 100,000 people at risk. On average, one expected life will be saved by the relocation of the landfill. As a group, the 100,000 residents are willing to pay $20 million ($20 × 100,000) for the one expected life that is saved. The economic value of this one expected life saved is consequently $2 million. This result is frequently termed the "value of life," even though this terminology implies in a somewhat misleading manner that what we are valuing is certain lives rather than statistical lives involving very small probabilities.

Another way of conceptualizing this calculation is to view it as simply ascertaining the value we are willing to pay per unit risk. Viewed in this manner, one estimates the value of a statistical life by dividing our willingness to pay for added safety ($20) by the risk increment that is involved (1/100,000), with the result being the same—$2 million.

It is important to recognize exactly what these tradeoffs mean. They only reflect attitudes toward small probabilities. They do not imply that we would accept certain death in return for $2 million, or even that we would accept a .5 probability of death for $1 million. Nor should we confuse these amounts with the appropriate level of compensation to our survivors should we die, as these amounts will generally be quite different, as will be explored in Chapter 5.

The pertinence of risk-dollar tradeoffs to valuing small changes in risk is not a substantial limitation. Most of the risks we face involve relatively small chances of death and other severe outcomes. Moreover, if we are faced with much greater risks, then we would still adopt the same willingness-to-pay approach except that the rate of tradeoff that was present for a very small risk reduction may not be what we would select if the risk change were quite different.

The relative orders of magnitude reflected in the estimates of the value of life are considerable. The empirical evidence on the value of life, which is reviewed in Chapters 3 and 4, suggests that the value of life of workers who have selected themselves into very high-risk jobs is on the order of $1 million, whereas workers in more representative jobs have estimated values of life in the range of $3 to $7 million. These numbers greatly exceed the workers' lifetime earnings—roughly by an order of magnitude. The economic value of life clearly extends well beyond the financial stakes involved. Moreover, there is no attempt by any external observer to limit the magnitude of these assessments. All we are asking is how much the individuals themselves value a particular risk reduction, and we will respect these values when designing social policies to protect them.

2.3 VALUING LIFE FOR POLICY DECISIONS

Adopting the willingness-to-pay approach and establishing empirical estimates considerably simplify the task of addressing value-of-life issues in policy contexts. For private decisions the dominant concern will be the private willingness-to-pay amount. For public choices it will be society's overall willingness to pay for the risk reduction. One would expect that the greatest benefit from a life-extension policy will be that received by the individual whose life is directly affected, so private valuations provide a good starting point for assessing the value of life. The extent and implications of altruistic concerns have yet to be estimated precisely.

Identified versus Statistical Lives

Consider the situation of identified lives that are highly publicized as being at risk. Society is willing to spend a considerable sum to rescue a child who falls down a well or a man who is trapped under a collapsed freeway after an earthquake. The valuation of identified lives involving 0–1 probabilities of life or death will, of course, be quite different from the valuation of statistical lives. On an economic basis, the willingness to pay per unit risk reduction should be lower for large risks than for small risks. In practice, we often observe the opposite. Society exhibits greater life valuations when saving identified lives than for policies with small effects on statistical lives.

Which reaction better reflects our true underlying risk valuations? From an economic standpoint, the statistical life valuation is the more correct approach to valuing statistical lives, but if our individual decision processes cannot deal effectively with probabilistic events, then the valuation of identified lives might be a more meaningful index of our preferences. Because value-of-life questions involve a complex mixture of morality, economics, and decision making under uncertainty, ascertaining the true underlying preference structure that should be used for policy purposes will often be difficult.

The dilemma in ascertaining our true preferences can be illustrated by the following example. Suppose that improved water treatment facilities will reduce the rate of a fatal form of cancer by 1/10,000 for a municipality of 20,000, so that on average two lives will be saved. Suppose that we knew in fact that exactly two lives would be saved, but we did not know whose they would be. Should our benefit value remain the same as when there were two statistical lives to be saved, as opposed to two lives saved with certainty? If we are applying a standard Bayesian decision theory approach, there should be no change.

Now suppose that the lives saved are known in advance to be Kira and Michael. Should our answer change? Strict application of willingness-to-pay principles suggests that the collective valuation of a 1/10,000 risk reduction by 20,000 people will exceed the value to 2 people of a risk reduction from 1.0 to 0. The value we are willing to pay per unit risk reduction is greater for small increments than larger changes since our resources become depleted when we must purchase a large decrease in risk. The role of altruism may, however, alter this relationship. In practice, the societal value for saving Kira's and Michael's lives may be greater since these are identified lives. Should society's valuation of these lives be allowed to reflect the identified aspect? A more appropriate and consistent basis for decision would result if we were to value two certain lives to be saved at random. However, it may be that the reality of dealing with probabilistic events may not be understood until there is more tangible evidence of the risk-reduction benefits. How, for example, would we modify our thinking if we placed the same value on the lives of Richard and Sally or any other pair of identified residents as we would on the lives of Kira and Michael? The reality that lives will actually be lost and that we are not dealing with abstract events may not be apparent until the prospective victims are identified.

Ascertaining the Pertinent Preferences

Ostensible concern with value-of-life outcomes may actually be related to the process by which these estimates are made. As Zeckhauser (1975) has observed, we often choose not to confront individual beliefs with respect to the life-extending decisions that we make. In many situations we may be forced to make a ceremonial commitment to life extension (e.g., unproductive medical expenditures), even though we do not believe that such expenditures can enhance life substantially.

Questions about true preferences also arise when we observe large discrepancies between the buying and selling prices for risk reduction. People often react with alarm to a risk increase but may not be willing to spend much to achieve a comparable risk reduction.[4] Substantial gaps cannot be reconciled with consistent, rational behavior. In such instances, which preferences should count—our complacency when faced with opportunities to reduce risk or our extreme reactions to risk increases?

Because of the special status of lifesaving decisions, planners in pursuit of some social good may attempt to impose their preferences. As the U.S. smoking population has dwindled, policy efforts to restrict smoking in public places have greatly increased. These restrictions have not emerged from a precise tallying of the risk reduction achieved against the decrease in welfare of smokers. Rather, each side has attempted to convert the smoking debate into a question of rights rather than policy merits. Is it the smokers or the nonsmokers who have the property rights in this particular instance?

Safety regulations present a less dramatic but more prevalent example of this imposition of preferences. Job safety standards reduce the risks faced by workers, but they also reduce the market-based compensation that workers receive. If the worker has knowingly struck a bargain with his employer for extra wages in return for the risk of the job, then regulations that decrease or eliminate this risk will reduce the worker's well-being, as he or she perceives it. The fact that policymakers would not accept the risk for the same tradeoff that workers are willing to accept does not imply that the market has failed or that the risk necessarily merits regulation. Such efforts at protection may not enhance the welfare of their intended beneficiaries.

Perhaps the most important concern is that the degree of volition of those bearing the risk plays a critical role. If we impose risks on people involuntarily and do not provide them with compensation, then our *ex ante* value-of-life measure may not be a compelling guide for policy.[5] This concern is, however, pertinent to all benefit valuation issues, not simply those involving the value of life.

Even if a risk is incurred voluntarily, society may be concerned if the level of the risk is high. Just as legislators have tried to put a floor under income levels by setting a minimum wage (although many economists claim that such efforts simply eliminate low-wage jobs), society may wish to have a ceiling on any one worker's level of risk. Nuclear power plant workers must rotate assignments so that no single worker receives too large a dose of radiation. Recently, there have been similar proposals to rotate airline flight crews to limit their radiation dosage. The resulting policy will not affect the total expected number of lives lost with a linear dose-response relationship, but no single worker will be substantially at risk. This example suggests that the motivations for societal action and the subsequent value of risk-reduction benefits may be highly complex, involving attributes other than the expected health impacts, such as the distribution of the risk.

The nature of societal interests driving these concerns with health status may lead to seemingly inconsistent policies. Society does little to interfere with most labor market operations, such as the determination of promotions and job assignments. But the same market processes giving rise to these outcomes also govern the allocation of labor market risks. These special concerns arise both because health risks are accorded special status and because the decision processes involving risks are likely to be particularly flawed. Clearly, however, we are much more concerned with a failure to assess the risk of death properly than with an overestimate of the likelihood of promotion. The stakes are greater, and the altruistic concerns of society with health are stronger as well.

2.4 RATIONALITY AND SELF-CONTROL

Smoking Behavior

The relationship between personal values and individual decision making involving risk is often unclear. Consider the case of cigarette smoking. Although a third of the U.S. adult population continues to smoke, most smokers either say they want to quit smoking or have attempted to quit in the past. A key economic issue is whose preferences should matter. Is the authentic self the smoker or the person who claims to want to be a nonsmoker? What does it mean when individuals express a desire to quit smoking? Are they physically dependent on nicotine, or is it the act of smoking that they cannot quit?

Nicotine chewing gum provides a ready substitute for those who want one, but it appears that most consumers enjoy smoking as a consumption decision. In 1988 R. J. Reynolds introduced the Premier cigarette. Externally indistinguishable from a traditional cigarette, the Premier had a burning charcoal ember at its tip which heated glycerine crystals coated with tobacco extract. The vapor from these crystals then passed through tobacco and was inhaled after going through a filter. Smokers of the Premier could enjoy the physical movements of holding a cigarette and the oral gratification achieved through cigarette smoking as well as the nicotine that smokers presumably desire. The Premier cigarette was available in regular and menthol flavors. Perhaps the only attribute on which the Premier fell short was its taste. The result was a marketing disaster, and the new product was withdrawn from the market.

The Premier provided an almost perfectly controlled experiment. The carcinogenic risks of cigarettes were eliminated, with the "look and feel" left intact.

The only drawback was in the cigarette's taste. Surely, if cigarette purchases were driven by "addiction" alone, this product would have dominated the market. It seems clear that some fundamental taste on the part of consumers for the smoking experience is at play.

In recent years the addiction label has been liberally applied to numerous behavioral phenomena.[6] Most residents of Los Angeles claim to want to move out of the city but do not. Similarly, millions of workers profess a desire to leave their jobs, but they do not quit. Self-help psychology paperbacks provide guidance for overcoming addictive relationships.

Two factors appear to be at work here. The first is that the individual would like to purge a particular activity of an undesirable attribute, such as the risk associated with smoking, but such unbundling is not possible. Professing a desire to quit smoking may really mean that one wishes to avoid a particular attribute of the product, while keeping all of the remaining attributes. Second, making changes—whether in smoking, diet, or exercise patterns—may impose important transactions costs.

To decide which of one's selves is the authentic self, it helps to consider risk-taking decisions in other contexts. If smoking decisions are rational, one would expect smokers to display a lower risk-dollar tradeoff than nonsmokers (unless the smoking decision is driven simply by a difference in the taste for cigarettes). An intriguing set of findings pertains to the variations in the job risk premiums workers require with respect to smoking status and seat belt use.[7] Workers on average receive compensation of $56,500 (1990 prices) for each statistical injury serious enough to lead to some loss of work.[8] However, the group of workers who are nonsmokers and who do wear seat belts require the greatest compensation for bearing the risk (equivalent to $95,220 per injury). Smokers on average receive compensation of roughly $30,781 per injury, or just over half of the comparable value for the entire sample of smoking and nonsmoking workers. Although these results do not imply that choices are fully rational, they do provide some evidence of consistency. In particular, the same individuals who accept the risks of smoking also are willing to accept a lower price in exchange for risking their lives on the job.

Consistent biases in risk perception cannot account for these findings. Could the results, for example, be attributable to people systematically underestimating the risks of smoking and risks from their jobs, thus gravitating to hazardous pursuits whose implications are not well understood? The wage-risk tradeoffs, however, are based on the risk assessments by the particular workers. If smokers underestimate all kinds of risks, the statistical impact will be a *larger* estimated wage premium per unit risk rather than the smaller premium that is observed. The given estimated wage premium will translate into a high value of injury when coupled with a low risk perception. One could advance the alternative hypothesis that smokers overestimate the risks they face, which would account for their smaller wage premiums for jobs. If, however, smokers systematically overassess risks, then their smoking behavior presumably is the result of a strong taste for smoking rather than a failure to appreciate the potential hazards of this activity.

A variety of factors consequently influence smoking behavior. First, smokers may have a different attitude toward risk, as reflected in their willingness to take risks other than those of cigarettes. Thus, there is at least some evidence that cigarette smoking is an action of one's authentic self. Second, there is also substantial evidence that people would like to quit smoking, but the full implications of the survey responses are not clear. Changes in preferences, changes in health status, or information acquisition concerning cigarette smoking all may be involved.

Irrational Behavior and the Value of Life

Such controversies extend well beyond the case of cigarette smoking. Self-control is an issue in many areas, and it is often necessary to identify the preferences that should matter from a policy standpoint. A substantial recent literature has documented a wide variety of anomalies in decisions involving risk, in which the task of distinguishing the authentic self is once again important.

Irrationality involving choices made under uncertainty often stems from underlying inadequacies in the way risk perceptions are formed. For example, individuals overestimate the risks associated with low-probability events; they overweight events that lead to complete elimination of the risk (the "certainty effect"); and they overreact to highly publicized and dramatic risks. The irrational behavior in these instances does not stem from the underlying preference structure but rather the risk perceptions. Chapters 6 and 7 will examine the source of these biases in detail. The result is risk-dollar tradeoffs that do not accurately reflect the preferences that individuals would have if they understood the risks better. As a practical matter, policymakers may have to overcome the political pressures generated by such preferences;[9] when formulating normative policy guidelines, however, one need not be concerned with excessive or inappropriate reactions stemming from inadequacies in risk perception.

More problematic are certain anomalies that cannot be attributed to simple misperception of the risk. One example is the phenomenon of regret.[10] Individuals may attach an additional negative payoff to an unfavorable lottery outcome above and beyond the stated terms of the lottery. Then decision making is complicated by making allowance for regret. Similarly, events associated with what I term the current "reference risk level"[11] may have special properties as well. People generally avoid lotteries that could lead to a higher risk level. The level of the risk within one's total risk portfolio is not the central issue. Rather, the main sensitivity is to an upward shift in a risk to which one has become accustomed.

These situations may involve a legitimate individual preference as opposed to a behavioral anomaly. To what extent should policies override these features of individual preferences? In addition, if individuals display various anomalous preferences, either in the market or in simulated market contexts presented by a survey, to what extent should we use these responses in formulating risk policy? Once risk policies have been framed in sound economic terms, making such distinctions will be a matter of increasing concern.

2.5 REGULATION OF GENETIC RISKS

One of the most sensitive areas of risk regulation pertains to genetic hazards. Controversies become particularly heated when risks are imposed involuntarily. To what extent, for example, should a woman be allowed to expose a fetus to potential birth defects as the result of her excessive drinking? Similarly, should pregnant women be allowed to work in situations involving the risk of potential birth defects (e.g., through exposure to lead in battery plants, or to excessive radiation)? In 1991 the U.S. Supreme Court ruled that employers could not discriminate by sex in placing workers on risky jobs. This decision will both increase the need to provide a safer work environment and increase the responsibility workers have for limiting their own genetic risks.[12]

One would expect the mother to take into account the interests of the child. However, if self-control is a problem when individuals make decisions in their own behalf, how can we be sure that they will behave correctly with respect to the future well-being of the unborn? Society has chosen not to leave these matters to individual discretion. Instead, we regulate risks and control access to jobs on the basis of the risk exposure. These regulations reflect a complex set of concerns involving irrationality as well as a legitimate concern with the health of others.

One policy problem often posed as a matter of ethics is whether pregnant women should be barred from particular hazardous jobs or whether instead the employer should be required to provide positions safe enough for any worker, including pregnant women. This policy decision seems to have been miscast as one of ethics when it is really differences in safety productivity that are more relevant. If some workers face a much higher degree of risk on the job, presumably the employer should not be required to reduce the risk so that it will be the same for all. Many factory jobs require heavy lifting, which can be done more safely by individuals with greater strength. To ensure that such positions would not impose dangerous back injury risks to any worker, all weight-lifting tasks would have to be subdivided into small increments.

The basic principle of allocating individuals to positions in the labor market is that individual differences in productivity should be exploited, not suppressed. This is the classic principle of comparative advantage. Differences in riskiness are just one aspect of productivity differences, and equalization of job risk is no more a matter of ethics than is equalization of other job attributes. Although I have long wished to be a Boston Celtic, I will be unable to fulfill this ambition until rules are instituted so that players who are nine inches shorter than Larry Bird and who cannot jump or shoot with any particular accuracy will be able to have the same productivity as people who can.[13] Indeed, we owe our high standard of living and our overall good health to the fact that society has been organized to exploit differences in talents.

The case of alcoholic beverages illustrates the undesirability of equalizing risk levels. Alcohol poses a much greater risk to pregnant women than to the adult population at large. The appropriate policy remedy is not to reduce the alcohol content of liquor so that it is equally safe for all to drink. Rather, the preferred policy course has been informational efforts aimed at reducing drinking by pregnant women. This approach recognizes that there is an inescapable heterogeneity in individual riskiness.

Changes in drinking patterns are, however, less costly to achieve than career shifts. When a woman who performs hazardous work becomes pregnant, transaction costs make it difficult for her to find a new job in the outside market. The employer can reduce those costs by providing alternative positions for employees who become pregnant. Because employers value workers' firm-specific skills, they have a strong interest in promoting such internal mobility.

The controversy surrounding pregnancy and hazardous jobs has focused not primarily on the situation of workers who already hold such jobs but rather on the question of initial access to the risky jobs. Women who plan to have children want the risk reduced so that they will face no greater risk on the job. Women who claim that they do not plan to have children want to choose better-paying but potentially hazardous employment. Since women's preferences as to becoming pregnant may change over time, irrespective of verbal commitments and prior intentions, the reluctance of employers to expose future unborn to major risks, and themselves to substantial future liability, appears quite appropriate. There is a tremendous moral hazard problem involved, particularly given the million-dollar stakes in tort liability awards.

Some women have suggested that they should be permitted access to the positions after providing evidence that they have been sterilized or are otherwise unable to become pregnant. Sterilization prerequisites for jobs have, quite legitimately, evoked substantial controversy. But it must be remembered that it is not the employer who forces the women to become sterilized. (Indeed, women often have other reasons to seek sterilization.) Rather, if workers choose this course it is because they value the higher wage rate they will receive in this position more than the loss associated with sterilization.

Almost all of the complaints on this issue have arisen from people who are seeking promotion to a higher-paying but potentially riskier job at the firm where they are currently employed. What is at stake here is not survival or avoidance of a poverty threshold, as hazard premiums average less than $1,000 annually for U.S. workers. Rather, the desire for economic advancement has generated a controversy over ethics and morality.

Such problems are likely to be less severe for entry-level jobs. Individuals seeking starting positions at firms have much greater mobility and many more diverse opportunities. Only when they have developed firm-specific expertise do workers become much more concerned with access to higher-paying positions. If society values access, it can approach this issue in the same manner used for the initial risk-dollar tradeoff. In particular, we must balance our willingness to pay for increased access against the associated efficiency loss and potential increased risk. These are not strictly ethical questions beyond economic analysis. Rather, making such tradeoffs lies at the heart of what economics is about.

Similar concerns regarding access occur in other contexts as well. Should we provide wheelchair ramps and parking spaces for the handicapped even when these policies fail a benefit-cost test? If the calculated benefits properly account for the entire value that society places on improved access, from an efficiency standpoint one cannot justify these efforts. The fundamental task is not to promote access at any price but to acquire a much better basis than we now have for evaluating the benefits of improved access. These benefits are legitimate but difficult to quantify, so that most policy decisions turn on speculative claims.

The ultimate policy question that must be addressed is what bases for discrimination are acceptable when differences in riskiness are present. Automobile insurance regulations generally preclude the use of race information in setting rates, and some states prohibit the use of age and sex information as well. Airplanes permit pregnant women to fly, even though the radiation risk to the fetus may be considerable and may not be well understood by the passenger. Overall, society has done very poorly at developing consistent guidelines for allocating risk and determining a sound basis for discriminating on the basis of differing riskiness. If we are to succeed in addressing these concerns, we must recognize that these are not simply issues of equity. Substantial efficiency gains can be reaped by proper allocation of risk, not only increasing productivity but more frequently saving lives and preventing birth defects.

2.6 AFFLUENCE AND THE VALUE OF LIFE

The starting point for any value-of-life discussion is the individual's own value of life. These values tend to be an increasing function of income. To what extent should we recognize this heterogeneity when making policy? Should one treat all individuals identically, as if they had the same values, or should we be guided by the values that the individuals themselves express?

Income Distribution at a Point in Time

Such distributional issues arise with all government programs, which inevitably benefit some parties more than others. Benefit assessment procedures are generally based on the willingness to pay of project beneficiaries, rather than on some systematic inflation of benefit values for the poor and compression of those for the wealthy. This approach does not mean that society has no concern for the poor, only that redistribution can be handled more efficiently through focused income transfer programs.

This kind of division of labor is consistent with the well-known Kaldor-Hicks compensation principle. If the policy is based on willingness-to-pay guidelines, then the parties that benefit can potentially compensate the losers from the policy. To override the willingness-to-pay values and tilt the policy mix toward risk reduction and environmental preservation, when the poor want education and housing, does not seem to be in anyone's best interests.

Most policies do not better the lot of some individuals at the expense of others but benefit one segment of the population disproportionately. Should we place a higher value on promoting airline safety, because of the relative affluence of the passengers, as compared with improved highway safety, which provides more broadly based benefits for the U.S. population? Reliance on willingness to pay would generate more stringent standards for airline safety, which in turn would raise the price that the (more affluent) airline passengers pay for their tickets. Somewhat paradoxically, however, the Federal Aviation Administration (FAA) sets the least stringent safety regulations of any federal agency, because FAA regulations were long based on the present value of victims' lost earnings, as opposed to willingness-to-pay estimates of the value of life. Rather than raise its standards in areas where the private valuation of the publicly provided benefits is high, the government has for the most part ignored these concerns.

In some situations, of course, it would be difficult or undesirable to make distinctions along income lines. The *Titanic* had enough lifeboats for the first-class passengers, but the other passengers apparently were expected to swim ashore. One could imagine an economic argument for making such distinctions, if the wealthier passengers were willing to pay the extra fare needed to support the purchase of lifeboats, whereas the less affluent passengers were not. Of course, there is no evidence that such a rational market process drove the *Titanic* lifeboat decision. In any case, such bargains will not hold up in practice, since once the catastrophe happens it is impossible to deny access to the lifeboats to those who did not pay. In situations that lead directly to a certainty of life or death rather than a small probability of death, denial of lifesaving alternatives based on income is highly controversial and understandably objectionable. For similar reasons, if medical support measures can preserve a life that would otherwise be lost, society spares little expense in doing so, whatever the patient's income.

Differences in safety protection are less troublesome when death is not an inevitable prospect but remains a more remote probability. Because of the heterogeneity in the value of life, market pressures have led to the introduction of air bags and antilock braking systems for the luxury car segment of the market. Cars such as the Mercedes-Benz and the Acura have introduced such safety-enhancing measures because their more affluent customers value them, whereas the Ford Escort and the Toyota Tercel have avoided such devices, which would lead to a dramatic relative price increase. There has been no public outcry that all cars should be equipped with the thousands of dollars worth of extra safety equipment as in the luxury class. It is highly unlikely that less affluent drivers would favor requirements that all cars meet the highest possible safety standards.

More observant airline passengers might notice the difference in buoyancy of the foam seat cusions provided to coach passengers and the inflatable life vests provided to those who ride in first class. Similarly, corporate jet fleets have invested in smoke hoods to better enable their executive passengers to escape a crash, whereas commercial airlines have not.

Recognizing the heterogeneity of the value of life could have substantial implications for the design and targeting of risk policies. The empirical studies to be examined in Chapter 4 indicate that for the range of risks now faced by American workers, risk valuations seem to be highly responsive to income (income elasticity is on the order of 1.0).[14] The role of individual income in assessing the value of life has long been accepted in legal contexts, where the basis for compensation is the present value of earnings or some other linear function of income, consumption, and taxes. As our estimates of the value of life become increasingly refined, policies will probably be designed to reflect these differences, thus replicating the outcomes that would be expected if individuals could express their attitudes toward risk in a market for safety.

Income Differences across Countries

Heterogeneity is particularly relevant to international trade policies. A desire to equalize risk levels throughout the world has led to proposals that the United States neither export products that violate any U.S. safety regulations nor import products from countries in which manufacturing processes are less safe than in the United States.[15] In practice, this policy would lead to a virtual ban on imports from the developing nations, which are in the greatest need of our economic support.

Worldwide standards for risk are not appropriate because individuals' attitudes toward risk are likely to vary considerably, and quite legitimately, depending on their countries' stage of development. Imposing the risk standards of an economically advanced society on less developed countries will reduce their welfare by retarding economic growth and the benefits it provides. The main reason for the United States' higher safety standards is not superior awareness of safety's importance but rather a greater ability to afford the luxury of greater safety. In many underdeveloped countries, increased income has a major impact on the individual's prospect of survival, and it would be highly detrimental to impose our current regulatory standards on societies that have quite rationally made different risk-taking decisions. Indeed, America made similar decisions in its earlier stages of development.

The rationale for controlling the risks of exported goods is stronger than the rationale for not importing goods produced unsafely. Two considerations with respect to the export of hazardous goods are most salient. First, there may be an informational problem if foreign consumers purchase goods, believing that they meet U.S. quality standards. Exportation of substandard products may lead to unexpected welfare losses and may have damaging effects on the perceived quality of other U.S. products that meet high quality standards. Second, if the U.S. producer is the sole world supplier of a product, then the foreign purchasers are not buying in a competitive market. In such a context they should not suffer the imposition of a substantial risk because of the market power of the U.S. producer.

Neither of these rationales for regulating the export of risky products assumes an obligation to produce equally safe products for all markets. The assessment of the adequacy of the risk hinges instead on identification of a market failure in the recipient country. In particular, is regulation of product risk warranted from the standpoint of improving product market efficiency in the importing country? The resulting policies will not be of a caveat emptor variety but instead will require a careful assessment of the rationale for regulation. Automatically imposing U.S. standards is not appropriate, but neither is having no standards whatsoever.

Age-Related Variations

Differences in the value of life also could arise with respect to age. The young have more to lose than the old, and the special societal concern with averting risks to children reflects this difference.[16] Fine-tuning lifesaving decisions to reflect differences in life expectancy between thirty- and fifty-year-olds may not be of great consequence because of the offsetting effects of wealth increases over a lifetime and the discounting of future utility streams.[17] In addition, most lifesaving policies benefit broad segments of the population—for example, all residents who drink water that may be contaminated by toxic wastes. Medical contexts offer the greatest potential for discrimination on the basis of age, but the issue has not become salient, because of the role of societal norms and patients' ability to pay for care through insurance and first-party payments.

Changes in Income over Time

Heterogeneity is also an issue with respect to valuing lives across time. If future generations are more affluent than we are, their value of life will be proportionally higher. Although in many cases we can simply let future generations spend more later, for irreversible effects on the environment or policies with long-term effects, decisions must be made now.

The growth of the benefit value over time will be indicated by the growth rate g, and the discount rate used will be r. If one recognizes the heterogeneity in the value of life, then the effective discount rate is approximately $1 + r - g$, but if one ignores the heterogeneity, the discount rate rises to $1 + r$. Even in the case in which heterogeneity is recognized, r will exceed g somewhat because of the presence of a pure rate-of-time preference for consumption now rather than later.[18] Thus, in each case there will be a positive rate of discount, but it will be greater when heterogeneity is suppressed than when it is recognized.

Recognition of heterogeneity in the valuation of life in this instance will foster more future-oriented policies. Policies addressing global warming and other long-term risks to society will appear more attractive. In contrast, if we ignore growth in the value of life over time as incomes rise, policies with deferred impacts will be put at a substantial disadvantage.

When making decisions with respect to our own internal welfare, we should not simply abstract from our own increases in well-being over time because we will be richer selves in twenty years. The more appropriate economic procedure would be to consider our valuation of risk reductions at the time they will occur. Similarly, appropriate recognition of heterogeneity will lead to more stringent, less short-sighted environmental and risk-regulation policies that will benefit future generations.

Appropriate recognition of the heterogeneity in the value of life could lead to either more stringent or less stringent risk-regulation policies, depending on the situation. Adopting a uniform valuation of life is in no way more responsible or more stringent from a risk-management standpoint. Appropriate recognition of the heterogeneity of the value of life will permit more sensible and consistent policy choices that are based on the benefits provided.

2.7 CONCLUSION

The value-of-life literature has gone through a number of stages. The main thrust of the early efforts was to get our thinking straight on the general value-of-life issue and to begin casting the fundamental tradeoff in meaningful economic terms. Much of the research throughout the 1970s was directed at developing an empirical basis for making these judgments, and in the 1980s we began to use these estimates for policy-making. Indeed, the value-of-life approach is now required by the U.S. Office of Management and Budget as a standard practice for all new major federal regulations.[19]

Once an unmentionable issue, value-of-life tradeoffs are now recognized as quite

amenable to economic analysis. The substantial magnitude of the empirical estimates of the value of life, together with the proper valuation of policies based on
willingness-to-pay principles (as opposed to earlier benefit techniques, such as lost
earnings), has led to much more ambitious risk-regulation efforts. Indeed, the first
major application of value-of-life principles, which will be examined in Chapter 14,
showed that the Occupational Safety and Health Administration's hazard communication standard offered benefits ten times greater than OSHA had originally
estimated using earnings-based measures of the value of life, enabling OSHA to
overcome the original objections of the Office of Management and Budget (OMB)
and to issue the regulation.

Proper application of value-of-life principles will not necessarily make risk regulations less ambitious. It will put them on a sounder economic basis, however, so
that we will allocate our resources to the most appropriate risk-reducing policies.

As techniques for refining value-of-life estimates improve and as the use of these
procedures spreads, more and more questions formerly seen as ethical issues will be
structured through this methodology. At a broad level, reliance on willingness-to-
pay principles and society's valuation of different outcomes raises no new ethical
concerns not present in any other benefits area.

The fact that many of these issues are amenable to economic analysis does not
imply that the answers are straightforward. One salient problem is the difficulty in
ferreting out individuals' true underlying preferences toward risk in situations where
their rationality is suspect. Society's willingness to make an appropriate commitment to the well-being of future generations is also likely to be controversial.

None of the major economic issues or policy debates will be resolved definitively
in the near future. However, the terms of the debate should be framed in a meaningful economic manner.

NOTES

1. See any standard text such as Stokey and Zeckhauser (1978).

2. Schelling (1968), p. 134, dismissed this widely used accounting approach altogether, observing that
"it is doubtful whether the interests of any consumers are represented in a calculation that treats a child
like an unfinished building or some expensive goods in process."

3. A discussion of self-control and determination of the authentic self appears in Schelling (1984a),
especially pp. 107–109, 111–112, and 152–153.

4. See Viscusi, Magat, and Huber (1987).

5. See Hammond (1982) for elaboration of this point.

6. Alan Schwartz (1989) provides an interesting perspective on legal policy issues raised by addiction.

7. See Hersch and Viscusi (1990).

8. All subsequent figures are in December 1990 prices as well.

9. This class of issues is discussed more fully in Chapter 9.

10. See Bell (1982) for an analysis of regret.

11. See Viscusi, Magat, and Huber (1987).

12. For a discussion of *Auto Workers v. Johnson Controls, Inc.* see the *Washington Post*, March 21,
1991, pp. A1, A14, A15.

13. It should also be noted that Larry Bird wishes he were three inches taller. See Bird (1989).

14. See Viscusi and Evans (1990).

15. For advocacy of each of these proposals, see Ashford (1976).

16. See Zeckhauser and Shepard (1976) for development of the quality-adjusted value of life, recognizing both the duration of life and its quality.

17. Estimates of the quantity-adjusted value of life consistent with small differences in the value of life for thirty- and fifty-year-olds appear in Moore and Viscusi (1990a).

18. Discounting issues are discussed in Fuchs and Zeckhauser (1987), Viscusi and Moore (1989), and Moore and Viscusi (1990a,b,c).

19. U.S. Office of Management and Budget (1988).

3

Evidence on the Value of Life:
Case Studies from the Labor Market

3.1 INTRODUCTION

A substantial body of research now addresses the value of individuals' risk-dollar tradeoffs, the focal point of the value-of-life debate. This chapter provides an introduction to this literature by considering in detail two studies from the labor market. This discussion provides a more detailed perspective on the nature of the empirical studies than does Chapter 4, which provides a comprehensive survey of the entire literature on the value of risks to life and health.

In this chapter, I have three principal concerns. First, I explore data on labor market behavior in order to obtain estimates of the values that individuals implicitly attach to death and injury through their employment decisions. By examining a few studies in detail, we will obtain some perspective on the nature of econometric efforts to derive a value of life. Second, I will discuss the pertinence of these estimates to policy evaluation. Investigations directed at obtaining an elusive value-of-life number are largely misdirected. Instead, analysts should be concerned with differences in individuals' values of life and health status and the implications that the resulting distribution of values has for government policy.

3.2 ESTIMATING THE VALUE OF LIFE

Adam Smith (1776) articulated the conceptual basis of this investigation two centuries ago when he observed that "the whole of the advantages and disadvantages of the different employments of labor and stock must, in the same neighborhood, be either perfectly equal or continually tending to equality." In other words, jobs that carry with them certain disadvantages must have other offsetting advantages such as higher wages that make them as attractive overall as jobs without these disadvantages. This "compensating wage differential" result holds whether or not individuals are risk-averse, that is, whether or not they will demand favorable odds to engage in a lottery. All that is required is that individuals prefer being healthy to being dead or injured.[1]

Although the underlying theory is not particularly controversial, it was only in the 1970s that it was first subjected to successful empirical tests. One principal difficulty is that the most attractive jobs in society tend to be well paid. Unless an analyst has sufficient information to be able to disentangle the role of different personal characteristics from the role of job attributes, including riskiness, the estimates of the wage premiums for risk will be seriously biased.

This section explores one set of empirical results to provide some sense of the methodology underlying the studies in this literature. Figure 3-1 illustrates the methodology that is surveyed in greater detail by Rosen (1986).[2] The vertical axis represents the wage rate, and the horizontal axis is the job risk. The curve WW represents the market offer curve (more technically, the envelope of the individual firms' offer curves). Firms are willing to pay workers a higher wage for jobs that pose a higher risk because fewer safety-related investments are involved. Put somewhat differently, if workers want to work on jobs with lower risk, firms will offer a lower wage rate due to the added costs that safe workplaces impose. The curves EU_1 and EU_2 represent constant expected utility loci for workers 1 and 2. All points along curve EU_1, for example, represent wage-risk combinations that give worker 1 the same expected utility level. The wage rate is an increasing function of the risk because workers require a compensating differential to face job risks. This result is quite general. The only assumption required is that workers would rather be healthy than not. One does not need to assume that workers are risk-averse in the sense of being unwilling to undertake financial gambles. The curve EU_1 represents the highest constant expected utility locus for worker 1 that this worker can achieve given the available wage opportunities, and EU_2 represents the highest constant expected utility level achievable by worker 2.

The points (p_1,w_1) and (p_2,w_2) represent the points of tangency of the expected utility curves with the market wage opportunities. These are the points that are observable using labor market data. In effect, we observe the wage-risk tradeoff along different points of tangency with the market opportunities curve. The econometric task is to estimate the locus of these wage-risk tradeoffs for the entire market. In effect, we fit a line through points such as these and estimate the curve that characterizes the wage-risk tradeoffs that prevail in the market. These points represent the market equilibrium for the entire set of workers, not the value that any particular worker would require to accept a greater risk level.[3] Thus, in the case of worker 1 a higher amount of wage compensation would be required along EU_1 to face the risk level p_2 than what worker 2 would require on EU_2. If the estimated wage-risk tradeoff curve for the market is linear, then the rate of tradeoff is the same for all workers at the points of tangency. However, for changes of more than a marginal amount from the current risk level, the risk-dollar tradeoff for different workers will not be the same since the tradeoff rate is measured along a constant expected utility locus, not the estimated market tradeoff curve.

The data set that will be used to assess the value of life is the University of Michigan's 1969–1970 Survey of Working Conditions (SWC). This survey provides detailed information concerning the individual and his or her job. The analysis here uses only the data on 496 full-time blue-collar workers in the SWC sample, since the survey questions focused primarily on the types of job characteristics pertinent to this group. Using the data provided in this survey, I constructed job hazard indices for each worker's job. The worker's earnings are then regressed on these job hazard indices, the worker's personal characteristics, and the job characteristics in order to

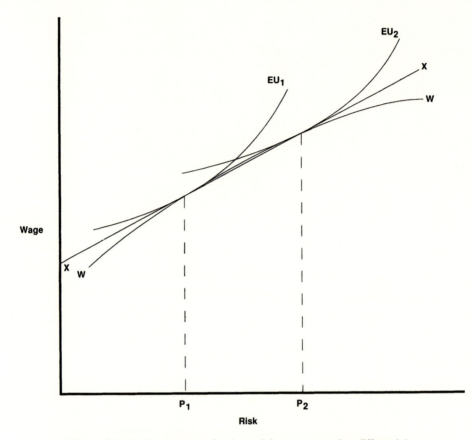

Figure 3.1 Market processes for determining compensating differentials

obtain the implicit monetary price workers receive for risks of death and injury. The results of this analysis are then used to estimate the dollar values that individuals attach to the loss of life or to a work injury.

The main independent variables of interest are of course the job hazard variables. The SWC includes a self-assessed hazard variable (DANGER) that has a value of 1 if the worker's job exposes him or her to dangerous or unhealthy conditions and a value of 0 otherwise. For purposes of this study, the DANGER variable is primarily used in constructing and refining hazard indices for the worker's job. Detailed examination of worker responses and the hazards cited indicated that the self-assessed hazard variable was consistent with the worker's occupation and industry. Workers' perceptions of hazards exhibited a strong positive correlation with the industry injury rate. Moreover, the estimated annual earnings premium for job risks was $375 (1969 prices) based on the self-perceived hazards variable and $420 based on the industry injury rate—a difference well within the bounds of error. All available evidence suggests that workers' subjective assessments of the risk are plausible. It is unlikely, however, that workers have perfect information about the risks posed by their jobs. The empirical implications of imperfect worker information are discussed below.

Using information about each worker's industry, 1969 Bureau of Labor Statistics (BLS) industry injury rate statistics were matched to the workers in the sample.[4] The most aggregative of these measures was INJURY RATE, the number of fatal or disabling on-the-job injuries per million hours worked in a particular worker's industry. An injury is defined as being "disabling" if it had "either caused some permanent impairment or made the worker unable to work at a regularly established job for at least 1 full day after the day of injury." Injuries are divided into three categories: death, permanent partial disability, and temporary total disability. On average, for the industries represented by the workers in the sample, death was 0.4 percent of all injuries. Permanent partial disability accounted for 2.9 percent of all injuries, and temporary total disability for the remaining 96.7 percent. For the purposes of this analysis, the two nonfatal injury rate classifications were pooled, for the data were not rich enough to distinguish the compensating differentials for all three types of hazards. The first of the disaggregative injury variables is DEATH, which is INJURY RATE multiplied by the percentage of injuries that were fatal in the worker's industry. Similarly, the variable NONFATAL was obtained by multiplying INJURY RATE by the percentage of nonfatal injuries.

Assuming an average workweek of forty hours and an average of fifty weeks worked per year, these hazard variables can be directly converted into annual probabilities of adverse outcomes.[5] On average, the workers in the sample faced an annual probability of 0.0319 of a fatal or nonfatal job injury, a 1.18×10^{-4} probability of death, and a 0.0317 probability of a nonfatal injury. These risks are a bit higher than the average for all manufacturing industries but lower than the hazard levels in many nonmanufacturing industries such as mining and transportation. They are, of course, incremental death and injury risks, over and above the risks the workers face in the normal course of daily life.

Three job risk variables were also constructed, using the information as to whether the worker considered his or her job hazardous, thereby reducing some of the measurement error associated with using an industrywide risk index. The variables INJURY RATE1, DEATH1, and NONFATAL1 were obtained by multiplying their former values by the 0 to 1 dummy variable DANGER. Thus, these variables are identical in value with INJURY RATE, DEATH, and NONFATAL except that they equal zero if the worker does not view his or her job as hazardous.

The earnings equation was estimated in both linear and semilogarithmic form; annual earnings (EARNINGS) and its natural logarithm (LOGEARNINGS) were the two dependent variables.[6] In addition to various combinations of job risk variables, each equation also contained twenty-two other independent variables. These included eleven dummy job characteristic variables reflecting the speed of work, whether the worker is a supervisor, overtime work, job security, whether the job requires that the worker make decisions, the presence of a training program, the number of other employees at the enterprise, and three dummy variables denoting the occupational group of the worker. The remaining independent variables pertained to regional economic conditions and the worker's personal characteristics, including age, race, sex, years of schooling, health status, job experience, and union membership.

It is assumed here that workers act as if the objective hazard indices correspond to their subjective assessments. Imperfect worker information generates underestimates of workers' implicit value of life for both econometric and economic reasons. First, if workers' probability assessments are randomly distributed about the true value, one encounters a conventional errors-in-variable situation in which the empirical estimates are biased downward. Second, suppose that workers' prior probability assessments correspond to the true risk of the job but that these assessments are imprecise. For normal employment situations in which workers face a sequence of lotteries on life and death and in which workers learn about the risks of the job through their on-the-job experiences, workers require less wage compensation for any mean level of risk as their initial judgment becomes less precise. The rationale for this result, which is formalized in Viscusi (1979a), is that the uncertain job offers potential gains from experimentation. If the uncertain job turns out to be very risky, the worker can quit. The empirical results consequently will understate workers' actual value of life and health.

Overall, the LOGEARNINGS equation provided a somewhat better fit. The linear form of the earnings equation implies a constant price per unit of job risk, and the semilogarithmic form implies a rising price. The death risk results are reported in Table 3-1. Six different specifications were estimated for both the EARNINGS and LOGEARNINGS variables. The principal differences among them are the other job risk variables that were included—the nonfatal injury rate or self-assessed dangers—and whether the hazard variables were nonzero only in instances in which the worker perceived his or her job as being hazardous. The most meaningful results are probably those given in lines 2 and 5 in Table 3-1, in which both the fatal and nonfatal components of the BLS injury rate are included in the equation. Throughout this first set of equations, the death risk coefficients tend to be somewhat lower for the job risk variables that are conditional on self-perceived hazards. These results, which were first reported in Viscusi (1978a), are noteworthy since they are the first estimates in the literature that take into account subjective risk perceptions and which successfully estimate premiums for both fatal and nonfatal risks. The estimates remain in the prices for the employment year of the survey 1969. In Chapter 4, all of these results are converted to 1990 dollars and presented as the findings in Viscusi (1978a).

The implied value-of-life estimates contained in Table 3-1 pertain to implicit values when there are low probabilities of risk. These magnitudes were computed in straightforward fashion. As noted earlier, each unit of the death risk variable corresponds to 50,000 deaths per year. Multiplication of the death risk coefficient for the EARNINGS equation by this number yields the value that individuals place on their life for small changes in the probability of death. The valuation estimates for the LOGEARNINGS equation were obtained similarly, taking into consideration the different functional form being used.[7]

The results from one equation to the next display striking similarity; most of the death risk equations in which other job risk variables are included indicate a value of life in the range of $1 to $1.5 million in 1969 dollars, or $3.6 to $5.4 million in

Table 3-1. Summary of Death Risk Regression Results[a]

Death risk variable	Other job risk variables included in equation	LOGEARNINGS results		EARNINGS results	
		Death risk coefficient (*std. error*)	Implied value of life	Death risk coefficient (*std. error*)	Implie value life
1. Industry death risk (DEATH)	—	0.00205 (0.00075)	1,595,000	35.39 (10.73)	1,769,
2. Industry death risk (DEATH)	Nonfatal injury rate (NONFATAL)	0.00153 (0.00088)	1,185,000	29.20 (12.69)	1,460,
3. Industry death risk (DEATH)	Self-assessed dangers (DANGER)	0.00183 (0.00075)	1,420,000	32.13 (10.81)	1,606,
4. Industry death risk conditional on self-perceived hazard (DEATH1)	—	0.00189 (0.00072)	1,490,000	34.08 (10.38)	1,704,
5. Industry death risk conditional on self-perceived hazard (DEATH1)	Nonfatal injury rate conditional on self-perceived hazard (NONFATAL1)	0.00076 (0.00093)	600,000	18.27 (13.33)	913.
6. Industry death risk conditional on self-perceived hazard (DEATH1)	Self-assessed dangers (DANGER)	0.00141 (0.00079)	1,080,000	27.93 (11.40)	1,396

[a]Complete regression results are not reported here, since they are similar to those reported in Viscusi (1979a); the difference is the inclusion of death risk and nonfatal injury risk variables in this analysis.

1990 dollars. These estimates clearly exceed the amount that a representative w er in the sample, with average annual earnings of $6,810 (1969 dollars), could to avoid certain death.

It is important, however, to note that such a magnitude is not what the valuat of-life figures represent. Rather, individuals act as if their lives were worth indicated amounts when they are faced with very small incremental risks of de An individual facing an annual additional death risk of 1.18×10^{-4} (the mean the sample) would receive additional wage compensation of $173 based on EARNINGS equation coefficient in line 2. The amount that a worker would pa eliminate the certainty of death is necessarily below the $1 to $1.5 million amo since the worker's wealth would be reduced as he or she purchased reductions ir risk of death. This decline in wealth in turn would reduce the value the indivic attached to his or her life, since one's willingness to incur such risks increase one's wealth declines. In short, there are likely to be important income effect that the implicit value of life for small changes in the probability of death greatly exceed the value workers would pay to avoid certain death.

In similar fashion, one can interpret the implied values of all injuries, inclu death. These values are reported in Table 3-2. Workers act as if they viewed

Table 3-2. Summary of Injury Risk Regression Results

Injury risk variable	Death risk variable not included in equation	LOGEARNINGS results		EARNINGS results	
		Injury risk coefficient (*std. error*)	Implied value of injury	Injury risk coefficient (*std. error*)	Implied value of injury
1. Unspecified job injury (INJURY RATE)	—	0.0040 (0.0016)	13,550	26.37 (10.14)	13,185
2. Unspecified job injury conditional on self-perceived hazard (INJURY RATE1)	—	0.0040 (0.0013)	13,550	27.72 (7.83)	13,860
3. Industry nonfatal injury rate (NON-FATAL)	Industry death rate (DEATH)	0.932E-5 (0.837E-5)	5,500	0.110 (0.121)	5,500
4. Industry nonfatal injury rate, conditional on self-perceived hazard (NONFATAL1)	Industry death conditional on self-perceived hazard (DEATH1)	0.136-4 (0.704E-5)	9,500	0.191 (0.101)	5,500

average industrial injury as equivalent to a \$13,000 to \$14,000 drop in income. This result refers to the distribution of all industrial injuries, of which 0.4 percent overall were fatalities, 2.9 percent permanent partial disabilities, and 96.7 percent temporary total disabilities. If the death risk premium is distinguished from that for nonfatal injuries, one obtains a value for nonfatal injuries in the \$6,000 to \$10,000 range. These results are instructive in that they indicate that, in dollar terms, a probability of death is regarded as being 100 times worse than an equal probability of a nonfatal injury.

The most immediate significance of the empirical results is their implication for labor market performance. If workers were not compensated adequately for the risks they incurred, one would conclude that the market did not function effectively, perhaps because of systematic individual misallocations. The theme of inadequate compensation runs throughout much of the popular literature on occupational safety.

As the empirical results indicate, the annual compensation for all job risks totals only about \$400. Unlike stuntmen and other workers who received clearly significant hazard premiums, blue-collar workers in the more hazardous occupations do not receive additional remuneration that is sufficiently great to be visible to the casual observer. It is also important to note, however, that the risks the workers incur are not very large; the probability of a fatal injury is only about 10^{-4}. To ascertain whether workers are accepting additional risks for amounts small enough to suggest some form of market failure, one should examine not the absolute level of compensation but the implicit values that workers associate with death or injury. The empirical results indicate that these magnitudes are quite impressive—on the order of \$1 to \$1.5 million for fatalities and \$10,000 for injuries (1969 dollars).

Although there is no way to ascertain whether these levels of compensation are above or below those that would prevail if workers were perfectly informed, the magnitudes are at least suggestive in that they indicate substantial wage compensation for job hazards.[8] These findings do not imply that the government should not intervene. They do indicate, however, that it is doubtful that one can base the case for intervention on the complete absence of compensation for risks of death and injury.

3.3 SHOULD ALL LABOR MARKET STUDIES YIELD SIMILAR RESULTS?

Thaler and Rosen's (1976) analysis of implicit valuations of life in the labor market yielded estimates of $220,000 ± $66,000 in 1969 dollars. Their study focused on 900 adult males in hazardous occupations. The death risk variable they used was the Society of Actuaries' incremental death risk for a group of thirty-seven narrowly defined occupations. This variable reflected the death risks of the occupation per se as well as the death risks that were unrelated to work but are correlated with the characteristics and life-styles and income levels of people in different occupations. As a result, the patterns of risk are surprising. Cooks face three times the death risk of firemen, elevator operators face twice the death risk of truck drivers or electricians, waiters face sixty-seven times the death risk of linemen or servicemen, and actors face a higher death risk than fishermen, foresters, power plant operatives, and individuals in many other more physically demanding occupations. Although narrowly defined occupational risk indices may be superior to BLS industry risk data, the inclusion of death risks unrelated to work makes it unclear which variable involves less measurement error.

If, as Thaler and Rosen suggest, the BLS injury rate involves more measurement error and if this error is random, my value-of-life estimates should underestimate the actual value by more than theirs. My figures, however, are already roughly five times the level of their results. Consequently, one cannot use measurement error as the explanation for this difference, because correction for this problem would make the estimates more disparate than they already are.

The principal difference in the death risk variables is that the BLS industry death risk variable pertains to a broad cross-section of industries, but the Society of Actuaries' measure pertains to only the most hazardous occupations that on average pose an annual death risk ten times larger than that faced in the SWC sample (10^{-3} versus 10^{-4}). The sample of workers in the Thaler and Rosen study includes only those who are least averse to job risks, but my analysis focuses on the entire blue-collar population.[9] Other than the risk level and occupational distribution the samples are quite similar. The most salient difference in the two studies is that the Thaler and Rosen analysis focuses on a group who have shown themselves to be less averse to severe death risks than the rest of the population.

Unlike standard consumer items, death risks do not command a single price. The risk is inextricably linked to the job; it cannot be divided to yield a constant price per unit of risk. Those individuals who are least averse to such risks are willing to accept a lower compensation per unit of risk than the rest of the working population. As a result, they are inclined to accept larger risks with lower wage premiums per unit of risk. Hence, the Thaler and Rosen analysis yields a lower implied value of life.

The final important difference in the analysis is that the results reported in Section 3.2 are the first value-of-life estimates obtained from equations in which other nonpecuniary job characteristics, such as nonfatal injuries and the speed of work, were included. To the extent that job risks are positively correlated with other unattractive job attributes, the omission of these attributes leads to overestimates of the value of life.

A suggestive estimate of the extent of the bias can be obtained by examining the results in Table 3-1. Omission of the nonfatal injury rate from the equations boosts the estimated value of life significantly. The increase ranges from 21 to 150 percent, depending on the equation in question. Omission of seven other job attribute variables alters the value-of-life estimates by much less—usually by about one-third and by as little as 1 percent for one equation.[10] A similar bias in other data sets could account for the fact that R. S. Smith's (1976) estimate of the BLS industry death risk premium yielded a value of life of $2.6 million, roughly double that found in this study. By similar reasoning, Thaler and Rosen's estimates may be too high, so that their value of life would actually have been less than one-fifth of the magnitude I found if additional job attribute variables had been included in their analysis.

3.4 THE HETEROGENEITY OF THE VALUE OF LIFE

Summarizing, the principal reason that my value of life estimates are several times larger than Thaler and Rosen's appears to be the difference in the level of the risk. Their analysis reflected the preferences of those who were least averse to risk and who consequently were in very risky jobs. One's natural inclination is to ask which estimate better reflects the value of life. Framing the issue in those familiar terms, however, is not the appropriate way to view value of life problems.

In particular, different members of the population attach different values to their life. Empirical analyses should not be directed at estimating an elusive value-of-life number; rather they should estimate the schedule of values for the entire population. The line VL in Figure 3-2 illustrates such a schedule. As the percentage of the population incurring the incremental risk increases, so does the marginal valuation of life. Those who price their life the cheapest are drawn into the market first; higher wages must be paid to lure additional workers into risky jobs. Thaler and Rosen (1976) focused on the lower tail of the population—those who appeared to value their life at approximately $200,000. The more representative blue-collar SWC sample yielded a value of roughly $1 million. Empirical estimates can most accurately be viewed as weighted averages of points along the marginal valuation-of-life curve for the population. If the sample contains disproportionately many workers from the occupations posing substantial risks, it generates lower average values of life and limb than if the sample is more representative. For simplicity, the empirical

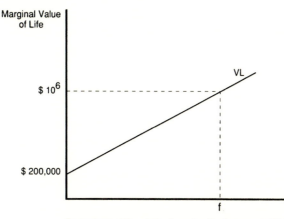

Figure 3.2 Relation of the value of life to the percentage of the population incurring the risk

results are illustrated as if they yielded single points on the curve rather than weighted averages of points along it. Thus, for Figure 3-2, Thaler and Rosen's results yield the intercept at \$200,000, but my findings correspond to a marginal value of \$$10^6$, with percentage f of the population incurring the risk.

The nature of the way the regression analysis averages workers' marginal valuations of life and limb can be illustrated with the aid of a numerical example and a bit of elementary statistics. Consider the sample of workers whose characteristics are summarized in Table 3-3. For simplicity, the only influences considered are the death risks posed by the job and the compensation for those risks, generating a model of the form[11]

$$y = \beta x.$$

Here x is the incremental death risk incurred by the worker, y is the earnings premium for this risk, and β is the implicit value of life. The implicit value of life for each of the three groups of workers is obtained by dividing y by x for the group, yielding values ranging from \$$0.2 \times 10^6$ to \$$1.5 \times 10^6$.

Suppose that the value of life estimate to be obtained is the simple average of

Table 3-3. Hypothetical Sample of Workers

	Group 1	Group 2	Group 3
Annual risk of death x_i	10^{-6}	10^{-5}	10^{-4}
Average total compensation y_i	\$1.50	\$10	\$20
Implicit value of life	\$$1.50 \times 10^6$	\$$10^6$	\$$0.2 \times 10^6$
Number in group	10	100	10

these marginal valuations, weighted according to the number of workers in each group. This approach would yield an average value of life equal to

$$\frac{1}{n} \sum_{i=1}^{n} \frac{y_i}{x_i} = \$9.75 \times 10^5.$$

It is important to recall that regression estimates do not yield a simple linear average of this type but rather produce an estimated value of life β given by

$$\beta = \frac{\sum_{i=1}^{n} y_i x_i}{\sum_{i=1}^{n} x_i^2} = \$2.73 \times 10^5.$$

Thus, the implied value-of-life estimates obtained in regression analyses are non-linear weighted averages of points along the value-of-life curve in Figure 3-1.

Investigations that seek a unique value of life rather than points on the value-of-life schedule implicitly assume that the value-of-life curves are flat. The stark difference, however, between the Thaler and Rosen results and those of this study as well as that of R. S. Smith (1976) combines with the investigation of likely biases in the analyses to suggest that individuals' valuations of life vary substantially.

3.5 HETEROGENEITY IN THE VALUE OF LIFE

Comparison of the value-of-life estimates for a representative sample of workers and for a sample of workers in high-risk jobs indicates that the value of life varies across individuals, as do preferences for other economic outcomes. The heterogeneity of the lives affected by government policies may also enter benefit valuation considerations. Should, for example, a large value be placed on the lives of individuals incurring the risk of nuclear power involuntarily or on coal miners who are cognizant of the risk they are facing and who receive additional wage premiums for those risks?

The discussion here will focus on results reported in Viscusi (1981) that represent the first successful empirical effort to ascertain the heterogeneity of individual values of life. The implicit values of injuries and deaths were obtained from compensating wage differential equations estimated for the 1976 survey year of the University of Michigan Panel Study of Income Dynamics (PSID). The analysis was restricted to the 3,977 full-time workers in the sample, that is, those who worked at least thirty hours per week.

The principal dependent variable was the worker's wage (in cents) per hour, where this variable has a mean of 503 and a standard deviation of 225. Interpreted on an annual basis, assuming that individuals work forty hours per week and fifty weeks per year, one obtains an average earnings amount of $10,060 per year. The wage equation was estimated using both the wage rate (in cents per hour) and its natural logarithm as the dependent variable.

The principal explanatory variables were those pertaining to the risk of the worker's job. Using information pertaining to the worker's industry and published BLS data, injury risk variables were constructed for each worker in the sample. The fatal injury risk variable, DEATH, is the frequency of fatalities in the worker's industry, measured in terms of deaths per 1,000 full-time workers.[12] To avoid measurement error problems arising from the small number of deaths in any particular year, the DEATH variable was constructed by averaging the industry death risk over the 1973 to 1976 period. The mean value of DEATH was .104, and its standard deviation was .108. On average, the workers in the sample faced an annual death risk of 1.04×10^{-4}. The square of this variable, DEATH × DEATH, was included in some equations in order to identify possible heterogeneity in the amount of compensation per unit of risk as the level of risk varied.

The nonfatal injury risk variable, NONFATAL, was the 1976 lost workday accident and illness injury rate for the worker's industry, minus the fatality rate for the comparable period. The lost workday injury and illness rate avoids the measurement error problems associated with the total accident and illness rate. The broader injury and illness measure is subject to greater discretion in terms of reporting adverse outcomes since the criteria for determining whether an injury or illness is to be recorded is not clear-cut for the less severe cases. Moreover, the lost workday cases are more comparable in severity to the injury measure used in the earlier results.

The risk measure NONFATAL had a mean of 3.20 and a standard deviation of 1.74. Since NONFATAL was scaled in terms of the number of lost workday accidents and illnesses per 100 full-time workers in the industry, each worker in the sample faced an annual risk of about 1/31 that he or she would incur an injury or illness of this type.

The square of the NONFATAL variable was also included in a variety of specifications to test for possible heterogeneity in compensation for nonfatal risk. Since the resulting coefficients were consistently small in magnitude and not statistically significant (at the usual levels), this variable was not included in any of the results reported below.

Finally, each equation included twenty-three additional variables reflecting the worker's personal characteristics (e.g., education, race, sex, and experience), job characteristics (e.g., coverage by a collective bargaining agreement and eight occupational dummy variables), and regional characteristics (e.g., the regional unemployment rate).

The principal regression coefficients of interest are summarized in Table 3-4.[13] All variants were estimated using both the wage and its natural logarithm as the dependent variables. In all of the equations considered, there was no evidence that the wage premiums/unit of risk for nonfatal worker injuries differed across the sample.

Using the wage premiums estimated and the associated risk levels, one can assess the implicit value that workers receive for injuries. These results will appear in Chapter 4 as Viscusi (1981). The results for the wage equation reported on the top

Table 3-4. Injury Risk Regression Results from Wage Equations

Coefficients and Regression Results		Standard Errors
Wage equation results:		
DEATH	+181.10	+368.57
	(26.10)	(75.84)
DEATH × DEATH	—	−386.55
		(146.91)
NONFATAL	+9.43	+8.81
	(1.78)	(1.79)
Log wage equation results:		
DEATH	+.311	+.509
	(.054)	(.156)
DEATH × DEATH	—	−.408
		(.303)
NONFATAL	+.021	+.021
	(.004)	(.004)

line of Table 3-5 were obtained in the following manner. The workers in the sample received an annual hazard premium of $694 for lost workday accidents. Since the average risk level was only .032, the average compensation for each accident was $694/.032, or $21,700 in 1978 (or $44,500 in December 1990 dollars).

No individual worker would necessarily accept the certainty of an accident for this amount, since the implicit value attached to an injury will usually vary depending on the level of the risk. However, a group of thirty-two workers including an average of one who will be injured will receive a mean total risk pay of $21,700 to compensate them for the additional risk incurred.

The implicit value of injuries obtained from the semilogarithmic specification of the earnings equation was calculated similarly and was $24,300 in 1978 (or $49,800 in December 1990 dollars). The range of injury values implied by these results is $22,000 to $24,000. These estimates are not too dissimilar from the $17,000 values (in 1978 prices) for the SWC sample of workers. Moreover, the risk premiums were estimated for different risk measures, as the BLS injury rate in the earlier study pertained to nonfatal disabling injuries reported on a voluntary basis, while the lost

Table 3-5. Implicit Values of Death and Injury with Constant Valuations

Implicit values	Amount in 1978 prices
Value of nonfatal injury	
Wage equation	$21.7 × 10³
Log wage equation	$24.3 × 10³[a]
Value of death	
Wage equation	$4.16 × 10⁶
Log wage equation	$3.20 × 10⁶[a]

[a]Estimates for this specification were evaluated at the mean variable levels for the sample.

workday injuries were reported on a mandatory basis by all firms. Thus, there was a slight change in the injury rate definition and a major change in reporting procedures.

The implicit value-of-life estimates obtained when only the linear form of the death risk variable was included in the equation ranged from \$3.2 to \$4.2 million in 1978 (or \$6.6 to \$8.5 million in December 1990 prices), as indicated in the bottom of Table 3-5. For the earlier BLS death risk variable and the SWC sample, the implicit value-of-life estimates ranged from \$2.1 to \$2.6 million for the equation comparable to those estimated here. Due to the greater measurement error involved in the earlier, voluntary reporting technique, one would expect the SWC estimates in the previous study to be biased downward. It may also be that the omission of the nonpecuniary characteristic variables for the PSID sample biases these results upward.

The primary matter of interest here is the heterogeneity in the value of life obtained when nonlinear death risk variables are included. The findings in Table 3-6 indicate the variation in these values, where the different quartile risk levels pertain to the entire private sector rather than the particular sample analyzed. It is especially striking that the majority of workers in the low-risk occupations place a similar value on their lives of \$8 million for the linear specification and \$5 million for the semilogarithmic wage equation. Indeed, the first and third quartile value-of-life estimates differ by only 2 to 3 percent.

The big discrepancy arises for workers in the high-risk jobs as their \$3 million value-of-life estimates are much lower than those for workers in slightly less risky jobs. A value-of-life estimate of \$400,000 in 1978 prices (or \$800,000 in December 1990 prices) was obtained by Thaler and Rosen (1976) for a sample of workers facing an annual death risk of 11×10^{-4}, or twice the risk of the highest average industry risk level considered here. Although the estimates in this study cannot be extrapolated reliably to such high levels of risk, the sharp decline in the value of life at high risk levels is consistent with the types of patterns found here. In short, the findings suggest that if all individuals in society were ranked in terms of the value placed on their lives, the value of life would rise quite rapidly as one considered people beyond the low-valuation group and then approach a constant level that is considerably larger than the values in the lower end of the range.

Table 3-6. Heterogeneity in the Value of Life

Risk Level	Annual Death Risk	Value of Life	
		(Wage Equation)	(Log Wage Equation)
First Quartile	$.48 \times 10^{-4}$	\$8.05 \times 10^6	\$5.01 \times 10^6
Second Quartile	$.54 \times 10^{-4}$	\$7.99 \times 10^6	\$4.99 \times 10^6
Third Quartile	$.70 \times 10^{-4}$	\$7.85 \times 10^6	\$4.93 \times 10^6
Fourth Quartile	6.18×10^{-4}	\$2.98 \times 10^6	\$2.82 \times 10^6
Sample Mean	1.04×10^{-4}	\$7.56 \times 10^6	\$4.83 \times 10^6

Note.
[a]Risk levels for each quartile pertain to the upper boundary of the quartile.

3.6 POLICY APPLICATIONS

Suppose that the pertinent schedule of values of life for the population has already been obtained through prior empirical work. The key question is how these schedules are to be used in the policy evaluation process in situations in which individuals incur risks voluntarily and involuntarily. Although the degree of volition involved spans a continuum of possibilities, for simplicity I focus on the polar cases of completely voluntary and completely involuntary risk.

The nature of the risk conveys important information about the implicit value of life and limb being assigned by the affected population. Other things being equal, it is those who place the lowest dollar value on the expected loss to their health who choose to incur the risk. If individuals choose to live in a flood-prone area, to drive cars while intoxicated, or to work at hazardous jobs, the government's assessment of the value of the health gains from safety regulation should be quite different from its assessment when no element of free choice is involved. The empirical estimates reported in Chapter 2, for example, indicated that smokers and those who do not wear seat belts value injuries less than those who engage in risk-averse behavior.

Suppose that the characteristics of the affected population are comparable with those of the SWC sample of workers that was examined and that the median value of life corresponds to that of the individual at point f in Figure 3-3. Consider the situation in which the risk is involuntary and affects the whole population. Then the use of the median individual's value of life gives correct estimates of the benefits of lifesaving activities if the value-of-life schedule is linear, as is CC; overstates the benefits if the schedule is concave, as is BB; or understates the benefits for schedule AA. The results for the PSID indicated that the curve BB reflects the actual population distribution of values. If the risk is voluntary and affects only half of the population, the use of the median individual's preferences at point f overstates the value of life irrespective of the shape of the value-of-life curve, since all other

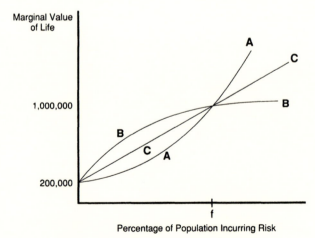

Figure 3.3 Possible value-of-life schedules

individuals who have chosen the risk value their lives at less than the amount for the median individual.

For the purposes of policy evaluation, it is the preferences of the average individual that matter in calculating consumers' surplus. The value of health-enhancing program benefits to project beneficiaries is computed by multiplying the number of lives saved or injuries prevented by the average value attached to these outcomes. In contrast, market outcomes reflect the preferences of the marginal worker. The valuation of life and limb of the worker who accepts the risky job and who is most averse to the hazards is instrumental in setting the wage rate, not the preferences of all the other inframarginal workers who would be willing to accept less than the going wage for the hazardous job.

3.7 CONCLUSION

Obtaining estimates of the risk-dollar tradeoff is feasible with the use of large sets of data on labor market behavior. In particular, it is possible to estimate the premiums received for both fatal and nonfatal job risk. These premiums can then be used to calculate the value per statistical death and per statistical injury that workers receive in return for facing these risks.

The empirical results presented in this chapter suggest that these values are quite substantial. The typical worker receives compensation for fatalities on the order of $1 to $2 million, and for nonfatal injuries on the order of $10,000, where these results are in 1969 prices. These tradeoffs are not universal constants but will vary with the individual characteristics in the sample. The results of estimates based on a sample of workers who knowingly engage in high-risk occupations yield smaller estimates of the value of life, as one would expect. Moreover, estimates of the heterogeneity of the value of life indicate that the value per statistical life steadily decreases as the average risk faced by the worker increases, which is a pattern one would expect in a rational labor market in which workers who are most willing to engage in risk-taking activity are most attracted to the hazardous occupations. Although the literature review in Chapter 4 will identify a broad range of subsequent studies that have addressed these issues using a variety of data sets for different countries, the essential thrust of these results has remained unchanged.

NOTES

1. A more formal statement of the underlying model is provided in Viscusi (1979a). The state-dependent utility model presented there is quite general. The ill-health state can be interpreted as either a fatal or a nonfatal job injury.

2. Also a forerunner of this line of work is the research on hedonic price indexes by Griliches (1971). See also Thaler and Rosen (1976).

3. Inframarginal workers earn an economic rent. The wage-risk tradeoff of the marginal worker is instrumental in establishing the wage rate the firm must pay and consequently the value of the risk reduction.

4. All injury rate data are from the injury and illness bulletin of the U.S. Department of Labor (1971b).

5. Since INJRATE is the number of fatalities and injuries per million hours, the number per 2,000 hours is INJRATE divided by 500. DEATH and NONFATAL are the percentages of INJRATE that are

fatal and nonfatal, i.e., DEATH + NONFATAL = 100 INJRATE. Hence, dividing each by 50,000 converts it to an annual probability.

6. Ideally, one would like to use the hourly wage as the dependent variable rather than total earnings, but the SWC did not provide wage data or other information, such as weeks worked, that would make it possible to construct a wage rate. Since the analysis focuses on full-time workers and includes an overtime work variable, this shortcoming is presumably not very serious.

7. These estimates were obtained with respect to a one-unit change in the death risk evaluated at the mean income level for the sample.

8. In addition to *ex ante* wage compensation, workers also receive substantial tax-free workers' compensation benefits—up to two-thirds of the worker's gross wages in most states—so that the injury results, in particular, underestimate the implicit values attached by the workers.

9. Their sample was selected on the basis of the availability of death risk data, which was provided only for the most hazardous occupations.

10. The seven variables omitted were all of the eleven job characteristic variables except the number of employees at the enterprise variable and the three occupational dummy variables.

11. The intercept for this simplified model is presumably zero, since workers receive no wage premium if they face no additional risk.

12. This death risk variable was based on a new reporting system introduced in the 1970s. It differs from the BLS death risk variable used earlier.

13. The fit for each of the four equations reported was quite similar, with an R^2 value of .57 for all of them. The semilogarithmic specification has a stronger justification in terms of the human capital theory linkage between earnings and schooling, but no comparable relationship has yet been derived for job risk and earnings.

4

A Survey of Values of Risks to Life and Health

4.1 INTRODUCTION

The wage-risk studies considered in Chapter 3 outline the basic approach that has been reflected in what is now a considerable literature on the valuation of risks to life and health. Over the past two decades, there have been a large number of studies using a variety of data sets to assess the tradeoff between worker wages and fatality risks. These studies address not only risks to U.S. workers but also the implicit values of life reflected in the behavior of workers in the United Kingdom, Australia, Canada, and Japan. A straightforward extension of these models has been to include a measure of nonfatal risks faced by the worker, enabling analysts to impute an implicit value per statistical injury in the workplace. There have also been attempts to analyze the price-risk tradeoff for several consumer products, yielding results somewhat similar to those reflected in wage equations.

In situations in which no market data are available, one can attempt to simulate the results of the market through a survey methodology. In particular, the usual survey approach is to ask how much consumers would be willing to pay for some risk reduction, assuming that some simulated market context has been created. This approach, which has been frequently referred to as the contingent valuation methodology, enables economists to ascertain the risk-dollar tradeoffs for outcomes as diverse as chronic bronchitis and the common cold.

This chapter provides a comprehensive survey of these different approaches to valuing fatal and nonfatal risks to life and health. In every case, the common element of these approaches is a concern with eliciting as precisely as possible the particular risk-dollar tradeoff pertinent to the individuals in the sample. These diverse results provide a strong empirical basis for establishing the appropriate tradeoff for risk-regulation policies, and these estimates are now widely used in a variety of regulatory contexts.[1]

4.2 REVIEW OF RISK TRADEOFFS
IN THE LABOR MARKET LITERATURE

Although the methodology for estimating the labor market value of life follows the general approach outlined in Chapter 3, there has been considerable variation in the literature in terms of the empirical estimates. Table 4-1 summarizes twenty-three of

Table 4-1. Summary of Labor Market Studies of the Value of Life

Author (year)	Sample	Risk variable	Mean risk	Nonfatal risk included?	Workers' comp included?	Average income level (1990 U.S.$)	Implicit value of life ($million)	Implicit value of life for air travelers ($million)
R. S. Smith (1974)	Industry data: census of manufacturers, U.S. Census, Employment and Earnings	Bureau of Labor Statistics (BLS)	NA[a]	Yes	No	22,640	7.2	11.0
Thaler and Rosen (1976)	Survey of Economic Opportunity	Society of Actuaries	.001	No	No	27,034	0.8	1.0
R. S. Smith (1976)	Current Population Survey (CPS), 1967, 1973	Bureau of Labor Statistics (BLS)	.0001	Yes, not signif.	No	NA	4.6	NA
Viscusi (1978a, 1979a)	Survey of Working Conditions, 1969–1970 (SWC)	BLS, subjective risk of job (SWC)	.0001	Yes, signif.	No	24,834	4.1	5.7
Brown (1980)	National Longitudinal Survey of Young Men 1966–1971, 1973	Society of Actuaries	.002	No	No	NA	1.5	NA
Viscusi (1981)	Panel Study of Income Dynamics, 1976	BLS	.0001	Yes, signif.	No	17,640	6.5	12.8
Olson (1981)	CPS	BLS	.0001	Yes, signif.	No	NA	5.2	NA
Marin and Psacharoopoulos (1982)	U.K. Office of Population Censuses and Surveys, 1977	Occupational mortality U.K.	.0001	No	No	11,287	2.8	8.1
Arnould and Nichols (1983)	U.S. Census	Society of Actuaries	.001	No	Yes	NA	0.9	NA
Butler (1983)	S.C. Workers' Compensation Data 1940/–1969	S.C. Workers' compensation claims data	.00005	No	Yes	NA	1.1	NA

Study	Data	Source						
Leigh and Folsom (1984)	Panel Study of Income Dynamics, 1974; Quality of Employment Survey, 1977	BLS	.0001	Yes	No	27,693, 28,734	9.7, 10.3	11.0, 11.7
Smith and Gilbert (1984)	Current Population Survey, 1978	BLS	NA	No	No	NA	0.7	NA
Dillingham (1985)	Quality of Employment Survey, 1977	BLS; Constructed by author	.00008, .00014	No	No	20,848	2.5–5.3; 0.9	4.2–8.8; 1.5
Leigh (1987)	Quality of Employment Survey, 1977; Current Population Survey, 1977	BLS	NA	No	No	NA	10.4	NA
Herzog and Schlottman (1987)	U.S. Census, 1970	BLS	NA	No	No	NA	9.1	NA
Moore and Viscusi (1988a)	Panel Study of Income Dynamics, 1982	BLS, NIOSH National Traumatic Occupational Fatality Survey	.00005, .00008	No	Yes	19,444	2.5, 7.3	4.6, 13.4
Moore and Viscusi (1988b)	Quality of Employment Survey, 1977	BLS, discounted expected life years lost; subjective risk of job (QES)	.00006	No	Yes	24,249	7.3	10.5
Garen (1988)	Panel Study of Income Dynamics, 1981–1982	BLS	NA	Yes	No	NA	13.5	NA
Cousineau, Lacroix, and Girard (1988)	Labor Canada Survey, 1979	Quebec Compensation Board	.00001	No	No	NA	3.6	NA
Viscusi and Moore (1989)	Panel Study of Income Dynamics, 1982	NIOSH (National Traumatic Occupational Fatality Survey), Structural Markov Model	.0001	No	No	19,194	7.8	14.1

(continued)

Table 4-1. (*Continued*)

Author (*year*)	Sample	Risk variable	Mean risk	Nonfatal risk included?	Workers' comp included?	Average income level (*1990 U.S.$*)	Implicit value of life (*$million*)	Implicit value of life for air travelers (*$million*)
Moore and Viscusi (1990b)	Panel Study of Income Dynamics, 1982	NIOSH National Traumatic Occupational Fatality Survey, Structural Life Cycle Model	.0001	No	No	19,194	16.2	29.4
Moore and Viscusi (1990c)	Panel Study of Income Dynamics, 1982	NIOSH National Traumatic Occupational Fatality Survey, Structural Integrated Life Cycle Model	.0001	Yes	Yes	19,194	16.2	29.4
Kniesner and Leeth (1991)	Two-digit mfg. data, Japan, 1986	Yearbook of Labor Statistics, Japan	.00003	Yes	No	34,989	7.6	7.5
	Two-digit mfg. data, Australia, by state, 1984–1985	Industrial accident data, Australia	.0001	Yes	Yes	18,177	3.3	6.3
	Current Population Survey, U.S., 1978	NIOSH (National Traumatic Occupational Fatality Survey)	.0004	Yes	Yes	26,226	0.6	0.8

Note: All values are in December 1990 dollars.

[a]NA = Not available.

the principal studies that have been undertaken to estimate the implicit value of life using labor market data. These studies appear in chronological order, beginning with 1974. Efforts to estimate compensating differentials before that time were largely unsuccessful because of the inadequacy of industrywide data to generate reliable estimates of wage differentials for risk. R. S. Smith (1974) successfully used industry-based data, but the other studies in the 1970s utilized individual worker data. Because of the positive income elasticity of the demand for good health, the more affluent workers will have safer jobs. The fact that the best jobs also tend to be the highest paid has long been observed by economists, and this relationship confounds any attempt to isolate wage premiums for risk. The advent of large micro data sets on individual worker behavior in the 1970s enabled economists to sort out the different influences at work. As Brown (1980) has observed, even large micro data sets do not always enable one to readily isolate the wage-risk tradeoff.

The studies listed in Table 4-1 differ in a variety of respects, including the data sets used as well as the nature of the specification. Perhaps the starkest difference consists of the structural estimation approach that is employed to differing degrees in the most recent studies. The initial studies in the literature consisted almost entirely of simple regressions of wage rates on risk levels. Beginning with Moore and Viscusi (1988b), there was an attempt to estimate the tradeoff for discounted expected life years lost rather than simply a death risk variable. This procedure was extended in their subsequent three studies listed in Table 4-1, in which specific functional forms were derived to relate the worker's wage rate to the nature of the lifetime job choice problem. These models are the most theoretically elegant, and they involve the most complex estimations.

These structural models are particularly insightful in illuminating more refined aspects of the lifetime job choice problem in situations involving fatality risks. Chief among the results is that the estimated implicit rate of discount that workers use in valuing death risks does not differ in a statistically significant manner from the prevailing rates of return in financial markets during the time periods under study. Thus, there is no evidence to indicate that we should use a different rate of discount when weighting the long-term health benefits of policies that affect life extension as compared with other benefit and cost components that these policies may have. An appropriate *real* rate of return based on market interest rates is a reasonable starting point for this procedure.

The additional information provided by the structural estimation approaches comes at a cost. The estimation procedures are quite complicated, and considerably greater demands are placed on the data. As a result, the risk-dollar tradeoff estimates tend to be less robust than in a more straightforward estimation approach. As a result, I will place greater reliance upon the more conventional wage equation estimates of the risk-wage tradeoff than on the findings yielded by the structural estimation models.

Although many of the studies listed in Table 4-1 consist primarily of replications and consistency checks on earlier results, a number of important innovations have occurred in the literature. The rows in Table 4-1 summarize the different dimensions of these studies. All except four of the studies rely upon large data sets on the U.S.

work force. R. S. Smith (1974) uses industry-level data; Marin and Psacharopoulos (1982) utilize data from the United Kingdom; Cousineau, Lacroix, and Girard (1988) analyze Canadian data; and Kniesner and Leeth (1991) analyze data from Japan, Australia, and the United States. All of these studies utilize national surveys of worker behavior, with the exception of R. S. Smith (1974) and the study by Butler (1983), which focuses on the performance in South Carolina using state workers' compensation data.

Because all of these surveys include most of the demographic and job characteristic information needed to estimate a reliable wage equation, the main distinguishing feature is the manner in which the risk variable is created. None of the sets of survey data listed include any objective measure of the risks posed by the worker's particular job. The University of Michigan's Survey of Working Conditions and Quality of Employment Survey each include a subjective risk variable. These data sets have been analyzed by Viscusi (1978a, 1979a), Dillingham (1985), Leigh (1987), and Moore and Viscusi (1988b), but not all of these researchers have utilized the subjective risk variable. The Michigan surveys included a question ascertaining whether the worker's job exposed him or her to dangerous or unhealthy conditions. The subjective risk-perception variable can be interacted with some objective measure of the risk to create a potentially more refined estimate of the risk variable. This procedure is followed in Viscusi (1978a, 1979a) and in Moore and Viscusi (1988b), each of which interacts a 0–1 subjective risk-perception variable for the worker's particular job with the BLS industry risk measure.

The dominant approach followed in the literature is to rely upon some published measure of the risk level by occupation or industry, and then to match this risk variable to the worker in the sample using information provided by the respondent on his or her job. The study by Thaler and Rosen (1976) utilized Society of Actuaries data pertaining to the risk associated with different occupations, as did Brown (1980) and Arnould and Nichols (1983). These data pertain primarily to high-risk occupations with average annual risks of death on the order of 1/1,000, which is roughly ten times the average for the U.S. workplace. To the extent that workers who select themselves into high-risk jobs have a lower risk-dollar tradeoff than do workers in higher-risk jobs, one would expect to obtain lower value-of-life estimates in studies that utilize these data, as Thaler and Rosen (1976) recognize. In addition, the Society of Actuaries data pertained to all incremental mortality risks associated with people in different occupations, not simply the job-specific risk. Thus, this variable also reflects risks other than those on the job, which would not be compensated through the wage mechanism.

Twelve of the studies listed in Table 4-1 utilize the U.S. Bureau of Labor Statistics risk data based on the risks associated with different industries. This risk measure has not been the same over time, however. Before the advent of the Occupational Safety and Health Administration, the reporting system for all injuries was different than after the establishment of OSHA, so that the occupational fatality risk data beginning in 1972 are not comparable to the risk data before 1972. The early studies in the literature, such as R. S. Smith (1974, 1976) and Viscusi (1978a, 1979a), utilize the pre-OSHA industrial fatality data, whereas the most recent studies utilizing BLS data have relied upon the post-OSHA data. The main deficiency of these data is that they pertain to an industrywide average risk and do not distinguish among the different jobs within that industry. In an effort to promote greater comparability of the risk measures with the jobs, various authors have restricted the sample composition by, for example, limiting it to only blue-collar workers for whom the risk data will be more pertinent. Additional limitations of the BLS data are that the reporting may not be complete, and there is a general belief that occupational diseases are not accurately captured in these data.

In an effort to reduce the measurement error associated with the fatality data, the National Institute of Occupational Safety and Health (NIOSH) instituted the National Traumatic Occupational Fatality Survey. This survey yielded a new set of data on industrial fatality rates that has been utilized in four recent studies by Michael Moore and myself, which are reported at the end of Table 4-1, and by Kniesner and Leeth (1991). In Moore and Viscusi (1988a) we compare the results obtained using the BLS and the NIOSH data as well as the data sets themselves. Although the risk level is higher in the NIOSH data than the BLS data, which suggests a more thorough tallying of the total number of occupational fatalities, there are other important differences as well. In particular, the comparison of results suggests that there are systematic differences in the reporting in the two sets of data. It is not simply the case that one can transform the BLS data into the NIOSH data through the use of a constant multiplicative scale factor. In practice, the main difference is that one obtains much higher estimates of the risk-wage tradeoff when using the NIOSH data than the BLS data, which is consistent with there being greater random measurement error with the BLS measure.

An important dimension on which these studies differ is in terms of the set of other job characteristic variables included in the equation. In particular, unless one includes variables other than job risk to capture the nonpecuniary aspects of the job, one cannot be confident that one is isolating wage premiums for risk as compared with compensating differentials for other unpleasant job characteristics. Most of the studies include some attempt to control for these influences through the inclusion of sets of occupational or industry dummy variables. In addition, several of these studies include a measure of the nonfatal risk associated with the job.

The studies by Viscusi (1978a, 1979a) were the first to obtain an estimate of a statistically significant value of compensation for injuries as well as fatalities. These studies also included a comprehensive set of nonpecuniary job characteristics, including whether the worker was a supervisor, the speed of work, whether the worker made decisions on the job, whether the job required the worker not make mistakes, job security, overtime work, worker training, and a series of dummy variables for the worker's industry and occupation.

The chief recent addition to the compensating differential equation has been the inclusion of a workers' compensation variable, beginning with the studies by Butler (1983), and by Arnould and Nichols (1983). Inclusion of a workers' compensation measure takes into account an important alternative for compensating job risks. In practice, inclusion of this variable serves to raise the estimated wage-risk tradeoff in the typical case. Although most studies in the literature have utilized state average benefit measures, beginning with Viscusi and Moore (1987) the compensating differential also included a worker-specific workers' compensation variable based

on the state benefit formulas in conjunction with the worker's demographic characteristics. Most importantly this variable also was interacted with the risk on the
worker's job so that the variable was the expected workers' compensation benefit
(or, more specifically, the expected replacement rate). Interaction of the probability
of receiving the benefits with the benefit level takes into account the fact that
workers who face no risk on the job would place zero value on workers' compensation.

As the average income level data included in Table 4-1 indicate, the composition
of the samples has varied considerably in terms of the income level of the workers.
This distinction is important because what these studies yield is an estimate of the
implicit wage-risk tradeoff—the implied value per statistical life—that is pertinent
to a particular segment of the population and cannot necessarily be generalized to
the population at large. In the case of the standard measure of economic damages
for accidents, the size of the loss is the present value of earnings, which varies
proportionally with the income level. The value of life from the standpoint of *ex
ante* prevention also varies with the income level. The estimates derived in Viscusi
and Evans (1990) suggest that the workers' implicit value of job injuries has an
income elasticity of approximately 1.0.

For purposes of illustration, let us assume that a comparable elasticity pertains to
fatality risks. One would expect the value-of-life estimates to rise roughly proportionally with the income level in the sample. Suppose we are valuing the benefits
from improved aviation safety. The average passenger on a U.S. airline has a
median income level of $32,840, which is considerably higher than the income
levels listed in Table 4-1.[2] If we extrapolate the results to the airline passenger
population using a unitary income elasticity, Thaler and Rosen's (1976) values for
this income group would rise to $1.0 million, and those in Viscusi (1978a, 1979a)
would rise to $5.7 million. The results from the United Kingdom by Marin and
Psacharopoulos (1982) would be even higher—$8.1 million—after making this
income adjustment. The final column in Table 4-1 summarizes the implied value-of-
life estimates for the typical airline passenger.

As the implicit value-of-life estimates in Table 4-1 indicate, the estimated wage-
risk tradeoff varies considerably across data sets and methodologies. There are a
number of reasons for this difference, one of which is that the mix of workers in
these samples is quite different. The value of life is not a universal constant, but it
reflects the wage-risk tradeoff that is pertinent to the preferences of the workers in a
particular sample.

In terms of picking a specific number, external observers could legitimately differ
in terms of the studies they most prefer. The most comprehensive earnings differential equation is that in Viscusi (1978a), but Moore and Viscusi (1988a) is potentially superior in that it includes the NIOSH risk measure. Its deficiencies as compared with Viscusi (1978a) are that it does not include a nonfatal risk variable or
extensive measures of the characteristics of the worker's job other than the fatality
risk so that the high estimated value of life may partially reflect omitted variables
bias.

Perhaps the best way to interpret these studies is that there is a value-of-life range
that is potentially pertinent. The quest for estimates of the value of life does not have

the same precision as nuclear physics. Rather than isolating a single best value-of-life number, a more appropriate policy approach would be to calculate the discounted costs per expected life saved and then to ascertain whether this figure is reasonable given the range of plausible value-of-life estimates that have been obtained in the literature.

4.3 THE IMPLICIT VALUE OF INJURY
BASED ON LABOR MARKET STUDIES

As in the case of fatalities, the principal source of evidence available pertaining to the risk-dollar tradeoff that individuals have with respect to nonfatal injuries is labor market data. What is the main matter of interest is the attitude individuals have toward accident prevention. Court awards are an *ex post* concept relating to insurance. Insurance issues are not totally unrelated to deterrence, and in the case of property damage losses they may be identical. However, for accidents involving serious personal injury the *ex post* compensation amounts will abstract from many of the important nonmonetary health losses that should be taken into account when valuing the benefits of policy improvements.

The methodology that is used to derive estimates of the implicit value of injury using labor market data parallels that for fatalities. The only difference is that we are now concerned with the wage premium for nonfatal risks rather than fatalities.

Ideally, one would like to distinguish the compensation for fatality risks from the compensation for nonfatal risks. Thus, we would like to include both a fatal risk measure and a nonfatal risk measure. In practice, including both of these variables has proven difficult, with the exception of a few studies.

The difficulties arise for two reasons. First, if there is a strong positive correlation between fatal and nonfatal risk measures for the industry, which are then matched to the individual worker, then it will be hard to disentangle the premiums associated with each of these risk measures. Second, recent studies have begun to rely upon the NIOSH fatal accident data rather than the U.S. Bureau of Labor Statistics (BLS) accident data. Since there is no nonfatal injury variable counterpart to the NIOSH data, whereas there was such a counterpart for the BLS data, there is no natural pair of variables gathered by government agencies that covers both classes of accidents. Attempts to include a NIOSH fatality risk measure in equations with BLS nonfatal risk measures have thus far not led to significant estimates for both sets of coefficients, perhaps due in part to the different reporting bases and methodologies used in gathering these accident statistics. Exclusion of the fatality risk measure from a nonfatal risk equation will tend to bias the estimates of the fatality risk premium upward, whereas random measurement error that arises from matching up an industry injury risk measure to an individual based on his or her reported industry will tend to bias the estimated value of the injuries downward.

The other main component of the earnings determination process for workers in hazardous jobs is workers' compensation. Differences across states in terms of the generosity of workers' compensation benefits will affect the premiums that workers receive for the hazards they face. The main effect of adding this variable is to improve the significance and increase the magnitude of the estimated coefficient on the nonfatal injury risk variable. However, in computing the implicit value of injuries in terms of the risk-dollar tradeoff, one must recognize that a higher injury rate will raise wage compensation through the risk premium effect, but it will lower wage compensation due to the workers' compensation offset from wages. Thus, there are two competing effects that must be taken into account when determining the net effect of risk levels on wages.

Table 4-2 summarizes seventeen studies that have successfully estimated the significant compensating differentials for job injury risk.[3] For fourteen of these studies it is possible to compute an implicit value of job injuries based on the data presented by the authors.[4]

The studies in Table 4-2 do not pertain to a homogeneous class of nonfatal injuries. In some cases the injuries reflect only those accidents that lead to a loss in work, whereas in other instances less severe injuries may be included. There are other differences as well, as some sets of injury data pertain to average reported industry risk levels, whereas others are the assessed injury amounts based on the worker's subjective perceptions.

The first of the injury variables used was the BLS injury rate data gathered before the advent of OSHA and the institution of the new reporting system. Injury reporting through 1970 was based on voluntary reports by the firm, which were then made mandatory in the 1970s. Studies using the pre-OSHA injury variable are those by Viscusi (1978a,b, 1979a). The second injury variable used is the total BLS reported accident rate, which is identical to the reported nonfatal accident rate. These statistics capture all job injuries, including those that are not severe enough to lead to the loss of a day of work. The studies that have used this variable include Viscusi (1981), Olson (1981), V. K. Smith (1983), Leigh and Folsom (1984), Viscusi and Moore (1987), and Garen (1988). To capture injuries of greater severity, some studies have used only the lost workday injury component of the reported BLS nonfatal accident statistics. These studies are those by Viscusi and Moore (1987) and Kniesner and Leeth (1991).

Two studies have used subjective risk-perception variables based on workers' assessed risk, where the risk scale presented to the workers was patterned after the BLS objective risk measure described above. In the case of Viscusi and O'Connor (1984), the reference scale was based on the overall reported BLS injury rate. In the case of Hersch and Viscusi (1990), the scale used was based on the BLS lost workday accident rate. Thus, these two studies provide the values of workers' subjective risk perceptions that are the counterparts of the two currently maintained BLS injury rate series.

Two other studies have utilized other risk data that are more specific in nature. Butler (1983) analyzed employment data for South Carolina workers derived from workers' compensation data for injuries that are severe enough to be filed in the workers' compensation system in South Carolina. French and Kendall (1991) used injury rate data gathered by the Federal Railroad Administration as their basis for deriving estimates of the implicit value of job injuries.

In all but two cases the approach was identical. The authors specify an equation in which the dependent variable is either the wage rate, the workers' annual earn-

Table 4-2. Summary of Labor Market Studies of Job Injuries

Author (year)	Sample	Nonfatal risk variable	Mean injury risk	Fatality risk included?	Workers' comp included?	Average income level (1990)	Implicit value of injury	Implicit value of injury for air traveler ($millions)
Viscusi (1978a, 1979a)	Survey of Working Conditions, 1969–1970	BLS nonfatal injury rate, 1969 (pre-OSHA)	.032	Yes	No	$24,800	$20,038–$38,560	$26,450–$50,899
Viscusi (1978b)	Survey of Working Conditions, 1969–1970	BLS nonfatal injury rate, 1969 (pre-OSHA)	.032	No	No	$24,800	$47,993–$49,322	$63,351–$65,105
Olson (1981)	Current Population Survey, 1973	BLS total lost workday accident rate, 1973	.035	Yes	No	$27,686	$18,725–$25,194	$22,283–$29,981
Viscusi (1981)	Panel Study of Income Dynamics, 1976	BLS lost workday injury rate, 1976	.032	Yes	No	$23,656	$46,200	$64,136
Butler (1983)	S.C. Workers' Compensation data, 1940–1969	S.C. Workers' Compensation injury days data	.061 (claims rate)	No	Yes	$12,403	$730/day	$1,933/day
Dorsey and Walzer (1983)	Current Population Survey, 1978	BLS nonfatal lost workday injury incidence rate, 1976	.030	Yes, in some equations	Yes	NA	Not reported, can't calculate	NA
V. K. Smith (1983)	Current Population Survey, 1978	BLS work injury rate	.078	No	No	$25,338	$27,675	$35,869

(continued)

Table 4-2. (*Continued*)

Author (*year*)	Sample	Nonfatal risk variable	Mean injury risk	Fatality risk included?	Workers' comp included?	Average income level (*1990*)	Implicit value of injury	Implicit value of injury for air traveler (*$millions*)
Leigh and Folsom (1984)	Panel Study of Income Dynamics, 1974; Quality of Employment Survey, 1977	BLS nonfatal injury rate	.074, .066	Yes	No	$27,693, $28,734	$77,547–$89,403	$92,281–$106,390
Viscusi and O'Connor (1984)	Authors' chemical worker survey, 1982	Workers' assessed injury and illness rate	.10	No	No	$29,357	$13,810–$17,761	$15,467–$19,892
Viscusi and Moore (1987)	Quality of Employment Survey, 1977	BLS lost workday injury rate, BLS total injury rate	.038, .097	No	Yes	$33,928	$55,100 lost workday accident; $21,800 for nonpecuniary loss—lost workday accident; $35,400 per accident	$53,447 lost workday accident; $21,146 for nonpecuniary loss—lost workday accident; $34,338 per accident
Biddle and Zarkin (1988)	Quality of Employment Survey, 1977	BLS nonfatal lost workday injury incidence rate, 1977	.037	No	No	$32,889	$131,495 (willing to accept), $121,550 (willing to pay)	$131,299 (willing to accept) $121,368 (willing to pay)

Study	Data/Sample	Injury rate measure	Rate					
Cousineau, Lacroix, and Girard (1988)	Labor Canada Survey, 1979	Quebec Compensation Board Occupational Injury Rates	.069	Yes	No	NA	Not reported, can't calculate	NA
Garen (1988)	Panel Study of Income Dynamics, 1981–1982	BLS nonfatal injury rate, 1980–1981	NA	Yes	No	NA	$21,021	NA
Hersch and Viscusi (1990)	Authors' survey in Eugene, Oregon 1987	Workers' assessed injury rate using BLS lost workday incidence rate scale	.059	No	No, same state	$17,078	$56,537 (full sample); $30,781 (smokers); $92,245 (seat belt users)	$108,551 (full sample); $59,100 (smokers); $177,110 (seat belt users)
Viscusi and Evans (1990)	Viscusi and O'Connor chemical worker survey, 1982	Utility function estimates using assessed injury and illness rate	.10	No	No	$29,482	$18,547 (marginal risk change); $28,880 (certain injury)	$20,660 (marginal risk change); $32,169 (certain injury)
French and Kendall (1991)	Current Population Survey, 1980, railroad industry only	Federal Railroad Administration injury data	.048	No	No	$36,097	$38,159	$34,716
Kniesner and Leeth (1991)	Current Population Survey, 1978	BLS lost workday accident rate	.055	Yes	Yes	$26,268	$47,281	$57,110

ings, or the natural logarithm of one of these two values. The authors then regress this variable against a series of variables pertaining to the workers' personal characteristics and job characteristics.

The two exceptions to this approach are those that have attempted to explore more fully the character of individuals' utility functions. Biddle and Zarkin (1988) attempted to impose greater structure on the estimation process by taking into account the constraints imposed by the tangency of individual utility functions with the market offer curve at the points along the offer curve that workers are willing to accept. Viscusi and Evans (1990) explicitly estimated individual utility functions for job injuries using baseline data pertaining to the assessed risk of the current job in conjunction with additional survey information pertaining to the wage compensation workers could receive after being given a hazard warning label that changed the character of their job, thus making it possible to observe two points along a constant expected utility locus.

The additional information provided by knowledge of the individual utility functions that is obtained in Viscusi and Evans (1990) is twofold. First, by showing that job accidents affect the structure of the utility function and lower the marginal utility of income, this paper documented the hypothesized discrepancy between the value of injuries from the standpoint of compensation and deterrence. The results have also shown for that data set that the difference between the willingness to accept values for risk increases and the willingness to pay amounts for risk reduction are very minor, so that from the standpoint of benefit assessment, utilization of the results from labor market studies should provide an accurate index of the benefit measure. Even substantial changes in the injury risk by, for example, $+.50$ will have only a modest effect on the implicit value of an injury.

Second, the paper estimated the income elasticity of the value of job injuries (measured in terms of the risk-dollar tradeoff) as being approximately 1.0. This estimate is the basis for the extrapolation of the value of injury statistics to reflect other income levels, such as the calculation of the values for airline passengers that appears in the final column of Table 4-2.

Let us consider some of the specific estimates that have been obtained. In the early studies using the pre-OSHA BLS injury data, Viscusi (1978a,b, 1979a) estimated the implicit value of injuries as being between $20,000 and $50,000. The values obtained using the BLS total accident rate are of roughly the same order of magnitude: $46,200 in Viscusi (1981), an average of $22,100 in Olson (1981), an average of $83,500 in Leigh and Folsom (1984), an average of $27,700 in V. K. Smith (1983), an average of $35,400 in Viscusi and Moore (1987), and $21,000 in Garen (1988). Most of these estimates are clustered in the $25,000 to $50,000 range.

The values for lost workday injuries tend to be somewhat greater. Viscusi and Moore (1987) report estimates for both the total accident rate and the lost workday accident rate for the same specifications, with the result being that the lost workday accident variable implies a value per injury of $55,100, as contrasted with a comparable estimate of $35,400 for the total accident measure. Kniesner and Leeth (1991) obtained comparable estimates of the implicit value of lost workday injury of

$47,300. The value of lost workday injuries consequently appears to be in the area of $50,000, or at the high end of the range for estimates for the implicit value of injuries overall.

The results in Viscusi and O'Connor (1984) for the total reported accident rate as subjectively assessed by the worker appear to be at the low end of the range for the market estimates, whereas the results for the subjectively assessed total lost work-day risk in Hersch and Viscusi (1990) appear to be closer to the estimated market values.

The Hersch and Viscusi (1990) study also provides estimates of differences in the implicit value of risk for different segments of the population. One would expect that individuals who have displayed a willingness to incur risks of other types would be more willing to bear risks on the job. This rational self-selection pattern is in fact borne out by the data. Smokers have a value per statistical job injury of $30,781, which is below the full sample value of $56,537. Seat belt users place a much higher implicit value on job injuries—$92,245. This heterogeneity in the value of riskiness corroborates the plausibility of the labor market studies.

The two studies that report estimated implicit values of injury obtained using other types of data also yield similar estimates. Butler's (1983) estimated value per day of injury is $730. For an average work injury in the United States that involves eighteen lost days of work, this value implies an implicit value per injury of $13,140. Butler's (1983) results imply a relatively low value of injury because they pertain to a low-income sample. For the typical airplane passenger, this injury value would be $34,794. The study of railroad worker injuries by French and Kendall (1991) yields an implicit value per injury of $38,200—or $34,716 for the typical airplane passenger's income level—which is very much in the range of the afore-mentioned studies of job injury.

4.4 OTHER MARKET EVIDENCE ON IMPLICIT TRADEOFFS

Since our objective is to obtain an estimate of the risk-dollar tradeoff, other market transactions that individuals make potentially could be utilized to obtain an estimate of this tradeoff value. We take a variety of risks in the course of our lives, including risks associated with consumption habits, transportation, and recreational activities. If one can identify the risk component of these actions and analyze the offsetting advantages that lead us to choose to engage in these pursuits, then potentially one can estimate the wage-risk tradeoff using data on behavior other than job decisions.

The advantage of labor market studies is that we observe the workers' income and wages, and we have reasonably reliable information on the risk levels as well, so that the two components of the tradeoff can be ascertained with some precision. Perhaps the main disadvantage of some of the studies outside the labor market is that it has often been necessary to impute values for at least one component of the tradeoff. For example, we may know the risk differences at stake, but we must estimate the dollar stakes involved in any particular instance. As a result, many of the studies to be discussed below should be regarded as very ingenious efforts to construct risk-dollar tradeoffs, but in terms of establishing an implicit value of a statistical life, they typically provide a less direct and potentially less reliable measure.

Table 4-3 summarizes the components of seven different studies in the literature. The tradeoffs involve the choice of highway speed, installation of smoke detectors, cigarette smoking decisions, property values, and automobile safety.

The study by Ghosh, Lees, and Seal (1975) utilized individual choice of highway speed, where the tradeoff involved the increased risk of death associated with greater speeds versus the time that would be saved. Two critical assumptions are that individuals understand the incremental mortality risk associated with different driving speeds, and that the opportunity cost of time is equal to the worker's wage rate. The opportunity cost assumption may be most questionable since some driving may have a low opportunity cost because it is actually enjoyable, whereas other driving in traffic jams may have an extremely high disutility. The study by Blomquist (1979) likewise utilizes the automobile safety context but focuses on the decision to wear a seat belt. The risk involved pertains to the reduced risk of fatality associated with the wearing of seat belts. Some analysts speculate that this risk may not be well understood given the low frequency of voluntary seat belt use.[5] The major open issue in this analysis is the value one should attach to the time and inconvenience costs of wearing a seat belt, which are not directly observable. The third auto safety study is that of Atkinson and Halvorsen (1990), who analyze price-risk tradeoffs using a hedonic price model that is comparable in approach to the hedonic wage-risk studies.

Dardis (1980) focuses on the decision to install a smoke detector, which reduces the risks of injuries and property damage associated with fires. The costs of smoke detectors were restricted to the expenses associated with purchase battery replacement. Installation costs were excluded. This study, which was highly aggregative in

Table 4-3. Summary of Value-of-Life Studies Based on Tradeoffs Outside the Labor Market

Author (*year*)	Nature of risk	Average income level	Implicit value of life (*$millions*)
Ghosh, Lees, and Seal (1975)	Highway speed/value of time tradeoff, 1973	NA	0.07
Blomquist (1979)	Automobile death risks/ seat belt use, 1972	29,840	1.2
Dardis (1980)	Smoke detector risk reduction, 1974–1979	NA	0.6
Portney (1981)	Property value response to air pollution risk, 1978	NA—value of life for 42-year-old male	0.8
Ippolito and Ippolito (1984)	Cigarette smoking cessation, 1980	NA	0.7
Garbacz (1987)	Smoke detector risk reduction, 1968–1985	NA	2.0
Atkinson and Halvorsen (1990)	Automobile accident risks/ price tradeoff, 1986	NA	4.0

Note: All values are in December 1990 dollars.

nature, analyzed the minimum value of a statistical life needed for installation of a smoke detector to be desirable. Portney (1981) focused on the effect of air pollution mortality risks on property values relying on data from Allegheny County, Pennsylvania. The property value effects are observable, but the critical assumption is that individuals understand the mortality risk from air pollution and the only aspect of air pollution that has value to them is the mortality risk. Morbidity effects and the undesirable visibility implications of air pollution are excluded.

Ippolito and Ippolito (1984) analyzed the effect of health hazard information on cigarette consumption. Their study does not derive an estimate of the value of life in the same sense as it has been used in the literature. Instead, they focus on what can be viewed as a marginal rate of substitution of wealth for life expectancy.[6]

Notwithstanding these various limitations of the studies outside the labor market, it is clear that people do make risk-dollar tradeoffs in contexts other than labor market decisions. This aspect of the studies should provide some reassurance, since one would expect individuals' value of life to be constant across different domains of decision. What is more disturbing is the comparatively low estimates of the value of life obtained using these various approaches, all of which suggest lower values than almost any of the studies in Table 4-1.

In some cases, the low estimates appear to be the result of a deliberate bias in the analysis. In particular, several studies made explicit reference to the early labor market value-of-life study done by Thaler and Rosen (1976) and often selected parameter values that could yield estimates of the value of life consistent with those obtained in the labor market literature, even though other ranges of assumptions might have been equally plausible. In addition, many of the value-of-life estimates may be biased downward because of the omission of key aspects of the disutility component of the risk tradeoff. Dardis (1980), for example, omits the installation cost of smoke detectors. In many instances one should regard these estimates as being the lower bounds on the value of life rather than estimates that are appropriate from the standpoint of policy analysis. It should be emphasized that almost all these limitations of the various studies are noted by the authors themselves. The studies are valuable in their own right but not for the purpose of establishing a value of life from the standpoint of government policy.

4.5 SURVEYS AND CONTINGENT VALUATION OF FATALITY RISKS

The principal limitation of compensating differential studies is that they do not pertain to all classes of risk that are of interest, and they may not always be sufficiently refined to enable us to perfectly isolate the risk-dollar tradeoff. Conceivably, one could construct a survey methodology that asks people for information concerning dollar amounts of compensation that they require to face added risk or that they would be willing to pay for reduced risk, thus obtaining the risk-dollar tradeoff directly. On theoretical grounds, this approach is clearly superior since it eliminates all of the intervening factors that may potentially be omitted and thus bias the analysis. The main disadvantage is that there is no assurance that one will obtain reliable answers to survey questions since, unlike market decisions, individuals may have less of an incentive to give an honest and thoughtful response to a survey question. Moreover, as I show in Viscusi (1990), individuals often do not take survey information at face value. In particular, respondents may not accurately process probability information presented to them, so that even though we may tell people risk information, their perception of that information and the risk-dollar tradeoff they are in fact making may be quite different from what the survey administrators believe it to be.

Despite these limitations, the survey methodology potentially is very useful, particularly in contexts in which good market data are not available. Moreover, the reliability of these surveys can be enhanced by constructing a survey context and utilization of a survey approach that does lead individuals to give meaningful answers to questions that they understand. Indeed, a well-executed survey should yield results similar to those obtained with labor market studies that are comparably well executed. That in fact has been the case. The survey valuations for job risks in Viscusi and O'Connor (1984) and in Gerking, de Haan, and Schulze (1988) each yield results from surveys that are very similar to the findings for the same sample with respect to job risks.

Two of the early studies listed in Table 4-4 were largely exploratory in nature. Acton (1973) ran a study of the valuation of post-heart attack lives using Harvard students as the survey administrators, yielding a sample of thirty-six. Similarly, Jones-Lee (1976) also did an exploratory study using a mail survey, to which there were thirty respondents. The final three studies in Table 4-4 were much larger in scale. The study by Gerking, de Haan, and Schulze (1988) focused on job fatality risks using a mail survey, whereas Jones-Lee (1989) and Viscusi, Magat, and Huber (1991b) each focused on different aspects of transportation risks. The studies by Gerking, de Haan, and Schulze (1988) and Jones-Lee (1989) each used variations of a standard type of contingent valuation approach in which respondents were asked how much they would be willing to pay for different hypothetical improvements in their well-being. The Gerking, de Haan, and Schulze (1988) study assessed the wage increases workers required for higher job fatality risks and the wage reductions they would be willing to accept for a lower risk of fatality. Similarly, the Jones-Lee (1989) study focused on individual willingness to pay for reduced motor accidents. The study by Viscusi, Magat, and Huber (1991b) also analyzed a risk-dollar tradeoff with automobile accident risks but utilized a different methodology. In particular, the survey presented subjects with a series of paired comparisons involving different areas in which to live and their associated risks of automobile accidents and cost of living. Respondents were presented with sequences of paired choices until indifference was obtained. The interactive computer program that was utilized to present these tradeoffs proceeded in iterative fashion until the risk-dollar tradeoff was ascertained. In contrast, the studies by Gerking, de Haan, and Schulze (1988), Jones-Lee (1989), and Miller and Guria (1991) proceeded using a one-step contingent valuation approach in which the respondent was simply asked directly what the associated dollar change would be in response to a specified risk change.

Each of these methodologies is potentially valid. The main issue is whether the respondents can deal more effectively with a particular type of question.[7] An additional potential advantage of the Viscusi, Magat, and Huber (1991b) approach is

Table 4-4. Summary of Value-of-Life Estimates Based on Survey Evidence

Author (*year*)	Nature of risk	Survey methodology	Average income level	Implicit value of life (*$millions*)
Acton (1973)	Improved ambulance service, post–heart attack lives	Willingness-to-pay question, door-to-door small Boston sample (36)	NA	.1
Jones-Lee (1976)	Airline safety and locational life expectancy risks	Mail survey willingness to accept increased risk, small (30) U.K. sample, 1975	NA	15.6
Gerking, de Haan, and Schulze (1988)	Job fatality risk	Willingness to pay, willingness to accept change in job risk in mail survey, 1984	NA	3.4 willingness to pay, 8.8 willingness to accept
Jones-Lee (1989)	Motor vehicle accidents	Willingness to pay for risk reduction, U.K. survey, 1982	NA	3.8
Viscusi, Magat, and Huber (1991b)	Automobile accident risks	Interactive computer program with pairwise auto risk–living cost tradeoffs until indifference achieved (1987)	43,771	2.7 (median) 9.7 (mean) (1987)
Miller and Guria (1991)	Traffic safety	Series of contingent valuation questions, New Zealand Survey, 1989–1990	NA	1.2

Note: All values are in December 1990 U.S. dollars.

that by presenting a series of paired choices to respondents one can run a variety of consistency checks to analyze the degree to which respondents are giving meaningful answers. Respondents who do not give consistent answers or who violate the basic laws of economic rationality can be singled out so that one can evaluate the degree to which respondents were engaged in the interview task.

The value-of-life estimates obtained from the three large-scale survey studies are fairly similar. The willingness-to-pay amounts obtained in all of these studies are in the range of approximately $3 million per statistical life. In the case of the Jones-Lee (1989) results in Table 4-4, the estimate pertains to the trimmed mean response, and the outliers have been excluded. The most pertinent estimates from the Viscusi, Magat, and Huber (1991) study are the median responses, because the mean figure is pushed upward by some extreme responses at the high end, which have not been trimmed from the sample in the reporting of these results. Nevertheless, it is striking that overall these statistics yield results that are quite similar to the range of value-of-life estimates obtained using labor market studies.

4.6 SURVEY VALUATIONS OF NONFATAL HEALTH RISKS

The survey approach has proven to be especially useful in valuing classes of risks not captured in labor market risk data, particularly nonfatal health risks. The first of the studies reported in Table 4-5 is by Viscusi and Magat (1987), who focus on individuals' valuations of the risks from bleach and drain opener, chloramine gassings, child poisonings, and hand burns, among others. These morbidity effects are by no means catastrophic in terms of their implications, and the estimated values attached to them by the respondents—in excess of $1 million in three cases—do not provide a reliable guide for benefit assessment. The main difficulty that this exploratory study highlighted is that when respondents are given information about very low-probability events, there is a tendency for them to overreact to these risks. Thus, individuals who are willing to pay one dollar to reduce the risk of bleach gassing by 1/1,000,000 will have an implicit value for the injury of $1 million. However, this response may not reflect the underlying risk-dollar tradeoff so much as it does the inability of individuals to deal with extremely low-probability events in a consistent and accurate manner. The evidence in the literature on psychology and economics indicates that there is such a tendency to overestimate the magnitude of low-probability events that are called to one's attention, which is what is being captured by this survey.

The subsequent study by Viscusi, Magat, and Huber (1987) dealt with a similar class of injuries but utilized a much more comprehensible risk level—on the order of 15/10,000 annually. The value of the morbidity effects such as skin poisonings and chloramine gassing is in a more reasonable range, as the health effects assessed in this study range in value from $700 to $3,500.

The study by Berger, et al. (1987) also addressed minor health problems, in this case the common cold. This study did not utilize risk-dollar tradeoffs but instead focused on the willingness to pay to avoid the certain outcome of one day of various kinds of illnesses. Individuals were willing to pay from $35 to avoid a stuffed-up sinus to $183 to avoid one day of heavy drowsiness. Although this study focused on the valuation of certain outcomes rather than the risk-dollar tradeoff, it is shown in Evans and Viscusi (1991) that minor health effects can be treated as a monetary loss equivalent so that valuation of such certain outcomes will give estimates comparable to assessing the risk-dollar tradeoff.

The study by Viscusi, Magat, and Forrest (1988) addressed the same class of household injuries that were considered in Viscusi and Magat (1987) and Viscusi, Magat, and Huber (1987). This study distinguished the private and altruistic valuations of the health outcome, where in this case the health outcome consisted of injury pairs that were prevented: inhalation and skin poisoning, and inhalation and child poisoning. The private values of these injury pairs ranged from $2,500 to $4,700.

Table 4-5. Summary of Valuations of Nonfatal Health Risks

Author (*year*)	Survey methodology	Average income level	Nature of risk	Value of health outcome
Viscusi and Magat (1987)	Paired comparison and contingent valuation interactive computer survey at mall, hardware store, 1984	$39,768	Bleach: chloramine gassings, child poisonings; drain opener: hand burns, child poisonings	$1.78 million (bleach gassing), $0.65 million (bleach poisoning), $1.60 million (drain opener hand burns), $1.06 million (drain opener and child poisoning)
Berger et al. (1987)	Contingent valuation interviews with 119 respondents, 1984–1985	NA	Certain outcome of one day of various illnesses	$98 (coughing spells), $35 (stuffed-up sinuses), $57 (throat congestion), $63 (itching eyes), $183 (heavy drowsiness), $140 (headaches), $62 (nausea)
Viscusi, Magat, and Huber (1987)	Contingent valuation computer survey at mall, hardware stores, 1986	$42,700	Morbidity risks of pesticide and toilet bowl cleaner, valuations for 15/10,000 risk decrease to zero	Insecticide $1,504 (skin poison), $1,742 (inhalation), $3,489 (child poisoning), toilet bowl cleaner $1,113 (gassing), $744 (eye burn), $1,232 (child poisoning)
Viscusi, Magat, and Forrest (1988)	Contingent valuation computer survey at mall, hardware stores, 1986	$44,554	Insecticide inhalation–skin poisoning, inhalation–child poisoning	Inhalation–skin poisoning $2,538 (private), $9,662 (N.C. altruism), $3,745 (U.S. altruism); Inhalation–child poisoning $4,709 (private), $17,592 (N.C. altruism), $5,197 (U.S. altruism)
Evans and Viscusi (1991)	Contingent valuation computer survey at mall, hardware stores, 1986	$32,700	Morbidity risks of pesticides and toilet bowl cleaner; utility function estimates of risk values; T values pertain to marginal risk-dollar tradeoffs, and L values per-	Insecticide: $761 (T), $755 (L) (skin poisoning), $1,047 (T), $1,036 (L) (inhalation–no kids), $2,575 (T) (inhalation–children), $3,207 (T), $2,877 (L) (child poisoning) Toilet bowl cleaner: $633 (T), $628 (L) (eye burn), $598 (T),

(continued)

Table 4-5. (*Continued*)

Author (*year*)	Survey methodology	Average income level	Nature of risk	Value of health outcome
			tain to monetary loss equivalents	$593 (L) (gassing–no kids), $717 (T), $709 (L) (gassing–children), $1,146 (T), $1,126 (L) (child poisoning)
Viscusi, Magat, and Huber (1991b)	Risk-risk and risk-dollar computer survey at mall, 1988	$41,000	Environmental risk of severe chronic bronchitis morbidity risk	.32 fatality risk or $904,000 risk-risk; $516,000 risk-dollar
Magat, Viscusi, and Huber (1991)	Risk-risk computer survey at mall, 1990	$35,700	Environmental risk of nonfatal nerve disease, fatal lymphoma, nonfatal lymphoma	$1.6 million (nerve disease), $2.6 million (nonfatal lymphoma), $4.1 million (fatal lymphoma)
Krupnick and Cropper (1992)	Viscusi-Magat-Huber (1991b) survey for sample with chronic lung disease, 1989	$39,744	Environmental risk of severe chronic bronchitis morbidity risk	$496,800–$691,200 (median)

What was noteworthy is the extent of the additional valuation due to individual altruism. Individuals' value per injury increases three to four times once one takes into account the valuation of risk reduction throughout one's state or residence, which will often include one's relatives. There is an additional but somewhat more muted altruistic benefit associated with a risk reduction that occurs nationwide. These numbers do not suggest that we should simply scale up the benefit values by such a factor. However, they do highlight the importance of undertaking additional studies to determine the extent of altruism for other risk contexts.

Viscusi, Magat, and Huber (1991b) considered a more severe class of outcomes involving chronic bronchitis. The value of risk reduction for this health outcome was assessed in two ways. In the first, respondents assessed the fatality risk equivalent of being exposed to the chance of chronic bronchitis. In general, respondents assess the risk of chronic bronchitis as being comparable to a lottery involving a .32 risk of an automobile accident. When presented with alternative lotteries involving automobile accident risks and chronic bronchitis risks, respondents displayed an ability to deal with these risks in a reliable manner, both because of the comparable level of the risk amounts and because they were trading off similar attributes. The implied value of preventing chronic bronchitis cases using this risk-risk approach was $904,000. Alternatively, using direct risk-dollar tradeoff questions involving differences in chronic bronchitis risks and differences in the cost of living, the implicit value per case of chronic bronchitis is $516,000.

Magat, Viscusi, and Huber (1991b) use similar methodology to assess the value of nerve disease and the value of both fatal and nonfatal lymphoma. The study used a questionnaire that establishes the value of these health outcomes in terms of automobile accident risks, which are assumed to have a value of $4 million per statistical life. The value of these health outcomes ranges from $1.6 to $2.6 million for nonfatal major diseases such as this.

The Evans and Viscusi (1991) study utilizes the Viscusi, Magat, and Huber (1987) data to estimate utility functions for different health effects. For these minor injuries, it is shown that one can treat the health outcomes as being tantamount to a monetary equivalent. In situations such as this, where the health outcome does not lower the marginal utility of income, the implicit value of the health outcome as measured by the risk-dollar tradeoff is the same as the optimal amount of insurance that one would choose on an *ex post* basis. These results highlight the fact that it is for major injuries, not all injuries, that one must recognize the changes in the structure of utility functions that are brought about by the injury.

The final study is that of Krupnick and Cropper (1992), which administered the Viscusi, Magat, and Huber (1991b) survey to a sample of individuals who actually experienced chronic lung disease. They obtained median estimates of the value of chronic bronchitis ranging from $496,800 to $691,200.

The usefulness of these various survey studies hinges on the degree to which they can replicate the kinds of choices that individuals would make in a market context if one existed. Surveys that present subjects with risk information that can be readily processed and with familiar tradeoffs that they are capable of addressing are more likely to succeed than those that do not have these attributes. Inability of respondents to process the survey information in a reliable manner can lead to results that provide a substantially misleading index of benefit values. In one case involving low-probability risks it is likely that failure of subjects to accurately perceive the risks involved inflated the benefit value by approximately a factor of 1,000. The need for care not only in structuring questions but in recognizing the cognitive limitations of respondents should be apparent.

4.7 POLICY IMPLICATIONS

Although the value-of-life literature is now roughly two decades old, the essential approach to the value of life became well established in the 1970s. The appropriate measure of the value of life from the standpoint of government policy is society's willingness to pay for the risk reduction, which is the same benefit formulation that one uses in all policy evaluation contexts.

Economists have had the greatest success in assessing the risk-dollar tradeoff using labor market data. Although the estimates of the risk-dollar tradeoff vary considerably depending on the population exposed to the risk, the nature of the risk, and similar factors, most of the reasonable estimates of the value of life are clustered in the $3 to $7 million range. Moreover, these estimates are for the population of exposed workers, who generally have lower incomes than the individuals being protected by broadly based risk regulations. Recognition of the income elasticity of the value of life will lead to the use of a different value of life depending on the population being protected.

The 1980s marked the first decade in which use of appropriate estimates of the value of life became widespread throughout the federal government. In large part through the efforts of the U.S. Office of Management and Budget, agencies such as OSHA and EPA began incorporating value-of-life estimates in terms of their benefit evaluations, whereas in earlier years the economic value of fatalities was noted or was treated in terms of the dollar cost alone. Recognition of the nonpecuniary aspects of life is an important advance.

The next major change that is needed is to establish an appropriate schedule of values of life that is pertinent for the differing populations at risk. Policies that protect groups who incur risks voluntarily, or policies that address the risks in very high-risk jobs for which the risks are well known and for which the workers are compensated should be treated quite differently than policies that protect populations who bear risks involuntarily or who have a very high aversion to incurring health risks.

The evidence from the labor market also provides average values for nonfatal injuries, principally those involving all workplace injuries that are severe enough to lead to a loss of work. Survey evidence on attitudes toward risk greatly expands the range of health outcomes that can be valued, but there is a continuing need to assess the validity of stated valuation amounts as compared to values captured in individual decisions.

NOTES

1. For a review of the federal guidelines on the valuation of health risks, see the U.S. Office of Management and Budget (1988, 1990).

2. See the Gallup Organization (1989).

3. Hamermesh and Wolfe (1990) obtain estimates of the wage premiums for the frequency and duration of injuries, but they do not report an estimate of the implicit value of an injury. They do find a stronger effect of injury duration than injury frequency.

4. For example, one cannot estimate the implicit value of an injury for a log wage equation without knowing the average wage level in the sample.

5. See Arnould and Grabowski (1981).

6. For a further discussion of Ippolito and Ippolito (1984), see Jones-Lee (1989).

7. An additional potential advantage of the Viscusi, Magat, and Huber (1991b) approach is that by presenting a series of paired choices to respondents one can run a variety of consistency checks to analyze the degree to which respondents are giving meaningful answers. Respondents who do not give consistent answers or who violate the basic laws of economic rationality can be singled out so that one can evaluate the degree to which respondents were engaged in the interview task.

5

Social Insurance for Work and Product Injuries

5.1 INTRODUCTION

Government policies designed to reduce risk are primarily concerned with the *ex ante* value of the statistical lives saved. In contrast, social insurance efforts primarily focus on the appropriate compensation amount after the accident has occurred. These functions are not entirely divisible since this *ex post* compensation may have important incentive effects for accident prevention. Moreover, an understanding of the appropriate principles for social insurance will enable us to better understand the differences between the appropriate value of life for compensation and prevention.

Two major social insurance efforts in the United States are the workers' compensation system for job risks and the product liability system for product injuries. Although one program is an administrative compensation system structure and the other operates through the courts, each has similar concerns with respect to providing effective insurance for the losses of accident victims.

Discussions of workers' compensation often assume that the reference point for effective insurance is full income replacement. Current replacement formulas, which generally provide for two-thirds earnings replacement, subject to various caps, floors, and limits, consequently leave an earnings gap that is reduced but not completely eliminated by the tax exemption accorded to workers' compensation benefits. Product liability awards tend to be more generous, compensating not only for the present value of earnings loss but also for noneconomic losses, such as pain and suffering. Although this approach is well established, the recent controversy over uncertain, and in some cases capricious, pain and suffering awards has led some observers to call for a cap on noneconomic damages. In each case, reform efforts are pushing benefit levels in the direction of full compensation of pecuniary loss.

The full-compensation social insurance target is sensible in the case of property damage losses, but it is not compelling when health outcomes are involved. Injuries may affect the structure of utility functions in a complex manner, altering the marginal utility one can derive from insurance compensation. An individual who has suffered severe brain damage, for example, may have substantial need for medical care, but there will be little welfare benefit from resources that are provided to foster additional consumption expenditures. Similarly, for many classes of utility functions, pain and suffering damages will impose the type of losses that individuals would not choose to insure if they were offered actuarially fair insurance for the risks of pain and suffering. Whether there should be pain and suffering compensation, and if so, in what amount, is a matter that hinges on the structure of utility functions, which is an empirical issue.

The focus of this chapter is on empirical implementation of the guidelines for social insurance that have been developed in the theoretical literature. In doing so I will adopt the simplifying assumption that our primary concern is the insurance function of these efforts. One component that will not be explored fully is that of moral hazard. Although the influence of moral hazard will be noted at appropriate junctures, the empirical evidence now available is not sufficiently precise to ascertain the responsiveness of such moral hazard effects to changes in the benefit structure.

The second major simplification is that the deterrence function of these social insurance efforts will not enter. If our objective were simply that of accident deterrence, the appropriate values of compensation would be the implicit values of life and health such as those used in selecting regulatory policies. Thus, an implicit value of life such as the $3 to $7 million dollars based on recent labor market evidence reviewed in Chapter 4 is an appropriate measure of the amount of compensation that would be justified in situations in which firms had no safety incentives other than those induced by such compensation. In such situations, establishing effective safety incentives through social insurance will lead to a tradeoff between the insurance and incentive objectives, as it will be desirable to overpay accident victims in order to bolster the safety incentive effects.[1] Rather than complicate the analysis with consideration of these influences, I will assume that safety incentives are handled by other government policies now in place, such as direct regulation of health and safety risks.

Even if we restrict our focus to social insurance, the task of establishing the appropriate social insurance level is not entirely straightforward. Although the theoretical basis for approaching these issues is almost two decades old,[2] the absence of firm empirical work in this area enables us to say little more than that there should be a relationship between the marginal utilities in different states, where it is not known how these marginal utilities are altered by the party's health state. As the results presented here will indicate, in some situations it is not necessary to know the utility function, as one can approach these issues using other information generated by market behavior. Workers' compensation and product liability operate within a market context. To the extent possible, one should take advantage of the information provided by the market to assess the adequacy of these social insurance efforts.

By utilizing labor market data on wage patterns, as in Section 5.2, one can assess the impact of workers' compensation on wage rates, thus establishing the tradeoff value that workers are willing to make between *ex ante* and *ex post* compensation. This worker tradeoff can then be compared with the terms of trade available in the market to assess whether current benefits are optimal and, if not, whether they are too high or too low. The tradeoff rates estimated indicate that the benefit levels in the United States were too low in the 1970s. An examination of subsequent tradeoff rates after benefits were increased indicates that there has been a narrowing in the gap between the current benefit level and the optimal social insurance amount. The extent of the departure from the optimal amount requires that one utilize more detailed information based on the structure of worker utility functions. Estimates of utility functions for a standard job injury, which are provided in Section 5.2, indicate that there is an inadequacy in the level of social insurance provided by workers' compensation, but that it is not substantial.

In the case of product risks, which is the subject of Section 5.3, the market-based evidence is much less detailed, in part because we have less information on consumption patterns than we do on employment patterns. Fortunately, the guidelines from labor market behavior are appropriate for considering product accidents of a similar character. In addition, Section 5.3 reports estimates of utility functions for minor health impacts associated with product risks. Temporary health effects do not alter the marginal utility of income but instead can be viewed as monetary loss equivalents. These findings indicate a legitimate economic demand for pain and suffering compensation from an insurance standpoint.

Section 5.4 reviews the trends in workers' compensation benefits and in product liability awards. Workers' compensation benefit changes have been the result of deliberate policy efforts to increase the adequacy of the program as a social insurance effort. In contrast, there has been no conscious policy choice to boost product liability awards, which have experienced increases that dwarf the increases in workers' compensation benefits. This escalation threatens the viability of the product liability system and has led to calls for draconian actions such as elimination of pain and suffering compensation altogether.

Although the results reported here do not completely resolve the task of designing the social insurance efforts optimally, they do enable us to say a great deal about their current performance and the direction in which the overall benefit structure should be shifted. Section 5.5 summarizes the major conclusions and highlights the main open areas for research.

5.2 INSURANCE FOR JOB INJURIES

Measures of Optimal Social Insurance

Most discussions of the appropriate levels of social insurance coverage do not have a precise reference point for assessing optimality. Discussions of the income-replacement role of social insurance often note that income replacement following an injury is generally less than complete, and they urge that the gap be eliminated. Even if insurance were the sole function of efforts such as workers' compensation, full coverage would not be optimal since severe injuries may alter the postinjury marginal utility of income.[3] The degree to which the optimal insurance amount departs from full coverage cannot be determined theoretically.

This section develops several empirical tests that will be applied to assess the adequacy of social insurance programs with respect to their insurance objective. The two main factors excluded from the analysis are moral hazard and safety incentive effects. Subsequently, I will provide a brief review of the evidence with respect to moral hazard, but the empirical research is not sufficiently advanced to enable one to use these results to pinpoint the effect on the optimal insurance amount. Similarly, the nascent stage of research on the safety incentive effects of social insurance limits efforts to obtain a more comprehensive measure of the optimal level of workers' compensation and similar efforts. The intent of the optimality measures provided here is to begin the process of developing theoretically sound tests of the optimality of social insurance that can be implemented on an empirical basis to provide explicit guidance for the policy choices in these areas.[4]

Attractive Labor Market Contracts

The first condition that will be applied to social insurance for labor market risks is that this insurance should be a component of a compensation mix sufficient to attract the worker to the job. The package of *ex ante* and *ex post* compensation must match the expected utility EU_0 that the worker can obtain elsewhere. Suppose the two possible states represent good health ($i = 1$) and injury ($i = 2$), where people would rather be healthy than injured. Income in state i is Y_i and utility in state i is given by $U^i(Y_i)$, where $U^1(X) > U^2(X)$, $U^1_x > 0$, $U^2_x > 0$, and it is usually assumed $U^1_x(X) > U^2_x(X)$, for any given income level X in each state, where the subscripts X denote derivatives.

It is the final marginal utility assumption that is most pivotal since it drives the structure of the social insurance effort. If an injury is tantamount to a monetary loss, so that

$$U^2(Y) = U^1(Y-L),$$

then full insurance is optimal. If the injury raises the marginal utility of income, then more than full income replacement is desirable. Injuries that reduce the marginal utility of income, such as death, should receive less than full income replacement.[5] In the absence of specific empirical evidence regarding the effect of the injury on the structure of utility functions, we can say very little about the appropriate level of insurance compensation.

To complete the labor market problem, let $(1-p)$ be the probability of state 1, p be the chance that the injury state 2 will prevail, and t be a proportional income tax rate. In the United States, wages Y_1, are taxed, but workers' compensation benefits Y_2 are not. To be attractive to the worker, the risky job must match the utility of some available job alternative, given by EU_0. As a result, one has for the marginal worker the condition

$$(1-p)U^1(Y_1(1-t)) + pU^2(Y_2) = EU_0.$$

The rate of tradeoff between wages Y_1 and workers' compensation Y_2 for such a job is given by

$$\frac{dY_1}{dY_2} = \frac{-\partial EU_0/\partial Y_2}{\partial EU_0/\partial Y_1} = \frac{-pU^2_X}{(1 - p)(1 - t)U^1_X} \tag{5.1}$$

The rate of the tradeoff between *ex ante* and *ex post* compensation equals the ratio of the expected marginal utilities in the two states, taking into account the favorable tax status of workers' compensation. Equation 5.1 will be the first of three main results used to assess the optimality of workers' compensation.

Efficient Insurance Protection

In addition to providing the correct mix of compensation that satisfies equation 5.1, an efficient social insurance effort will also provide the optimal level of insurance given the terms on which insurance is available.[6] Let h be an insurance loading factor, where h = 1 if the insurance effort is actuarially fair. In addition, let z be the worker's marginal product and δ be an index of whether the injury affects the worker's productivity after an injury; $\delta = 1$ if the employee cannot work after an injury, $\delta = 0$ if the injury has no effect on the worker's productivity, and $0 < \delta < 1$ if there is a partial productivity effect.

The compensation package must satisfy the actuarial constraint given by

$$(1-\delta p)z = (1-p)Y_1 + hpY_2.$$

As a result, one can write the efficient compensation design as

$$\begin{aligned} \text{Max } V = &(1 - p)U^1[(1 - t)Y_1] + pU^2(Y_2) \\ \underset{Y_1,Y_2,\lambda}{} \\ &-\lambda[(1 - p)Y_1 + hpY_2 - (1 - \delta p)z]. \end{aligned}$$

In addition to the actuarial constraint, this leads to the condition

$$U_x^2 = (1-t)hU_x^1. \tag{5.2}$$

In the absence of taxes and insurance loading one will equate the marginal utility of income in each state, a well known result. The favorable tax status of workers' compensation boosts the required marginal utility of income when not injured that is required to equal any given value of U_x^2, and loading has the opposite effect. In the absence of insurance loading and taxes, one equates the marginal utility of income in each state, leading to full insurance of financial losses and insurance that provides less (more) than full income replacement if the injury reduces (raises) the marginal utility of income.

Optimal Insurance and Attractive Labor Market Contracts

It is useful to combine the results for the efficient compensation package in equation 5.1 and optimal insurance in equation 5.2. Substituting for the value of U_x^2 from equation 5.2 into equation 5.1 and canceling the common terms in the numerator and denominator yields

$$\frac{dY_1}{dY_2} = \frac{-ph}{1 - p}, \tag{5.3}$$

or

$$\frac{dY_1}{dY_2} = \frac{-p}{(1 - p)}$$

if insurance is actuarially fair.

Equation 5.3 consequently provides a test of the optimality for workers' compensation based on the observed rate of tradeoff between wages and workers' compensation, dY_1/dY_2. If this tradeoff equals the term on the right side of equation 5.3, insurance is optimal. If the wage offset rate is greater in absolute magnitude than the right-hand term, social insurance is underprovided since workers are willing to substitute wages for workers' compensation at a greater rate than is required by the terms of trade. The level of social insurance is excessive if the wage offset is smaller in absolute value than $-ph/(1-p)$.

Market Tests

Wage-Workers' Compensation Tradeoff

Equation 5.3 enables one to readily ascertain the rate of tradeoff using available labor market data. In particular, wage equation estimates with a properly specified workers' compensation variable provide an empirical measure of dY_1/dY_2. Since p and h are also observable, all of the components of equation 5.3 can be assessed empirically.

Table 5-1 summarizes the results for three different data sets, the first two of which will be of concern here. The first set of data is the University of Michigan Quality of Employment Survey (QES; 1977), which includes detailed employment and job attribute information. The second survey is the University of Michigan Panel Study of Income Dynamics (PSID; 1982), which pertains to employment year 1981. The sample sizes used in the analysis were 485 (QES) and 1,106 (PSID).

Table 5-1. Summary of Wage-Workers' Compensation Tradeoff Results[a]

	Quality of employment 1977	Panel Study of Income Dynamics 1982	Viscusi-O'Connor chemical worker survey
Employment year	1976	1981	1982
Actuarially fair reference point tradeoff	−.04	−.05	−.09
Reference point tradeoff with loading	−.05	−.06	−.11
Observed tradeoff dY_1/dY_2	−.12	−.08	−.15
Observed tradeoff/actuarially fair tradeoff	3.0	1.6	1.7
Observed tradeoff/loading tradeoff	2.4	1.3	1.4
Implications	Inadequate	Inadequate but closer to optimal	Inadequate but closer to optimal

[a]These results are based on labor market estimates reported in Viscusi and Moore (1987) for the 1977 QES, Moore and Viscusi (1990a) for the 1982 PSID, and Viscusi and Evans (1990) for the chemical worker survey.

Although the risk levels are similar in both years, the time period spanned by the two survey years was one of considerable change for the U.S. workers' compensation program. Benefit levels increased in the 1970s and early 1980s so that the adequacy of benefits was believed to be much greater. If the methodology for assessing the adequacy of workers' compensation is valid, the increased benefit level should be reflected in the tradeoff rates.

The risk levels for each worker were based on U.S. Bureau of Labor Statistics data on lost workday injury rates by industry, which were then matched to workers based on their industry responses. The relative odds of injury and no injury range from .04 to .05 for the two samples. Prevailing loading rates for the workers' compensation program imply a value of h that averages 1.25. As a result, the reference point tradeoff with loading reported in the third row of Table 5-1 is a bit higher than the value assuming actuarially fair insurance.

The fourth row of Table 5-1 gives the observed tradeoff rates. Consider first the 1977 QES results. Workers sacrifice twelve cents in wages for each additional dollar of workers' compensation benefits, whereas the tradeoffs based on the prevailing terms of trade range from four cents (actuarially fair) to five cents (current loading) per dollar. The observed tradeoff ranges from 2.4 to 3.0 times the tradeoff reference point, indicating that the level of social insurance is underprovided.

The substantial wage offsets are noteworthy from a second standpoint as well. Social insurance efforts that are provided in a market context should not be viewed as a simple net drain on a firm's resources. Since these benefits are valued by the recipients, the wage offset reduces the net cost of these efforts below the cost of the premiums. Indeed, these estimates imply that the U.S. workers' compensation system more than pays for itself since the wage offsets exceed the value of the premiums (see Moore and Viscusi [1990a]). This result is not implausible since risk-averse individuals will value their insurance at more than its actuarial cost unless they are overinsured.

The results for the early 1980s reported in the second column of Table 5-1 indicate very similar tradeoff reference points since the risk levels are similar. The wage-workers' compensation tradeoff rate has, however, gone from $-.12$ to $-.08$, which is a figure that is closer to the optimal tradeoff amount.

This movement in the tradeoff toward the optimal level is consistent with the expanded role of this social insurance effort over that period. Premiums rose by 62.2 percent over that five-year period, in part because of the more generous benefit levels and greater rates of earnings replacement.[7] It should also be noted that this period was one of extraordinary price inflation, as the consumer price index rose by 59.8 percent.[8] Although premium increases outstripped the rate of price increase, wages did not, as average hourly earnings increased by only 49.5 percent. Thus, there was a shift in the compensation mix as workers' compensation assumed a comparatively greater role.

Tests Based on Utility Functions
Although wage equations are one methodology for assessing short-run labor supply, if one had knowledge of worker utility functions, then one could calculate the same tradeoff value but using the information contained in the character of individual

preferences rather than the direct estimates of the tradeoff rates. Although one cannot go beyond estimating tradeoff rates with available market data, the experimental data on workers' responses to chemical labels developed by Viscusi and O'Connor (1984) provide information on two wage-risk combinations on a worker's constant expected utility locus. The first point is the worker's current job, and the second is the wage the worker requires to work at a high-risk position. These data, which are based on a 1982 survey of workers at four different chemical plants, enable one to estimate simple functional forms for worker utility functions.

The risk measure for the sample is based on workers' subjective risk perceptions for which the worker used a metric identical to the U.S. Bureau of Labor Statistics injury and illness rate scale. The main difference is that the subjective worker perceptions also reflected health risks, which are quite important in the chemical industry but are not adequately captured by government statistics, which tend to primarily reflect acute safety hazards. The overall assessed probability of injury of .084 leads to a reference tradeoff value of $-p/(1-p)$ of -0.09 in the actuarially fair insurance case and a tradeoff $-hp/(1-p)$ of $-.11$ with current loading rates.

For this sample, worker utility functions were estimated in Viscusi and Evans (1990) to be $\ln Y$ when injured and $1.077 \ln Y$ when healthy, so that an injury reduced the marginal utility of income. Although other more general preference structures could not be estimated with the available data, the results implied by the logarithmic form were consistent with findings using a flexible functional form (Taylor's series expansion) and were not rejected after performing a specification test.

The additional parameters needed to estimate all of the components of equation 5.1 for optimal labor market contracts are the replacement rate or (.637), the tax rate t (.124), and the weekly earnings amount ($392.13). Substituting these values into equation 5.1, one has the result that

$$\frac{dY_1}{dY_2} = -.15.$$

As before, the rate of tradeoff indicates that social insurance is being under-provided. However, if we take the ratio of the observed tradeoff to the reference point tradeoffs, the results reported in the final column of Table 5-1 are very similar to those in the second column. Thus, the tradeoff rates obtained using utility functions and equation 5.1 yield the same relative discrepancy between observed tradeoff rates and the reference point values as is obtained using direct estimates of wage-workers' compensation tradeoffs in conjunction with equation 5.3. Although the risk levels differ because of the different industry mix, the degree of optimality of the workers' compensation benefit structure is similar under both approaches.

Knowledge of the utility functions also enables one to assess the discrepancy in the marginal utility of income in the two states, as in equation 5.2, thus providing a third perspective on the optimality of workers' compensation. The marginal utility of income in good health U_x^1 is .0031, as compared with a marginal utility of income in ill health U_x^2 of .0040. After making adjustments for the role of taxes and loading, one obtains the result that

$$U_x^2 = .0040 > (1-t)hU_x^1 = .0033.$$

The high marginal utility of income in the ill-health state indicates that too few resources have been transferred to individuals in the postaccident situation. The general spirit of the conclusion implied by estimation of equation 5.2 reinforces the results implied by equations 5.1 and 5.3. Although these tests are not entirely independent, they do provide alternative perspectives on the character and consequences of the insurance inadequacy.

Optimal Insurance

Knowledge of the utility functions enables one to ascertain not only that the level of social insurance is below the optimal amount, but it also makes it possible to ascertain the optimal level of insurance coverage.[9] For the empirical values discussed above, one obtains the result that the optimal insurance replacement rate is 0.68 with the current degree of loading. If one were to examine the earnings replacement rate for an idealized world of actuarially fair insurance, it would rise to 0.85.

Each of these values exceeds current earnings replacement rates. For the sample of chemical workers used to generate the utility function estimates, the replacement rate is .64. Moreover, the primary earnings replacement specified in workers' compensation statutes is .67, but this amount is subject to a variety of complicating factors such as benefit ceilings and floors. The overall range of workers' compensation benefits does not appear to be greatly out of line with what is implied with optimal insurance, even though the direction of error indicates that benefits are underprovided. Moreover, these results are for an average job injury, so that there may be significant differences depending on injury type.

It is particularly striking, however, that the optimal reference point is not full earnings replacement. The role of the effect of injuries on the structure of utility functions reduces this value to .85, and the presence of insurance loading has an additional effect that lowers the optimal replacement rate to approximately two-thirds of worker earnings.

Social Efficiency and the Role of Taxes

The desirability of workers' compensation to workers stems in part from the fact that these benefits are accorded favorable tax status. If this tax exemption stems from recognition of an altruistic externality, then inclusion of the current role of taxes is appropriate. In addition, the tax exemption may represent an administrative convenience, as one could either provide $1 in benefits subject to tax or equivalently provide $0.876 in untaxable benefits. Thus, a two-thirds earnings replacement rate not subject to tax is equivalent to a .76 earnings replacement rate that would be taxed.

Of the three equations used to test for the optimality of social insurance, only the first two are changed by recognition of taxes. The third equation pertaining to the rate of tradeoff implied by optimal contracts and insurance remains unchanged. The labor market contract equation 5.1 becomes

$$\frac{dY_1}{dY_2} = \frac{-pU_x^2}{(1-p)U_x^1}$$

and the efficient insurance condition equation 5.2 is now

$$U_x^2 = hU_x^1.$$

The wage-workers' compensation tradeoff implied by equation 5.4 is closer to the optimal insurance tradeoff reference point (equation 5.3) than before. In particular, the presence of taxes makes workers less willing to trade off wages for workers' compensation, as dY_1/dY_2 is $-.13$, as compared with its earlier value of $-.15$.

Similarly, the marginal utility difference in the two states is narrowed. Although U_x^2 remains at .0040, the value of hU_x^1 is now .0038, which is approximately the same. What these two results suggest is that in the absence of a tax exemption for workers' compensation benefits there would be a substantial improvement in the measures of the adequacy of benefit levels.

Moral Hazard

The optimal level of insurance will be reduced to the extent that higher levels of moral hazard concerns are influential.[10] Four types of such effects can be distinguished. The first is that of *ex ante* injury hazard. The presence of workers' compensation reduces the extent of financial loss associated with an injury, thus diminishing the economic incentive of victims to take care.

Two elements must be present for this form of moral hazard to be of consequence. First, worker actions have to be an important contributor to job safety, and second, the worker's choice of the level of precautions must be responsive to the level of workers' compensation provided.

In terms of the link of worker behavior to safety, a variety of studies using different methodologies for apportioning responsibility have all indicated a strong link of job accidents to worker actions. In particular, as documented in Viscusi (1983), worker behavior accounts for 35 percent of workers' compensation cases in Wisconsin, 95 percent of the workers' compensation cases in the state of Pennsylvania, the majority of deaths experienced by deep-sea divers in the North Sea, 63 percent of the accidents in the United States that are monitored by the National Safety Council, and half of the deaths on oil and gas well-drilling rigs. By almost any measure, the role of worker actions in contributing to safety problems is clearly substantial.

The second behavioral link to workers' compensation is, however, much more tenuous. Consider the tradeoffs facing the worker. One gains in leisure time after experiencing a job accident, but there is generally a loss in income as well as a substantial decrease in health status. In the case of job fatalities, higher workers' compensation levels are likely to have little effect on incentives for workers to avoid such risks in view of their substantial implicit values of life reflected in the wages they receive. In addition, in the case of fatalities, the worker will not be alive to reap the additional utility from the higher benefit levels, and the bequest motive is unlikely to be so strong as to have a substantial influence.

The more typical job injury that does not involve a fatality also imposes a noneconomic loss. Using wage equation estimates to assess the implicit nonmonetary value of an injury by setting the replacement rate equal to 1.0, Viscusi and Moore (1987) report that the nonmonetary value of a typical job injury is in the range of $17,000 to $26,000. Higher levels of workers' compensation benefits can diminish the financial loss associated with an injury, but the nonpecuniary losses will remain considerable. Overall, it seems unlikely that moral hazard of the form in which workers' compensation dampens workers' safety incentives is likely to be a major factor in setting the optimal level of workers' compensation benefits.

A second form of moral hazard might be termed *ex ante* causality hazard, which is that it may be difficult to identify which accidents are caused by the job. The workers' compensation system in the United States compensates all workers irrespective of fault, but the accident or illness must be job-related. Causality is particularly difficult to ascertain in the case of injuries whose presence or timing is difficult to monitor. Workers, for example, are more likely to experience back injuries on Monday (see R. S. Smith [1990]), but it is not clear whether this phenomenon represents a legitimate accident pattern or simply a consequence of workers reporting injuries that occurred over the weekend on the first day of work so that they can obtain insurance coverage for their injury. The greatest causality problems lie with respect to dimly understood health hazards, such as cancer, which often involve long time lags and multiple causality. Compensation of all lung cancer cases of workers in the asbestos industry would cost an order of magnitude more than simply compensating only those cases specifically attributable to asbestos exposures, if they could be identified.[11] For the most part, workers' compensation systems have sidestepped these difficult causality issues by simply not compensating diseases.

What matters from the standpoint of setting the optimal insurance level is not whether there are causality problems such as this, but instead whether they are likely to be responsive to the level at which workers' compensation benefits are set. In particular, to what extent will the number of illegitimate claims increase in response to higher levels of workers' compensation benefits? This relationship is surely positive, but its magnitude is uncertain.

A third form of moral hazard might be termed *ex post* treatment hazard. In the standard medical insurance context a frequent form of moral hazard encountered is that individuals might choose to receive unnecessary care or more generally to undergo costly treatments with a low probability of success. These difficulties are substantially alleviated by stringent controls imposed on the types and costs of treatment that one can receive.

The final form of moral hazard that is of interest is what one can term *ex post* duration hazard. As the benefit structure becomes more lucrative, individuals' incentives to return to work are diminished. Of all the forms of moral hazard, this appears to be the one of greatest consequence.[12] In particular, the elasticity of the duration of benefits with respect to the generosity of benefit levels is one of the most salient, practical problems faced by the workers' compensation system. Recent estimates in Meyer, Viscusi, and Durbin (1990) suggest that the elasticity of spell duration to benefit levels is in the range of 0.3 to 0.4. Efforts to provide optimal levels of insurance must be tempered with the moral hazard problems that arise with respect to prolonging the period over which benefits are paid out.

5.3 PRODUCT RISK INSURANCE

Context and Objectives

Whereas the workers' compensation program is a publicly run social insurance effort, the insurance for product risks in the United States is not carried out through a conventional insurance program. Rather, injured parties must file lawsuits against the producers of the product involved in the injury, and the rules of common law will dictate whether the individual will be compensated.

The most important difference between workers' compensation and compensation provided through the liability system is that the workers' compensation system is not based on employer fault, whereas product liability is explicitly linked to the attributes of the product, principally strict liability and negligence standards. Conceivably, the two types of social insurance system could have been set up in the same manner. One could, for example, have established a product liability insurance system that paid injured parties irrespective of producer fault. Such an effort would obviously impose much greater costs, and more importantly there would be substantial potential for abuse. Was the individual actually using the product at the time of the accident? What was its causal role? The court system resolves such issues.

Once a firm has been found to be liable for the injury, the amount of damages that are levied often is quite substantial. Individuals can receive compensation for both pecuniary and nonpecuniary losses. The main pecuniary loss components include lost earnings and medical expenses, where we will focus on the lost earnings component since that is the main concern of this paper. Although the formulas for providing compensation vary across states, the general approach tends to be fairly similar, with minor differences for the treatment of taxes and the role of discounting. The general approach now used in the United States courts is to compensate the survivors of fatally injured victims for the present value of their earnings loss minus the value of any consumption share of the deceased. Estimates of the consumption share generally put that value in the vicinity of 30 percent, so that this formula serves to provide for roughly two-thirds replacement of the present value of lost earnings.[13] In the case of individuals who are injured but survive the accident, the compensation formula provides for payment of the present value of the lost earnings. This formula is consequently more generous than is the standard workers' compensation benefit formula that consists of two-thirds wage replacement.

Several differences should be noted, however. First, whereas workers' compensation benefits are not taxed, court awards are subject to tax, thus eliminating about half of the difference in the compensation levels.[14] In addition, there is greater certainty that one will receive a workers' compensation award that will be paid irrespective of fault than the chance that one will obtain a successful product liability judgment. Finally, the amount of any product liability award received by the victim must be reduced by the size of any legal fees, which under commonly adopted contingent fee arrangements in the United States generally account for roughly one-third of all payments. In terms of the financial loss component, the net effect is that the product liability awards for economic loss are not starkly different from workers' compensation benefits in terms of the extent of earnings replacement under the standard formulas that are used.

A second class of compensation that is provided for victims of product injuries is compensation for noneconomic damages. The chief components of such damages are compensation for the pain and suffering incurred by the accident victim as well as compensation for the survivors of an accident victim for loss of consortium. As the empirical evidence reported below will indicate, the amount of compensation for these components of loss is often quite substantial. Any justification for such compensation on insurance grounds must hinge on a belief that the accident raises the marginal utility of income to the accident victim. Although this assumption was not borne out in the estimates of worker utility functions presented in Section 5.2, the discussion below explores other empirical results consistent with this assumption.

Optimal Insurance Reference Points

For injuries that are comparable in severity to job injuries, one can apply the same kind of analysis utilized in Section 5.2 to obtain the appropriate replacement rate. Partial replacement of the earnings loss will generally be optimal. Moreover, any differences that arise in the analysis with respect to products and jobs arise only from the tax treatment of workers' compensation and product liability awards. There appears to be no legitimate economic reason for making a distinction across these two forms of consumption in terms of the degree to which they should be taxed. Each of these programs provides insurance compensation to injured parties, and from a social insurance standpoint it matters little whether the causal factor was a consumer product or a feature of the workplace environment.

Another concern arises with respect to the differing severity mix of the types of injuries that may be involved. To receive compensation for a job accident, the injury must be severe enough to result in a loss of employment and/or medical expenses associated with the accident. Product liability awards need not be based on such an employment loss as, for example, an individual can sue for the pain and suffering experienced from chemical poisoning even though there was no loss of work or out-of-pocket medical expense.

To refine the assessment of how we should insure different types of injuries, Table 5-2 presents utility function estimates for a variety of minor product injuries. Whereas the utility functions involving job risks were based on survey data pertaining to hazard warnings for chemical workers, these estimates were generated using survey data on consumer attitudes toward potentially hazardous products. The two products used in the study were pesticide and toilet bowl cleaner. For each product individuals were asked how much they would be willing to pay in exchange for products of different riskiness.

Because of the more extensive nature of the data, the utility functions that could be estimated were more elaborate than in the worker case, as it was possible to estimate a utility function in the ill-health state of the form

$$U^2(Y) = \beta \ln(Y-L),$$

where $U^1(Y)$ can be set equal to $\ln Y$ with no loss of generality.

Under this specification of the utility function following an injury, there are two possible components to the loss. The loss may include a financial loss equivalent, and it can also include a term β that reflects an effect on the marginal utility of income so that both the structure and the level of utility can be influenced.

The results reported in Table 5-2 indicate that these injuries tend to be treated largely as equivalent to financial losses. Two samples were asked questions with respect to these risks, a sample of individuals who did not have young children as well as a sample with young children. In the case of the sample with young children, the child poisoning risk associated with toilet bowl cleaner was included in the survey instead of the risk of eye burns. Similarly for the insecticide subsample, child poisoning risks were included for the sample with young children and skin poisoning risks were included for the sample without young children. These risk categories constitute the major risks posed by these products. Moreover, the descriptions of the injuries indicated that the effects were largely temporary in nature. One could safely conclude that the injuries were much less severe than, for example, the risk of a job accident that was serious enough to cause one to receive workers' compensation benefits.

The estimates provided in Table 5-2 indicate that the utility functions were affected very little by the injury as the β coefficient is significantly different from 1.0 in only one case—insecticide inhalation for respondents with young children. Even in that case, the discrepancy is not substantial. The monetary loss equivalent values reported in the second column of results in Table 5-2 indicate an injury range from a value of $486 for toilet bowl gassings (without young children) to a value of $2,538 for insecticide child poisonings for respondents with children. A noteworthy feature of the results is that the responses were higher for individuals with young children, which may reflect a belief that the risk is higher in such households than the average risk level, and it may reflect an altruistic concern for children.

The third column of results in Table 5-2 provides the calculation of the optimal insurance amount assuming that actuarially fair insurance is available. The proce-

Table 5-2. Utility Functions for Minor Product Injuries

	$U^2(Y)$ β	$= \beta\ln(Y - L)$ L^a	Optimal fair insurance	Replacement rate
Sample without young children:				
Insecticide inhalation	.9998	849	842	.99
Insecticide skin poisoning	.9996	619	605	.98
Toilet bowl cleaner gassing	.9999	486	482	.99
Toilet bowl cleaner eye burn	.9997	515	504	.98
Sample with young children:				
Insecticide inhalation	.9983[a]	1,433	1,373	.96
Insecticide child poisoning	.9984	2,538	2,482	.98
Toilet bowl cleaner gassing	1.0002	581	588	1.01
Toilet bowl cleaner child poisoning	1.0004	923	937	1.02

[a]All loss coefficients are statistically significant at the 5 percent level, and one b coefficient is significantly different from 1.0. The coefficient estimates in columns 1 and 2 are drawn from Evans and Viscusi (1991).

dure used was to assess the level of insurance compensation that would give the injured party the same marginal utility of income as their income level, which averaged $35,300. The optimal insurance amounts differ very little from the magnitude of the financial loss equivalent, with the greatest differences being for child poisoning from insecticide, for which there is a $56 difference, and insecticide inhalations, for which the difference is $60. It should be noted that only in the case of insecticide inhalation is the β coefficient significantly different from 1.0, so that in all other cases one cannot reject the result that utility functions are consistent with an optimal insurance value that provides for full replacement of the monetary loss equivalent of the accident. The optimal fair insurance levels that are calculated for the point estimates of the utility functions cannot be distinguished statistically from a system of insurance that compensates individuals for the loss L except in the situation of insecticide inhalation, where there is a significant effect on marginal utility.

The optimal replacement rates for the financial loss equivalents given in the final column of Table 5-2 indicate that the optimal replacement rate is very close to 1.0, as the lowest value observed in the set of results for insecticide inhalation, which has a replacement rate of .96.

The general theme of these results is that individuals did not regard product injuries as fundamentally affecting the structure of their utility; these injuries did impose a welfare loss that people viewed as being equivalent to a monetary loss. Moreover, this loss has an associated optimal insurance amount that is close to full replacement of its value. The striking aspect about these results is that the survey was set up in such a manner that there would be no out-of-pocket medical or other costs associated with an injury. Whereas pain and suffering damages would not be insured under the worker utility functions estimated in Section 5.2, these consumer utility functions for minor injuries do indicate a demand for pain and suffering insurance. Moreover, even though insurance was not found to be desirable for the typical job injury, job injuries such as severe burns or paraplegia might be of the type that an individual would choose to receive additional insurance compensation after the injury if one could structure such an insurance plan. Thus, one cannot rule out altogether the appropriateness of pain and suffering compensation for injuries, where this judgment is based on social insurance concerns alone. This result contrasts with the standard assumption that dominates the entire literature on pain and suffering and tort liability reform more generally, which is that individuals would never choose to purchase insurance for pain and suffering damages.[15]

The findings in Table 5-2 indicate that further evidence of the character of individual preferences in response to different classes of injuries is central to the optimal design of our social insurance efforts. Our confidence in the less than full replacement of worker earnings through workers' compensation is economically consistent with a belief that damages for pain and suffering serve no legitimate insurance function. However, one cannot necessarily assume that pain and suffering losses are not an insurable component of the injury simply because individuals do not now purchase insurance policies that provide for pain and suffering compensation. The absence of such policies may not reflect a feature of the individual utility functions but instead may be a consequence of the difficulty of monitoring the pain and suffering that individuals experience, so that there would be a severe moral hazard problem in ascertaining the level of pain and suffering experienced. Within the context of a narrowly defined tort liability action, the determination of the presence of pain and suffering, which is typically an adjunct to the medical expenses and other losses for which the individual has received compensation, poses many fewer difficulties in terms of assessing the legitimacy of the loss that is claimed.

A more problematic aspect of pain and suffering compensation is that it is not now based on any analytic approach to determining optimal insurance amounts. Rather, juries are simply given vague guidance that the injured party should receive some pecuniary return for the injury that has been suffered. A more desirable approach would be to link the amount of pain and suffering compensation with the optimal insurance amount that an individual would choose to purchase based on estimates obtained using the utility function such as those estimated in Table 5-2.

Performance of Product Liability as Social Insurance

To assess the insurance function of product liability, I will use a sample of over 10,000 closed product liability claims from the 1977 Insurance Services Office Product Liability Closed Claims Survey. These data remain the most detailed available information on the performance of product liability on a claim-specific basis. The sample includes over 10,000 closed claims and is quite comprehensive in terms of the scope of its coverage. In situations in which the claim is dropped, which occurs in 19 percent of all cases, we have no data on insurance compensation. This does not mean that the individual receives no compensation at all in dropped claims. Multiple claims may have been filed against different producers. What may be at issue is who ultimately will be responsible for the liability, not whether the individual will have received compensation for the injury. Many of these claims, for example, represent subrogation actions whereby a firm is trying to obtain reimbursement from some other company of injury payments it has made. In addition, in a fault-based system, many of the claims that are dropped will be those in which the liability case is relatively weak. Since four-fifths of the claims are successful, on an expected value basis the rate of income replacement will continue to be quite substantial even if one ignores questions regarding the legitimacy of the claims that are dropped.

The amount of damages paid cannot be distinguished in terms of whether these damages were paid by earnings losses or medical expenses. The most that one can do is ascertain the total amount of damages awarded as well as the amount of economic losses that were claimed. For the sample of cases involving bodily injury considered here, the three components of economic loss are lost earnings, medical expenses, and other economic damages. These estimates are used to construct the loss ranges in the first column of Table 5-3. These values are in 1977 prices; to convert them to 1991 dollars, one should roughly double all dollar amounts. For each loss range, I calculated the replacement rate, which is the ratio of the amount of compensation received to the value of the economic loss. These calculations for cases settled out of court and for cases resulting in a successful verdict on behalf of the plaintiff appear in columns 2 and 3 of Table 5-3.

The pattern in terms of the replacement rates is fairly similar in both classes of claims. For small values of claims, the replacement rate is often well in excess of

Table 5-3. Product Liability Replacement
Rates by Loss Range

	Replacement rate	
Loss range	Settled out of court	Won court verdict
1–10,000	7.09	19.39
10,001–25,000	3.09	4.56
25,001–50,000	1.96	2.73
50,001–100,000	2.58	1.69
100,001–200,000	0.60	1.56
200,001–500,000	0.58	2.22
500,001–1,000,000	0.43	0.44
Over 1,000,001	0.26	0.05

1.0, and the amount of replacement is generally a declining function of the size of the stated loss. Out-of-court settlements exceed economic damages for all claims with a loss range of $100,000 or less, and court awards exceed economic losses for claims of $500,000 or less.

The decline in the level of replacement rates at the high end of the loss range may be due in part to the possible overstatement of such losses. Cases in which the value of economic losses is overstated will tend to be disproportionately clustered at the bottom end of the set of loss ranges. As a result, these low replacement rates may not reflect a low level of insurance of these claims but rather a measurement problem with respect to the true economic losses experienced in each particular case.

Overall, the pattern is quite different from that of workers' compensation, which generally provides for less than full compensation for the earnings losses of job accident victims. In the case of product liability awards, the norm is overcompensation of financial losses. In the case of claims settled out of court, only 2 percent of claims received compensation values that were less than the amount of financial losses, and for successful court verdicts, an identical 2 percent received compensation below the amount of economic losses. In view of the small number of claims for which there is only partial compensation, the apparent legal standard is such that the insurance provided exceeds the economic loss.

The amount of payment for such noneconomic losses is summarized for different injury groups in Table 5-4. Different categories of injuries are listed in column 1, where the injury categories that are most prominent in terms of noneconomic loss, chiefly pain and suffering, are brain damage and para/quadriplegia. The first two columns of statistics provide information for all claims in which there is some positive bodily injury payment. The average value of noneconomic loss ranged from a low of $422 for dermatitis to a high of $82,129 for brain damage. Although the fraction of claims for any particular injury receiving compensation for noneconomic loss varies, for the most part this fraction is in the vicinity of one-half. Approximately half of all the damages received for bodily injury losses consist of payment for noneconomic loss.

Table 5-4. Noneconomic Losses for Nonfatal Accidents

	Claims with positive bodily injury payments		Claims with positive noneconomic loss	
	Mean noneconomic loss	Fraction of payment for noneconomic loss	Mean noneconomic loss	Fraction of noneconomic loss
Amputation	30,733	.50	41,568	.68
Asphyxiation	1,743	.52	2,490	.74
Brain damage	82,179	.41	141,348	.71
Bruise	2,546	.49	3,502	.68
Burn	22,319	.57	26,653	.69
Cancer	26,652	.53	31,094	.62
Concussion	6,372	.52	8,097	.66
Dermatitis	422	.41	639	.63
Dislocation	11,327	.42	18,124	.67
Disease—other	4,957	.46	6,360	.60
Electrical shock	4,184	.50	5,661	.68
Fracture	5,693	.30	11,071	.58
Laceration	3,356	.51	4,455	.68
Para/quadriplegia	71,447	.24	142,894	.48
Poison	443	.49	614	.64
Respiratory	18,140	.40	35,416	.77
Sprain/strain	10,476	.50	13,721	.65
Other	3,710	.35	6,924	.64

The final two columns of Table 5-4 indicate that for claims in which there was a positive value of compensation for noneconomic losses, the mean noneconomic loss compensation was, as expected, much greater. In this case, the low value of noneconomic loss compensation is $614 for poisonings, with the high value of $142,894 for para/quadriplegia. Given that an individual receives payment for noneconomic loss, roughly two-thirds of all of the compensation that is received appears to be for noneconomic as opposed to economic damages.

Substantial anecdotal evidence suggests that awards for pain and suffering are on the rise. The widespread belief in such a trend has led to a variety of tort liability reform efforts at the state level. In addition, the U.S. Department of Justice has proposed restrictions on pain and suffering awards.[16]

One difficulty with the class of compensation is that in the absence of a firm legal basis for establishing such compensation, there will be a tendency for the award structure to be uncertain and for there to be inequities across cases. Detailed analysis of patterns of compensation for noneconomic loss indicates that there is a systematic relationship between these payments and various measures of injury severity, although one would be hard-pressed to argue that these awards are at a social optimum. Perhaps the most instructive finding is that the noneconomic loss is $614 (in 1977 prices) or $1,090 (in 1985 prices) for poisonings, which is in line with the insurance values indicated in Table 5-2 (in 1985 prices) for poisoning-related injuries associated with products. These estimates lie roughly in the middle of the range of estimates reported in Table 5-2. This figure is certainly in line with the general order of magnitude implied by the utility function estimates.

Further exploration of the shape of other utility functions for different classes of injuries is required before one can dismiss pain and suffering compensation as lacking any basis in an insurance objective. Although it is likely that there are many classes of severe injuries for which the effect of the injury on one's ability to derive utility from additional expenditures implies that the level of social insurance should provide for less than full compensation of earnings loss, one cannot necessarily conclude that this will always be the case or that social insurance systems that make provision for noneconomic losses are inappropriate.

5.4 THE VIABILITY OF SOCIAL INSURANCE

Workers' Compensation

As benefit levels are increased, the cost of workers' compensation is boosted as well. Although the cost of workers' compensation could escalate as a result of unintended changes brought about by responses to modifications in the benefit structure, for the most part the performance of workers' compensation has been what one would have expected given the effort to raise the adequacy of benefits.

Table 5-5 summarizes trends in three different types of costs for workers' compensation. The first column of statistics provides information on the percentage change in premiums, which is then broken out into the contributory role of benefits increases (column 2) and experience review (column 3), which includes not only changes in items such as taxes but, more importantly, changes attributable to shifts either in the level of risks or in the duration of the benefit periods. The final column of statistics in Table 5-5 gives information on trends in the overall premium level.

The major shifts in the benefit structure occurred from 1972 to 1976 and 1982 to 1983. The increases that took place in the mid-1970s are particularly noteworthy since these were the results of efforts to close the gap in terms of income replacement. In particular, the perceived inadequacy of benefits led to efforts to bolster the social insurance function of the workers' compensation program. Based on the evidence in Section 5.2, it appears that these efforts have been reasonably successful, as the level of benefits seems to be roughly in line with what one would expect in terms of an effective social insurance effort.

The trends in the experience review component of premiums suggest that there may, however, be a moral hazard link between benefit structure and experience rating. For example, the benefit increases in 1972 to 1976 were followed by a similar three-year jump in the experience review component from 1975 to 1978. Similarly, the benefit increase in 1982 was followed by a like pattern from 1985.

Overall, however, the workers' compensation system seems to be performing reasonably well as a social insurance program. The two main problem areas that remain are those that can be traced to monitorability and moral hazard. A continuing problem is that of permanent partial disability benefits, as these individuals have experienced an injury but are also likely to be affected by the work disincentives of more generous social insurance benefits.[17] There have been substantial changes in

Table 5-5. Percentage Changes in Workers' Compensation

Year	Benefits and premiums		Percentage benefits component
	Change in premiums overall	Experience review	
1970	1.5	−1.3	2.8
1971	2.1	−0.8	2.9
1972	7.2	1.2	5.9
1973	7.4	1.0	6.3
1974	8.2	2.2	5.9
1975	15.3	7.1	7.7
1976	17.0	9.7	6.7
1977	11.2	9.2	1.8
1978	11.3	7.2	3.8
1979	6.4	4.2	2.1
1980	2.9	0.2	2.7
1981	−2.1	−5.0	3.1
1982	−1.4	−5.5	4.3
1983	1.7	−3.1	5.0
1984	0.4	−2.2	2.7
1985	12.2	10.3	1.7
1986	8.9	7.5	1.3
1987	9.6	8.8	0.7
1988	8.1	6.8	1.2
1969–1988	258.8	68.7	109.1
1980–1988	110.1	24.2	39.9

Source: National Council on Compensation Insurance, *Annual Statistical Bulletin* (New York: National Council on Compensation Insurance, 1989). Data for 1988 are for first three quarters.

the structure of permanent partial disability in an effort to address this difficult tradeoff problem, but given the nature of the economic problem it is likely to be of continuing concern. The second problem area is that of the increased role of occupational disease. The causality problems here raise the fundamental issue of what role, if any, the workers' compensation system should play in compensating illnesses that have a tenuous link to workplace exposures. Although such concerns remain, overall the system is not undergoing any period of crisis.

Product Liability

In contrast, the product liability system has undergone a major upheaval, particularly in the 1980s. The general view is that this social insurance effort is out of control. Among the more prominent symptoms of the product liability crisis are the tripling in general liability premiums from 1984 to 1986 as well as the evidence of denials of coverage. The main difference in the social insurance of product-related risks and job risks is that the structure of social insurance for product risks is not as much a consequence of a conscious policy choice. Liability doctrines are influenced by the evolution of common law, and the overall approach to compensation (e.g., present value of lost earnings and pain and suffering compensation) is influenced by state statutes. However, there is considerable discretion for juries to set compensation levels, and in the important area of noneconomic damages there are effectively no guidelines whatsoever for setting the compensation values. Whereas the workers' compensation system is a tightly organized administrative insurance effort with explicit benefit guidelines for various categories of injuries, tort liability cases are decided on an ad hoc basis with very little structure imposed on the damage amounts.

The trends in verdicts that have been awarded under this system, summarized in Table 5-6, indicate that there has been a dramatic change over the past decade. Although the survey of court cases used throughout these statistics does not include all litigation, it is the largest such sample now available on litigation trends. The overall pattern of verdict levels is unmistakable. The median verdict experienced a 188 percent increase from 1981 to 1987, which is almost a tripling in the median verdict level. The pattern of mean verdict levels is also uneven because of the role of outliers as well as the small sample, but the trend is strongly upward. Average verdicts in product liability cases rose by 389 percent from 1980 to 1988, so that the average award increased almost by a factor of 5 within a seven-year period.

The rise in verdict amounts will in turn raise the incentives of injured parties to pursue litigation. The number of product liability cases in federal courts rose from 2,393 in 1975 to 13,145 in 1987. Although changes in liability doctrine contributed to the caseload, the more generous jury verdicts no doubt also contributed to the growth-industry status of product liability litigation.

The dramatic escalation in verdicts, litigation, and premiums suggests that at the very least there should be an examination of the structure of product liability compensation to see whether in fact it is serving as an effective social insurance effort. The first concern is with respect to whether the degree of income replacement under product liability is appropriate. The overall pattern of overpaying small losses and underpaying large losses might be appropriate if severe injuries diminish the marginal utility of income so that less than full compensation is desirable. In

Table 5-6. Percentage Changes in Product Liability Verdicts

	Percentage change	
	Median verdict	Mean verdict
1981	51	42
1982	−12	6
1983	0	46
1984	0	18
1985	50	−26
1986	56	6
1987	−37	14
1988	−6	16
1980–1989	80	173

Source: Figures calculated using information from Jury Verdict Research (1990).

addition, the nature of pain and suffering for small losses should be such that the individuals would have insured such losses for it to be desirable to provide such compensation.

The patterns of compensation that have been adopted do not seem to have been developed based on any analytic basis of any kind. Rather, small losses tend to be overcompensated since claimants wish to recoup their legal fees, and insurers are eager to close out relatively minor cases that impose administrative costs. The tendency to underpay large losses may not be so much a conscious decision to take into account the diminished marginal utility of income with severe injuries as it may be a reflection in the measurement error associated with reported loss values, which may be overstated for large losses. The one exception is that of fatalities, where the practice of deducting the consumption share of the deceased represents an effort to adjust for the most severe case in which an injury will affect one's marginal utility of expenditures.

What is lacking is a methodological approach for determining the appropriate award level. Focusing on the present value of lost earnings, which will then be taxed, may be appropriate, but it differs from the workers' compensation approach of two-thirds earnings replacement, which is not taxed. Additional information on utility function structure could assist in fine-tuning these two compensation approaches.

A more difficult area that is much more out of control is the pain and suffering and other compensation for noneconomic damages. Although the current system is not necessarily random or capricious, it does not appear to be particularly sound, and there is need for additional economic guidance in this area.

5.5 CONCLUSION

The primary intent of this paper was not to develop specific results for either workers' compensation or product liability but rather to indicate how some of the principles that have been developed in the theoretical literature can be of greater consequence. Investigation of the empirical implications of many of the theoretical guidelines that have been developed makes it possible to go beyond simply indicating general patterns of influence and factors that should be considered to give more explicit guidance for policy design.

The greater availability of information regarding employment patterns enables us to draw more precise conclusions with respect to workers' compensation than for product liability. Since workers' compensation will be a valued component of a worker's compensation package, there will be a market adjustment in response to this social insurance. This wage offset is of interest not only because it reduces the net cost to employers of the social insurance program but also because it can be used as a measure to indicate whether the tradeoff rate expressed through the labor market actions of workers is within a range one would expect given the price structure of the social insurance effort in relation to the terms of trade it provides between wages and workers' compensation. The wage-workers' compensation tradeoff results indicate some inadequacy of benefits in the 1970s but a narrowing of this gap in the 1980s.

Information on the specific structure of worker utility functions reinforced these results with respect to the optimality of social insurance. Moreover, it is possible to calculate the optimal level of income replacement under workers' compensation, which is greater than but not too dissimilar from the level now in place.

One also can utilize the implications of the workers' compensation results to assess the adequacy of social insurance provided by product liability. By these criteria, product liability awards may appear to be overly generous for small injuries and may provide for undercompensation of serious injuries. This conclusion may reflect in part the role of fatalities and measurement error, so it is not entirely clear that severe injuries are necessarily undercompensated.

Perhaps the most striking aspect of product liability awards is that in addition to compensation for pecuniary losses there is additional compensation for non-economic loss, chiefly pain and suffering. Estimates of consumer utility function for minor health risks indicate that the utility function structure may be of the form such that the injury is tantamount to a monetary loss equivalent. In that case, insurance of pain and suffering losses would be desirable, but the findings for the more severe job injuries indicate that the insurance demand for pain and suffering is not likely to be the case for all classes of injuries. The product liability system does not distinguish which injuries should receive pain and suffering and which should not except by ruling out pain and suffering awards for utility loss experienced after one's death. The alarming escalation in product liability awards may be attributable at least in part to the imprecise economic foundations for establishing the levels of such compensation. Reform advocates and legal scholars have long recommended greater structure for compensation values. Further developments in economic analysis of these issues should enable economists to assist in providing more explicit guidance for such a new award structure.

The findings reported here raise an important class of issues but do not necessarily resolve them. A number of major areas in which extension of our knowledge is needed are clearly evident. Chief among these are estimation of utility functions for a variety of health outcomes, determination of the relationship between actual benefits paid for particular kinds of injuries and the formal benefits structures that were used in this chapter, and incorporation of the role of moral hazard in an explicit manner. As we continue to make additional progress on these issues, the determination of the structure of social insurance efforts will be increasingly a task in the economists' domain.

NOTES

This paper was originally given as the Inaugural Geneva Risk Economics Lecture sponsored by the Geneva Association for Risk and Insurance in Paris, September 18, 1989. I would like to thank Eric Briys and Pascale Viala for both their helpful comments and their hospitality.

1. The optimal tradeoff is analyzed in product risk contexts by Spence (1977) and in the job risk context by Viscusi (1980). The spirit of this result can be traced to the medical insurance analysis in Zeckhauser (1970).

2. Among the earliest treatments, see Zeckhauser (1970, 1973) and Arrow (1974).

3. This observation was first made in the case of fatalities by Eisner and Strotz (1961). Other studies generating this result include, among others: Cook and Graham (1977), Karni (1985), Keeney and Raiffa (1976), Shavell (1987), and Viscusi (1979a).

4. This is one insurance issue for which there has long been an economic consensus.

5. This development is an elaboration of the test described in Viscusi and Moore (1987).

6. For description of these terms, see Viscusi and Moore (1987) and Moore and Viscusi (1990a).

7. Data are drawn from the National Council on Compensation Insurance, Annual Statistical Bulletin, 1989, p. 7.

8. Council of Economic Advisors (1989), p. 373.

9. The main policy parameter that is manipulated in order to govern the insurance function is the income replacement rate r. The optimal value of r maximized the worker's expected utility subject to the actuarial constraint, which we can take into consideration through the insurance price hp/(1-p). As a result, one has

$$\max_r V = (1-p)1.077 \ln \{Y[1-(hpr/(1-p))](1-t)\} + p \ln Yr.$$

In computing such optimality, one should note that the choice of the insurance level is not the result of a worker optimation. Some of the consequences of this distinction are explored in Briys, Kahane, and Kroll (1988).

10. The role of moral hazard has been discussed in such early treatments as Zeckhauser (1970).

11. See Viscusi (1984b).

12. See also Butler and Worrall (1985) for estimates of this effect.

13. See Cheit (1961) for an early study of this issue.

14. Tax treatments of court awards differ by jurisdiction and by whether the award is a lump sum or a structured settlement whereby payments are made over a period of time.

15. An eloquent and economically cogent case against pain and suffering is provided by Schwartz (1988). A somewhat different legal perspective based on alternative economic assumptions appears in Weiler (1989).

16. See the U.S. Department of Justice (1986).

17. Berkowitz and Burton (1987) and Weiler (1986) discuss these issues in detail.

PART II

**Rationality and Individual
Responses to Risk**

6

Rational Models of Biases in Risk Perception

6.1 RISK PERCEPTIONS AND ECONOMIC BEHAVIOR

For there to be a risk-dollar tradeoff, the individuals exposed to the risk must have some awareness that they are making a tradeoff. Unfortunately, we do not enter the world with perfect information. There are, however, opportunities to learn about risks over time.

A fundamental aspect of risk perception in the economics literature is the ability of individuals to incorporate new information reliably in forming their probabilistic judgments. Workers learn from their job search efforts, consumers learn about the products they prefer, and investors acquire sufficient information about future price shifts to eliminate arbitrage possibilities.

There has been increasing interest in whether these normative models of individual choice under uncertainty accord with actual behavior. These concerns have been much greater than in other economic contexts because of the particularly severe demands such decisions place on the rationality of the decision maker. The limitations of these decisions have widespread consequences, as they provide the rationale for many government efforts to regulate the risks people face. This chapter explores these risk-perception issues using a Bayesian decision framework, which is the most prominent model of rational decision making in learning contexts.

6.2 RISK PERCEPTIONS AND MARKET DECISIONS

Ideally, individuals should fully understand the risks they face before making decisions with probabilistic outcomes. In most instances, extensive experimental evidence is not available, so that individuals must rely on their subjective probabilistic judgments of the risk. Such assessments will clearly not always be accurate and may be systematically biased as well. Precise analysis of the nature and extent of such biases is impeded by the paucity of data on individuals' probability assessments and the actual risks that they face.

Evidence on worker risk perceptions reported in Viscusi (1979a) focused on survey data for which I linked an objective risk index (the BLS injury rate for the worker's industry) and a measure of the worker's subjective risk perceptions—a dummy variable for whether or not the worker's job exposed him or her to dangerous or unhealthy conditions. The expected positive correlation was observed, but such evidence can only be suggestive because the workers did not scale the risks in probabilistic terms. It is, however, noteworthy that one obtains the same estimate of the annual compensating differential for job risks using the worker's subjective perceptions as one does using an objective measure of the risk.

More generally, the studies reviewed in Chapters 3 and 4 indicated the presence of substantial compensating differentials for risk in the labor market as well as other risk-taking contexts. If risk perceptions were equal to zero, no risk premiums would be observed since individuals would be indifferent to the risks they faced. These findings do not rule out the presence of perceptional biases, but they do indicate that the most extreme characterizations of perceptional biases are not warranted.

To refine this evidence, in Viscusi and O'Connor (1984) we presented over 300 chemical workers with a linear scale that they would use to rate the hazards of their jobs. This scale was constructed in a manner that made it possible for us to compare workers' responses to objective measures of the chemical industry risk. In particular, each rating could be converted into an equivalent level for the BLS injury and illness rate. Overall, workers' subjective risk assessments were above the reported injury and illness rate for the chemical industry, which one would expect since health risks are notoriously underreported.

The survey then presented workers with a hazard warning label for a chemical that they were told would replace the chemicals with which they currently worked. One of the chemicals—sodium bicarbonate—was household baking soda. A shift to this chemical eliminated the disease risks associated with the job so that only the accident risks remained. It is particularly noteworthy that once the long-term chemical hazards were excluded from consideration the subjective risk perceptions were identically equal to the published accident rates. Although one would be hard-pressed to claim that such a fortuitous result implies that all job risk perceptions are unbiased, there does appear to be a strong correspondence between actual and perceived risks for a major class of risks that people face.

When asked to rate their job risks using a linear scale or when asked about whether or not their jobs pose a hazard, most respondents gave plausible risk-perceptions assessments. These assessments are much more accurate than the responses in studies that frame the risk perception issue in relative terms (for example, whether or not the respondent believes he or she is an above-average-risk driver), where systematic optimism has been observed. Some observed biases in past studies may be due to the manner in which the risk-perception question is framed rather than to any underlying shortcoming in individual behavior.

6.3 PERCEPTIONS OF LETHAL EVENTS

A widely cited result in the risk perception literature is that individuals assessing risks of fatality overassess the risks of low-probability events (e.g., smallpox, tornadoes, botulism) and underassess the risks of high-probability events (e.g., diabetes, heart disease, and stroke).

Table 6-1 summarizes the results of the Lichtenstein et al. (1978) study of individual assessments of different fatality risks, which was the seminal study demon-

Table 6-1. Perceived versus Actual Risks

	Perceived risk/actual risk	
Cause of death	Motor vehicle risk reference point	Electrocution risk reference point
Smallpox	—[a]	—[a]
Poisoning by vitamins	1.27	1.16
Botulism	1.97	1.96
Measles	1.39	1.47
Fireworks	1.54	1.26
Smallpox vaccination	.17	.22
Whooping cough	.69	.62
Polio	.80	.55
Venomous bite or sting	1.67	1.85
Tornado	1.82	2.86
Lightning	.32	.37
Nonvenomous animal	.71	.54
Flood	1.77	2.71
Excess cold	.81	.73
Syphilis	1.15	1.05
Pregnancy, childbirth, and abortion	2.98	2.78
Infectious hepatitis	1.19	.80
Appendicitis	1.03	.87
Electrocution	.65	1.96
Motor-train collision	.74	.95
Asthma	.65	.47
Firearms	1.26	1.42
Poisoning	.96	.92
Tuberculosis	.59	.43
Fire and flames	1.62	1.86
Drowning	.85	.91
Leukemia	.81	.92
Accidental falls	.68	1.03
Homicide	2.10	1.30
Emphysema	.69	.86
Suicide	1.42	.97
Breast cancer	.66	.61
Diabetes	.34	.22
Motor vehicle accident	6.34	5.76
Lung cancer	1.00	1.33
Stomach cancer	.43	.26
All accidents	6.77	9.32
Stroke	.54	.31
All cancer	1.70	2.00
Heart disease	.49	.51
All disease	.75	1.14

[a]Base risk is zero, so ratio is not defined.

Source: Lichtenstein et al. (1978), p. 564.

strating this bias. In the survey the authors presented respondents with information concerning the fatality rate for one particular risk. In the case of one sample, the interviewer gave the respondent information concerning the motor vehicle risk level, and for another sample the respondents received information concerning electrocution risks. The ratio of the respondents' perceived risks to the estimated value of the actual risks posed by these different causes of death appears in the two columns of Table 6-1. Although the pattern is somewhat uneven, for the most part there is a tendency to overestimate the lower risks in the table and to underestimate the larger risks. This general pattern is borne out in a more formal statistical analysis of the findings and has become one of the central results in the literature on biases and risk perception.

No explanation has been given for this pattern of bias, other than to observe that it is a feature of individual behavior. Slovic, Fischhoff, and Lichtenstein (1982) do, however, note that some overassessed risks are those that have been highly publicized—a result quite consistent with a rational learning process. This explanation addresses a few outliers, not the general nature of risk perceptions.

An understanding of this phenomenon requires, however, that one have a meaningful reference point for assessing the character of risk perceptions. The approach here will utilize a model of rational learning, in particular, a Bayesian decision framework.

The first building block of this approach is the treatment of individuals' risk perceptions. I will characterize these perceptions by a beta distribution, which I will parameterize as follows.[1] Before being informed of the class of fatality risks he or she is considering, the individual starts with a prior risk p, which has an associated precision γ. Being informed that the risk is in category i (e.g., heart disease) will trigger information that the individual has acquired concerning the risk category, which is equivalent to observing s_i deaths in ξ_i trials, where I will assume that s_i is the true risk (e.g., learning is unbiased). As a result, the posterior risk assessment p_i^* can be written as

$$p_i^* = (\gamma p + \xi_i s_i)/(\gamma + \xi_i).$$

If we let ψ_i be the relative informational content of the new information compared to the prior (i.e., ξ_i/γ), then p_i^* can be rewritten as

$$p_i^* = (p + \psi_i s_i)/(1 + \psi_i). \qquad (6.1)$$

The individual's risk perception will be a linear function of his or her prior beliefs.

If the relative amount of information ψ_i acquired about the risk is independent of s_i, then the pattern observed will be that illustrated in Figure 6-1. Risks below that of the prior p will be revised downward, and risks above that of the prior will be revised upward. Unless individuals acquire full information rather than partial information, low-probability events will be overassessed and high-probability events will tend to be underassessed, as psychologists have observed.

Testing for Bias

Let us consider first the consistency of the risk-perception results with the pattern sketched in Figure 6-1. The perceived risk p_i^* pertains to the assessed frequency

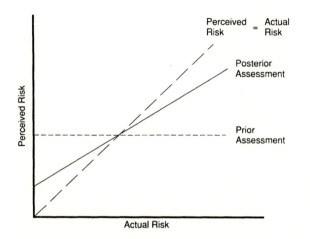

Figure 6.1 Nature of the updating process

of the risk category i, and s_i is the actual frequency. The units have been selected so that the frequency is in terms of the absolute number of deaths for every 205 million people. Recall that in the administration of the survey, the samples were divided into two groups. One group was given the actual motor vehicle accident frequency rate, while the other was given the electrocution frequency rate. Since these risk anchors influence the perceived risks, separate equations for each group were estimated.

Table 6-2 reports results obtained by regressing the perceived frequency rate on the actual rate and the square of this rate to ascertain whether the relationship follows the pattern in Figure 6-1. The data were drawn from the original Lichtenstein et al. (1978) study. The coefficient of the actual frequency rate is statistically significant and that of the square of this term is not, which is consistent with the expected linear relationship. The weight placed on the actual risk level is not, however, close to 1, which suggests that there is not a strong relationship between actual and perceived risk levels.

A more appropriate test for risk-related bias is not whether there is overassessment of small risks and underassessment of large risks, which we should expect, but

Table 6-2. Regression of Perceived Accident Frequency on Actual Frequency

	Coefficients (*standard errors*)	
Explanatory variable	Motor vehicle subsample	Electrocution subsample
Intercept	3,087.9	3,784.8
	(2,600.5)	(2,586.1)
Actual frequency	0.070	0.087
	(0.029)	(0.029)
(Actual frequency)^2	$-1.0E-8$	$-2.6E-8$
	(1.8E-8)	(1.8E-8)
$\bar{R}^2$	0.52	0.45

whether or not there is a risk-related variation in the relative weight ψ_i placed on new information. Do individuals, for example, incorporate the true risk information to a greater degree for small risks rather than large risks?

To test whether ψ_i is correlated with s_i, we must first construct a measure of the relative informational content ψ_i associated with each risk group. The prior risk that would be assigned to any accident group before knowing its identity will be approximated in two ways. First, the respondent may have used the anchor supplied in the survey (motor vehicle accidents or electrocutions) as his prior value of p. The second approach is an Akerlof (1970) lemons-type model whereby I will use the average risk level across all of the fatality risk groups. This average value will change depending on the subsample used. Three subsamples will be considered: the full sample of forty-one risks, the full sample excluding the category for which respondents were given the risk information, and the full sample less the anchor risk categories and three aggregate groups (all diseases, all cancers, and all accidents). The value of the s_i used is the true frequency rate. As a result, the ψ_i level reflects the relative emphasis the respondent implicitly places on the true risk level when forming his or her perceived risk judgments for each risk.

Table 6-3 summarizes the results of the regression of the different ψ_i values on s_i, where each equation also included a constant term. All of the estimated coefficients of s_i are well below their standard errors in all cases so that there is no statistically significant relationship between ψ_i and s_i. The degree to which individuals learn and incorporate new risk information is unaffected by the level of the risk, as one would expect within a Bayesian framework.

These results by no means fully demonstrate that individuals are Bayesian decision makers. What they do accomplish is to provide an explanation of observed biases in risk perception other than simply noting that a bias exists. The observed bias is quite consistent with a Bayesian learning model. Moreover, a more meaningful test of risk-related bias based on the relative weight placed on information used in revising the prior indicates no systematic bias. Although the risk perceptions guiding individual decisions may not be fully accurate, some of the observed discrepancies are consistent with a rational learning model.

Overall, the evidence suggests that individuals may have reasonably accurate

Table 6-3. Regression of ψ_i on Actual Frequency

Prior information	Frequency coefficients (*standard errors*)		
	Full sample	Full sample exclusive of anchor group	Specific risks
Motor vehicle accidents	−.276E-3	−0.279E-3	−0.861E-3
	(0.881E-3)	(0.892E-3)	(2.267E-3)
Electrocutions	−0.282E-5	−0.293E-5	−0.724E-5
	(0.461E-5)	(0.466E-5)	(0.121E-5)
Average risk (motor vehicle subsample)	−0.432E-3	−0.440E-3	−0.568E-3
	(1.38E-3)	(1.411E-3)	(1.496E-3)
Average risk (electrocutions)	−0.198E-3	−0.214E-3	−0.226E-3
	(0.557E-3)	(0.578E-3)	(0.618E-3)

perceptions of risks that have a fundamental impact on their welfare. Risk perceptions for other more remote hazards are less precise, and the observed biases are exactly what one would expect from a rational, Bayesian learning process. The inadequacies in risk perception also do not appear to be clear-cut in either direction. The overestimation of small risks and underestimation of large risks represents a more complex type of market failure than is reflected in the usual economic models incorporating biases in risk perception, which typically assume that risks are underestimated.

6.4 THE ROLE OF LEARNING

The cornerstone of the Bayesian approach is the learning process by which individuals update their risk perceptions. This learning process was implicitly involved in the formation of the risk perceptions discussed above. In Viscusi (1979a), I analyzed the consistency of workers' risk perceptions with the possibility of on-the-job learning using cross-sectional data. Workers who had experienced a job injury or viewed other working conditions as being unpleasant were more likely to view their jobs as being dangerous, controlling for the industry risk level and related factors. One cannot be confident based on this evidence that workers do in fact learn, since the results may simply reflect the correlation of high initial risk assessments with risky job attributes.

To explore the evolution of workers' risk judgments, in Viscusi and O'Connor (1984) we undertook an experiment with chemical workers at four plants. Each worker was shown a label for a chemical (either sodium bicarbonate, chloroacetophenone, asbestos, or TNT) and was told that this chemical would replace the chemicals on his or her present job. Workers' risk perceptions responded in the expected manner, falling for sodium bicarbonate and rising for the other three chemicals. Since the true job-specific risks posed by these substances and the worker's other job risks are not fully understood, the most that could be concluded is that the prior probability assessments were revised in the correct direction.

Based on the worker responses, it was possible to estimate the key parameters in equation 6.1 that are associated with the label's impact—the risk s_i implied by the label and its relative informational content ψ_i. Table 6-4 reports the estimated risk and informational content values based on two alternative specifications. In the

Table 6-4. Risks and Informational Content of Warning Labels

	Risk		Informational content	
	s_i *(linear)*	s_i *(log-odds)*	ψ_i *(linear)*	ψ_i *(log-odds)*
Sodium bicarbonate	.038	.042	3.72	4.98
Chloroacetophenone	.239	.274	1.29	0.83
Asbestos	.289	.325	6.43	2.80
TNT	.317	.315	31.36	40.67

Source: Viscusi and O'Connor (1984), p. 952.

linear model, the perceived risk level is the dependent variable; for the log-odds results it is the log-odds of the perceived risk that is the dependent variable. The results are similar in each case. Except for sodium bicarbonate, the implied risks s_i did not differ greatly. There was, however, a substantial difference in the relative informational content ψ_i of the hazard warnings. The unfamiliar chemical chloroacetophenone had a ψ_i value of 1.3, implying an informational content just above that of the worker's prior, whereas TNT had a dominant ψ_i value of 31.4. The warning message for the more familiar hazard triggered the greatest informational effect, as one would expect.

These results suggest that people can process risk information in the expected direction, but that it is the informational content of the message, not simply the associated risk level, that is instrumental. The ineffectiveness of informational campaigns to promote seat belt use and to eliminate cigarette smoking are not unexpected, since the new information contained in such ads is not great. These efforts might be viewed more accurately as being policies of exhortation rather than information.

While available evidence suggests that individual learning about risks can often play an important economic role, this learning process may not be ideal. The critical reviews by Tversky and Kahneman (1974), Arrow (1982), and Fischhoff and Beyth-Marom (1983) have identified a number of systematic shortcomings. Individuals tend to exaggerate the completeness of hypothesis sets, ignore the base-rate frequency of outcomes, and more generally fail to fully understand the laws of probability. Individuals may behave in the general spirit of Bayesian decision makers in the learning process, but this behavior does not conform identically with an optimal learning process. The degree to which the various shortcomings identified in laboratory experiments affect market behavior involving risks has not yet been ascertained.

6.5 RISK PERCEPTIONS, LEARNING, AND INDIVIDUAL BEHAVIOR

A number of studies have linked higher wages to job risks and lower prices to product risks. This is the most basic test of rational decisions involving uncertainty, and the supporting evidence is strong and quite diverse. Although the risk level is the only feature of the job risk that is of consequence in a single-period model, in a multiperiod model in which there is the possibility of terminating the job either through a job change or one's death, I have shown that the precision of the risk judgments is an additional concern. The underlying rationale is that in this class of two-armed bandit models, loose prior beliefs are preferred because they offer the potential for greater gains from experimentation with the uncertain job.

Consider two jobs. Job 1 poses a risk 0.5 of injury every year, where this risk is known with precision. Job 2 has uncertain properties. Either the worker will definitely suffer an injury every year, or he will definitely be free of injury. Moreover, the riskiness of this job is assumed to be the same over time. Job 2 has more uncertain properties and in the initial period it offers the same subjective risk 0.5 of injury as does Job 1. However, Job 2 is more attractive in a long-term context because the worker can stay on the job if it turns out to be safe, and he or she can switch to Job 1 if it is not. In general, the more uncertain risk is preferable, for any given initial risk level, because of the opportunities for experimentation it provides.

A refined test of this relationship is possible using the chemical worker survey data. As predicted, chemical labels associated with higher ψ_i values (i.e., more precise risks) lead to higher worker reservation wages, as do labels with higher s_i values. Both the risk level and its precision affect a lottery's attractiveness if one is incurring a sequence of such lotteries that may be terminated conditional on an unfavorable outcome.

Although these results are consistent with optimal behavior in uncertain contexts with learning, not all observed risk-dollar tradeoffs imply that decisions are accurate. In Viscusi and Magat (1987) we examined consumer attitudes toward low-probability events (on the order of $1/100,000$ risk annually), associated with risks of different adverse health outcomes. The results suggested implausibly large risk-dollar tradeoffs. For example, there was an implied externality value to society at large of roughly \$200,000 to prevent an expected hand burn from drain cleaner that would be temporary but severe enough to require medical treatment. Individuals clearly have difficulty making decisions involving low-probability events, and in this instance there is evidence of excessive valuation of the risks. These biases in turn may lead to alarmist decisions and excessive governmental regulation. In other cases the low risk may be ignored, creating biases of the opposite nature.

Once learning is introduced as an element, individuals will continually reassess the appropriateness of the risks and its rewards in relation to their other opportunities. The tendency of individuals to experiment with activities posing dimly understood risk will be fostered by the structure of the statistical decision problem. Individuals will display a predilection for risky jobs and other lottery sequences associated with loose priors since these offer the greatest gains from experimentation.

As predicted by these two-armed bandit models, there is a significant relationship between job risks and worker decisions to switch jobs once significantly adverse information is acquired. Results for five data sets reported in Viscusi (1979a,b) indicate that job risks raise worker quit rates, boost quit intentions and job-search activities, and shorten paths of employment at the firm, controlling for health status and a variety of other factors. Indeed, job risks account for as much as one-third of all manufacturing quit rates.

In addition to the positive effect of the risk level on quitting, the aforementioned work on chemical labeling produced a positive influence of the relative precision ψ_i of the risk information on quit behavior. This impact is also consistent with the optimal experimentation process since more precisely understood risks are less attractive because of the diminished value of the experimentation process associated with them. The overall job choice process is consistent with a model in which individuals start jobs with imperfect information, revise these beliefs in Bayesian fashion based on their on-the-job experiences, and alter their job choice if this information is sufficiently adverse.

Consumers likewise respond to risk information in an adaptive manner. In our study of consumer product labeling—Viscusi and Magat (1987)—we found that labels including risk warnings increased the frequency of consumer precautions by up to 33 percent, as compared with labels without warnings. These results may understate the role of learning to the extent that consumers' prior beliefs have been conditioned by past knowledge of the product. For example, even without a hazard warning, more than half of all consumers would store drain cleaner in a location to which children did not have easy access.

Overall, individuals do not possess perfect information about the risks they face, but they do have opportunities to revise these beliefs based on their experiences. Many of the observed behavior patterns are consistent with the principal predictions of a Bayesian learning process and subsequent adaptive behavior.

6.6 CONCLUSION

Although much risk-taking behavior is broadly consistent with a Bayesian framework, these decisions do not always coincide with optimal behavior. As with other optimizing models in economics, Bayesian decision models represent an often powerful tool but also a tool that may not accurately reflect how decisions are made. The expected utility hypothesis that is central to these models has long been questioned. In some contexts, inconsistencies in individual choices have been observed. There also appears to be asymmetric treatment of gains and losses, as well as special attention paid to certain outcomes. Moreover, in an actual market context in which one would have expected risk-averse consumers to purchase heavily subsidized flood and earthquake insurance, Kunreuther et al. (1978) have shown that they failed to do so.[2] As a result, individuals may respond in a manner that is broadly consistent with Bayesian decision theory, but the normative guidelines of that theory may not always be met.

Nevertheless, Bayesian models remain a useful optimizing framework for analyzing economic behavior. In some cases, the existing biases in behavior may be predicted by proper application of the Bayesian model. In others, there may be shortcomings in the manner in which individuals make decisions.

The implications of these inadequacies for the nature of the market failure are not always clear-cut. Risks may be ignored, leading to a supraoptimal level of risk, or they may be overassessed, as shown in studies of small fatality risks. The nature of the market failure is likely to be more complex than is captured in standard models of imperfect information. There may be either inadequate or excessive attention to risks, depending on the particular context.

NOTES

1. Assuming a normal distribution yields the same functional forms as below, but it imposes more restrictions with respect to the shape of the distribution.

2. One possible explanation of Kunreuther's result is that the risks in his study were not called to consumers' attention, whereas Magat and I focused on identified risks.

7

Behavioral Anomalies and Paradoxes in Choices under Uncertainty

7.1 INTRODUCTION

Since World War II, expected utility theory has become the dominant economic paradigm for analyzing choices under uncertainty. This prominence in the economics literature has been coupled with an expanding body of research providing empirical tests of different components of the theory. A major theme of the work, much of which has consisted of experimental studies by psychologists, has been that expected utility theory does not provide a reliable predictive guide to behavior. These studies observe that individual choices are often inconsistent, violating one or more of the von Neumann-Morgenstern (1953) axioms. In addition, the Bayesian formulations of the model, such as those of Savage (1972) and Raiffa (1968), have been challenged because individuals' probabilistic beliefs often do not conform with those hypothesized in the model.[1] Some of these perceptional biases were the focus of the previous chapter.

If the implications of the literature on the irrationality of choices under uncertainty are correct, market outcomes will be seriously flawed. Moreover, in many of these instances safety levels will be inadequate and there will be a rationale for government intervention. If, however, people respond irrationally to risk, the reliance on individual responses to government policies may not promote safety. If people cannot process hazard warning information and cannot make rational protective decisions after safety measures such as seat belts are mandated, then the set of effective government policies will be restricted. This chapter explores these anomalies and assesses their implications for government risk policy and choice under uncertainty more generally. The analysis of these issues is more methodological in nature than in the previous chapters. The concluding section of this chapter summarizes the main findings that are of interest from the standpoint of analyzing behavior under uncertainty and its implications for risk policy.

There are two possible responses to the wave of research on the irrationality of risky decisions. First, one could reject the evidence contradicting the conventional expected utility theory as not being representative of economic behavior. The deviations from rationality typically pertain to experimental contexts rather than market contexts, and if there is a market imperfection, there is still no evidence that the deviation from full rationality is large. Moreover, there is much empirical evidence regarding risk-taking and insurance behavior that is consistent with the expected utility model. This defense of the conventional analysis is often pertinent, particularly with respect to some of the more speculative experimental results, but as a general response it is inadequate. As economists such as Arrow (1982) have observed, the mounting evidence contradicting the expected utility model does present a legitimate challenge to the theory that cannot be dismissed out of hand.

The second approach to this research is to accept its implications and abandon or amend the conventional model. A widely discussed alternative framework is that of prospect theory developed by Kahneman and Tversky (1979). Their innovative analysis alters the expected utility framework by adopting a utility function with a distinctive shape and abandoning the linear probability weights on the payoffs. Tversky and Kahneman (1986) have cast this framework as an alternative to the expected utility model rather than as an amendment of it, since they claim that "deviations of actual behavior from the normative model are . . . too fundamental to be accommodated by relaxing the normative system." A less sweeping modification of the expected utility model is that of Machina (1982), who drops the independence axiom but still preserves many of the essential features and predictions of the expected utility framework.[2] The amendments to the standard model by Kahneman and Tversky, Machina, and others make it possible to reconcile some aberrant phenomena such as the Allais paradox with rational behavior.

When judging the performance of the expected utility model in comparison to alternative approaches, it is essential to place comparable demands on the competing theories. The expected utility model has quite specific empirical predictions and, as a result, can be potentially invalidated in an empirical test. In contrast, alternatives such as prospect theory have much less formal structures that can be used to establish unambiguous predictions and as a consequence are better able to avoid paradoxes and empirical inconsistencies. Under the prospect theory approach, the framing and editing processes do not have an associated theory that is sufficiently precise to generate unambiguous predictions, and the preference and valuation functions have unspecified nonlinear shapes that allow great leeway in terms of behavior that is potentially consistent with the model. This flexibility greatly diminishes the predictive power of the theory so that in many instances one is limited to *post hoc ergo propter hoc* explanations of behavior.

The framework to be developed here, termed *prospective reference theory* (PRT), stems from the standard expected utility model, but rather than amending or dropping any of its basic assumptions regarding choice, the manner in which probabilities enter the analysis is altered. The concern here with perceptional elements shares many concerns with the approach taken in prospect theory, but unlike that analysis this formulation will be consistent with a quasi-Bayesian learning process. Depending on one's orientation, one can view this model as being a modified prospect theory model with a Bayesian structure imposed on the risk perceptions, or an expected utility model in which stated probabilities are rated as imperfect information and are then processed in Bayesian fashion. This approach shares with the prospect theory model an emphasis on empirical regularities in the nature of the risk perceptions, which may contribute to apparent inconsistencies in decisions. Thus, it is the nature of risk perceptions rather than inadequacies in the way that choices are made that accounts for the observed anomalies in behavior.

The genesis of this research is a series of three empirical analyses of risk perceptions and individual behavior. In Viscusi and O'Connor (1984), the risk-perception function that will be used in this chapter to explain the experimental paradoxes was found to provide an excellent characterization of workers' risk perceptions when these workers were presented with chemical labels. In particular, the beta distribution parameters that were estimated had the predicted effect when included in a wage equation, as workers demanded compensating differentials for higher risk levels and for more precisely understood risks. A second basis of the theory is the empirical results on biases in risk perception discussed in Chapter 6. Application of Bayesian risk perception function to data gathered by psychologists with respect to perceptions of fatality risks provided an alternative and a "more rational" explanation of the observed patterns. As will be discussed below, the observed variation in the bias in risk perceptions with respect to differences in the level of the risk is exactly what one would predict based on a Bayesian learning model. Most recently, the analysis of consumers' responses to risk changes follows the same general types of patterns that the risk perception studies suggest should be evidenced in market outcomes. The relationship of these empirical studies to the analysis of economic paradoxes will be articulated further below.

The basic assumption driving the analysis is that individuals' attitudes toward uncertain prospects are influenced by a reference risk level. These reference risks may involve an assumption that each lottery outcome is equally likely or, in the case of lottery outcomes with which the individual has some related experience, the probability assessment could differ across payoffs. The reference risk in effect serves as the individual's prior probability. When presented with a new lottery, the probabilistic belief is updated in standard Bayesian fashion from this reference point. Even in the case of the experimental lotteries, the individual may not place absolute confidence in stated probabilities but instead may act as if he or she has received imperfect information that is used to update his or her probabilistic beliefs from the reference risk level.

The resulting formulation is well behaved in that the perceived probabilities have the same mathematical properties as a standard probability measure. This attractive property arises because the assessed probabilities involve no more than ascertaining the posterior probability assessment using a standard Bayesian framework. Since the PRT model does not alter any of the basic principles of rational choice, it is also consistent with empirical evidence supporting the expected utility model. Moreover, unlike the standard framework, it explains the Allais paradox and a wide variety of other phenomena cited as contradicting the standard expected utility model.

The PRT model also has considerable power, since it predicts many of the empirical regularities that have been adopted as assumptions within the prospect theory framework or other models of choice under uncertainty. What is perhaps most striking is that most of the deviant phenomena identified as paradoxes in the literature are predicted by the theory. This feature is a stronger property than having a model with theoretical predictions that are ambiguous and as a consequence can be potentially reconciled with any pattern of observed behavior under special circumstances. Under the prospect theory approach, the main emphasis is on summarizing the various forms of irrational behavior that have been observed and to identify the broad character of systematic empirical regularities. The approach taken here will be the opposite in that a theoretical framework will be developed that predicts the empirical regularities rather than using the observed regularities as the essential components of a descriptive theory.

The importance of this distinction lies at the heart of what economic models can contribute. The ultimate purpose of such models is to predict behavior in circumstances for which we have not yet observed behavior. If the predictive power of a theory is limited to situations that have been observed previously, then the power of the theory will be severely limited. Moreover, a theory based solely on empirical regularities can never be invalidated and as a result can never serve as a true theory of decisions in any fundamental sense.

Section 7.2 will discuss the nature of the formation of probabilistic perceptions for the symmetric reference point situation in which all lottery outcomes are assessed initially as being equally probable. This reformulation of the perceptional concerns leads to modification of the standard axioms of expected utility but does not require a modification of any of the choice-related properties. As is indicated in Section 7.3, lotteries continue to be valued by linear function of the utility of the payoffs, but the specific functional form need not be equivalent to the traditional expected utility value. The nature of these differences and some of the general properties of expected utility within prospective reference theory are also discussed in Section 7.3. Section 7.4 indicates how the PRT model can be used to reconcile a wide variety of divergent phenomena with rational behavior. These aberrations include different variants of the Allais paradox, the overweighting of low-probability events, the existence of certainty premiums for complete elimination of a risk, and several other phenomena that have played a prominent role in challenges to the rational model. The PRT approach consequently predicts a wide range of empirical phenomena that have played a dominant role in the literature on the rationality of choice under uncertainty. As observed in the concluding Section 7.5, the PRT approach by no means exhausts all forms of irrational behavior that have been observed. Nevertheless, it does provide a logically consistent framework that retains the key elements of the standard expected utility model while also recognizing the role of cognitive processes within a rational information-processing framework. Appendix 7A develops the assumptions of the theory more formally.

7.2. PROSPECTIVE REFERENCE THEORY

The Formation of Perceptions

Before discussing the role of reference risk in perception formation, it is instructive to review the elements of the Bayesian approach. Individual risk perceptions will be characterized using a beta probability distribution. For lotteries involving two possible outcomes, the standard beta distribution will be used to characterize risk perceptions. With more than two outcomes, the multivariate generalization of the beta distribution—the Dirichlet distribution—will be employed.[3] The beta family of distributions is highly flexible and can assume a wide variety of skewed or symmetric shapes. Moreover, it is ideally suited to analyzing independent and identically distributed Bernoulli trials. To the extent that one can view probabilities in a lottery as equivalent to some mixture in a hypothetical urn from which one makes a random draw, as in Raiffa (1968), the stochastic process assumed here corresponds to the thought experiment that is utilized by the advocates of a Bayesian expected utility framework.

The particular parameterization of the distribution developed here is useful in empirical tests of the bivariate version of the model. Consider a multivariate outcome situation where there are n possible outcomes. Let the prior probability of outcome i be q_i, and let the individual observe ξ trials of which a fraction p_i are outcome i. Let γ be a parameter of the prior distribution corresponding to the informational content of the individual's prior beliefs. Then the posterior probability p_i^* outcome i is given by

$$p_i^* = \frac{\gamma q_i + \xi p_i}{\gamma + \xi}. \tag{7.1}$$

The individual acts as if he or she has observed γ trials in forming his prior q_i. He then observes ξ trials, and his posterior probability is a simple weighted average of q_i and p_i, where the weights correspond to the fraction of his total information associated with his prior probability and with the experiment he has observed. In contexts using data on individual behavior, it is often feasible to estimate ξ/γ—the relative informational content of the experiment,[4] as discussed in Section 6.4.

The perceptional structure of prospective reference theory utilizes this basic framework but introduces an additional stage in the preference-formation process. Suppose that an individual faces a lottery on some prize, and he or she is told that p is the chance of winning the prize. He will not treat this probabilistic information as fully informative but will view it as providing incomplete information that he uses in standard Bayesian fashion to update his prior probability of success—which is here termed his *reference* risk.

The framework is consistent with two possible scenarios. First, the individual may be legitimately suspicious of supposedly "hard" probabilities, particularly if he or she does not have full confidence in the experiment being performed. The second possibility is that this behavior may reflect an inherent aspect of individuals' information processing whereby individuals act as if risk information is imperfect. Thus, the functioning of individuals' cognitive processes may lead to this partial learning phenomenon. Even under this second interpretation, however, the processing of the information and subsequent decisions will be assumed to occur in a rational, Bayesian manner that is augmented by the role of reference risks. Although the discussion in this section focuses on the situation in which there are symmetric reference points for all lottery outcomes, each of the above interpretations of reference points is consistent with multiple reference points that depend on the lottery outcome, the decision context, and the nature of the risk.

Consider a lottery with possible payoffs $(A_1, A_2, \ldots, A_n)$ where each payoff A_i has a stated probability $p_i (0 < p_i < 1)$ that satisfies

$$\sum_{i=1}^{n} p_i = 1. \qquad (7.2)$$

In the symmetric-reference-point case, the individual views each possible outcome as being equally likely, so the reference point is $1/n$. (See Appendix 7B for an extension of the model to asymmetric reference points.) The informational content γ of the prior probability and the lottery information ξ are assumed to be the same for all payoffs, although this assumption could easily be relaxed in situations where there is a rationale for doing so. The perceived probability function P modifies the stated probability in a Bayesian manner, where

$$P(p_i) = \frac{\gamma(1/n) + \xi p_i}{\gamma + \xi}. \qquad (7.3)$$

In situations in which informational content ξ varies by payoff, the notation $P(p_i, \xi_i)$ will be used.

The two extreme informational cases lead to dominance of one component of the perception function. If γ equals zero or if ξ/γ is arbitrarily large, then the perceptions equal the stated probabilities p_i, and the results are the same as in conventional decision models in which the probabilities are taken at face value. Similarly, if ξ/γ equals zero, the individual places no weight on the lottery information and is guided solely by the reference risk.

The two p_i values that merit special treatment are the two cases of certainty, where $p_i = 0$ or 1. The certainty situation is easier to process, so to the extent that reference points play a role because of cognitive limitations, they will be less prominent in this case. Similarly, if it is individuals' underlying distrust of the accuracy of probabilistic information that is the driving force behind reference effects, the introduction of certainty should eliminate these concerns. Both of these factors lead credible lottery descriptions of certain events to be treated at face value, so that

$$P(0) = 0 \text{ and } P(1) = 1. \qquad (7.4)$$

There may, however, be exceptional cases in which the lottery descriptions are not fully credible, and therefore the respondent may have a reason to believe that the stated certainty is only a rough approximation. For the n-payoff case, where the payoff for certain events is included among the n payoffs, we will then have the value

$$P(0) = \frac{\gamma(1/n)}{\gamma + \xi},$$

and

$$P(1) = \frac{\gamma(1/n) + \xi}{\gamma + \xi}.$$

The discussion below will focus on the usual situation in which equation 7.4 holds, on the assumption that the certain events will be treated differently for the reasons stated above.

Thus, the role of reference effects is to convert a stated probability into a perceived probability following equations 7.3 and 7.4. In effect, reference effects introduce an earlier stage into a Bayesian learning process in situations that are normally considered to be simple situations in which lottery descriptions provide full information. The introduction of the reference risk state into the learning process by no means precludes subsequent stages of experimentation. Consider a situation in which an individual can acquire information regarding some lottery with probability p_i of outcome A. In the usual case, the p_i value serves as the prior probability, whereas within the prospective reference theory model the $P(p_i)$ value serves this function. Having made this modification, analysis of any situation of information acquisition proceeds in the usual fashion.

Properties of Perceptions with Reference Points

Except for the two certainty cases, perceived probabilities can be characterized by a linear function of the stated probabilities, as is illustrated in Figure 7-1 for the symmetric reference point case. For some value p_f, stated and perceived values are equal. For the symmetric rewards case, p_f equals $1/n$ so that, for example, p_i equals .5 for the binary outcome case. Low probabilities below p_f are perceived as being larger than their stated values, and high probabilities above p_f are perceived as being smaller than their stated values. Changes in the reference point due, for example, to an increase in the number of lottery outcomes alter the vertical intercept and result in parallel shifts of the perceived probability line. Increases in the informational

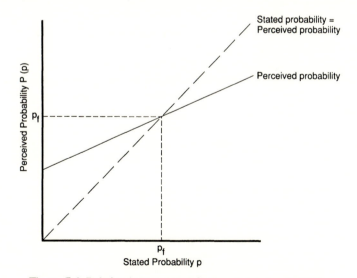

Figure 7.1 Relation between perceived and stated probabilities

content ξ of the lottery rotate the perception function counterclockwise until in the limiting case of $\xi \to \infty$ it coincides with the 45° line. Similarly, boosting γ raises the weight on the prior probability so that as γ/ξ rises the perception line becomes horizontal, and the stated probability p plays no role.

The reference perception function is well behaved. Each perceived probability is in the appropriate range, where $0 \leq P(p_i) \leq 1$ for all p_i. In addition, perceived probabilities are additive. Suppose that there are n possible outcomes, where none of these has a p_i value of 0 or 1. Then

$$\sum_{i=1}^{n} P(p_i) = \sum_{i=1}^{n} \frac{\gamma(1/n) + \xi p_i}{\gamma + \xi} = 1,$$

from equation 7.2. Suppose there is some outcome A_{n+1} for which the stated p_i equals 0. In that situation in which the certain information is credible, outcome A_{n+1} is simply ignored and each of the remaining outcomes has an associated probability 1/n. If outcome A_{n+1} has a p_i value of 1, all other outcomes drop out of the analysis. It matters little whether one assigns a reference probability $1/(n + 1)$ to events A_1 through A_n coupled with an arbitrarily large value of ξ/γ, or alternatively one views the decision maker as pruning the analysis to consider only outcomes with a finite probability of occurrence.[5]

The reference probability function accords generally with observed patterns of risk perception, as will be discussed in Section 7.4. It follows the form analyzed with respect to the chemical labeling study of worker risk perceptions and the study of fatality risk perceptions, each of which was discussed in Chapter 6. In the latter case, equation 7.3 was the functional form used to investigate these perceptions, as will be discussed further in Section 7.3.

There is an additional parallel with Kahneman and Tversky's prospect theory model (1979) in which their decision weight function $\pi(p_i)$ serves an analogous role to the reference risk perception function $P(p_i)$. Their approach is similarly based on the widely observed empirical phenomenon that individuals tend to overestimate low probability events and underestimate high probabilities. As in their formulation, the perception of certain events is not altered here (equation 7.4), and the perception of intermediate risks is transformed through a risk-perception function.

Several differences with the prospect theory approach are noteworthy.[6] First, the reference risk perception function is generated by a rational Bayesian updating process from a reference risk level that is specified precisely, whereas decision weights reflect empirical patterns for which there is presently no well-defined theory for predicting their precise shape. Prospect theory does not impose any restrictions or make any predictions with respect to the location of the crossover point p_f, the steepness of the curvature of the $\pi(p)$ function, or the exact behavior of this function as one approaches the extreme probability values 0 and 1. Second, decision weights are a nonlinear function rather than a linear function, which will lead to inherent inconsistency with the expected utility model. Third, whereas reference risk perceptions are additive, decision weights need not be. Indeed, Kahneman and Tversky (1979) stress that "decision weights are not probabilities: they do not obey the probability axioms and they should not be interpreted as measures of degree of belief. . . . π is not a probability measure and it will be shown later that $\pi(p) + \pi(1 - p)$ is typically less than unity." They term this subadditivity *subcertainty*.

A second line of related research is the psychology literature on anchoring. Experimental studies suggest that probability assessments may be anchored in some initial value that usually stems from the wording of the questionnaire. Individuals then adjust their perceptions partially from the anchor toward the true probability.[7] These anchors are analogous in spirit to reference risk levels, except that they are not as well behaved. For example, whereas reference probability levels sum to 1 across all states, anchors need not. Moreover, the existence of anchors is typically treated as evidence of irrationality. To the extent that anchoring models have been estimated empirically, it has been with nonlinear functions that are usually subadditive.[8] Thus, anchoring models are viewed as alternatives to a Bayesian framework. Discussions of anchoring touch on some of the same phenomena as does the reference risk-perception analysis, so that each approach addresses a similar class of concerns. However, the methodological approach is non-Bayesian, the choices usually violate the principles of rationality, and the empirical properties are quite different.

7.3 PROPERTIES OF INDIVIDUAL DECISIONS

General Implications for Expected Utility Theory

If we let EU*(L) denote the expected utility of Lottery L within PRT and $U(A^i)$ denote the utility value of payoff A_i, then the value of a lottery will be determined by

$$EU^*(L) = \sum_{i=1}^{n} P(p_i)U(A_i),$$

which is analogous to the standard expected utility value

$$\cdot EU(L) = \sum_{i=1}^{n} p_i U(A_i).$$

Thus, the principal amendments to the expected utility model are the replacement of actual probabilities by perceived probabilities and the specification of how these perceptions are formed when facing compound lotteries.[9]

Since the reference perception function $P(p_i)$ is a linear transformation of p_i, expected utility remains a linear function of the utilities. More specifically, using equation 7.3 we can express EU*(L) as

$$EU^*(L) = \frac{\gamma}{\gamma + \xi} \left[\sum_{i=1}^{n} (1/n)U(A_i) \right] + \frac{\xi}{\gamma + \xi} \left[\sum_{i=1}^{n} p_i U(A_i) \right].$$

If we define $EU_0(L)$ as the utility of a random lottery on the payoffs in lottery L, or

$$EU_0(L) = \sum_{i=1}^{n} (1/n)U(A_i),$$

then we can write

$$EU^*(L) = \frac{\gamma}{\gamma + \xi} [EU_0(L)] + \frac{\xi}{\gamma + \xi} [EU(L)]. \tag{7.5}$$

Thus, expected utility is a weighted average of the rewards one would obtain from a random lottery on the payoffs and the conventional expected utility value. The weights are the relative information content $\gamma/(\gamma + \xi)$ associated with the reference probability and the relative informational content $\xi/(\gamma + \xi)$ of the stated lottery.

Whether the individual's expected utility is higher or lower within the PRT approach hinges on whether the random lottery offers higher or lower expected rewards than with the expected utility model. After some algebraic manipulation, the difference is given by

$$EU^*(L) - EU(L) = \frac{\gamma}{\gamma + \xi} [EU_0(L) - EU(L)].$$

Thus, the difference is the gap between $EU_0(L)$ and $EU(L)$, weighted by the fraction of the informational content associated with the reference point. For γ equal to zero, there is no difference in the approaches, since the role of the reference point drops out. If ξ equals zero, the reference risk perceptions dominate and the change in expected utility equals the difference between EU_0 and $EU(L)$.

A slight modification of this relationship can also be used to compare two different lotteries. Suppose that lottery A is of the form $(p_1, A_1; \ldots ; p_n, A_n)$ and lottery B is of the form $(q_1, B_1; \ldots ; q_m, B_m)$, where m need not equal n. Upon taking differences, one obtains the result that

$$EU^*(A) - EU^*(B) = \frac{\gamma}{\gamma + \xi} [EU_0(A) - EU_0(B)] + \frac{\xi}{\gamma + \xi} [EU(A) - EU(B)].$$

The difference in expected values equals the difference in the expected utility from a random lottery weighted by the fraction of the informational content associated with the reference probability plus the conventional expected utility difference weighted by the fraction of the informational content associated with the lottery.

Because reference risk perceptions dampen the influence of the stated terms of a lottery, changes in lottery probabilities have less effect than they otherwise would. Consider a binary lottery with a top prize A_1 and a bottom prize A_2, so that we can set $U(A_1)$ equal to 1 and $U(A_2)$ equal to 0. In a standard expected utility framework, boosting the chance of receiving A_1 from $.5p$ to p will increase the expected utility of the lottery by $.5p$. In contrast, with reference probabilities playing a role, the change in the perceived probability of success will only be

$$P(p) - P(.5p) = \frac{.5\gamma + \xi p}{\gamma + \xi} - \frac{.5\gamma + .5\xi p}{\gamma + \xi} = \frac{.5\xi p}{\gamma + \xi} < .5p.$$

As ξ/γ rises, the relative informational content of the lottery increases so that in the limiting case the change in expected lottery utility equals $.5p$.

The PRT formulation also highlights the importance of lottery framing—an issue that has been a major theme in the psychology literature. Consider the two lotteries $L_1 = (1/2,0;1/2,1)$ and $L_2 = (1/2,0;1/4,1;1/4,1-\epsilon)$. Lottery L_1 stochastically dominates L_2 in terms of the stated lottery terms, and in the limiting case ($\xi/\gamma \rightarrow \infty$) individuals will prefer L_1. This dominance does not hold in terms of the perceived lottery attractiveness, and for sufficiently small ϵ lottery L_2 will be preferred. The source of the preference is that by creating a new state with a positive reward, individuals will tend to assign a lower prior probability (1/3 rather than 1/2) to the chance of no positive payoff. This change in the prior will be reflected at least in part in individuals' perceived probabilities of lottery outcomes.

Such behavior is by no means unreasonable, nor does it represent a logical inconsistency. Consider the limiting case of imperfectly informative lottery information. If one were given no probability information but were simply told that there is a lottery with payoffs [0,1] and another lottery with three possible payoffs $[0,1,1-\epsilon]$, then if one treated each state as being equally likely, the second lottery would be preferred, since it offers a 2/3 chance of a payoff of roughly 1, whereas the first option offers a 1/2 chance of such a reward. Within the realm of the perceived properties of lotteries, stochastic dominance is not violated. Discussions of rationality and consistency must take place given the manner in which lottery information is processed by the decision maker, which may differ from how the lottery terms are stated. A noteworthy aspect of the role of framing is that within the context of prospective reference theory, the influence of lottery framing is linked to quite precise empirical predictions. In contrast, psychological models of behavioral choice have noted the importance of framing effects but thus far have offered no systematic basis for predicting their influence.

Relative Odds and Compound Lotteries

Several of the principal predictions of the prospective-reference approach hinge on the effect on ratios and products of probabilities. In the usual case, altering the scale of relative probabilities is not consequential. Thus, the ratio of probabilities $.6/.3$ is associated with the same relative odds as $.8/.4$. The perceived probabilities may not, however, be the same, since $P(.6)/P(.3)$ may not equal $P(.8)/P(.4)$.

Consider the general issue of how altering the probability ratio p/q by some scale fraction α will alter the probability ratio, where α is not so large that either αp or αq exceeds 1. In the symmetric n-outcome case, we have the result that

$$\frac{\partial}{\partial \alpha} \frac{P(\alpha p)}{P(\alpha q)} = \frac{\gamma\xi(1/n)(p - q)}{[\gamma(1/n) + \xi q\alpha]^2}. \tag{7.6}$$

For values of $p = q$, the odds ratio is unaffected by α and always equals 1; for $p > q$, increasing α raises the discrepancy in the relative odds by increasing the weight on the lottery probability p, which exceeds q, compared with the reference risk $1/n$, which is the same in both cases. The opposite result occurs for $p < q$, since raising α in this case reduces the odds ratio.

These results consequently include as a special case the prediction that

$$\frac{P(p)}{P(q)} \leq \frac{P(\alpha p)}{P(\alpha q)},\tag{7.7}$$

for $p < q$ and $\alpha < 1$. Reducing the influence on the stated probability through the factor α and thus increasing the weight on the reference probabilities, which are equal, will tend to equalize the odds ratio in this case. Thus, as we make the component probabilities in a ratio of probabilities smaller, the probabilities are viewed as more similar. For example, the value of $.002/.004$ is viewed as being closer to 1 than is $.2/.4$.

Equation 7.7 is a rewritten form of Kahneman and Tversky's (1979) "general principle underlying substitution axiom violations." In their analysis, they have observed that as an empirical regularity individuals behave in accordance with equation 7.7. Thus, many prominent experimental phenomena such as the Allais paradox, which will be addressed in Section 7.3, can be traced to their relationship. The PRT approach can be viewed as providing a theoretical basis for the prospect theory analysis. Equation 7.7 is a prediction of the PRT model, whereas within prospect theory it is an empirical regularity incorporated as an assumption.[10]

The compounding of lotteries is also affected by the role of reference probabilities. Lottery 1 and lottery 2 in Figure 7-2, which are equivalent under expected utility theory, will consequently be perceived differently.

A variant on this compounding issue is whether it is desirable to introduce additional compounding of the lottery on some prize. Suppose that there is a probability pq that the prize will be rewarded. Should the lottery be framed in a manner so that pq is the announced probability of winning, or should the lottery be staged in a sequence in which there will be some probability p that one will enter round 2 of the lottery with a subsequent chance q of success? In effect, one would win a lottery ticket on a lottery ticket. Thus the two alternative choices are the lotteries sketched in Figure 7-3. If lottery 2 is preferred to lottery 1, one could continue to enhance its attractiveness by introducing an arbitrarily large number of stages.

Unlike the more symmetric compounding case in Figure 7.2, compounding a lottery on the chance to win a prize is always undesirable. In particular, the condition $P(pq) > P(p)P(q)$ can be rewritten as

$$\frac{.5\gamma + \xi pq}{\gamma + \xi} > \frac{(.5\gamma + \xi p)}{(\gamma + \xi)}\frac{(.5\gamma + \xi q)}{(\gamma + \xi)},$$

which reduces to

$$1 + 2pq > p + q,$$

which always holds for permissible values of p and q.

Although it will be shown subsequently that individuals will tend to overestimate

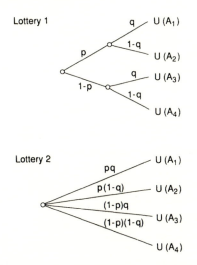

Figure 7.2 Compound versus simple lotteries

low probability events, the introduction of additional compounding that in effect subdivides a probability into the product of successively smaller probabilities will lower the perceived chance of success. This property accords with typical lottery structures, which award prizes rather than lottery tickets for a subsequent stage. To the extent that such phenomena of compound lottery tickets are observed, one must appeal to other economic factors such as the utility associated with anticipation for lotteries resolved over time.

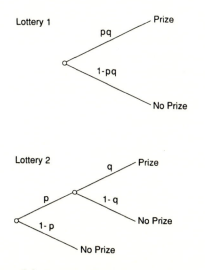

Figure 7.3 Compounding a lottery on a prize

7.4 APPLICATIONS TO EMPIRICAL
AND EXPERIMENTAL PHENOMENA

Before examining the application of the model to various aberrant phenomena that have been observed, it should be emphasized that the PRT framework is consistent with the wide body of empirical evidence supporting the subjective expected utility framework. Since the prospective reference theory model includes expected utility theory as a special case for which ξ/γ is arbitrarily large, as one might expect for frequently repeated market transactions, there is no need to reconcile the theory with existing evidence in support of the expected utility model. As a result, the emphasis here will be on highlighting how the model explains phenomena that contradict the expected utility model.

Overweighting of Low Probabilities and Certainty

The influential study by Lichtenstein et al. (1978) demonstrated that individuals tend to overassess low probability events and underassess high probability events. This risk-related bias is a central theme in the psychology of risk literature, and it has been incorporated as an assumption in Kahneman and Tversky's (1979) prospect theory model. Whereas the usual explanation offered for this phenomenon is that it reflects a form of irrationality, in the PRT approach it is viewed as the consequence of a conventional Bayesian learning process.

A bias of this type is exactly what one would predict from the prospective reference theory framework. From equation 7.3,

$$P(p) > p \qquad \text{if } p < 1/n$$

and

$$P(p) < p \qquad \text{if } p > 1/n,$$

which is the observed pattern. In Chapter 6, the functional form in equation 7.3 was fitted to the original Lichtenstein et al. (1978) data, and observed behavior was shown to be consistent with a rational Bayesian updating process from an initial reference risk. The apparent bias in risk perceptions is exactly what one would expect with a rational Bayesian learning process in which only partial information has been acquired. The critical test of rationality is whether there is a risk-related bias in the degree of learning. In particular, is there a probability-related difference in the degree of updating ξ/γ from the reference risk toward the actual probabilities? For the Lichtenstein et al. (1978) sample, it was shown in Chapter 6 that there is no statistically significant bias of this sort.

One manifestation of this overestimation of low probabilities is that individuals will be willing to pay a certainty premium for reductions of risk that completely eliminate the risk. Thus, any given incremental risk reduction Δp will be more highly valued if this reduction leads to zero risk than if it achieves only partial risk reduction, whereas standard economic models predict that the last incremental risk reduction should be less highly valued.

There are two types of experimental evidence in support of this phenomenon. The first consists of studies such as Kahneman and Tversky (1979).[11] Experimental subjects prefer hypothetical insurance policies that reduce the risk from p/2 to 0 to policies that reduce the risk from p to p/2. This result is a direct consequence of the nature of the risk change. Since P(0) is assumed to be a full information probability equal to 0, we have $P(p) - P(p/2) < P(p/2) - P(0)$, since

$$\frac{.5\gamma + p\xi}{\gamma + \xi} - \frac{.5\gamma + .5p\xi}{\gamma + \xi} < \frac{.5\gamma + .5p\xi}{\gamma + \xi} - 0,$$

as one can readily verify. The driving force behind this effect in the present analysis and in prospect theory is that a zero probability is treated at face value, and hence there is a jump in the perceived probability. If 0 were treated as imperfect information with the same reference risk probability .5 and the same weight ξ as the other outcome, no certainty effect would be observed. Thus, the existence of certainty premiums is consistent with the PRT formulation in which certain events with probability 0 or 1 are viewed as being fully informative.

Similarly, an analysis of consumer valuations of product risk reductions in a quasi-market experiment with over 1,500 consumers also reveals the existence of certainty premiums. The results in Table 7.1 present consumers' willingness to pay for incremental risk reductions of 5/10,000, where these results are given for four injury pairs and three different starting risk values. Consumers initially display diminishing marginal valuations of risk reduction for the reduction in the product risk rate from 15/10,000 to 10/10,000 and then to 5/10,000. However, the valuation of the last incremental risk reduction that eliminates the risk completely is valued by a greater amount than the preceding increment. This result contradicts a standard expected utility model but accords with PRT and with approaches such as prospect theory. More generally, one would predict that individuals will tend to overreact to small risks, such as the chance of a Tylenol poisoning due to product tampering or the risk of being a victim of a terrorist act while vacationing in Europe.

The Representativeness Heuristic

Since the PRT approach is a quasi-Bayesian approach, psychological evidence that contradicts the validity of the Bayesian updating process poses a potentially critical

Table 7-1. Consumers' Marginal Valuations of Reducing Both Risks by a Probability of 5 Injuries per 10,000

Starting risk (*injuries/10,000 bottles*)	Marginal willingness to pay (*dollars/bottle*) (*standard errors of mean*)			
	Inhalation–skin poisoning	Inhalation–child poisoning	Gassing eye burn	Child poisoning–gassing
15	1.04	1.84	0.65	0.99
	(0.10)	(0.35)	(0.04)	(0.15)
10	0.34	0.54	0.19	0.24
	(0.05)	(0.12)	(0.03)	(0.11)
5	2.41	5.71	0.83	0.99
	(0.14)	(1.05)	(0.10)	(0.12)

Source: Mean values are from Viscusi, Magat, and Huber (1987). I generated the standard errors.

challenge to the framework. Chief among these difficulties is evidence in support of the representativeness heuristic, whereby respondents assessing the chance that an event belonging to class A or class B tend to place less weight on the base rate conditions than Bayes's theorem requires.

Consider the following example from Tversky and Kahneman (1974). Under scenario 1, subjects are given a personal description of a worker that is intended to be worthless information, and are told that the group from which the description was drawn consisted of seventy lawyers and thirty engineers. In effect, individuals tended to ignore the prior probabilities regarding the mix of engineers and lawyers, treating this ratio as closer to 50–50 than the 70–30 and 30–70 splits.[12]

This apparent dampening of the difference in the assessed probabilities is what PRT predicts. If the occupational mix information were equivalent to 100 draws from an urn, ξ would equal 100. Using this value of ξ,

$$P(\text{engineer} \mid 70 \text{ engineers, } 30 \text{ lawyers}) = \frac{.5\gamma + .7(100)}{\gamma + 100},$$

and

$$P(\text{engineer} \mid 30 \text{ engineers, } 70 \text{ lawyers}) = \frac{.5\gamma + .3(100)}{\gamma + 100}.$$

The ratio of the assessed probabilities in the two situations satisfies the condition

$$1 \leq \frac{P(\text{engineer} \mid 70 \text{ engineers, } 30 \text{ lawyers})}{P(\text{engineer} \mid 30 \text{ engineers, } 70 \text{ lawyers})} = \frac{.5\gamma + 70}{.5\gamma + 30} \leq \frac{.7}{.3}.$$

For high values of γ for which there is relatively low weight placed on the occupational mix information, the probability ratio approaches 1, which is what has been observed experimentally.

In a variant of this study undertaken by Grether (1980), subjects placed greater reliance on the mix information as the experiment was repeated. The PRT approach predicts such behavior, since as subjects have more experience with the experimental information and are given feedback that indicates that the information is accurate, then the relative weight ξ/γ placed on the base occupational mix information will rise. Under this interpretation, the information presented becomes more credible with repetition. The alternative explanation that individuals learn how to play with repetition is not required. Experimental subjects may be fully rational from the outset.

The Allais Paradox

The most prevalent class of experimental phenomena contradicting the expected utility model consists of various violations of the substitution axiom. When a particular lottery L is substituted into another lottery context, the apparent valuation of lottery L often changes. The well-known Allais paradox epitomizes this phenomenon, which has been replicated in a variety of experimental contexts with different lottery structures. Since all of these phenomena involve the same principle of substitution axiom violations in equation 7.7, the original version of the Allais paradox will be discussed here.[13]

In the original Allais paradox, subjects exhibited the following preferences:

$$P(1)U(100) > P(.10)U(500) + P(.89)U(100) + P(.01)U(0), \quad (7.8)$$

and

$$P(.11)U(100) + P(.89)U(0) < P(.10)U(500) + P(.90)U(0). \quad (7.9)$$

Within the standard expected utility framework in which $P(p) = p$, the only difference between these two sets of lottery pairs is that $.89\ U(10)$ has been subtracted from both sides of equation 7.8 to produce equation 7.9. Yet the preferences have been reversed. If, however, we substitute the PRT values for the perceived probabilities, equations 7.8 and 7.9 become

$$U(100) > \frac{(.33\gamma + .1\xi)}{(\gamma + \xi)} U(500) + \frac{(.33\gamma + .89\xi)}{\gamma + \xi} U(100) + \frac{(.33\gamma + .01\xi)}{\gamma + \xi} U(0), \quad (7.10)$$

and

$$\frac{(.5\gamma + .11\xi)}{\gamma + \xi} U(100) + \frac{(.5\gamma + .89\xi)}{\gamma + \xi} U(0)$$

$$< \frac{(.5\gamma + .1\xi)}{\gamma + \xi} U(500) + \frac{(.5\gamma + .9\xi)}{\gamma + \xi} U(0). \quad (7.11)$$

If we set $U(0) = 0$, then we can rewrite equation 7.10 as

$$U(100) > \frac{.33\gamma + .1\xi}{.67\gamma + .11\xi} U(500), \quad (7.12)$$

and equation 7.11 becomes

$$U(100) < \frac{.5\gamma + .1\xi}{.5\gamma + .11\xi} U(500). \quad (7.13)$$

Conditions 7.12 and 7.13 are not contradictory, provided that

$$\frac{.5\gamma + .1\xi}{.5\gamma + .11\xi} > \frac{.33\gamma + .1\xi}{.67\gamma + .11\xi},$$

which is always true except in the full information case where ξ is infinite, in which case a strict equality prevails.

Thus, the PRT approach is a framework that is more than possibly consistent with the Allais paradox. It *predicts* that such a phenomenon will always occur except for fully informative probabilities. The underlying rationale for this version of the Allais paradox is that $P(1)$ equals 1, whereas the other probabilities are governed by equation 7.4. Although a certainty effect is dominant in this case, other substitution axiom violations without a certainty effect can be reconciled using equation 7.7. The PRT explanation for the Allais paradox stems from the manner in which information is perceived and processed. This paradoxical behavior is predicted by the theory rather than being potentially consistent with the theory.[14]

Compound Lotteries and the Isolation Effect

Other phenomena that are prominent in the psychology literature and that can be addressed with the symmetric PRT model are inconsistencies that arise with compound lotteries.[15] Under the first scenario, an individual is told that there is a .75 chance of 0 and a .25 probability of facing a second lottery in which he or she will have a choice between (.8,4000;.2,0) and (1.0,3000). Respondents prefer the certain reward of 3000 in round 2. Under the expected utility framework, this lottery sequence can be expressed as a choice between (.2,4000;.8,0) and (.25,3000;.75,0), where the second lottery is preferred when the lotteries are described sequentially. When offered this lottery choice directly, however, individuals reverse their preferences, since they now prefer to take the chance to win the prize of 4000. The manner in which the different lotteries are decomposed and edited in these two cases is termed the *isolation effect* in prospect theory.[16]

The PRT formulation of preference formation (and assumption 3 concerning perceptions of compound lotteries—see Appendix 7A) reflects an approach similar to that of prospect theory. More specifically, setting $U(0) = 0$, under the first scenario respondents exhibit the preferences

$$U(3000) > \frac{.5\gamma + .8\xi}{\gamma + \xi} U(4000),$$

and under the second scenario

$$\frac{.5\gamma + .2\xi}{\gamma + \xi} U(4000) > \frac{.5\gamma + .25\xi}{\gamma + \xi} U(3000).$$

One can verify that these inequalities will hold for all nonzero values of γ. This class of phenomena contradicts the expected utility framework but will always occur in the PRT model. The driving force of the effect is the assumption that, when confronting compound lotteries, each individual probability will be processed separately using the reference probability function. Thus, the editing and perceptual explanations that have been offered in the literature are incorporated in the PRT model in an explicit manner that yield unambiguous predictions regarding how individuals will process complex lottery information.

7.5 CONCLUSIONS

The recent literature in economics and psychology, particularly that dealing with what has been termed *prospect theory*, has identified a wide variety of systematic violations of the expected utility model. These violations were first observed with respect to hypothetical experiments, but recent evidence suggests that they are of consequence for economic behavior as well.

If our objective is to develop a model with descriptive as well as prescriptive validity, then some modification of expected utility theory is required. The issue is which alternative framework we should adopt and how big a departure from the full-rationality case we wish to make. Perhaps the major drawback of abandoning a well-defined theory is that the alternative may have less predictive validity. To take the extreme case, one might simply summarize recent evidence as indicating that people are irrational. Such a judgment may be correct as far as it goes, but it does not indicate the nature of the departure from rationality or enable us to predict the patterns of behavior in new situations.

By introducing the role of a reference risk from which individuals revise their probability assessments when presented probabilistic information, one can generalize the expected utility model to address these phenomena without altering its fundamental character. This modification incorporates many of the concerns raised in the literature, but it also embodies a quasi-Bayesian structure that is consistent with empirical evidence in support of expected utility theory. Since the expected utility framework is a special case of the PRT model, there is no need to reconcile the two frameworks.

The PRT model with symmetric reference points has substantial predictive power, since the value of the reference point is specified. This framework is particularly applicable to phenomena that have been observed in experimental contexts. Among phenomena that are predicted by the PRT symmetric reference risk model are the following: overweighting of low probabilities, premiums for certain eliminations of a risk, the representativeness heuristic, and the Allais paradox and related violations of the substitution axiom. This substantial power to predict these aberrant phenomena distinguishes the PRT approach from many alternative models designed to explain apparently irrational behavior.

Researchers in psychology, and the developers of prospect theory in particular, have played a valuable role in highlighting systematic behavioral deviations from the standard expected utility model. The PRT model does not address all of the challenges that have been advanced against the expected utility model. Nevertheless, it does resolve a wide range of difficulties that have played a prominent role in the literature, while at the same time retaining the attractive features of a rational model of economic choice uncertainty. If we let individuals' risk perceptions reflect the perceptual problems and information inadequacies that affect decisions, then the subsequent behavior accords quite closely with rational economic behavior.

The anomalous aspects of behavior that are observed may not always reflect irrationalities in the way decisions are made, but rather may reflect a quite rational response to a world in which information about the risks we face is limited. The subsequent decisions are not, however, fully efficient, particularly if we use as our reference point the maximization of expected utility in a world of full information. These inadequacies have fundamental implications for the design of social risk policy, which will be explored in the next chapter.

Appendix 7A
Implications for Expected Utility Theory:
The Symmetric Reference Risk Case

The modifications required to incorporate reference-risk perceptions in the standard axioms of expected utility theory do not disturb its basic structure. In effect, one need only introduce a previous informational stage before the evaluation of any lottery. One's assessment of the lottery is then governed by the posterior probability of each outcome obtained using the reference perception as the prior probability, which is a quasi-Bayesian procedure.

One has considerable leeway in choosing the set of axioms for expected utility, including, for example, those of Arrow (1971) and Savage (1972). The specific formulation affects the degree of generality of the theory, but there are many strong parallels in the structure of assumptions. Here the assumptions employed by Luce and Raiffa (1957), which sacrifice some generality but are pertinent to the discrete lottery outcome situation adopted here, will be utilized. The set of assumptions adopted closely parallels the Luce and Raiffa (1957) framework. The fundamental changes that drive the distinctive aspects of this chapter's approach pertain to how individuals form their risk assessments (assumption 2) and how they process probability information presented in a compound lottery (assumption 3).

The first assumption, which is identical to that in the Luce and Raiffa (1957) formulation, is that individuals can order alternative lottery outcomes and do so in a transitive manner:

Assumption 1 (ordering of alternatives). The preference or indifference ordering, $\geq$, holds between any two prizes, and it is transitive. Formally, for any A_i and A_j, either $A_i \geq A_j$, or $A_j \geq A_i$, and if $A_i \geq A_j$ and $A_j \geq A_k$ then $A_i \geq A_k$.

The second assumption, concerning lottery perceptions, is a new and pivotal addition to the axiom set, since it presents a departure from the normal situation in which stated lottery probabilities are treated at face value. In effect, probabilities are processed through a Bayesian cognitive filter. In the symmetric reference point case with n prizes, individuals will employ their posterior assessment of the risk as their perceived probability, using $1/n$ as their prior probability and the stated value $(p_1,A_1; p_2,A_2)$ will be used to denote a lottery that offers a chance p_1 of prize A_1 and a chance p_2 of prize A_2. More specifically, we have the following:

Assumption 2 (lottery perceptions). A stated lottery L defined by $L = (p_1,A_1; p_2,A_2; \ldots ; p_n,A_n)$ is perceived by the decision maker as $L^* = (P(p_1),A_1; P(p_2),A_2; \ldots ; P(p_n),A_n)$, where

$$P(p_i) = \frac{\gamma(1/n) + \xi p_i}{\gamma + \xi}.$$

Since γ and ξ are nonnegative constants and the p_i values sum to 1, the perceived probabilities $P(p_i)$ also sum to 1. The reference perception formulation here assumes that reference points are symmetric. Both the informational content γ and the prior probability $1/n$ of each outcome are assumed to be identical. This assumption can be relaxed, but there is little basis for doing so for the types of lotteries considered in much of the experimental literature on decision making. Similarly, ξ could vary according to different payoffs if the new information about different components of the lottery differed, but this is not likely to be the case for abstract experimental lotteries. The assumptions made about the symmetry of reference perceptions make the predictions of the model less ambiguous than if γ, ξ, and the perceived prior probability all varied across payoffs. In this instance, the informational requirements needed by an external observer wishing to make behavioral predictions would be far greater.

The next assumption concerning the reduction of compound lotteries parallels more traditional formulations, except that individuals convert each component probability into a perceived probability.

Assumption 3 (reduction of compound lotteries). One is indifferent between a compound lottery and a simple lottery on the A_i's computed using the ordinary probability calculus, where all stated probabilities p_i are viewed as $P(p_i)$. If stated lottery $L(i)$ is defined as $L(i) = (p_1(i),A_1;p_2(i),A_2; \ldots ; p_n(i),A_n)$, for $i = 1,2, \ldots ,m$, and the associated perceived lottery is defined as $L^*(i) = (P(p_1(i)),A_1; P(p_2(i)),A_2; \ldots ; P(p_n(i)),A_n)$, then the compound lottery $(s_1,L(1); s_2,L(2); \ldots ; s_m,L(m))$ will be equivalent to some simple full information (i.e., $P(r_i) = r_i$) lottery $(r_1,A_1;r_2,A_2; \ldots ; r_n,A_n)$, where $r_j = P(s_1)P(p_j(1)) + P(s_2)P(p_j(2)) + \ldots + P(s_m)P(p_j(m))$.

Although this assumption represents a direct generalization of the standard approach to the reference perception situation, its implications are by no means innocuous. Suppose, for example, the individual faces a lottery with the compound probabilities s and p. The assumption here is that the individual will first process these probabilities through the reference perception function and then multiply them rather than performing these operations in the opposite order. Thus, $P(s)P(p) \neq P(sp)$, so that the result will be different than if the compounding operation were done first. The validity of this assumption is an empirical issue. A principal implication is that the framing of compound lotteries will be consequential—a result that has often been stressed in the psychology literature.[17] Presenting a reduced compound lottery will be perceived differently than the series of individual lotteries.

The next assumption pertaining to the continuity of lottery outcomes is a direct analogue of the standard formulation.

Assumption 4 (continuity). Each prize A_i is indifferent to some lottery on A_1 (highest-ranked outcome) and A_n (lowest-ranked outcome). One can construct a full-information lottery with a probability of u_i of A_1 such that A_i is indifferent to $[u_i;A_1;(1 - u_i),A_n] = \hat{A}_i$ for some u_i, where $A_1 > A_i > A_n$.

This assumption that a full-information reference lottery exists is somewhat stronger than what is required, since there will be an infinity of partial-information lotteries with finite ξ_i that will also suffice as the reference lottery. If, however, γ/ξ_i were very large, it might not be possible to vary the perceived reference probability sufficiently to establish an equivalent reference lottery. Since this reference lottery procedure is only a hypothetical thought experiment for establishing a utility metric, it suffices to assume that we can construct a lottery so that individuals will perceive the probability of A_i as being u_i. Rather than index the preference payoffs according to both a stated probability and some precision parameter, they will be stated in terms of the full-information lottery counterparts or, equivalently, in terms of their perceived probabilities.

Assumption 5 (substitutability). In any lottery L, $\hat{A}_i$ is substitutable for A_i, that is, $(p_1,A_1; \ldots ; p_i,A_i; \ldots ; p_n,A_n)$ is indifferent to $(p_1,A_1; \ldots ; p_i,\hat{A}_i; \ldots ; p_n,A_n)$.

Clearly, this substitutability hinges on individuals perceiving compound lotteries in the manner described in assumption 4. Otherwise, the value of the lottery might change upon substitution, leading to potential inconsistencies.

The next assumptions are identical to the Luce and Raiffa (1957) formulation, except that assumption 7 has been modified to take into account the formulation of risk perceptions.

Assumption 6 (transitivity). Preference and indifference among lottery tickets are transitive relations.

Assumption 7 (monotonicity). A lottery $(p,A_1; (1 - p)A_n)$ is preferred or indifferent to $(p',A_1; 1 - p',A_n)$ if and only if $P(p) \geq P(p')$.

It should be noted that if the lotteries share a common value of ξ, the requirement in assumption 7 is simply that $p \geq P(p')$.

These assumptions ensure that each payoff can be replaced by a lottery on the highest- and lowest-valued payoffs, which establishes the utility metric. Through the reduction of compound lotteries, we can reduce any lottery into a simple lottery on the highest- and lowest-valued payoffs, which, by assumption 7, can be ranked according to the probability of receiving payoff A_1. Thus, following the standard reasoning, we are led to a variant on the basic result.

Expected utility theorem. If the preference or indifference relation satisfied assumptions 1 through 7, there are numbers u_i associated with basic prizes A_i such that for two lotteries L and L' the magnitudes of the expected values $P(p_1)u_1 + P(p_2)u_2 + \ldots + P(p_n)u_n$ and $P(p'_1)u_1 + P(p'_2)u_2 + \ldots + P(p'_n)u_n$ reflect the preference between lotteries.

Appendix 7B

Extension to multiple reference points

Multiple Reference Risks

The symmetric reference risk model provides a framework for analysis of individuals confronting abstract lotteries and situations in which we have no basis for determining how individuals' prior beliefs differ from a random chance at a particular outcome. In most decision contexts, however, the individual has some prior experience regarding a particular event, so that his or her assessed prior probability of outcome i will not be 1/n, but some other value π_i. This value π_i may be influenced by past observations of such events, inferences based on similar events, and related factors.[18] This appendix will describe how the analysis can be modified to incorporate such phenomena.

If we abstract from differences in informational content across events, the assessed probability of event i will be

$$P(p_i) = \frac{\gamma \pi_i + \xi p_i}{\gamma + \xi}.$$

The values of γ and ξ can also be permitted to vary by events, but doing so complicates the analysis and is not needed for any of the specific examples considered. Generalizing the analysis to permit differing degrees of informational content across events is also possible.

The nature of the formation of probability assessments is, however, not completely straightforward. Consider the following three lotteries. In lottery 1, there is a 50–50 chance that the individual will win a car, or (.5,car;.5,0). For concreteness, suppose that the individual's past experience with such lotteries has been unfavorable, so that the π(car) value is below .5, resulting in P(.5,car) < .5. In lottery 2, the top prize is a boat, or (.5,boat;.5,0). For analogous reasons, suppose that π(boat) value is below .5, so that P(.5,boat) < .5. In lottery 3, the individual will win either a car or a boat, or (.5,car;.5,boat).

There are three possible solutions. First, if the π values are consistent across lotteries, then P(.5,car) + P(.5,boat) < 1, violating additivity. One method for resolving the inconsistency across lotteries 1 through 3 is to assume that individuals have common prior probabilities, not multiple prior probabilities, so that both π(car) and π(boat) equal .5. Such an assumption excludes any meaningful role for individuals' prior information, however. A second solution to the inconsistency involves the perception of a different lottery than is stated. If the individual believed that there was a nonzero chance that those offering the lottery would renege on either prize, giving him or her perhaps a 0 payoff, then in effect the lottery has been misrepresented. Once the payoff 0 is included, the assessed probabilities can sum to

1. One could develop the analysis below based on this assumption, but there would be an indeterminacy regarding the value of the omitted payoff.

An approach to resolving potential inconsistencies that will be adopted here is to assume that the π values depend not only on the individual prize but also on the other prize in the particular lottery. Thus, the chance that the individual will receive a boat hinges on what alternative prizes he or she might also receive. The role of individual learning pertains to the entire lottery structure, not just one payoff. In this instance, the set of possible payoffs is taken at face value, but the assessed probability of any particular prize depends on the entire set of prizes in that lottery.

Consider a standard lottery of the form $(p_1,A_1; p_2,A_2; \ldots ; p_n,A_n)$. In this case, the individual acts as if he or she has the prior probability $\pi(A_i; A_1, \ldots , A_{i-1},A_{i+1}, \ldots , A_n)$, which will be denoted by π_i in situations where the set of pertinent payoffs is unambiguous. These prior probabilities are assumed to be nonnegative and to sum to 1.

The perceived probability $P(p_i,A_i; A_1, \ldots , A_{i-1},A_{i+1}, \ldots , A_n)$ will be denoted by P_i, where

$$P_i = \frac{\gamma \pi_i + \xi p_i}{\gamma + \xi} .$$ (7.14)

It follows from the assumed properties of π_i that

$$\sum_{i=1}^{n} P_i = 1.$$

In the multiple reference point case, the reference point π_i satisfies all of the usual properties of a probability measure, as do the P_i values.

The change in the perceptional formulation of the reference points leaves the basic assumptions largely unchanged. Assumption 3 for lottery perceptions is modified by replacing the $P(p_i)$ equation by equation 7.14. Two additional assumptions are also critically involved—in particular, those pertaining to the reduction of compound lotteries and substitutability. In each case, the role of contextual factors could potentially cause intractable difficulties.

One can resolve such problems by making π_i depend only on the particular lottery embedded within a larger decision tree. For example, suppose there is a compound lottery in which there is a chance s of facing the lottery $(p_1,A_1;1 - p_1,A_2)$ and a chance $1 - s$ of receiving A_3. Then the reference points for A_1 and A_2 are assumed to be independent of A_3, making it possible to substitute equivalent lotteries and to reduce a compound lottery in which the influence of the reference point is retained. This assumption is in the same spirit as the earlier assumption regarding the perception of compound lotteries in accordance with the isolation effect.

Thus, in reducing compound lotteries under assumption 3, one continues to assume that the compound probabilities consist of the product of two probabilities, each of which has been transformed using the reference probability formulation, except that $P(p_i(i))$ is calculated using the multiple reference point equation 7.14.

Similarly, the substitutability assumption can be generalized directly, since a shift in the context of a particular lottery is irrelevant because the other branches of the decision tree are assumed to be irrelevant. One must, however, impose the additional assumption that the substitution of equivalent utility items does not alter the reference point. Consider two lotteries—$(p,A_1;1 - p,A_2)$ and $(p,A_1;1 - p,A_3)$. If the individual is indifferent between A_2 and A_3, then $\pi(A_1;A_2)$ must equal $\pi(A_1;A_3)$.

The Ellsberg Paradox

The multiple reference point model can be used to explain one of the most basic and well-known violations of rational behavior—the Ellsberg paradox.[19] Consider the following basic version of the Ellsberg paradox. Urn 1 has 100 red and black balls, but the mix is not known. Urn 2 has 100 balls, 50 of which are red and 50 of which are black. You can win a $100 prize if you correctly pick the ball color for the urn you choose. The observed behavior is that people are indifferent between drawing a red ball or black ball from urn 1. They would rather draw a red ball from urn 2 than from urn 1 and would rather draw a black ball from urn 2 than from 1. These patterns of preferences are inconsistent unless the assessed probabilities for the uncertain urn are subadditive.

Rather than defining events in terms of colors of balls, define them in terms of drawing the color ball associated with the awarding of $100. Thus, the individual has some prior probability $\pi(\$100;0) < .5$ of winning the prize when there are two ball colors involved. Moreover, to achieve additivity, $\pi(\$100;0)$ and $\pi(0;\$100)$ must sum to 1. There are two possible interpretations of this prior probability. First, the individual may believe that the experiment is being manipulated against him or her in some manner, thus leading to a below average chance of success. Thus, even converting his or her chance of success to a "hard" probability by choosing the ball color based on the tossing of a fair coin, as suggested by Raiffa (1961), may not be effective if he or she believes that the presence of ambiguity creates greater opportunities for manipulation of the experiment. Second, based on past experience with lotteries the participant may be pessimistic of the chance of winning regardless of the ball color he or she picks. This belief may be a quite rational reflection of the individual's past experiences, since almost all available lotteries are at actuarially unfair odds.

The perceived probability of drawing a winning ball will be given by

$$P(.5) = \frac{\gamma\pi(\$100;0) + .5\xi}{\gamma + \xi}.$$

For urn 1, the value of ξ is 100, and $P(.5) < .5$, as is observed. For urn 2, the value of ξ exceeds 100, and if the individual takes the experiment at face value, then $\xi \rightarrow \infty$, and the resulting value of $P(.5)$ will exceed that for urn 1 and will equal .5 in the full-information case. Thus, the precision of the information associated with urn 2 eliminates the role of the pessimistic reference risk $\pi(\$100;0)$.

The traditional explanation for the Ellsberg paradox is that individuals slant ambiguous probabilities downward, leading to subadditivity. No such subadditivity is required, however. In a multiple reference point model in which individuals' reference points reflect a chance of winning the prize below what would occur with a random lottery, the observed behavior will occur. One would expect $\pi(\$100;0)$ to be below .5, given the actuarially unfair nature of available lotteries with which the individual has had experience.

NOTES

1. It should be noted, however, that claims regarding the predictive validity of the theory vary. For example, Raiffa (1968) emphasizes the normative purposes of the model as a guide to decision making, whereas Savage (1972) notes that even though "the behavior of people does often flagrantly depart from the theory," the framework may nevertheless be useful as a predictive guide since "a theory is not to be altogether rejected because it is not absolutely true."

2. Other discussions of violations of the expected utility model and alternatives to it appear in Allais (1953), Bell (1982), Einhorn and Hogarth (1985,1986), Ellsberg (1961), Fischhoff, et al. (1981), Fischhoff and Beyth-Marom (1983), Grether (1980), Hogarth and Kunreuther (1985), Kahneman and Tversky (1982), Raiffa (1961), Viscusi (1985a,b), Viscusi, Magat, and Huber (1987), Viscusi and O'Connor (1984), and Zeckhauser (1986).

3. The Dirichlet distribution reduces to a standard beta distribution in the bivariate case. For further discussion of the Dirichlet distribution, see Johnson and Kotz (1972), pp. 231–235.

4. The value of ξ/γ has been estimated in Viscusi (1985a) and in Viscusi and O'Connor (1984), whereas ξ and γ could not be estimated.

5. In the unusual cases in which outcomes with stated certainty p_i values of 0 and 1 are really viewed as being subject to a stochastic process, one simply incorporates the expanded set of possible outcomes into the reference probabilities. With both such events included, for example, the reference probability becomes $1/(n+2)$, where n is the number of lottery outcomes with associated p_i values between 0 and 1. As before, the perceived probabilities sum to 1.

6. In addition to the difference cited below, decision weights also may not be well defined near 0 or 1, since Kahneman and Tversky (1979) omit any decision weight values near 0 or 1 from their graph of the decision weight function (1979), Figure 4, p. 283.

7. For a discussion of anchoring phenomena, see Tversky and Kahneman (1974), pp. 14–18; Slovic, Fischhoff, and Lichtenstein (1982), pp. 481–482; and Einhorn and Hogarth (1985,1986).

8. See, for example, Einhorn and Hogarth (1985).

9. These changes are based on assumptions 2 and 3 discussed in Appendix 7A.

10. Kahneman and Tversky (1979) describe this property as the "empirical generalization concerning the manner in which the substitution axiom is violated . . . This property is incorporated into an alternative theory. . . ."

11. In addition to the example here, their problems 14 and 14' involve a similar principle and can also be explained with the PRT framework.

12. This neglect was context-dependent, since it was greater when a description of the worker was provided than when it was not. This pattern suggests that the informational content ξ that respondents associate with the information provided concerning the mix of workers may be reduced by the provision of other information provided in the experiments that may lead respondents to, in effect, ignore or discount the veracity of the occupational mix information.

13. One can readily verify that these other cases can be reconciled with the PRT approach. See, in particular, problems 1–8 in Kahneman and Tversky (1979), which exemplify this phenomenon, as does the certainty effect considered in Section 7.4 of this chapter.

14. The prospect theory explanation is similar in spirit, except that the paradox is not a prediction of the theory. Other possible explanations following different approaches appear in Machina (1982), Luce and Raiffa (1957), and Bell (1982).

15. See Kahnemann and Tversky (1979), pp. 271–273. The particular phenomenon was observed by Tversky in earlier work.

16. *Ibid.*, p. 271.

17. See, for example, the studies by Tversky and Kahneman (1982) and Kahneman and Tversky (1979).

18. For a discussion of these influences, see Slovic, Fischhoff, and Lichtenstein (1982).

19. See both the original article by Ellsberg (1961), the illuminating discussion by Raiffa (1961), and the modern revivals of this phenomenon by Einhorn and Hogarth (1985, 1986), and Hogarth and Kunreuther (1985).

8

Sources of Inconsistency in Societal
Responses to Health Risks

8.1 INTRODUCTION

Society responds in extreme and often inconsistent ways to health risks. In many instances, the pattern observed is one of overreaction. The Tylenol tampering incidents of the early 1980s drastically reduced the national sales of this product even though the seven reported deaths were all in the Chicago area. Isolated terrorist incidents periodically choke off the consumer demand for European travel, and the Food and Drug Administration banned the sale of tens of millions of dollars of Chilean fruit based on evidence of low levels of cyanide that was possibly injected into two grapes. More generally, there is evidence that individuals respond in an alarmist manner to increases in the risks they face even though these increases may be rather small.

Recall the results in Chapter 7 pertaining to consumer willingness to pay for risk reductions associated with insecticides and toilet bowl cleaner. The total willingness to pay for risk reductions on the order of 5/10,000 was relatively modest. When these same respondents were subsequently asked how much of a price decrease they would require to accept an increase in risk of 5/10,000, all respondents in the pretest indicated that the product would be too risky to buy. As a result, the survey used a modified variant of the question in which the risk only increased by 1/10,000.

The results from this survey are summarized in Table 8-1. Somewhat surprisingly, for the overwhelming majority of the sample, in every case the product is now viewed as being too risky to purchase once the risk has risen by 1/10,000. These results are for the same groups of individuals who in Chapter 7 were willing to pay as little as $1.67 for a reduction in the gassing–eye burn injuries from 15/10,000 to 0. When faced with a risk increase of 1/10,000, 61.5 percent of these respondents would not be willing to take any price cut to purchase the product, and those who are willing to accept a price discount to buy the product would require a price reduction of $5.52 per bottle to purchase it. This striking asymmetry in responses cannot be traced to a legitimate difference between willingness to pay and willingness to accept amounts and cannot be reconciled with conventional models of risk taking.[1]

Although one might be tempted to generalize from such events to conclude that

Table 8-1. Responses to Risk Increase ($+1$, $+1$) Valuation Questions[a]

Injury pair	Percentage for whom product is too risky to purchase	Mean value (*$/bottle*) of positive responses
Inhalation–skin poisoning	77.2	2.86
Inhalation–child poisoning	68.1	3.19
Eyeburns–gassing	61.5	5.52
Gassing–child poisoning	74.3	1.28

[a]This question asked subjects what price discount they would require on the new product to accept an additional risk of 1/10,000 for both injuries, starting with risks of 15 injuries per 10,000 bottles sold for both injuries.
Source: Viscusi, Magat, and Huber (1987), p. 477.

there is always universal overreaction to risk, other patterns of behavior reflect errors of the opposite type. Individuals continue to fail to wear seat belts as often as they should, given the health benefits and the costs involved (see Arnould and Grabowski [1981]). Similarly, society has until recently devoted insufficient attention to the long-run environmental problems that we face, including acid rain and the greenhouse effect. Our inaction with respect to these risks can hardly be characterized as a rational response or an overreaction to risk.

There are three possible explanations of such diverse phenomena. First, one could simply dismiss this behavior as being the result of inconsistent and irrational behavior. Second, one could devise ad hoc explanations of why individuals underreact in some instances and overreact in others. A third possibility is to reconcile this seemingly inconsistent behavior with a consistent theoretical framework. In this chapter I will follow the third approach, in which I will discuss how the theoretical model of Chapter 7 can address the observed character of individual risk decisions.

8.2 THE PATTERN OF RISK PERCEPTIONS

The genesis of my approach stems from the relationship between perceived and actual risks. Figure 8-1 sketches the relationship that has been borne out in studies of risk perception analyzed in Chapter 6. At probability levels below F_0, individuals tend to overestimate the risk level, whereas for large risks above F_0 there is a tendency toward underestimation. Individuals consequently exaggerate the risks posed by rare events, such as the chance of being hit by lightning, and underassess the truly major risks, such as the chance of death by heart attack or stroke. In addition, the discontinuity of preferences at the zero risk level indicates that there will be a substantial jump in the perceived risk level once the risk rises from being zero to some nonzero level of risk.

This basic pattern of risk perception was incorporated within the prospective reference theory model discussed in Chapter 7. The principal modification in standard choice models is that one replaces the individual's actual probability q with some perceived probability $\pi(q)$. For example, using a beta probability distribution, if q is the risk of an accident, then we can write $\pi(q) = (\gamma p + \delta q)/(\gamma + \delta)$, where p denotes the reference risk level, q denotes the risk associated with the particular

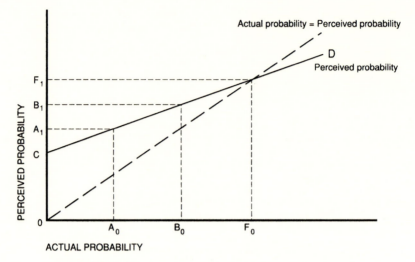

Figure 8.1 Relation between actual and perceived probabilities

event, γ is the informational content associated with p, and δ is the informational content associated with q.

This formulation is consistent with a Bayesian learning model in which the reference risk p corresponds to the decision maker's prior probability assessment. In the context of accidental death risks, this probability could, for example, be the average risk being addressed in the survey. In the context of laboratory experiments, the probability associated with the lottery outcome could be the probability that would prevail if the respondent did not take the experiment description as being fully informative but instead placed some weight on a prior probability in which all outcomes in a lottery were equally likely.

Application of this approach to the anomalies that have been observed in the literature produces quite powerful results. One can reconcile a large and diverse array of types of irrational behavior with the standard expected utility model upon making this transformation. Moreover, what is most striking is that this formulation *predicts* such behavior as opposed to being potentially consistent with these anomalies. For example, the methodology predicts that the Allais paradox will prevail, that there will be a certainty effect in which individuals value risk reductions that achieve complete certainty more greatly than they should, and many other prominent violations of the standard expected utility theory.

8.3 IMPLICATIONS FOR RISK-TAKING BEHAVIOR

Consider a binary lottery situation in which an individual faces a probability q of injury or death and a probability of $1-q$ of remaining healthy, where the perceived probability is given by $\pi(q)$. In the good health state utility is given by $U(I)$, and in the ill health state utility is given by V(I−L), where I is the income level and L is a monetary loss (possibly 0) associated with ill health. For any given level of income, the individual is assumed to rather be healthy than not and to be risk-averse. I will also assume that the marginal utility of income is at least as great when one is healthy as when one is not, which has been borne out empirically in the case of job risks.[2]

Let Y be the compensation, such as a price cut for a risky product or a wage premium for a hazardous job, that is necessary to maintain the individual's expected utility level at U_0, or

$$U_0 = (1 - \pi(q))U(I+Y) + \pi(q)V(I+Y-L). \qquad (8.1)$$

The first tradeoff that will be considered is how the required compensation Y varies with the extent of the loss. Total differentiation of equation 8.1 yields the result that

$$\frac{dY}{dL} = \frac{\pi(q)V'}{(1 - \pi(q))U' + \pi(q)V'} > 0. \qquad (8.2)$$

As the loss increases, the required compensation Y rises. The more important issue is the extent to which dY/dL is altered by the introduction of perceptional biases. For situations in Figure 8-1 in which q is below F_0, $\pi(q)$ will exceed q, implying that dY/dL will be increased by the biases in risk perception for small risks. Similarly, the required compensation will be decreased by the perceptional biases for high risk levels.

The analogous result for the effect of changes in the risk level q are somewhat more complex, and it is more instructive to consider them within the context of concrete economic actions that will alter the risk level. In particular, suppose that we have opportunities for both insurance and self-protection. In the case of self-protection, one can take a precautionary expenditure c that will influence the risk component q, but the reference risk component p will be unaffected so that we have $\pi(q(c)) = (\gamma p + \delta q(c))/(\gamma + \delta)$. In addition, one can choose to purchase an amount of insurance x for a unit price of s, leading to the optimization problem

$$\underset{c,x}{\text{Max}} \ Z = (1 - \pi)U(I - sx - c) + \pi V(I - L - sx + x - c). \qquad (8.3)$$

The condition for optimal insurance is given by

$$U' = \frac{\pi}{q} \frac{(1 - s)}{(1 - \pi)} V'. \qquad (8.4)$$

Consider the actuarially fair insurance case, where s = q. For $\pi(q) > q$, the right side of equation 8.4 will be larger than in the unbiased case, implying that a lower marginal utility of income in state 2 is needed to establish the optimal insurance amount. A lower marginal utility of income is associated with a higher level of insurance, so that for the risk levels below F_0 in Figure 8-1 there will be an incentive to overinsure as compared with the unbiased case. For the points above F_0, there will be an incentive to underinsure.

Risk perception biases have a more complex effect on safety precautions. The requirement for optimal self-protection is that

$$\frac{-dq}{dc} = \frac{\gamma + \delta}{\delta} \frac{[(1 - \pi(q))U' + \pi(q)V']}{U - V}. \tag{8.5}$$

The value $-dq/dc$ indicates the marginal productivity of precautionary behavior in influencing the risk level.

The requirement on the marginal productivity of safety precautions as reflected in the right side of equation 8.5 is affected in two ways by perceptional biases. The informational content term $(\gamma + \delta)/\delta$, which exceeds 1.0, induces a lower level of precautions by requiring a higher marginal productivity $-dq/dc$. In situations of optimal insurance ($U' = V'$), the net effect will be to diminish the level of precautions selected. When there is not full insurance, the results become more ambiguous because the effect of the risk perception biases on the level of insurance and the expected marginal utility of income hinge on how much marginal utilities are altered when one departs from the optimal insurance amount and on whether the size of any such effect outweighs the role of the informational weight term. If, however, the dominant effect is that the biases in risk perceptions raise the required marginal productivity of safety expenditures, as in the optimal insurance case, then risk perception biases will always reduce precautionary expenditures.

The nature of the different influences can be summarized using Figure 8-1. Overall attitudes toward risk and the desirability of insurance will be governed by the relationship between the perceived and actual probabilities. For $q < F_0$, risks are overestimated, and there will be a tendency to overinsure and to be overly cautious in discrete responses to risk. For large risks, $q > F_0$, the reaction will be the opposite. From the standpoint of continuous choices affecting safety, however, what is primarily relevant is the slope of CD, not the level of the probability, although this continues to enter the expected marginal utility. Since the perception function $\pi(q)$ flattens out the relationship between perceived and actual probabilities, the marginal efficacy of safety expenditures is reduced. A precaution that reduces a risk from B_0 to A_0 in Figure 8-1 has a more modest effect of reducing the perceived risk from B_1 to A_1. The risk perception function consequently mutes the perceived impact that safety precautions will have for all levels of risk.

These different competing effects indicate why one might have quite conflicting reactions to the same level of risk. Why, for example, do we respond in often alarmist ways to the various low-probability health risks that are called to our attention, yet we fail to take appropriate safety precautions, such as seat belt use, that are available to us? Although a variety of explanations are possible, the character of the risk perception biases alone is sufficient to explain these seemingly contradictory phenomena. The level of the risk may be overestimated, but the risk-perception function may also serve to dampen the perceived efficacy of safety precautions so that when we have available actions offering incremental reductions in risk, we underrespond.

Although this conclusion is true for marginal changes in riskiness, if there are available strategies that will completely eliminate the risk, then there will be no such dampening in the response. In particular, if we can reduce the risk to zero, we not only obtain a value of the marginal perceived risk-reduction probability along CD, but we also achieve the additional bonus in terms of the perceived risk reduction of 0C. Thus, there will be a predilection for policies that achieve the complete certainty of risk reduction. This predilection is borne out in studies of consumer evaluation of product safety, as consumers are willing to pay much more for the final incremental reduction in risk to zero than they are for the earlier risk reductions of equal magnitude, even though economic theory would predict the opposite. Stringent government regulations, such as the Delaney Clause's requirement that no nonzero carcinogenic food additives be permitted, is likewise consistent with this orientation.

The character of the bias is dependent on the nature of the risky decision. Individuals tend to overreact to identified increases in the risk level from its accustomed amount. The study of consumer valuations of product safety summarized in Table 8-1 indicate that individuals were willing to pay moderate amounts for product risk reductions of fifteen injuries per 10,000 bottles of insecticide or toilet bowl cleaner used per year, but when faced with a product risk increase of $1/10,000$ most consumers were unwilling to buy the product at all, and those who were demanded a considerable price discount. In this context, the risky choice focused on changes in the risk from the current risk reference point to which consumers had become accustomed. In the case in which consumers are focusing on the risk increase of a product, the jump in the perceived probability indicated by the segment 0C in Figure 8-1 is the pertinent perceived risk increase from a marginal shift in the product risk. Even if there were a risk decrease of similar magnitude to the risk increase, there would be no reason to believe that consumers would respond in symmetric fashion because the reference risk probability p that individuals have with respect to the risks posed by product improvements as opposed to deteriorations in product quality may be quite different.

8.4 THE EFFECTS OF RISK AMBIGUITY

Alarmist responses to increases in risk are not the only example of excessive reactions to risk. When informed about various potential hazards that might befall them in situations in which there is risk ambiguity, individuals generally place too much weight on the worst-case possibility. Rather than simply averaging the types of information presented to them, they tend to place excessive weight on the worst possible outcome.

An example of how this type of bias arises has been documented within the context of environmental risks by Viscusi, Magat, and Huber (1991a). In this study, we informed respondents who had the prospect of moving to some new Area A that there is some uncertainty in terms of the risk per million of nerve disease. For Panel 1 of sixty-five respondents, we informed them that there had been two scientific studies indicating that the risks per million were 150 cases and 200 cases, respectively. The midpoint of this range is 175. Respondents were then asked what they viewed as being an equivalent risk in Area B, if there is no uncertainty that would be involved in the Area B risk. In this situation, they indicated that the equivalent risk was 178, which is not too dissimilar from the midpoint of the range given to them for Area A.

If, however, we increase the size of the risk ambiguity, while at the same time not affecting the midpoint, the reactions become much more extreme. In particular, for Panel B the possible risks per million in Area A were 110 cases and 240 cases. As the results in Table 8-2 indicate, the equivalent from the standpoint of the respondents was 191 cases per million, indicating that overall the respondents viewed this as a much less desirable situation even though the midpoint risk estimate had remained unchanged. Perhaps the most dramatic is that thirteen of the fifty-eight respondents viewed the risk equivalent to this pair of ambiguous risk studies as being 240 cases per million, which was the high end of the risk range indicated to them. Thus, there is an emphasis and myopic focus on the worst-case outcome, much more than can be justified by the types of information given to them with respect to the studies.

Other biases arise in the case of risk ambiguity as well. The order in which the subjects process the information pertaining to the studies is of consequence, even in a situation in which there is no temporal order for the studies. What these and similar types of errors in behavior suggest is that the nature of individual responses to risk is going to be quite sensitive to the character of the information presented and the manner of presentation. We cannot assume that individuals will be fully rational in the manner in which they process the information, but we can attempt to identify systematic biases. In this instance, there appears to be substantial "ambiguous belief aversion" as individuals attempt to avoid situations in which very risky outcomes could befall them even if the cost of doing so is to accept a higher average risk level. In this situation, as in the case of overreacting to increases in the risk, respondents tend to approach such contexts with a substantial degree of skepticism. The guiding principal underlining their responses appears to be an extension of Murphy's Law: if anything can go wrong, people believe it will.

One example of the role of risk ambiguity pertains to the information that was disseminated in the early 1990s concerning the cancer risks from breast implants.

Table 8-2. Risk Ambiguity Aversion and the Size of the Nerve Disease Risk Spread

Risk levels in Area A	Sample size	Median	Mean	Standard error of mean	Minimum (#)	Maximum (#)
Panel 1: Risk ambiguity						
150,200	65	175.00	178.35	1.24	150.50 (1)	200.00 (1)
Panel 2: Size of spread effect						
110,240	58	180.00	191.08	3.95	115.00 (1)	240.00 (13)

Source: W. K. Viscusi, W. A. Magat, and J. Huber (1991), Table 1.

The U.S. Food and Drug Administration estimates that the lifetime cancer risk from the implants is between 1/10,000 and 1/1,000,000. However, some scientists claim the risk may be as high as 1/50 to 1/500. These estimates at the high end of the range seem to have been the dominant ones in terms of influencing the public's response to this risk information.[3]

8.5 DISCOUNTING DEFERRED EFFECTS

The decision problems that individuals face involving risk are compounded by the task of appropriately discounting these outcomes. Although it has long been speculated that individuals behave myopically, there is no systematic evidence that this is the case. Studies of worker valuations of death risks, such as Viscusi and Moore (1989), indicate that the implicit rates of interest with which workers discount the years of life at risk on the job are consistent with rational behavior. Our point estimates of the implied discount rates are in the vicinity of 11 percent, which is somewhat high, but the standard errors on these estimates are sufficient to include other market reference points, such as prevailing mortgage interest rates.

In many respects, examining revealed preferences toward risks to their welfare at different periods of time may represent a best-case scenario. A more important issue from the standpoint of policy is how we will address effects that will influence not only our own well-being but also that of our children and future generations. The U.S. Office of Management and Budget (1988) has long specified a 10 percent rate of discount as the main reference point for such calculations—an approach that will drastically reduce the attractiveness of policies such as those that reduce cancer risks or have long-term implications for our ecological well-being.

Although there have been a variety of battles over the appropriate discount rate, insufficient attention has been paid to the implications of the productivity assumptions that underlie such discount rate estimates. In particular, if the appropriate rate of discount is in fact 10 percent, then the rate of expected productivity growth in the economy also must be quite substantial to justify such a high rate. This growth will boost the income of future generations, which in turn will raise the value that they attach to the risk-reduction benefits. The estimates in Viscusi and Evans (1990) reported in Chapter 4 indicate that the elasticity of the implicit value of job injuries with respect to income is 1.0, and if this relationship generalizes to other health impacts then it implies that an increase in income will increase the risk reduction benefit values proportionally. Valuing health risks through use of high discount rates should not drastically affect the attractiveness of policies with long- term implications provided that the benefit values are adjusted appropriately.

Perhaps the main shortcoming is that individuals are likely to place an inefficiently low weight on benefits to future generations. Moreover, our social institutions have thus far proven to be very poor at long range planning, as there is a predilection for responding to more imminent crises. Indeed, if it had not been for the hot summer of 1988, it is unlikely that addressing the greenhouse effect would even be on our national agenda.

As in the case of risk-perception biases, the most disturbing aspect of these potential market failures is that the government policies intended to eliminate the shortcomings often appear to be driven by the same sets of influences.

NOTES

1. One possible explanation is that the perceived probability that subjects assess for the risk is much greater than the 1/10,000 risk increase that they were told.

2. See Viscusi and Evans (1990).

3. *New York Times*, March 16, 1991, p. B8.

PART III
Risk Regulation

9

Risk within Reason[1]

9.1 INTRODUCTION

Society's system for managing risks to life and limb is deeply flawed. We overreact to some risks and virtually ignore others. Often too much weight is placed on risks of low probability but high salience (such as those posed by trace carcinogens or terrorist action); risks of commission rather than omission; and risks, such as those associated with frontier technologies, whose magnitude is difficult to estimate. Too little effort is spent ameliorating voluntary risks, such as those involving automobiles and diet. When the bearers of risk do not share in the costs of reduction, moreover, extravagance is likely.

Part of the problem is that we rely on a mix of individual, corporate, and government decisions to respond to risk. Our traditional coordinating mechanisms—markets and government action—are crippled by inadequate information, costly decision-making processes, and the need to accommodate citizens' misperceptions, sometimes arising from imbalances in media attention.

Risk can never be entirely eliminated from life, and reductions come at a price (in dollars, foregone pleasures, or both). Our current muddled approach makes it difficult to reach wise, well-informed decisions as to the preferred balance of risk and cost. Some risks we ignore; some small ones we regulate stringently. Worse, our overreaction to very small risks impedes the kind of technological progress that has historically brought dramatic improvements in both health and material well-being. In addition, we are likely to misdirect our efforts, for example, by focusing on risks that command attention in the political process, such as newly identified carcinogens, rather than those where the greatest gains in well-being are available, such as individual life-style choices.[2]

Our regulatory efforts focus too much on equipment and physical processes, too little on human error and venality. We may set stringent emission standards, which impose high costs per unit of environmental quality gained, yet ignore the haphazard operation of nuclear weapons plants.

Evidently willing to expend substantial resources to reduce risk, our society seems reluctant to look closely at the bargains it has struck. Unless we reorient our risk-management policies, we will continue to pay more than we should for health gains that are less than we could achieve.

The success of risk-management policies should be judged in terms of their effect on expected utility.[3] In practice, the choices made by human beings under uncertainty frequently do not conform to the prescriptions of expected utility theory. Upon reflection, however, most people would accept the theory's axiomatic underpinnings. (There is no well-developed competing prescriptive theory for choice under uncertainty.)

The formulation of risk policy should then begin by asking what outcomes would result from perfectly functioning market processes if individuals behaved so as to maximize their own expected utility. What level of adverse side effects from pharmaceuticals would be acceptable if we knew the risk and could take the time and effort to make sound decisions? Our hypothetical market should be open to future generations. If they could compensate the present generation for preserving resources and the environment, what environmental decisions would we make today? Such a thought experiment should guide our efforts to bequeath posterity an efficient mix of technological capabilities, environmental quality, and cultural attainments.

9.2 HUMAN FALLIBILITY IN RESPONSES TO RISKS

Decisions involving risks illustrate the limits of human rationality, as a substantial recent literature documents.[4] Perhaps the most fundamental problem is that individuals have great difficulty comprehending extremely low-probability events, such as differentiating a risk of 10^{-7} from a risk 100 times as large, 10^{-5}. When assessing such risks, even scientists may not appreciate how much greater the payoff is that comes from addressing the larger probability.

The numerous decision-making problems that arise with respect to small probabilities are individually of little consequence. Expected welfare loss from any single error may well be negligible. Aggregated, however, low-probability events make up a large part of an individual's risk level. Even truly substantial risks, such as the chance of death from a stroke—roughly 1/2,000 annually averaged over the population—are usually influenced by a myriad of decisions, each of which has only a small probabilistic impact on our longevity. Systematic errors in these decisions might have an enormous cumulative effect.

Mistakes in Estimation

Whereas people generally overestimate the likelihood of low-probability events (death by tornado), they underestimate higher risk levels (heart disease or stroke).[5] We are particularly likely to overestimate previously unrecognized risks in the aftermath of an unfavorable outcome.[6] Such perceptual biases account for the emotional public response to such events as Three Mile Island, or occasional incidents of deliberate poisoning of foodstuffs or medicines.

Risk perceptions may also be affected by the visibility of a risk, by fear associated with it, and by the extent to which individuals believe they can exercise control over it. Consider the greenhouse effect. Although global warming is a prime concern of the Environmental Protection Agency, it ranks only twenty-third among the U.S. public's environmental concerns.[7] The high risk of automobile fatality—car accidents kill one in 5,000 Americans each year[8]—might perhaps be reduced significantly if drivers informed with a more realistic sense of what they can and cannot do to control the risk drank less alcohol and wore seat belts more often.

Because experience tells us little about low-probability risks, we appropriately examine correlated indicators that pose less serious problems. For example, the record high temperatures of 1988 may or may not have been signals of an impending greenhouse effect.[9] Unfortunately, such signals are seldom as informative as canaries in the coal mine. Adverse events may occur without warning; witness the San Francisco earthquake in October 1989. Moreover, happenstance warnings may bear little relation to the magnitude, likelihood, or nature of a problem. Forest management efforts should not have to await the chance burning of national parks and forests.

Distortions in Monetary Valuation

Economic valuations of risk also tend to be distorted by underlying misweighting of risks. For example, from an expected utility perspective, individuals generally place too high a value on preventing increases in a risk from its current level (the so-called status quo bias or reference risk effect.[10] These tendencies are reflected in government policy. Products causing new forms of cancer tend to arouse greater public concern, and new technologies are often regulated much more strictly than are old technologies and familiar risks.[11] Man-made carcinogens are carefully scrutinized, while much higher levels of natural carcinogens may be tolerated. Because of this imbalance, we pay more dollars for our products and end up with greater risks to our lives.

Studies of consumers show that many individuals would be willing to pay a premium for the assured elimination of a risk.[12] The Russian roulette problem illustrates. Consider two alternative scenarios for a forced round of play. In the first, you have the option to purchase and remove one bullet from a gun that has three bullets in its six chambers. How much would you pay for this reduction in risk? (Assume you are unmarried, with no children.) In the second situation, the gun has only a single bullet. How much would you pay to buy back this bullet? From an economic standpoint, you should always be willing to pay at least as much and typically more in the first situation since there is some chance you will be killed by one of the remaining bullets, in which case money is worthless (or worth less).[13] However, experiments find respondents are typically willing to pay more when a single bullet is in the gun, because its removal will ensure survival.[14]

The Chilean grape scare provides a recent example of a risk that does not lend itself to statistical estimation or scientific assessment. Neither the government nor consumers could estimate how much consumers' risk was increased by the discovery of traces of cyanide in two Chilean grapes in Philadelphia.[15] When precise scientific judgments concerning probabilities are elusive, regret is likely to play a significant role.[16] If societal norms were flouted, regret would be greater still. (Few of us would leave a baby sleeping alone in a house while we drove off on a ten-minute errand, even though car-crash risks are much greater than home risks.) Hindsight is frequently able to identify why an individual or society should have known certain risk estimates were far too low, as we "learned" from the highway collapse during the San Francisco earthquake. Regret is less of an issue when consequences cannot be tied back to a particular risk exposure or a particular decision maker.

The valuation of a risk is likely to depend on how the risk is generated. We tolerate voluntarily assumed risks more than those, such as environmental hazards, over which we have no control. We regard acts of commission as much more serious than acts of omission. In pharmaceutical screening, for example, the Food and Drug Administration (FDA) worries more about introducing harmful new drugs than about missing opportunities for risk reduction offered by new pharmaceutical products.[17]

Agency Dilemmas

Problems of risk perception and valuation may become entangled with so-called agency problems. What rules apply when one individual or organization (the agent) makes risk decisions on behalf of another (the principal)? Should the agent replicate shortcomings in the principal's decision-making capabilities? Suppose there is one chance in 10,000 that a drug will have adverse consequences as severe as those of thalidomide. If the drug offers significant health benefits, it may be best for society to permit this risk—particularly since approving the drug would generate information useful in risk assessment, and the decision could be reversed if appropriate. Yet in practice, the FDA (society's agent) would probably not make such a decision, because of its bias toward avoiding new risks.[18]

Society's pattern of lopsided tradeoffs between errors of omission and commission persists for at least two reasons. First, apart from people's levels of risk, their consumption of information is relevant. When a federal agency demonstrates that it will not take chances with individual health, that reassurance alone enhances individual welfare. Conversely, a perception that the government tolerates risks to the public might be more damaging than the risks themselves. Second, it is easier to observe the costs of bad drugs that are approved than to assess the foregone benefits of good drugs that were not introduced. (Note, however, that potential beneficiaries, such as the users of saccharin and AIDS victims, sometimes put substantial pressure on the FDA to compromise normally stringent procedures for approving food additives and drugs.)[19]

How should we proceed once we admit that individuals do not react to many risks "correctly"? We might ask the government to make many more decisions. It is not clear, however, that the government itself is well equipped to compute certain risks accurately or to make sensible decisions once that information is obtained. Alternatively, we could shift decision-making authority to those best qualified to make particular kinds of choices. Here, however, the problem arises that the preferences of those making a decision might not be the same as those affected by it. A third possibility would be to develop processes enabling both agents and principals to participate in risk-related decisions, but there is little evidence that such processes would produce convergence. Finally, we might try to improve individuals' decision making skills by providing them, for example, with expert-certified information, much as accounting firms verify the accuracy of reported financial data.

The Informational Approach

Society's objective should be to foster informed consumer choice. With respect to cigarette smoking, for example, this may not be the same thing as seeking a smoke-free society. (Note that research linking aflatoxin and cancer risks[20] has not moved the Surgeon General to call for a peanut butter–free society.) Politically, of course, the passive smoking concern may be a trump card, rendering it irrelevant whether the risk imposed on others is substantial or negligible.

Hazard warnings are often used to convey risk information. Congress has mandated labels for cigarettes, artificial sweeteners, and alcoholic beverages. Federal agencies impose labeling requirements for consumer products, workplace risks, and pesticides. Informational efforts work in conjunction with market forces rather than attempting to supersede them.

Individuals may have difficulty processing risk information, however.[21] Overambitious information efforts may outstrip decision-making capabilities (e.g., California Proposition 65,[22] which requires warnings for products that expose consumers to annual risks of cancer of 1 in 7 million). The dangers are underreaction, overreaction, and nonreaction—a complete dismissal of the risk information effort. Sound decisions are unlikely to result. Indeed, the supposition of informed consent is called into question.

More general human cognitive limitations also work against detailed informational efforts. If a warning label contains more than a handful of items, or if warnings proliferate, problems of information overload arise.[23]

In a democratic society, one should hesitate to override the legitimate preferences of segments of the population, taking care not to dismiss diversity of taste as mere nonrational choice. Where there is broad consensus on a rational course of action, however, and either the cost of providing information is high or individuals cannot process the information adequately, then mandatory requirements may be preferable to risk information efforts. Laws requiring the use of seat belts are one possible example.

Individuals often fail to interpret risks or value their consequences accurately. Government efforts may escape some of these biases but are often thrown off course by political pressures and agency losses. The consequence is that our risk portfolio enjoys no legitimacy and satisfies no one. The first step toward a remedy is to develop a broad-based understanding of the nature of risk.

9.3 REASON AND INFORMATION ABOUT RISK

Information on risk is generated through several mechanisms. The most salient source is scientific research, but information can also be gained through experience, and knowledge of such information can be increased by distributing it more widely.

Risk, Uncertainty, and Ignorance

It is helpful to distinguish among risk, uncertainty, and ignorance. In the situation of risk, we know the states of the world that may prevail (a flipped coin will show one of two faces) and the precise probability of each state (heads and tails are equally likely). In the case of uncertainty, we may not even be able to define what states of the world are possible.

The real world is rife with uncertainty. Even if we can make direct environmental measurements (e.g., for atmospheric pollution), interpretation of our observations may be problematic.[24] Does an unusually high temperature this year indicate an upward trend, or does it represent random variation around an unchanging mean?

As our technological capabilities grow and economic activity imposes further strains on the environment, we will increasingly find ourselves in situations of ignorance. As we enter apparently benign but uncharted territory, we cannot be confident that if there were threats, we would detect them. Many individual decisions, as well as scientific risk analyses, are afflicted by ignorance. California studies of transportation safety in the event of an earthquake, for example, failed to capture the full range of effects that may have led to the highway damage experienced in October 1989.[25] Under ignorance, the potential for bad societal decisions is particularly great. Conceivably, for example, environmental releases of genetically engineered organisms might alter the current ecological balance in ways we cannot anticipate.[26]

Some observers insist that we simply cannot take such risks; others argue for weighing potential benefits the activity might bring. In many areas, fundamental scientific research may shed light on what states of the world may prevail and with what probability. But while we wait, we must decide (if only negatively, by default) on the basis of our limited information whether to deploy experimental drugs that might save lives, innovative organisms that might preserve threatened ecosystems, and controversial technologies such as nuclear power, which reduces the environmental risks from reliance on fossil fuels but creates another class of hazards.

Learning about Risks

Information by its very nature tends to be a public good; it can be acquired by another party without destroying its productive value to those who already possess it. Small countries, for example, make use of the information generated by large countries, say in drug regulation. Since generating information is often a costly process, there can be a temptation to hold back from making the effort, in the hope of free riding. Society has designed various mechanisms to promote the development of information; governments support research and development and issue patents, which protect the private value of information. Information on risk levels, however, cannot be patented. Without government participation, too little will be produced.

Risk information may be generated through experience. An employee can observe the injuries suffered by his or her coworkers in various jobs. Since the annual odds that a typical worker will experience an injury leading to one lost day of work per year are 3/100, even an individual observer will find some basis for making inferences about risk. In many cases, unfortunately, society may never learn how risky a process is, because it will change before we get enough experience. With an estimated 10^{-7} annual risk, it would take years of widespread observation to learn whether the risk is even an order of magnitude higher or lower than we initially believed. In addition, carcinogenic risks are often coupled with long time lags and multiple causal factors, so that precise inferences are not possible.

In such situations, it is rarely feasible to await the outcome of direct observations. One strategy would be to look instead for symptoms of high levels of risk. Thus, to assess whether we have underestimated the probability of a nuclear meltdown, we might ascertain whether our component estimates of the probability of a pipe break or human error were substantially too low. Alternatively, we can look to parallel risk estimates to see whether they have been proven too high or too low, which would tell us about potential biases in risk-estimation technology.

Resolving Discrepancies

Discrepancies in probabilistic beliefs provide an economic rationale for betting, and in many important instances, markets for such bets exist. Beliefs about economic prospects are exercised every day in markets for stocks and bonds, foreign exchange, and commodity futures.[27] The recent scientific debate over cold fusion might have been resolved more rapidly if the participants had made similar bets, thus providing information to each other and to bystanders.

Other societal mechanisms are also used to resolve informational differences. Adversary processes such as those of the judicial system, or a science court with an expert on each side, can air opposing viewpoints but, unlike markets, they will not reveal the weight of opinion on the two sides.

Markets and Their Absence

Markets generate information used by the world at large, not just by those who trade. Assessments of risk may be adjusted through market processes, but only to the extent that they are reflected in prices. After a disaster in one chemical plant, for example, investors may hastily unload all chemical company stocks. If their implicit valuation of chemical company risk is too pessimistic, more realistic appraisers will find bargains and bid up share prices to an appropriate level. In a more mundane fashion, futures prices tell decision makers the expected future price of oil, and insurance premiums reveal information about assessed levels of risk.

For many important risk decisions, however, market mechanisms are not useful means of conveying risk information. Whereas a poorly operated business will lose its ability to produce for the market, no one will take over decision making for an adult who underinvests in his own health. Poaching on the poor decisions of others—a critical factor ensuring efficient production in economic markets—is simply not possible.

Many informational asymmetries are not resolved successfully through markets. Firms may have better notions of the risks posed by their products or employment than do the individuals who bear these risks, and individual purchasers of insurance policies may be better informed than the firm about the likely claims they will make under these policies. Ideally, everyone would have an incentive to convey information honestly and truthfully. In reality, however, a firm marketing a potentially hazardous good in a world with a capricious tort system may have too much to lose by informing consumers of the risky characteristics of its products.

Making the Most of Uncertainty

Information is valuable when it accurately represents the risks posed. For one-time-only decisions, from the standpoint of Bayesian decision making, the mean assessment of the probability of each outcome is all that matters, for that gives the likelihood with which the outcome will be received. For example, with option I there is a 10 percent chance that a 0.01 risk is imposed and a 90 percent chance that no risk is imposed. With option II, there is a 100 percent chance of a 0.002 risk. Option I should be preferred since its mean risk, $0.1 \times 0.01 + 0.9 \times 0 = 0.001$, is lower than for option II.[28]

In situations of learning and sequential decisions, the precision of the estimate also matters. Paradoxically, imprecisely known probabilities are more favorable, as some simple examples illustrate. Suppose you must choose between two alternative medical treatments. Choice A is known to cure half the patients to whom it is applied. Choice B is an experimental treatment that is equally likely to be either perfect or worthless. In each case, the probability of a cure is 0.5. On a one-time-out basis the two options are equally attractive.

With two patients in sequential trials, however, the correct strategy is to pursue B. If the first patient recovers, give the second the same treatment; otherwise switch to A. With this strategy, on average one and one-fourth of two patients will recover, as opposed to only one out of two if the better-known treatment A is chosen at the outset. (This is equivalent to the simplest version of the classic two-armed bandit problem.)[29] In any choice between a certain and an uncertain risk of an adverse outcome, if the initial mean value for the probability is the same, the uncertain risk is preferable when learning and adaptive behavior after experience are possible.

Now suppose the experimental treatment is treatment C, which will turn out to be either a total failure or a 90 percent cure (with both possibilities equally likely). Trying C rather than A will be preferable (offering an expected 1.13 cures),[30] but now the first patient will face unfavorable odds with experimental treatment C (0.45 rather than 0.5 with A). If randomization is not possible, or if the first patient objects, perhaps even after a lottery is conducted, ethical norms would require offering the patient treatment A. This argument has been illogically extended to suggest that even if experimental treatment C looks better than established treatment A, we may find out it was worse, and we should therefore stick with A. In the medical context, patient interest provides an antidote to such misconceptions. Many experimental technologies are not blessed with such a counterweight.

Regulatory Efforts and Misplaced Conservatism

Government efforts at developing risk information are not guided by the formal statistical properties of the risk but rather by administrative procedures incorporating various types of "conservatism." Although risk-assessment biases may operate in both directions,[31] most approved procedures tend to overstate the actual risk.[32] In regulating toxic substances, for example, results from the most sensitive animal species are often used, and government agencies such as the EPA routinely focus on the upper end of the 95 percent confidence interval as the risk level rather than use the mean of the distribution. A series of such conservative assumptions (e.g., on exposure or focusing on the most sensitive humans) can overstate the mean probability of an unfavorable outcome by several orders of magnitude.

If lives are at stake, should we not be conservative when risk estimates are known to be uncertain? In fact, conservatism of this nature is undesirable for three reasons. First, these conservative biases often are not uniform across risks, so that comparative risk judgments may be in error. If we focus on reducing risks for which standard errors are large with respect to their level, then we will save fewer expected lives than if we were guided by the mean of our probability distribution on the risk level. In effect, society will be curtailing the wrong risks, ones that offer less expected health improvement than other available options, for the resources and benefits foregone. The bias that results will cut against new technologies and innovative products. Second, stringent regulation of uncertain risks destroys opportunities for learning, ignoring the lesson of the medical treatment example above. Third and most fundamental, tilting risk assessments in a conservative direction confuses the informational and decision aspects of research about risks. A conceptually sound form of conservatism would have the decision maker (not the risk estimator) adjust the weights on the consequences. Adjusting the probabilities amounts to lying to ourselves about what we expect.

9.4 TOWARD REASONABLE POLICIES TOWARD RISK

Restrictions on a risky activity, such as exposure limits or restrictions in use, should be based on the relative gains and losses of the activity as compared with its alternatives. In thinking about these tradeoffs, one should remember that improvements in mortality and morbidity have come primarily from technological progress and a higher standard of living, not from government regulation or private forbearance.[33] A dramatic case in point is that of postwar Japan, where mortality rates have fallen for all age groups. Over the period 1955–1975, with a rapid rise in the standard of living, mortality rates for men aged 65–69 fell 32 percent; men aged 25–29 had a 64 percent drop.[34] Sustained economic development also seems to be the principal factor in explaining mortality gains in the United States. In contrast, risk-regulation policies often provide few major dividends.[35]

It is useful to think about risk-averting policy in terms of the rates of tradeoff involved, such as the cost per expected life saved. Using this lives-saved standard of value highlights the most effective means of promoting our risk reduction objective.[36] The cost-effectiveness of existing regulations ranges widely, from $200,000 per life saved for airplane cabin fire protection to as much as $132 million per life saved for a 1979 regulation of DES in cattle feed.[37] These wide discrepancies reflect differences among agencies in their risk-cost balancing as well as differences in the character of risk-reducing opportunities. The Federal Aviation Administration has traditionally undervalued lives, looking only at lost earnings, whereas food additive regulations and EPA ambient air quality standards are set without consideration of cost. Elimination of such interagency imbalances would foster better control of risks at less cost.

The fundamental policy question is how far to proceed with lifesaving expenditures. Economists are accused, sometimes with justification, of concluding too quickly that policy choice to promote the saving of lives is merely a question of setting an appropriate price. In contrast, society often is insensitive to the tradeoffs that must be made. Indeed, 80 percent of respondents polled two months after the Exxon *Valdez* oil spill indicated a willingness to pursue greater environmental protection "regardless of cost."[38] Ultimately, however, society must decide how much of a resource commitment it will make.

Learning from Market Outcomes

Market outcomes provide a natural starting point for obtaining information on how risk-reduction policies are valued by their beneficiaries. Health risks are important components of goods and services sold on markets, providing an approach to valuation. Wage differentials for high-risk occupations imply a value of several million dollars for each expected death in the workplace.[39]

Market data for many risk outcomes are not available, in part because government policies are largely directed at situations in which the market is believed not to function effectively, or at all. Thus, we have little price information to guide us when deciding, for example, whether society's resources would be better used to reduce rates of birth defects or to promote better nutrition, or to reduce oil spills from tankers.

The policies for which no market reference is possible are the very ones in which current practice may be furthest from the optimum. How much, for example, is it worth to prevent a low-level risk of genetic damage? Such valuation questions have received little careful consideration. When risks are received collectively, as when a sewage treatment plant or prison is placed in a community, little is learned about valuation, since compensation is rarely paid.[40] The result has been severe inequity for the unfortunate few, and a democratic society that cannot find places to site essential though noxious facilities.

Finding Appropriate Roles

The government's responsibility in generating and using risk information involves structuring a decision process in which individuals and societal institutions work together. Policy choice in a democratic society is, however, complicated by discrepancies between lay and expert opinion. In some situations, the government must decide whether to intervene to overcome apparent limitations on individual choices. But it can be difficult to distinguish irrationality from legitimate citizen preferences. Are people who do not wear seat belts irrational? What about those who wolf down animal fats? Analogous questions arise with respect to policy emphasis. To what extent should the government focus on risks that are of particular concern to its citizens, who may be misinformed and subject to severe errors in perceptions and valuation of risk? Government agencies, subject to political pressures, may find it difficult to set their course in the direction indicated by dispassionate analysis of risks and overall benefits to society.

As science advances and our ability to detect risks improves, our opportunities for influencing risks have proliferated. To date we have proceeded haphazardly, responding to each risk in turn, whether it arises from a new technology, is revealed by scientific investigation, or is catapulted to prominence by media attention. This is not a sensible strategy for making balanced decisions across the entire spectrum of risks.

We need to acknowledge that risks to life and limb are inherent in modern society—indeed in life itself—and that systematic strategies for assessing and responding to risks are overdue. Such strategies will involve significant reassignment of decision-making responsibilities. Individuals should do more for themselves, paying greater attention, for example, to their diets and driving habits. Governments should focus less on microscopic contingencies, and more on human mistakes and misdeeds, the source of far greater risks.

NOTES

1. This chapter was coauthored with Richard J. Zeckhauser and first appeared in *Science*, Vol. 248 (May 4, 1990), pp. 559–564.

2. The role of life-style is discussed by Fuchs (1974), particularly pp. 52–54, who assesses the stark differences in mortality between high-living Nevada and sober Utah.

3. Under certainty, a mere ranking of outcomes is sufficient to determine the best choice. Choices under uncertainty require a more refined, cardinal metric to decide, for example: Is A preferred to a 50–50 chance of B or C? Expected utility theory, due to von Neumann and Morgenstern (1953), enables us to address such questions. Savage (1954) added an axiomatic approach for incorporating subjective probabilities, thus producing a complete prescriptive basis for rational choice under uncertainty.

4. Kunreuther et al. (1978), Tversky and Kahneman (1981), Slovic (1987), Machina (1987), Fischhoff et al. (1981), and Viscusi and Magat (1987).

5. See Fischhoff et al. (1981).

6. See Viscusi and Magat (1987).

7. Baxter and Allen (1989), cited in the *New York Times*, May 22, 1989, p. B7.

8. National Safety Council (1985).

9. Schneider (1989), Roberts (1988), Kerr (1989). For a general assessment of risk and uncertainty, see Wilson and Crouch (1987).

10. See Viscusi, Magat, and Huber (1987) and Samuelson and Zeckhauser (1988).

11. Huber (1983).

12. See Viscusi, Magat, and Huber (1987).

13. Let p be the initial probability of survival, q be the increased probability of survival, purchased at cost z, $U(Y)$ be the utility of income if alive, where $U'(Y) > 0$, and $U(Death) = 0$, independent of income. Assuming expected utility maximization, by definition Z satisfies $pU(Y) + (1-p)U(Death) = (p+q)U(Y-Z)+(1-p-q)U(Death)$, or setting $U(Death) = 0$, $pU(Y) = (p+q)U(Y-Z)$. Totally differentiating, one has

$$\frac{dZ}{dp} = \frac{U(Y - Z) - U(Y)}{(p + q)U'(Y - Z)} < 0.$$

14. See Viscusi, Magat, and Huber (1987).

15. *Wall Street Journal*, March 17, 1989, B12.

16. Bell (1982).

17. Grabowski and Vernon (1983).

18. Ibid.

19. Booth (1988). For example, the drug grancyclovir, used to treat a blindness-threatening eye infection suffered by one in four AIDS victims, was approved for use although it had not completed full clinical testing. "Progress and Placebos," *Wall Street Journal*, June 29, 1989, p. A14, observed some difficulties with our counterbalancing political force approach to drug (and risk) regulation: "Should families of Alzheimer's patients follow the AIDS precedent, busing in about 1,000 of their demented parents to roam the agency's grounds outside of Washington for the benefit of television?"

20. Ames, Magaw, and Gold (1987).

21. See Viscusi, Magat, and Huber (1987).

22. Roberts (1989a).

23. Viscusi and Magat (1987).

24. See Schneider (1989), Roberts (1988), and Kerr (1989).

25. Egan (1989) reported: "'The collapse came as a horrible surprise to us all,' said Robert J. Gore, assistant director of the California Department of Transportation. . . . The Bay Bridge lost a 250 ton section in the earthquake and Mr. Roberts (chief structural engineer for the State Transportation Department) said the standards for it had proved primitive. The collapse was due to 2 million pounds of force shearing off anchor bolts, he said. That's far in excess of what anyone would have calculated,' he said."

26. Roberts (1989b), pp. 1134, 1141.

27. A prominent theory—the so-called efficient markets hypothesis—holds that publicly available information about a firm will be transmitted rapidly into market outcomes as the stock price fully adjusts to reflect the influence of this information. See Fama et al. (1969). Arrow (1982) cites empirical evidence on futures markets, indicating that the operation of these markets may not be ideal.

28. Pratt, Raiffa, and Schlaifer (1965).

29. Berry and Fristedt (1985).

30. When C is bad, 0.5 people are saved on average. When C is good, 90 percent of the trials succeed and 1.9 people are saved on the average; 10 percent of the trials fail and after the switch to A, 0.5 people are saved on average. The expected value is 1.13.

31. Roberts (1989c), Lave (1987), and Lave (1982).

32. Nichols and Zeckhauser (1986).

33. Wildavsky (1988).

34. Data provided by Ministry of Health and Welfare, Japan.

35. Council of Economic Advisors (1987) recently concluded, "In many cases, government control of risk is neither efficient nor effective," p. 207.

36. If very good information is available, one can employ the more refined measure of cost per quality-adjusted life year (QALY) saved, thus taking into account both the number of person-years gained and their quality. See Zeckhauser and Shepard (1976).

37. See Morrall (1986).

38. A *New York Times*/CBS News Poll asked people if they agreed with the statement "Protecting the environment is so important that requirements and standards cannot be too high, and continuing environmental improvements must be made regardless of cost." Seventy-four percent of the public supported the statement in April 1989, shortly after the Exxon *Valdez* spill, while 80 percent agreed with it two months later. The *Times* concluded, "Public support for greater environmental efforts regardless of cost has soared since the Exxon *Valdez* oil spill in Alaska," *New York Times*, July 2, 1989, p. A18.

39. See Viscusi (1983). More generally, see Chapters 3 and 4 of this book.

40. Little heed has been paid to innovative suggestions, such as the proposal of O'Hare, Bacow, and Sanderson (1983) that communities submit negative bids for accepting noxious facilities.

10

Cotton Dust Regulation:
An OSHA Success Story?

10.1 INTRODUCTION

A pivotal regulation in the history of the Occupational Safety and Health Administration is its standard to limit the cotton dust exposures of textile workers. This regulation was the subject of a major internal battle within the Carter administration, served as the focal point of a fundamental U.S. Supreme Court decision in the risk-regulation area, and was the target of a controversial reassessment under the Reagan administration.

The source of the controversy can be traced to several factors. The cotton dust standard is an important regulation from the standpoint of the economic costs it imposes on the textile industry. But the presence of a significant cost impact does not distinguish this regulation. Of much greater significance is the link to worker health, where the health impact in question is a lung disease called byssinosis. Many experts have challenged whether or not there is a causal link between cotton dust and byssinosis. Some have observed that if there is such a link, protective equipment such as dust masks would be a more cost-effective response than equipment to control the level of cotton dust in the textile plant.

Another factor that has distinguished the controversy over the cotton dust standard is the extent of the analysis to which that standard has been exposed since its adoption. Although it is now routine practice to assess the merits of newly proposed OSHA regulations, they are not usually accorded careful scrutiny once they have been issued. In contrast, the OSHA cotton dust standard was the object of an extensive reassessment during 1982 and 1983, which was much more detailed than the initial analysis. Although firms were not required to be in compliance until 1984, most of the expenditures needed to achieve compliance had been made. The retrospective assessment of the costs and health impacts of these efforts provide a detailed perspective on the impact of OSHA regulations.

Examination of a particular case study of OSHA regulations offers a number of advantages over a broader assessment of differences in industry risk levels, such as that in Chapters 11 and 12. By focusing on a particular industry it will be possible to assess the specific changes in the workplace technology that were instituted in response to the regulation. Moreover, we will be able to examine the way in which workplace characteristics have been altered as firms have achieved compliance with regulations. This regulation deals with a class of occupational diseases that are difficult to monitor and do not get captured in the reported statistics on injuries and illnesses. However, by considering the change in workers' environmental exposures in conjunction with scientifically established dose-response relationships, we will be able to estimate the observed impacts of OSHA on worker health that would otherwise go undetected. This analysis at the micro level will show that for this particular area of OSHA regulation, the agency's activities have been quite influential.

10.2 GENESIS OF THE STANDARD

OSHA's cotton dust standard was issued in June 1978.[1] The source of the concern behind OSHA's initiative derived from the link between cotton dust and the disease byssinosis, which Ralph Nader labeled "brown lung" disease in an effort to draw a parallel with the "black lung" risks faced by coal miners.

Byssinosis is not a disease with uniform health effects but instead consists of several stages, with differing degrees of severity.[2] Grade 1/2 byssinosis involves chest tightness or breathing difficulties on the first day of the workweek, normally Monday mornings. Grade 1 byssinosis involves occasional chest tightness or breathing difficulties on every Monday. If the worker experiences such problems on other days as well, he or she is placed in Grade 2. Finally, workers suffering from Grade 2 symptoms and who show evidence of permanent incapacity are placed in Grade 3. In addition to byssinosis grades of this type for current and recent workers, there are also cases of partial and total disability that have been identified among retired cotton textile workers.

The disease generally involves a progression through a series of grades, and, with the exception of cases in Grade 3 and cases involving actual disabilities, all of these health impacts may be reversible.[3] When transferred to non-cotton-dust areas, workers who fall into the low byssinosis grades are likely to lose the symptoms of the disease. Rotation of this type is now widespread in the textile industry.

Only Grade 3 byssinosis and cases entailing disabilities clearly involve chronic health effects, notably diminished lung capacity. According to the evidence, this reduction of lung function is not a prelude to some other ailment, such as lung cancer. The worker does not face a major risk of early death, and the employee is not disabled to the same extent as are victims of severe accidents, such as those who have lost the use of their limbs. Diminished lung capacity and occasional coughing is not a trivial ailment, but it is not as severe as many other targets of OSHA regulation.

The link of chronic byssinosis effects to cotton dust is also controversial because the relevant medical evidence on the nature of the causal link is not conclusive.[4] Is cotton dust the cause of byssinosis, or is it some agent correlated with the presence of cotton dust? The link is difficult to distinguish because of the high rates of cigarette smoking among textile mill workers and the small number of chronic byssinosis cases. Indeed, the major studies that have been conducted on the relationships between cotton dust and byssinosis do not even attempt to distinguish the Grade 3 cases or disabilities, since many of these more severe effects are not apparent until after the worker has retired.[5] Because the available medical evidence is imprecise, various suggestions have been made to refine the evidence, including the possibility of conducting experiments at plants not yet in compliance with the standard.[6]

It is expected that the largest impact of the cotton dust standard will be in preventing the less serious grades of byssinosis. According to estimates, over two-thirds of all cases that will be prevented by the standard fall in Grades 1/2 and 1. Of the remaining cases prevented, only a small number can be said to entail the prevention of serious ailments. Overall it is expected that under 7 percent of all cases of byssinosis at any one time involve total disability, and these occur with a substantial time lag of up to three decades.

There have been other reasons for assuming that the byssinosis threat might be exaggerated. Available studies of the relationships between cotton dust exposures and worker health had taken as their reference point the work practices of the textile industry in 1970 rather than their practices at the time of the standard's introduction.[7] Moreover, they have failed to explore the possibilities of reducing the risk by means other than reducing the cotton dust in the plant's atmosphere. For instance, if there were medical surveillance of workers coupled with a sufficiently vigorous policy of rotation, all chronic byssinosis cases could be prevented. A much more ambitious rotation policy could prevent all Grade 2 cases as well. To reduce the frequency of rotation, workers exposed to cotton dust could be required to wear protective equipment such as disposable cotton masks during the periods of work when the cotton dust levels were high.

OSHA has preferred not to rely on alternatives such as the use of masks and the rotation of workers because of unions' aversion to solutions that entail the use of such equipment; the unions' position has been that it is preferable to make the work environment safe whenever possible. Behind that position has been the widely recognized fact that workers themselves commonly object to wearing protective devices if any alternative control method exists.

The 1978 cotton dust standard did more than simply prescribe limits for the amount of cotton dust in the plant environment. It adopted a mix of approaches to regulating this hazard.[8] The standard provides for engineering controls, medical surveillance, and respirators in situations of extreme exposure, such as during maintenance activities. The most novel aspect of the standard is that it is not uniform for all exposed worker groups. The standard establishes a permissible exposure limit for respirable cotton dust particles of 200 micrograms per cubic meter of air (200 $\mu g/m^3$) for yarn manufacturing, 750 $\mu g/m^3$ for slashing and weaving operations, and 500 $\mu g/m^3$ for all other processes. OSHA required that the medical surveillance provisions should be in place by mid-1979, but firms had until March 1984 to comply with the exposure limits.

This variation in standards is dictated partly by the cost differences that are entailed in controlling cotton dust at different stages of processing and partly by the differences in the severity of the types of cotton dust exposure encountered at each stage. Table 10-1 presents data based on OSHA's analysis of the differences at the time the cotton standard was adopted. The figures in Table 10-1 purport to show what the incremental cost would be for preventing one additional case of byssinosis

Table 10-1. Incremental Cost Per Year of Preventing an Additional Case of Byssinosis at Three Exposure Levels as of 1978[a]

	Exposure level (*in µg cotton dust particles/m³ air*)		
State of processing	500	200	100
Yarn preparation	56	593	6,268
Mill slashing and weaving	22	1,338	1,867

[a]In thousands of dollars.
Source: W. K. Viscusi (1983), p. 125.

at different exposure levels. (As we shall presently see, actual costs incurred have proven to be quite different from those that were predicted.) As the table shows, the projected marginal cost per case rises much more rapidly for mill slashing and weaving than it does for yarn preparation.

OSHA's decision to impose a tighter standard for yarn preparation is consistent with the key principle that where a given risk such as byssinosis arises from two different sources, expenditures made to reduce the risk from each of the two sources ought to be equal at the margin in order to maximize the overall effectiveness of those expenditures. The standards selected represent an application of that principle. However, in order to equalize the marginal costs per byssinosis case, the 200-µg/m³ standard for yarn preparation should be coupled with a standard for mill slashing and weaving of under 400-µg/m³ rather than the more relaxed 750-µg/m³ level that was selected. Although the precise basis for OSHA's differentiation is unclear, that feature of the standard may have been the result of either of two factors: It may have been an attempt to equalize the risk of cotton dust exposure,[9] or it may have been an effort to set standards at the level of stringency that could be achieved without vastly increasing the costs of compliance.

The data in Table 10-1 suggest that on a prospective basis the overall efficacy of the standard in promoting worker health did not appear to be very high. In the case of yarn preparation, where the marginal costs are greatest, the costs per year of preventing an additional case of byssinosis comes to almost $600,000. Since the great majority of these ailments involve only inconsequential health effects (Grades 1/2 and 1), these cost levels appear to be extraordinarily high. If we include only cases of Grade 2 byssinosis or higher, the costs per year rise to almost $2 million (1978 prices) per case prevented. This figure is comparable to some of the value-of-life estimates that were reviewed in Chapter 4. The high projected cost levels for the health benefits achieved and the availability of alternative policies that might be more cost-effective led to an extended debate over the efficacy of the standard.

Economists in the Carter White House opposed the standard after it had been proposed by OSHA.[10] Led by the chairman of the Council of Economic Advisors, Charles Schultze, they were successful in obtaining President Carter's support in a decision not to issue the standard. After a subsequent appeal by Secretary of Labor

Marshall, the president reversed his earlier decision and decided to issue the regulation.

The attempt to block the cotton dust standard then shifted to the courts. The American Textile Manufacturers' Institute challenged the OSHA standard on the grounds that the benefits were not commensurate with the costs. In a landmark decision that had a major effect on all risk-regulation agencies, the U.S. Supreme Court upheld the standard and explicitly ruled out the use of a benefit-cost test. The court concluded that OSHA had to promote risk reduction as long as there was a technical possibility of compliance, a criterion that the court interpreted as meaning "capable of being done."[11]

In actual practice, the Supreme Court's criterion has little practical meaning. Almost any risk can be reduced further through additional expenditures. As the data in Table 10-1 indicate, tighter standards could have been imposed, albeit at higher costs. Studies prepared subsequent to 1978 confirmed, for instance, that the standard for yarn preparation could be tightened considerably at a cost double that incurred in achieving the OSHA standard.[12] Any question of feasibility, therefore, cannot escape recognizing cost considerations.

The U.S. Supreme Court's decision that OSHA's legislative mandate prohibits the use of a benefit-cost test has had widespread ramifications. Before the issuance of that decision, Carter's White House staff routinely had applied a cost-effectiveness test to the proposed measures of the regulatory agencies and had urged them to take greater cognizance of the relationship of benefits to costs. Under Present Reagan's Executive Order 11291, the Office of Management and Budget attempted to impose a benefit-cost test on new regulations, but in recognition of the Supreme Court decision it specifically exempted cases that "violated the agency's legislation." Accordingly, agencies may sometimes disregard the balancing of benefits and costs, as in the case of the EPA ambient air standards for which the Clean Air Act specifically prohibits any consideration of costs.

As part of the Reagan administration's review of potentially unproductive regulations, OSHA undertook a full reassessment of the merits of the cotton dust standard. This review included an analysis of the cost-effectiveness of loosening or tightening the standard as well as the efficacy of mandating the use of protective equipment, such as the use of cotton dust masks.[13] Although the use of such masks for a few hours a day in high-exposure situations coupled with a rotation policy would often produce the same benefits as a cotton dust standard, OSHA did not pursue this option; the agency's general aversion to solutions that leave the environmental source of the hazard unchanged continued to dictate its recommendations.

It is clear that the costs of the mask-and-rotation approach would be below the costs of changing the workplace technology. There might, however, be problems of enforcement and discomfiture for the workers.[14] But there is some evidence that even if such factors are taken into account, the mask-and-rotation alternative would still be a more cost-effective approach except in extreme exposure situations.

Because OSHA has required that such masks be worn as a temporary measure in situations where compliance had not yet been achieved, some experience with the approach already exists. In 1978, for example, 35 percent of all workers exposed to cotton dust were required to wear dust masks; yet no serious problems of worker noncompliance with the regulation have been reported.[15] To be sure, some problems would still arise if the widespread use of masks were mandated. Some types of masks, notably those required in high-exposure areas, may not fit the worker's face, particularly for workers with full beards. Workers may surreptitiously discard their masks if they find them uncomfortable. But the costs associated with overcoming such problems appear of an order of magnitude that does not impair the relative cost-effectiveness of this politically unattractive alternative.

Among the various important lessons to be drawn from the country's experience with the cotton dust standard is the fact that industry's responses to such standards will not be simple. During the Carter administration, the American Textile Manufacturers Institute (ATMI), composed mainly of the larger firms in the industry, had expressed bitter opposition to the application of the cotton dust standard, and it took its case to the U.S. Supreme Court. During the Reagan administration's reassessment of the standard, ATMI continued to request a relaxation of the standard, but it focused its lobbying effort with OSHA almost exclusively on the details of the monitoring and surveillance provisions. The Office of Management and Budget pressed for the more cost-effective protective equipment and rotation approach and, after the interagency debate had reached Vice President Bush, OMB explicitly requested the industry's support for that alternative. But ATMI failed to act in support of OMB. That failure was probably a consequence of the substantial investments already made to comply with the standard; the industry had already made almost two-thirds of the expenditures needed to achieve compliance.[16] Moreover, the large firms that dominate ATMI, already largely in compliance, could use the standard to squeeze some of the smaller competitors that had not yet reached the same level of compliance. As a result, after OSHA had given the cotton dust standard a more thorough retrospective assessment than any other OSHA regulation has yet received, the agency did not alter the essential features of the standard.

10.3 COSTS AND CONSEQUENCES

The source of much of the political controversy over the cotton dust standard was the high levels of costs that would be imposed. To meet the cotton dust exposure limits, firms often had to make substantial changes in their production technology. In some instances, these modifications would be made without basically altering the existing technology. Ventilation and air filtration equipment most often fit this characterization. When these measures were not sufficient to ensure compliance, however, firms had to make more fundamental changes in their technology, and many firms used this opportunity to overhaul their plant and equipment.

One particular case of such changes was in the operations in which the cotton bales are opened, the cotton is cleaned and blended, and the fiber is converted into a continuous piece (carding). Firms replaced lower speed cards with higher speed cards, equipping the new cards with up-to-date dust-control features. Firms also introduced automatic opening systems, chute feed systems for cards, and automatic systems for waste collection.[17] According to a 1983 estimate, the industry would

spend about $171 million on ventilation equipment and $428 million on new production equipment between 1978 and the time when full compliance is achieved.[18]

Although many of these investments are perhaps being triggered by the standard,
most of them have been undertaken in order to increase productivity. For instance,
about $353 million of the $428 million of new production equipment was intended
for that purpose, rather than to meet the standard. Consequently, capital costs
specifically attributable to the standard will amount to only $246 million by the time
compliance is achieved. Most of the remaining costs associated with reducing
cotton dust exposure have been energy costs and labor costs, which are directly
related to the operation of the ventilation equipment and the production equipment.
If one converts these capital costs and operating costs to an equivalent annual
expenditure, the total comes to $53 million.[19]

What effects on the health of workers can be discerned? The usual starting point
for analyzing any such impact is to examine reported rates of occupational injuries
and illnesses. In the textile industry as in other industries, the illness data do not
exist in a long and continuous time series. Moreover, byssinosis cases, representing
illnesses rather than accidents, are notoriously underreported. The less severe
grades of byssinosis do not have sufficiently adverse effects to lead to lost workdays
or to other consequences that might be reflected in the statistics. Chronic byssinosis
cases only emerge after a considerable period of exposure, so that the effects of the
new standard in reducing the incidence of such cases would not yet be apparent.

As a result, the limited data on illnesses can only be suggestive.[20] From 1978 to
1982, the incidence of reported work-related illnesses in the textile mill products
industry dropped from 1.9 cases per 1000 workers to 1.5 cases per 1000 workers.
Over that same period, the rate of illnesses per 1000 workers involving at least one
lost day of work dropped from 0.6 to 0.5. In each instance, the trend is in the
expected direction if the standard has had a favorable effect. However, the coverage
of series of this kind is notoriously incomplete, and it is likely that only a fraction of
the byssinosis cases are captured in the statistics.

In my efforts to measure the effects of the standard upon the health of workers, I
uncovered one unanticipated phenomenon that could well be characteristic of other
cases involving the introduction of machinery on a large scale. Byssinosis cases
represent an illness, not an injury. But the more typical analysis of OSHA's role
concentrates on injuries as well as illnesses. Accordingly, following the usual design of OSHA-related studies, I analyzed the injury and illness rates of the textile
mill products industry for what clues they might offer. Figure 10-1, which portrays
the rates of injuries and illnesses among workers in the industry that entailed at least
one lost day of work, presents some quite unexpected results.

Somewhat contrary to expectations, the measure exhibits an alarming upward
jump in 1978, the year the standard was introduced. Not until 1982 does it return to
the level prevailing in 1976 and 1977. The fact that the measure remained high for
four consecutive years suggests that the increase was not a random aberration but
the result of a substantial change in the risks to which workers were exposed in the
textile industry.

One possibility to be considered, of course, was that the increase in risk was a

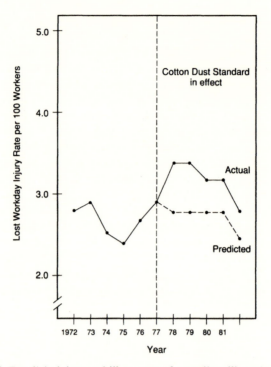

Figure 10.1 Trends in injury and illness rates for textile mill products industry

phenomenon associated with cyclical fluctuations in the industry. Using data for the period 1960–1982, I explored that possibility with some care. The details of my statistical analysis appear in Appendix 10A. In essence, I used the experience of 1960–1977, the years before the introduction of the standard, to predict the risk level that should have been expected from 1978 to 1982, given the level of activity of the industry, the proportion of female employees in the industry, and the proportion of production workers in the industry in each of those years.

The statistical manipulations generate the "predicted" values shown in Figure 10-1. As the data in Appendix 10A show, each of the variables mentioned did have their expected relation to rates of injury and illness involving a lost workday but taken together they predicted a significantly lower rate for the period after 1977 than in fact occurred. That low expected value, it should be noted, was due in part to the fact that the U.S. textile industry, unlike the country as a whole, did not experience an upswing in 1978 and 1979.[21] Over the 1978–1982 period, the reported accidents and illnesses exceeded the predicted figure by 19,000, or 13 percent.

There are several conjectures one might advance to explain the increase in injury rates. First, the higher level of lost workday accidents may have been a consequence of the new technologies that were introduced in connection with meeting the standard. These technologies often involve faster production speeds and higher productivity both in yarn preparation and in weaving. The pattern shown in Figure 10-1 is consistent with the hypothesis that the new equipment may have led to a temporary increase in accidents associated with a learning period.

However, as noted earlier, less than one-fifth of the new production equipment purchased from 1978 to 1982 was directly related to compliance with the standard,[22] the rest being a response to the fact that modernization of the industry's equipment had been long overdue. The safety implications of adjustment to new technologies merit further exploration, but it seems unlikely that the cotton dust regulation alone was responsible for this increase in accidents.

A second possible explanation for the accident increase is that the imposition of the cotton dust standard made firms more vigilant in their reporting of injuries and illnesses; the initial years of OSHA regulation, for example, had apparently led to a sharp increase in the reporting of injuries. Nevertheless, that hypothesis does not seem very plausible. OSHA's imposition of the cotton standard was not accompanied by any evidence of increased vigilance on its part. In the years following the introduction of the standard, the number of inspections per worker declined somewhat, and the total penalties per worker imposed by OSHA inspectors remained unchanged.[23] Besides, if the announcement of the new standard had stimulated more complete reporting, the statistical effect would not have greatly affected the data on the incidence of reported accidents involving lost workdays since the identification of these injuries is less a matter of discretion than the overall accident rate. If any tie existed between the adoption of the standard and an increase in reporting coverage, it may have been through the fact that the larger and more modern firms expanded their operations while many older plants ceased operations in reaction to the introduction of the standard. As a rule, larger firms are known to be more vigilant in reporting injuries.

Because the illness-and-injury data suffer from such obvious limitations as a guide to the effectiveness of the standards in controlling byssinosis, I turned to other measures that might be reflecting this relationship. The data on worker quit behavior offered an alternative possibility. According to my statistical studies using several sets of data, about one-third of the difference in quit rate levels among different manufacturing industries is accounted for by variations in the risks that workers experience in those industries.[24] If the cotton dust standard were effective, therefore, one would expect to see some decline in the quit rates experienced by the textile industry. To be sure, the relationship might not be very strong. Severe byssinosis cases, as we observed earlier, are a long time in gestation. On the other hand, milder forms of byssinosis occur more rapidly and are more rapidly reversible, so that one would expect workers to be aware of the improvement in their health that resulted from a decrease in the cotton dust exposure.

The solid line in Figure 10-2 represents the quit rate trend in the textile industry from 1972 to 1981; after that year, the Bureau of Labor Statistics suspended collection of the turnover data. After the advent of the cotton dust standard, the quit rate rose for one year, then resumed a downward trend that had dominated through most of the 1970s. The "predicted" rates in Figure 10-2, portrayed by a dotted line, were derived by a procedure similar to that used earlier, when predicting the injury and illness rates of the textile products industry; the details of that estimating process appear in Appendix 10A.

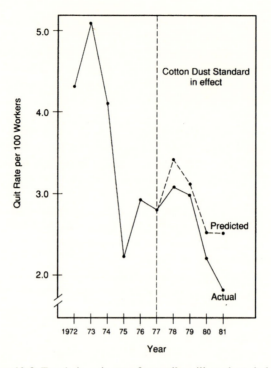

Figure 10.2 Trends in quit rates for textile mill products industry

In order to derive these estimates, I hypothesized that worker quit rates would be positively related to the injury rate and to the fraction of female employees in the industry. Higher wages should reduce the quit rate, and there should be an increase in quit rates during cyclical upturns, such upturns being reflected in hours worked and overtime hours worked per week. For the years 1960–1977, the data conformed closely to expectations, with the fraction of female employees, wages, and overtime hours making the largest contributions; the resulting equations provided the basis for the "predicted" data from 1978 to 1981.

Of course, many workers' decisions to quit may be motivated not by actual changes in their health but by their perception of the effect the job will ultimately have on their health. Similarly, because byssinosis is not disabling or severely limiting in its early stages, some workers suffering from the disease will refuse to quit. The evidence for quit rates consequently does not provide a measure of the health impact per se. The quit rate results in conjunction with the limited data on illnesses are consistent with the view that the cotton dust standard had a beneficial health effect, but they do not enable us to calculate the magnitude of the effect.

10.4 ESTIMATING COST-EFFECTIVENESS

Although each of the approaches that have been presented so far offers some basis for estimating the cost effectiveness of the cotton dust standard, there is another approach that lends itself more readily to such a calculation. In this approach, we begin by estimating the health effects of the cotton dust standard from two kinds of data: the number of workers operating or expected to operate in textile product factories after 1978, and field medical studies on the relative incidence of byssinosis under different conditions of exposure to cotton dust. Coupling these two sets of data, we can produce estimates of the number of cases of byssinosis, according to year of onset and grade of severity, that could be expected to be prevented by the standard. As noted above, these health relationships do not take into account the role played by medical surveillance and worker rotation, both of which increased in the 1970s; as a result, the estimates may overstate the impact of the changes in the workplace technology. But to some extent medical surveillance and other measures were undertaken in response to the standard; accordingly, the data may be interpreted as providing an estimate of the overall impact of all of the features of the regulation.

Table 10-2 summarizes the estimates of the reduction in byssinosis cases between 1978 and 1982 brought about by introduction of the standard, as well as the additional reductions to be anticipated after 1984, the year when full compliance was to be achieved. Although OSHA did not require that firms comply with the cotton dust exposure requirements until 1984, firms had made sufficient changes by 1982 to justify the assumption that over two-thirds of the anticipated reduction in byssinosis cases was already occurring in that year. In short, the estimates suggest that the firms' health-related investments were already having a substantial impact.

According to estimates of this sort, the number of byssinosis cases eliminated annually when full compliance is in effect will be over 9,000, although over half of these are in the less severe Grades 1/2 and 1. The total number of disabling cases eventually eliminated per year is about 1,700, of which about 500 are total disabilities. The severe cases prevented by the standard will not be among active workers but among workers who have retired, and the reduction will not be apparent for many years because of the long lags involved.

In order to assess the efficacy of the standard, it is necessary to obtain some measure of the costs. The costs of the program from 1978 to 1982 could be estimated from sources already described, and the incremental costs after the deadline year, 1984, could also be estimated. Similarly, the benefits in each year can be estimated using results along the lines of those in Table 10-2. In each case, one

Table 10-2. Estimated Reduction in Byssinosis Cases
Associated with Introduction of Cotton Dust Standard

Type of case	Number of cases reduced per year, 1978–1982	Total cases reduced per year with full compliance[a]
Byssinosis Grades 1/2 and 1	3,517	5,047
Byssinosis over Grade 1	1,634	2,349
Partial disabilities	843	1,210
Total disabilities	339	487

[a]The results pertain to the steady-state outcome.

Source: Exhibit 5-8 of Centaur Associates (1983) and calculations by the author. Also note that the author served as the principal outside consultant on the Centaur study.

should discount the deferred impacts appropriately to take into account the different timing of the effects. Most of the costs are immediate, whereas the benefits are deferred, particularly for the more severe health effects. The discounting rate used for this purpose was 10 percent.[25]

Table 10-3 summarizes the result of these calculations for different grades of byssinosis. Obviously, these cost estimates exclude the costs of any increased accidents that may have resulted from the change in workplace technologies, but given the tenuous nature of the link between those accidents and the cotton dust standard, that exclusion seems justified. The average costs per case prevented will be higher with full compliance than for the 1978–82 period. This pattern reflects the expectation that the cost per case is likely to be higher for firms that were not yet in compliance by 1982 than for those in compliance by that date; a similar pattern is found in other regulatory contexts, and it is to be expected on theoretical grounds.[26]

It is instructive to compare the estimates in Table 10-3 with those that had been prepared in 1978, shown in Table 10-1. The cost per reduced case year shown in Table 10-3 is roughly $9,000, which is only a fraction of the various 1978 projections.

The 1978 projections appear to have been high for a number of reasons, including various methodological differences in the estimates of benefits. By far the most important difference was that OSHA and firms in the industry had initially overestimated their compliance costs. Based on discussions with industry officials, OSHA originally projected that the capital costs would be $971 million in 1982 prices but by 1983 these estimates were lowered to $246 million.[27] It is widely believed that benefit estimates are usually less precise than are the cost estimates. Experience in the cotton dust case suggests that cost estimates merit close scrutiny as well.

The estimates in Table 10-3 provide measures of the costs of preventing byssinosis cases, distinguishing between cases of increasing severity. Some of the patterns in the table are noteworthy. Grades 1/2 and 1 of the byssinosis disease, it will be remembered, manifest themselves by some difficulty in breathing on the first day of the workweek, a difficulty that is reversible by changing the environment. Such cases are preventable at a cost of $10,000 per case per year, which is below the

Table 10-3. Estimated Cost per Year of Preventing One Case of Byssinosis by Introduction of Cotton Dust Standard

Type of case	Costs in $thousands	
	Years 1978–1982	With full compliance
All cases	9	9
Total byssinosis cases over Grade 1 and disabilities	50	54
Total partial and total disabilities	350	378
Total disabilities	1,220	1,318

Source: Exhibit 5-9 of Centaur Associates (1983) and calculations by the author. Also note that the author served as the principal outside consultant on the Centaur study.

estimate of $25,000 of the value placed by workers on avoiding a serious accident, as revealed in their wage-risk tradeoffs.[28] At face value, the costs seem somewhat disproportionate to the benefits. It should be noted, too, that the costs of avoiding a case of partial or total disability also seem high—$378,000 per year for cases of partial disability and over $1,000,000 per year for total disability alone. These magnitudes are comparable to some of the lower estimates obtained for the implicit value of life (see Chapter 4).

The cotton dust standard appears most clearly justified for its effects in preventing moderately serious cases, those that fall in Grade 2 and above; these cases, it will be remembered, involve some loss of lung function throughout the workweek. Even in such cases, however, it takes a cost of $54,000 per year to avoid the symptoms involved.

The fundamental regulatory policy issue, however, is not so much whether workers' health should be better protected but whether the cotton dust standard approach is the most cost-effective means of achieving that result. In absolute terms the standard is a relatively costly means to promote worker health. Moreover, as was observed earlier, the relative costs of the standard are high compared with an option that utilizes protective equipment such as masks in conjunction with the rotation of workers. The chief cost of the alternative is likely to be the discomfort to workers of wearing the masks. But these would need to be worn only a few hours a day in most cases, so the level of extra wage compensation needed to make the protective equipment option preferable to workers may not be great.

Perhaps the greatest impediment to the introduction of equipment solutions such as these may not be unions' opposition to such measures but rather OSHA's failure to fashion a mechanism for ensuring that there is adequate financial compensation for the affected workers. In a competitive market, the wages for jobs involving the use of protective devices such as masks will presumably rise to take into account the associated discomfort. Formalizing such compensation, however, creates an apparent link between the compensation and the change in workplace conditions, thereby improving the chances that workers will accept the change.

Such market-oriented compensation schemes have not been used in the regulation of labor markets. But they may have been used in other regulatory situations; airlines that overbook now offer compensation to bumped passengers or to volunteers who will accept the bumping in return for the compensation. Financial compensation could play a similar beneficial role in promoting safety policies for workers in situations such as those posed by the cotton dust hazard.

10.5 *EX ANTE* VERSUS *EX POST* REGULATORY ANALYSIS[29]

The cotton dust regulation marked the first instance of a health and safety standard that received a comprehensive regulatory analysis both before and after it was issued. The Research Triangle Institute (RTI) prepared the initial study of the prospective effects of the regulation in 1976, and Centaur Associates prepared a retrospective assessment of the standard in 1983. I was a coauthor and the principal outside consultant on the Centaur report.[30] Outside consulting firms, not the agencies themselves, are generally responsible for the substance of all analyses of major proposed federal regulations.

Since *ex ante* regulatory analyses are a frequent target of policy debate, it is useful to assess how accurate the initial RTI assessments were. What were the biases and sources of error in the analysis? Were there any systematic deficiencies that should alert us to potential pitfalls in future regulatory analyses? Table 10-4 summarizes the differences in the *ex ante* and *ex post* assessments of the cotton dust standard.

Although the cotton dust standard may be an expensive means for promoting worker health, it is less expensive than was believed initially. In order to achieve the

Table 10-4. Summary of Changes in Regulatory Analysis: Nature of Assumptions

Component	OSHA/RTI prospective analysis	OSHA/Centaur retrospective analysis
Population at risk	233,000 workers (RTI); over 300,000 workers in 1978 (OSHA)	105,000 workers in 1978
Exposed population	Based on worker turnover (confused monthly and annual turnover rates)	Based on steady-state worker population
Exposure assumption	1,000 $\mu g/m^3$ cotton dust	Actual exposure levels
Dose-response relationships	Merchant et al. byssinosis study (1973a,b)	Merchant et al. study (1973a,b) and Beck et al. retirement and disability study (1981)
Health impacts considered	Byssinosis, not distinguished by severity; considered only worker population turnover rate (incorrectly stated)	Byssinosis cases of different severity grades, partial and total disabilities; considered active-worker population and retired population aged 45 and over
Duration of health impacts	Not considered	Analyzed case years to distinguish impacts of different duration
Lags of discounting	Not considered	Ten years for byssinosis grades above 1; 25 years for disabilities (also sensitivity analysis on lag time)
Procedure to estimate costs of standard	Projected costs assuming 1,000 $\mu g/m^3$ exposures	Actual historical costs and estimated future costs using actual exposure levels to meet alternative standards
Total estimated investment costs	$1.4 billion[a] capital costs to meet current standard	$269 million[a] capital costs to meet current standards
Estimated annual operating costs associated with investment	$173 million[a]	$29 million[a]
Cost-effectiveness measures	Not computed but can be calculated using data in report	Indices calculated for impacts of differing severity and with sensitivity analysis

[a] 1982 dollars.

Source: P. W. Kolp and W. K. Viscusi (1986), in V. Kerry Smith, ed., p. 125.

existing OSHA cotton dust standard when starting from conditions present in the cotton textile industry prior to 1978, the marginal cost per byssinosis and disability case year prevented is about $8,340 when assuming a real discount rate of 10 percent and a relatively long lag time for development of the more serious health effects related to cotton dust exposure. Improvement at approximately the historical cost-effectiveness rate is still possible by continuing to implement the current standard. In contrast, the original prospective marginal cost per case of byssinosis prevented was estimated at $593,000 (in 1980 dollars) for yarn processing, which is the main segment of cotton operations affected by the standard. The initial analysis underestimated the standard's cost-effectiveness based on this retrospective assessment of the actual costs imposed by the standard.

The apparent improved efficacy of the standard can be traced to several factors involved in performing the two regulatory analyses. These differences are summarized in Table 10-4 and will only be highlighted here. First, there were factual errors in the initial prospective analysis, such as the confusion of the monthly and annual turnover rates. The only major lesson one can draw here is the importance of exercising care, since simple errors affected the results by an order of magnitude or more, thus distorting the entire analysis.

Second, there were conceptual shortcomings in the original analysis. These deficiencies stemmed from the difficulties posed by applying dose-response relationships to a changing worker population. Since the applicable relationships were linear, the most straightforward approach was to estimate the health effects for the steady-state population. The differing length of the ailments associated with cotton dust exposure also posed difficulties, but by converting the health effects into case years comparability could be established. Finally, the lags involved in the more serious health effects also needed to be addressed, which was accomplished by discounting these deferred impacts.

Many of the foregoing shortcomings in the original OSHA/RTI analysis represent substantial deficiencies that could have been corrected by undertaking a sound analysis initially. Other differences pertain to factors that were not known at the time of OSHA's initial prospective assessment but became known once some information had been acquired about the standard.

The first such difference was in terms of the costs of the standard. Capital costs were overestimated by a factor of 5 in the initial analysis for two reasons. The analysts assumed that the cotton dust exposure starting point for firms was the previous level of the OSHA standard, whereas in fact the exposures averaged less than this limit. In addition, the engineering studies done to ascertain the cost of controls were not in line with the actual costs. This was in part because of an overestimate of the numbers of plants and worker exposures to be controlled. A more thorough survey and analysis of the industry would have avoided these overestimates and may have uncovered the more likely (and less costly) methods that the industry actually used to control exposure to cotton dust.

The benefits associated with the standard were refined in the retrospective analysis in two ways. First, there was a better understanding of how many workers were in fact exposed to cotton dust levels of differing severity. The actual population at risk was under half what was believed initially and was exposed to a lower level of cotton dust than OSHA believed. Both difficulties were avoidable with a survey and related analyses of the cotton textile industry.

The second benefit refinement stemmed from an improvement in our information about the health effects. At the time the standard was promulgated, no study had yet identified any permanent health impacts for former cotton dust workers. The study by Beck et al. (1981) made it possible to estimate the impact of the standard on disabilities among older and retired workers. Since these health effects are the most severe impacts involved, inclusion of them in the analysis increases the value one places on the benefits of the standard.

A final addition to the scientific basis of the standard was a report by the National Research Council (1982) that questioned whether or not there was a causal link between cotton dust and chronic byssinosis. Suppose that cotton dust per se is not the cause of byssinosis, but rather the cause is some chemical agent correlated with the presence of cotton dust. So long as the cotton dust standard reduces whatever causal agent is involved in generating byssinosis it will be effective. Nevertheless, this report should be a signal of the importance of continued assessment of a standard's efficacy.

Overall, results of the prospective analysis of the cotton dust standard bore little relationship to its actual performance based on an OSHA study of the five years of experience since the advent of the standard. Although the health effects or risk-assessment aspects of the analysis have been greatly altered by the retrospective analysis, there are equal or greater deficiencies throughout all aspects of the original prospective assessment. The usual concerns about the uncertainties involved in prospective regulatory analyses are in many respects too narrow. Not only are there well-known uncertainties involved in the risk assessment, but many of the aspects of a regulatory analysis that are believed to be known with precision are not. This was especially true of the initial cost analysis of the cotton dust standard. One should consequently not adopt the simplistic view that the risk assessment components are more speculative than cost estimates but instead should exercise care in preparing and interpreting all of the aspects of the analysis.

Uncertainty is present in all aspects of a study of the costs and effects of health and environmental risks. Decision makers can develop reasonable strategies to diminish risk only to the degree that more accurate estimates of costs and effects result from regulatory analyses of proposed policies. In the cotton dust case, a more thorough initial survey and microeconomic analysis of the textile industry combined with a sound method for aggregating and comparing costs and health effects could have improved the certainty and accuracy of the results. This failure to prepare sound regulatory analyses as a basis for policy design does not appear to be an isolated case. This instance underscores the importance of expending sufficient time and resources in initial assessments of health and environmental risks that will have major public policy implications and national impacts. In the cotton dust case, a substantial overstatement of costs in the original analysis was partly compensated for by an overstatement of expected health effects. These kinds of errors need not be similar in magnitude or direction. The fact that the most cost-effective cotton dust standard was apparently chosen from among alternate proposals can be primarily attributed to luck. The bitter debate over the standard can be traced in part to faulty regulatory analysis that exaggerated the burdens imposed.

10.6 CONCLUSION

As a general rule, OSHA regulations are not widely believed to have significantly influenced health and safety in the factory. In the cotton dust case, however, the data suggest that the standard is having a considerable impact. Data on the relationship between exposure doses and disease incidence, as well as the fragmentary illness data and the evidence based on worker turnover, suggest that the risks of byssinosis have been reduced dramatically. Such beneficial effects will not, however, be apparent in accident rate statistics, which are the focus of Chapters 11 and 12 as well as almost all other assessments of OSHA's efficacy.

The current exposure levels are not the lowest that are "capable of being done," and if one were to follow the U.S. Supreme Court's guidance, a tightening of the standard would be warranted. Such an action, however, would not generate health benefits commensurate with the value that workers place upon them. Indeed, there are at least two grounds for concluding that the present standard is not an efficacious means for promoting worker health. One is its cost, which is remarkably high in comparison with any value that can be reasonably placed upon its achievements. The second is the fact that a much cheaper alternative is available.

In defense of the standard, however, it should be noted that the standard has proven to be much more cost-effective than was anticipated originally, in large part because the costs of compliance were greatly exaggerated. The overestimation of the costs of compliance should be a signal of the potential biases in industry-based compliance cost assessments and should highlight the importance of increased attention to the cost estimates in regulatory analyses. Both the benefit and cost estimates of regulations merit careful scrutiny.

The prospect for any change in the standard, however, is not great. Now that the large firms in the industry are in compliance, they no longer advocate changes in the regulation. Presumably, the reason is that the capital costs of achieving compliance represent a barrier to the entry of newcomers into the industry. This is simply one more illustration of the familiar point that surviving firms often have a strong vested interest in the continuation of a regulatory system.

Appendix 10A

Injury Rate and Quit Regression Results

The forecasted lost workday injury and illness rates in Figure 10-1 and the fore-casted quit rates in Figure 10-2 were each based on a regression equation estimated for the preregulation period, which was then used to predict the postregulatory experience.

The time period for the injury rate equation to be estimated was 1960 to 1977.[31] Because of the change in the injury rate data series after the advent of OSHA, I merged the pre-OSHA and post-OSHA series after placing them on a comparable basis.[32] The dependent variable in the analysis was the log-odds of the lost workday rate (i.e., the natural logarithm of the lost workday accident rate divided by 100 minus this rate), which avoids the otherwise constrained nature of an accident rate variable, which cannot be outside the interval [0,100].

The explanatory variables are intended to capture both cyclical influences and changes in the technology of the industry. The cyclical variable is average hours per week, which should be positively related to the risk level in this industry. Each of these variables is strongly related to the types of cotton processing operations regulated by the standard. This pattern is somewhat unusual because unlike most industries where the riskier blue-collar jobs are held by males, in textile mills women often have very hazardous jobs. Finally, a lagged dependent variable has been included as a proxy for the current stock of health and safety capital in the industry.

The regression results in Table 10-A1 follow the expected patterns, with cyclical

Table 10A-1. Regression Equation for the Log-Odds of Injuries and Illness Involving at Least One Lost Workday in the Textile Mill Products Industry, 1960–1977

	Coefficients (standard errors)
Independent variables:	
Intercept	−13.86
	(4.77)
Average weekly hours of labor force in industry	0.041
	(0.013)
Fraction of female employees in industry	6.81
	(2.41)
Fraction of production workers in industry	5.25
	(3.58)
Lagged dependent variable:	
ln $[IR_{t-1}/(100 - IR_{t-1})]$	−0.113
	(0.242)
Summary statistic:	
$\bar{R}^2$	0.78

Table 10A-2. Regression Equation for the Log-Odds of the Quit Rate in the Textile Mill Products Industry, 1960–1977

	Coefficients (*standard errors*)
Intercept	33.08
	(38.17)
Injury rate in industry	0.21
	(0.39)
Fraction of female employees in industry	15.53
	(9.43)
ln (wage rate in industry)	−0.91
	(0.32)
ln (average weekly hours in industry)	−12.83
	(9.76)
ln (average weekly overtime hours)	2.54
	(1.06)
Summary statistic:	
$\bar{R}^2$	0.90

and technological mix variables performing the strongest. This preregulation equation is used to forecast the predicted risk levels after 1977, and these predicted values are given by the dashed line in Figure 10–1.

The prediction of worker quit rates in Figure 10–2 was quite similar. To isolate the effect of the standard, I used an equation patterned after my analyses of manufacturing quit rates.[33] The dependent variable was the log-odds of the quit rate. Worker quitting should be positively related to the injury rate and to the fraction of female employees, which serves in part as a proxy for the job mix. Higher wages should diminish quitting, and there should be increased turnover during cyclical upturns as reflected in the work hours and overtime hours variables. The significant coefficients in Table 10-A2 follow the expected patterns, with the fraction of female employees, wages, and overtime hours being the most instrumental. This equation, estimated for the pre-OSHA period, was used to predict quit rates after imposition of the standard. The predicted quit levels are those shown in Figure 10–2 by the dashed line.

NOTES

1. *Federal Register* (1978), 122(43):27350–27399.
2. These stages were devised by Schilling et al. (1963), and amended by Merchant et al. (1973a,b).
3. See Schilling et al. (1963), and Merchant et al. (1973a,b). There is some debate over the implications of Grade 2 byssinosis, which may pose a small risk of early death among retirees.
4. For a critical review of the medical evidence and a summary of the weakness of the evidence supporting the causal link, see the National Research Council (1982).
5. See Merchant et al. (1973a,b).
6. Such experiments remain controversial and thus far have not been initiated.
7. Even these health-impact estimates may be too high. The relationships between cotton dust exposures and worker health (i.e., the dose-response relationships) in the medical literature are based on individuals with long work lives at high levels of cotton dust exposure, thereby being somewhat unrepresentative of workers in the mills at the present time. See Morrall (1981a), pp. 92–108.

8. *Federal Register* (1978).

9. See Morrall (1981a) for support of this view.

10. See particularly Litan and Nordhaus (1983) and Viscusi (1983).

11. *American Textile Manufacturers Institute v. Donovan*, 452 U.S. 490 (1981).

12. The total annualized cost of the tigher standard would be $222 million, compared with $91.9 million for the present standard. These estimates were calculated using data from the report by Centaur Associates (1983), Vol. 1.

13. The report that emerged from this effort is that by Centaur Associates (1983).

14. The protection factor for such masks is quite high since they have 93 to 99 percent filter efficiency for removing the dust from the air. See Merchant et al. (1973b).

15. For dust mask usage data, see the Centaur report (1983), pp. 4–41.

16. This estimate was calculated using data from Centaur Associates (1983), pp. 6–7, 6–10.

17. Centaur Associates (1983), p. 4–4. The Centaur study was based on a telephone survey of 170 textile firms and a field survey of fourteen plants.

18. *Ibid.*, pp. 1–8.

19. *Ibid.*, pp. 6–7.

20. The data in this paragraph are drawn from U.S. Bureau of Labor Statistics, *Occupational Injuries and Illnesses in the United States by Industry* (1980, 1984).

21. See U.S. Department of Labor, *Employment and Earnings*, various issues.

22. See the Centaur report (1983), p. 1–8. The limited data that do exist on the nature of the capital expenditures related to compliance with the regulation are suggestive of a possible link with the rise in accidents. For example, sales of new cotton system cards rose from 800 in 1977 to 1,500 by 1982. See the Centaur report (1983), p. 4–18.

23. These patterns are based on unpublished OSHA computer printouts generated for the author.

24. See Viscusi (1979a, 1983).

25. A sensitivity analysis using lower and more reasonable discount rates yields similar results in terms of relative cost-effectiveness. The 10 percent rate is stressed, since the original study was prepared for OSHA, and OMB requires a 10 percent rate.

26. See Viscusi and Zeckhauser (1979), pp. 437–456.

27. The prospective estimates appear in the *Federal Register* (1978) 122(43):27369, and the 1983 estimates appear in Centaur Associates (1983), pp. 1–8.

28. See Viscusi (1983).

29. This section was coauthored with Paul W. Kolp.

30. Paul Kolp (benefits) and John Birdsong (costs) were the key Centaur economists.

31. This equation was patterned after equation 11.11 in Chapter 11.

32. More specifically, I predicted the injury rate (IR) for 1972 using the pre-OSHA data and used the ratio of the observed IR_{72} to this predicted value to scale up the pre-OSHA variable. Although the resulting data series is not ideal, the cotton dust standard occurs sufficiently after 1972 and the IR shift in 1978 is so stark that the results are not greatly sensitive to the data series merger.

33. See Viscusi (1979a), pp. 189–197.

11

The Impact of Occupational Safety and Health Regulation, 1972–1975

11.1 INTRODUCTION

Since the passage of the Occupational Safety and Health Act of 1970, there has been a steady decline in the injury rate for manufacturing workers. This favorable trend has been widely cited as evidence of the effectiveness of the regulatory activities of the Occupational Safety and Health Administration. This chapter provides both a conceptual analysis of the likely effects of regulation and analyzes the determinants of health and safety investments and industry injury rates over the 1972–75 period.

Section 11.2 provides the conceptual basis of the investigation. It is shown that OSHA enforcement efforts will raise enterprise investments in work quality, which in turn will diminish workers' safety-enhancing actions. The analysis indicates that the expected penalty levels currently imposed should increase health and safety investments by the firm and diminish worker injuries and illnesses. The net effect depends on the severity of the penalties. If penalties are too severe, the regulations may be counterproductive. Section 11.3 incorporates these results in the empirical model to be estimated and describes the data sample that will be used. In Sections 11.4 and 11.5, I analyze the impact of OSHA enforcement on health and safety investments and job hazards for a large cross-section of industries over a four-year period. As indicated in the concluding Section 11.6, the expected penalty levels imposed by OSHA in the early 1970s appear to have been too low to have had a perceptible effect on either enterprise decisions or health and safety outcomes.

11.2 CONCEPTUAL ANALYSIS OF OCCUPATIONAL HEALTH AND SAFETY REGULATION

Existing analyses of health and safety regulation treat occupational risk levels as choice variables to be manipulated by the firm.[1] Regulations such as those imposed by OSHA either place constraints on hazard levels in the case of complete compliance or else impose expected penalties that increase with the level of the hazard. Although models of this type have produced many profitable insights, they neglect the role of worker actions in the production of health and safety. The care and speed with which an individual works, as well as actions that are not directly related to his or her job (e.g., smoking), influence the likelihood of adverse health and safety outcomes, just as does a high concentration of asbestos fibers or an unguarded punch press. A Wisconsin study of the determinants of accidents concluded that 45 percent of all work accidents resulted from worker actions, 30 percent were caused by transitory hazards, and the remaining 25 percent were due to identifiable physical characteristics of the workplace.[2]

The structure of the influences to be analyzed is as follows. For firms not in compliance with OSHA regulations, OSHA policies impose expected penalties that diminish with the level of work quality provided by the enterprise. This penalty structure influences the enterprise's choice of work-quality inputs. In making its decisions the firm must also take into account the influence of its choice of work-quality inputs on the behavior of workers, which in conjunction with the work-quality inputs determines the health and safety level at the firm. The key analytic question is how regulation influences the decisions of workers and firms and ultimately the production of health and safety at the enterprise.

The conceptual analysis consists of three parts. First, I shall consider the behavior of individual workers to determine the nature of worker response to different work quality inputs by the firm. Second, this worker reaction function will be incorporated into a general model of enterprise decisions in which the effect of health and safety regulations on firms' decisions will be analyzed. Finally, I shall explore the implications of the enterprise and worker responses to regulation for the production of workplace safety.

In Appendix 11A, it is shown that as the quality q of the work environment provided by the firm is increased, workers will diminish their level of safety-enhancing actions e that affect either the probability of an accident or the size of the loss. For example, workers may get more careless if the company adds guards or safety cables to a machine. A similar behavioral response by consumers reacting to product safety regulations will be the focus of Chapter 13.

This effect is sketched in Figure 11-1. At some initial work quality environment level, the worker selects an optimal level of safety effort e* determined by the interaction of the marginal benefit (MB) and marginal cost (MC) curves for the provision of safety effort by the worker.[3] If the firm improves the quality of the work environment, the marginal benefit of preventive actions on the part of the worker will be diminished and the marginal costs increased, shifting these curves to MB' and MC', respectively, and resulting in a lower safety effort level e**. This incentive effect gives rise to the worker effort reaction function e(q), where $de/dq < 0$, which will be incorporated in the enterprise's decision problem.

Since OSHA policies primarily affect capital investments in safety and health, I shall treat the regulatory policy as generating a capital cost in terms of health and safety investments, which in turn influence the safety level at the firm. If workplace health and safety are increased by this change in the technology, I assume that output similarly is raised. If regulation affected workplace operations rather than health and safety investments, a different formulation would be warranted. For example, slowing down the speed of the assembly line would not generate a capital cost, but it would reduce output. Safety-enhancing measures of that type would diminish production rather than increase it. Consequently, one must modify the

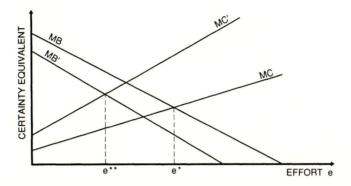

Figure 11.1 Effect of improved work environment on workers' safety-enhancing efforts

analysis below to consider modes of workplace regulation different from those now employed.

The two inputs to the production of health and safety are the enterprise's work quality input q and the safety-enhancing worker actions e(q), which are dependent on the level of q. The employment health and safety levels S consequently can be represented by

$$S(q) = r(q, e(q)), \tag{11.1}$$

where S is negatively related to the probability p of an accident for a hypothetical worker.

The enterprise's production of its output is dependent on both the size of its work force L and the safety level so that the production function is F(L, S(q)). Each input has a positive and diminishing marginal product. Higher levels of health and safety increase output by diminishing the disruptive effects of injuries and by increasing the stability of the work force by reducing worker quitting.[4] The price of the output is 1, and the capital stock other than the stock of health and safety capital is fixed.

There are three types of costs that are incurred. First, the enterprise wage bill equals Lw(S(q)), where a lower wage is required as the safety level is increased. The intervening safety function S that relates q to w is now made explicit, since it will be utilized in the analysis of enterprise decisions. In the model of individual choice, the actions by the individual were assumed not to influence the wage rate. In effect, the work force is treated as being sufficiently large that actions by one individual do not influence the aggregate safety level, whereas collective worker actions and their influence on workplace health and safety are of importance.

The second form of enterprise expenditure is a cost c for each unit of work quality input that it provides. The price represents the rental price for health and safety capital. The influence of depreciation on the price of capital is subsumed in the value of c.

Third, for firms not in compliance with health and safety standards, regulation imposes additional costs related to work quality. Let q* equal the work environment standard. For firms in compliance (q ≥ q*), the expected penalty level is zero.[5]

Firms in violation of the standards ($q < q^*$) risk an expected penalty if the infraction is discovered.[6] Let $G(q,q^*,t)$ be the expected cost associated with noncompliance including all direct (e.g., fines) and indirect (e.g., legal fees) costs, where t is an index of OSHA enforcement activities such as the level of inspections or penalties. The expected penalty is assumed not to diminish as the extent of the violation increases, i.e., $G_q \leq 0$ and $G_q^* \geq 0$. Moreover, increases in t raise either the probability of inspection, the probability of a violation given an inspection, or the level of the penalty for violations so that $G_t > 0$. Finally, investments in the work environment are more desirable as the regulatory activity increases, i.e., $G_{qt} < 0$.

The firm's objective is to select L and q to maximize its profit π, which is given by

$$\pi = F(L,S(q)) - Lw(S(q)) - cq$$

for firms in compliance ($q \geq q^*$), and

$$\pi = F(L,S(q)) - Lw(S(q)) - cq - G(q,q^*,t)$$

for firms not in compliance with the standards ($q < q^*$). Since OSHA regulations do not affect behavior of firms in compliance, I shall focus only on π for the case where $q < q^*$. The resulting first-order conditions are that

$$\pi_L = 0 = F_L - w, \tag{11.2}$$

and

$$\pi_q = 0 = F_S S_q - L w_S S_q - c - G_q \tag{11.3}$$

which can be rewritten as

$$c + G_q = S_q(F_S - Lw_S). \tag{11.4}$$

The principal matter of interest is how more stringent regulatory activities affect the behavior of enterprises not in compliance. Let H be the Hessian determinant that has a positive value at an interior maximum. Upon total differentiation of equations 11.2 and 11.3, one can solve for $\partial q/\partial t$ to obtain

$$\frac{\partial q}{\partial t} = \frac{F_{LL} G_{qt}}{H} > 0.[7]$$

More intensive enforcement activities will raise the enterprise's level of investment in work quality, which in turn has a negative impact on the safety-enhancing actions undertaken by workers.

The implications of these influences for health and safety outcomes depend upon the shape of the work-quality production function and the relative magnitude of the impacts on enterprise and worker actions. Although there may be the technological possibility that S_q could be positive, negative, or zero, an optimizing firm at an interior solution must behave in a manner that satisfies equation 11.4. For firms in compliance (q ≥ q*), G_q is zero, so that S_q must be positive since both c and F_S − Lw_S are necessarily positive. Similarly, if workers' original safety effort levels e equal zero, higher levels of q cannot lead to further reduction in effort, so that the e(q) term in the expansion for S in equation 11.1 drops out, implying that S_q will be positive.

When these corner solutions do not pertain, the sign of S_q depends on the relative magnitudes of c and G_q. For marginal expected penalty reductions equal to the price of work-quality inputs (i.e., $c = -G_q$), the marginal effect of regulation on safety is zero since S_q equals zero. The effect of a better environment is offset by a reduction in workers' safety effort. For low expected penalties (i.e., $c > -G_q$), more intensive enforcement will increase the production of health and safety. For very stringent penalties (i.e., $c < -G_q$), hazards must necessarily increase since S_q must be negative.[8] The reduction of worker effort resulting from an increase in q induced by stricter enforcement will have an effect opposite that which was intended owing to the diminished safety-enhancing actions by workers. Although it will be shown in the following section that present expected penalties are too low to be in the counter-productive region, this result highlights a potential danger for future policy.

11.3. THE EMPIRICAL FRAMEWORK AND DATA

Framework for Empirical Analysis

The expected positive effect of OSHA on enterprise safety investments and job safety can be incorporated in an empirical framework that recognizes the decision lags associated with the capital investment decisions involved. Here I shall derive the general function forms of the partial adjustment model to be estimated. A health and safety investment equation and an occupational hazard equation are derived in this section. Since the nature of the tests for OSHA's impact depends in part on the nature of the data, I shall not discuss such issues in detail until Sections 11.4 and 11.5.

Consider a representative industry (or firm) in year t. Let q_t be the current stock of health and safety capital per worker in year t, and let the worker injury and illness rate variable be $LOGIR_t$.[9] The job risk variable $LOGIR_t$ is related to the health and safety capital variable by the function R that is inversely related to the safety function S, so that

$$LOGIR_t = R(q_t).\text{[10]} \qquad (11.5)$$

A principal result of the conceptual analysis in Section 10.2 was that higher levels of q_t would decrease $LOGIR_t$ for expected OSHA penalty levels such as those now utilized, implying a negative functional relationship between $LOGIR_t$ and q_t.

The enterprise influences its injury rate by investing in its health and safety capital stock. Investments in health and safety capital are represented by the variable $INVEST_t$. These investments are assumed to be determined by the following partial adjustment model. Let δ be the depreciation rate of the current capital stock, and let q_t^* be the desired safety capital stock per worker in year t. Owing to the costs of adjusting the level of the capital stock and organizational delays, the firm increases its capital stock by a fraction λ of the desired increase, where $0 < \lambda \leq 1$, so that

$$\text{INVEST}_t = q_t - q_{t-1} = \lambda[q_t^* - (1 - \delta)q_{t-1}].^{11} \tag{11.6}$$

The object of the empirical analysis in Section 11.4 will be to estimate this investment equation. However, the values of q_t^* and q_{t-1} are not observable. Let the desired health and safety capital stock per worker be a function of worker characteristics, the firm's technology, and OSHA enforcement efforts. In particular, let q_t^* be given by

$$q_t^* = \alpha_0 + \beta_1 Z_t + \beta_2 \text{LOGIR}_{t-1} + \sum_{i=0}^{n} \gamma_i \text{OSHA}_{t-i}. \tag{11.7}$$

The variable Z_t is a vector of worker and enterprise characteristics that describe the preferences and risk-proneness of the firm's workforce, the occupational mix, and the technology of the workplace; β_1 is the vector of coefficients for these variables. Although these values are not observed until year t, many of these variables, such as those relating to the occupational mix, are dictated by longer-term considerations such as the technology in the industry. The technology is also reflected in the lagged values of the injury rate. Owing to the well-known lags in capital investment decisions of one to two years, it is unlikely that contemporaneous injury rate values would affect such plans, creating potential simultaneity problems. The coefficient β_2 should be negative since the technological characteristics that yielded a high optimal injury rate in the past should decrease the desirability of investments in health and safety. Finally, the enterprise will attempt to reduce the expected OSHA penalty costs (OSHA_t). These expectations are based on a distributed lag on past OSHA enforcement activities, as represented by the final term in equation 11.7. It is assumed that OSHA enforcement efforts are determined by prior considerations, such as the previous year's injury rate.[12] More stringent enforcement efforts will increase the desired health and safety stock, implying that the γ_i's should be positive.

The value of q_{t-1} can be ascertained by employing equation 11.5 for the period $t-1$, or

$$\text{LOGIR}_{t-1} = R(q_{t-1}).$$

Inverting this function yields

$$q_{t-1} = R^{-1}(\text{LOGIR}_{t-1}).$$

If the function R is a linear function of q with a negative slope, one obtains

$$q_{t-1} = \alpha_1 + \beta_3 \text{LOGIR}_{t-1}, \tag{11.8}$$

where β_3 is negative. Subsumed in the constant term is the mean influence of all other determinants of the relationship between q and LOGIR.[13]

Substituting the values for q_t^* and q_{t-1} from equations 11.7 and 11.8 into equation 11.6 yields an investment equation

$$\text{INVEST}_t = \lambda \left[\left(\alpha_0 + \beta_1 Z_t + \beta_2 \text{LOGIR}_{t-1} + \sum_{i=0}^{n} \gamma_i \text{OSHA}_{t-1} \right) \right.$$

$$\left. - (1 - \delta)(\alpha_1 + \beta_3 \text{LOGIR}_{t-1}) \right] + u_t,$$

where u_t is the random error term. This investment equation can be rewritten as

$$\text{INVEST}_t = (\lambda\alpha_0 - \lambda(1 - \delta)\alpha_1) + \lambda\beta_1 Z_t + \lambda(\beta_2 - (1 - \delta)\beta_3)\text{LOGIR}_{t-1}$$

$$+ \sum_{i=0}^{n} \lambda\gamma_i \text{OSHA}_{t-1} + U_t. \tag{11.9}$$

After relabeling the coefficients, this equation takes the final form to be estimated

$$\text{INVEST}_t = \alpha' + \beta_1' Z_t + \beta_2' \text{LOGIR}_{t-1} + \sum_{i=0}^{n} \gamma_i' \text{OSHA}_{t-1} + u_t'. \tag{11.10}$$

The expected signs of these coefficients can be determined by analyzing the underlying structure of the model that generated them. The signs of the coefficients in the vector β_1' of the variables describing the worker characteristics and the technology are the same as those of β_1 in equation 11.7, which expresses the determinants of the desired stock of health and safety capital. Similarly, the signs of the γ_i' coefficients should be positive since multiplying the positive γ_i coefficients from the q_t^* equation 11.7 by the positive factor λ will not alter their expected signs.

Matters are somewhat different with respect to the sign of the LOGIR_{t-1} coefficient for β_2', which is ambiguous. The ambiguity derives from the fact that a large LOGIR_{t-1} may imply either that the desired level of health and safety capital is low or that the actual safety capital stock level is low. Since the level of investment is determined by the weighted difference of these two similar effects, the sign of β_2' is ambiguous. More specifically, the value of β_2' equals $\lambda(\beta_2 - (1 - \delta)\beta_3)$, where both λ and $(1 - \delta)$ are positive. The coefficient β_2, which was introduced in equation 11.7, would be expected to have a negative sign to the extent that high values of LOGIR_{t-1} reflect the fact that the optimal technology selected by the firm involves substantial worker risks. However, high levels of LOGIR_{t-1} reflect the fact the optimal technology selected by the firm involves substantial worker risks. However, high levels of LOGIR_{t-1} also may be a measure of a low level of the previous period's stock of health and safety capital, as β_3 was assumed to be negative in the discussion of equation 11.8. The sign of β_2', which depends on the net influence of the weighted difference of these two negative coefficients, cannot be ascertained on a conceptual basis. The structure of the investment equation implied by equation 11.10 forms the basis of the empirical work in Section 11.4.

The occupational hazard equation to be estimated is much simpler to derive, since I have assumed that the structure of the model is recursive, with job risks influenced by the present stock of safety capital and other variables determined either by prior decision by the firm or by exogenous cyclical factors.[14] Rewriting the $LOGIR_t$ equation 11.5 in more detail yields

$$LOGIR_t = R(q_t) = R(INVEST_t + (1 - \delta)q_{t-1}).$$

The function R depends on the industry's technology, the characteristics of workers and their accident propensities, modes of workplace operation, and similar factors. The equation to be estimated in any year t is given by

$$LOGIR_t = \alpha^* + \beta_1^* Z_t + \beta_2^* INVEST_t$$

$$+ \beta_3^* LOGIR_{t-1} + \sum_{i=0}^{n} \gamma_i^* OSHA_{t-1} + u_t^*. \qquad (11.11)$$

The vector Z_t consists of characteristics of workers and the technology that affects injuries, such as the percentage of production workers or the hours of work. Health and safety investment levels should have a negative effect on injuries. The lagged injury rate variable $LOGIR_{t-1}^*$ can be viewed as a proxy for the previous period's stock of health and safety capital as before so that β_3^* is expected to have a positive sign.

The OSHA coefficients γ_i^* should be negative if OSHA affects workplace operations and worker actions in a safety-enhancing manner. The semireduced form estimates of γ_i^* obtained when $INVEST_t$ is omitted will reflect both the direct effect of OSHA on injuries and the indirect effect through the agency's impact on health and safety investments.

An Overview of OSHA

Table 11-1 summarizes the quantitative aspects of OSHA operations. Although OSHA's budget has displayed continued increases, rising to $130 million by 1977, the size and scope of the agency's operations are relatively modest by federal standards. Enforcement expenditures have constituted an increasing share of all allocations—totaling over 80 percent by 1975—with the average expenditure per inspection being roughly $1,000 in that year. The remaining 20 percent of the OSHA budget is allocated to oversight of the enforcement efforts and the evaluation and promulgation of health and safety standards. Establishment and enforcement of safety regulations is the sole major activity of the agency.

As the analysis in Section 11.2 indicated, it is the expected penalty that is the principal OSHA policy parameter of interest. The expected penalty amount is the product of the probability of an inspection, the number of violations per inspection, and the average penalty per violation. None of these magnitudes is very large.[15]

Over the five-year period being considered, there were 286,159 inspections. The total number of enterprises within OSHA's jurisdiction is at least 3.6 million.[16] The average number of inspections per enterprise was 0.079 over the five-year period, or

Table 11-1. OSHA Activities and Expenditures, 1971–1975

	1971	1972	1973	1974	1975
Total budget (*in thousands*)	$25,537	$52,629	$69,891	$86,207	$109,594
Enforcement budget (*in thousands*)	$10,172	$19,235	$38,543	$66,991	$88,287
Inspections	14,500	36,100	67,153	79,605	88,801
Compliance rate	28%	28%	26%	24%	21%
Violations	35,800	125,400	224,786	308,702	367,401
Citations	9,500	23,900	43,099	58,338	68,955
Proposed penalties (*in thousands*)	$738	$3,121	$6,059	$6,950	$10,411
Manufacturing inju- ry rate[a]	—	0.156	0.153	0.146	0.130

[a]Injury rate figures for 1971 are not available owing to the change in the injury rate reporting system during that year.

Source: Data supplied by the Occupational Safety and Health Administration.

roughly 0.02 on an annual basis. The probability that an enterprise would be visited by an OSHA inspector in any particular year is actually less than 1/50 since a substantial number of inspections (40 percent in 1975) are repeat and follow-up inspections at enterprises already visited.

Since the probability of inspection is negligible, the penalties for inspected enterprises must be very severe for there to be an effective financial incentive for enterprises to comply with OSHA regulations. The average number of standards violations cited per inspection was only 3.7, and the average penalty per violation was only $25.68 from 1971 to 1975. Viewed somewhat differently, the average OSHA penalty per establishment was $7.58 over the period examined, or $1.52 annually.

The expected penalty levels are in the range where the net influence of OSHA policies on health and safety should be positive, as was indicated by the analysis in Section 11.2. However, the financial incentives created by OSHA are at such a low level that there is unlikely to be any empirically observable impact. The analysis of the possibly counterproductive effect of very high penalties clearly is more pertinent to evaluation of prospective policy reform than to the empirical assessment of OSHA's impact to date.

Moreover, even if present efforts did create effective financial incentives, such activities are not necessarily desirable. Virtually all OSHA violations are for readily monitorable hazards that will generate compensating wage differentials.[17] Fewer than 1 percent of all violations in any year have been for less apparent health hazards (i.e., toxic and hazardous substances). Indeed, for FY1976 there were eight times as many procedural violations for improperly completed forms and similar offenses as there were for this important health category. Evidence of an impact of OSHA on hazards would not necessarily imply that the agency's activities were beneficial.

Despite the weak OSHA enforcement effort, worker injury and illness rates have been declining. As indicated in the bottom line of Table 11-1, the manufacturing injury and illness rate per full-time worker declined by 17 percent from 1972 to 1975. The empirical analysis will be directed in large part toward assessing OSHA's influence on this trend.

The Sample and the Variables

Most of OSHA's activities are reflected in the sample of industries whose characteristics are summarized in Table 11-2. All variables are expressed in real terms, where the base year is 1972.[18] The sample consists of 22 two-digit industries in 1972 and 61 two-digit and three-digit industries in 1973–1975. Although the industries represented are primarily in the manufacturing sector, many nonmanufacturing industries, such as construction, are also represented. The sample is quite comprehensive, as 84 percent of the workers in industries within OSHA's jurisdiction are included.[19]

The job risk variable is based on the industry rate variable INJRATE, which represents the annual number of recordable injuries and illnesses per full-time worker for the industries in the sample.[20] The absolute level and trend of this BLS injury rate variable are comparable with those of the manufacturing injury rate,

Table 11-2. Summary of Sample Characteristics

Variable	Mean and standard deviation			
	1972	1973	1974	1975
INJRATE	0.152	0.151	0.145	0.132
	(0.076)	(0.063)	(0.057)	(0.054)
INSPECT	83.87	122.41	151.88	184.46
	(96.20)	(84.43)	(93.02)	(108.25)
PENALTY	130.25	116.59	109.93	165.34
	(390.27)	(87.02)	(74.24)	(103.26)
INVEST	0.131	0.098	0.120	0.121
	(0.164)	(0.142)	(0.178)	(0.205)
EMPLOY	1,695.22	837.46	857.63	820.78
	(4,040.57)	(2,588.79)	(2,694.11)	(2,691.7)
PCNGEMP	3.89	5.02	1.44	−6.56
	(8.31)	(3.98)	(5.18)	(7.25)
HOURS	41.10	41.48	40.79	39.72
	(1.50)	(1.89)	(1.83)	(4.29)
OVERTIME	2.75	3.39	2.92	2.35
	(1.83)	(1.93)	(1.67)	(1.39)
FEMALE	21.50	23.40	23.80	23.50
	(13.63)	(16.30)	(16.17)	(15.77)
PRODN	73.87	74.48	74.55	72.78
	(10.14)	(10.78)	(11.80)	(11.82)
Sample size	22	61	61	61
Planned year	—	1977	1978	1979
PLANINV		0.140	0.155	0.132
		(0.167)	(0.278)	(0.241)
Sample size	—	61	61	61

which is reported in the bottom line of Table 11-1. Since this variable includes only occupational injuries and illnesses reported during a particular year, many health hazards that have long-term implications and are often difficult to attribute to a specific cause will be systematically neglected. This omission should not hinder any attempts to assess OSHA's impact, since fewer than 1 percent of all violations for any year from 1972 to 1975 were for toxic and hazardous substances. The preponderance of all violations were for the types of readily monitorable safety hazards that are accurately reflected in the available data.

In the subsequent analysis, the injury rate variable will be employed in its log-odds form, where

$$\text{LOGIR} = \ln\left[\frac{\text{INJRATE}}{1 - \text{INJRATE}}\right],$$

so that the injury variable will not be constrained to the [0,1] interval. If the injury frequency is interpreted as a probability that a worker will be injured, then LOGIR can be viewed as the logit of an injury.

The two other variables that will serve as dependent variables in the subsequent analysis are INVEST, which is thousands of dollars invested per worker in employee safety and health, and PLANINV, which is the level of health and safety investment (in thousands per worker) planned for year $t + 4$. These variables were calculated by dividing the actual or planned health and safety investment levels (in millions) from the McGraw-Hill *Annual Survey of Investment in Employee Safety and Health* by the level of employment (EMPLOY) in thousands for the industry.[21]

Both variables are on a per worker basis so as to adjust for differences in industry size. Over the 1973–1975 period in which the sample size is the same, INVEST displayed a modest increase of about 20 percent and PLANINV rose in 1974 but was somewhat lower in 1975 than in 1973.

The two OSHA policy variables are the number of inspections per hundred thousand workers in the industry (INSPECT) and the total proposed penalties per thousand workers in the industry (PENALTY), each of which is hypothesized to have a positive effect on health and safety investments. If inspection-related costs other than penalties are dominant (e.g., legal fees, paperwork, and the nuisance value of inspectors), INSPECT will serve as a better measure of the expected costs than will PENALTY. These measures of OSHA's enforcement efforts were created using unpublished data on inspections and penalties by industry provided by OSHA. Data are available only for OSHA activities from 1972 to 1975, so that the influence of early OSHA enforcement efforts will not be reflected in the analysis.[22] This shortcoming should not be too great, since enforcement efforts in 1971 were minimal, as they represent only 5 percent of the inspections, 3 percent of the violations, and 5 percent of the citations from 1971 to 1975 (see Table 11-1). Moreover, the substantial decision and implementation lags associated with the capital-intensive changes in technology stipulated by OSHA suggest that it is unlikely that there was a major and rapid impact from the creation of OSHA and its early activities in 1971.

A variety of worker and enterprise characteristic variables will be included in the analysis. The expected signs of these variables will be discussed in greater detail in the subsequent sections. It should be noted that while the effects are clear-cut for some variables, others capture aspects of both the mix of worker characteristics and job types, so that their impact cannot be readily ascertained. Owing to the inherent limitations of aggregative data in distinguishing such influences, many of the variables described below should be regarded as subsidiary control variables rather than as variables directly related to the central hypotheses of this study.

The percentage of female workers in the industry (FEMALE) and the percentage of production workers (PRODN) will reflect low-risk and high-risk job mixes, respectively.[23] These worker characteristics variables were supplemented with three U.S. Census (1973) cross-sectional variables, pertaining to the age and racial mix of the industry. The percentage of black workers in the industry (BLACK) should be negatively related to health and safety investment levels and positively related to the level of hazard since blacks' lower level of wealth increases their willingness to accept risks, diminishing the incentive to improve workplace conditions.[24]

Variables pertaining to the percentage of workers aged 24 and under (AGE24−) and the percentage aged 45 and over (AGE45+) were included to reflect age-related differences in job types and accident propensities.[25] Work injuries are a decreasing function of age overall and display an inverted U-shaped relationship within broad occupational groups.[26] Although the influences reflected by the age variables are quite diverse, the dominant effect appears to be that older workers are concentrated in lower-risk occupations, such as professional workers.[27]

The three variables capturing cyclical influences are the percentage change in employment in the industry (PCNGEMP), hours of work per week (HOURS), and overtime hours per week (OVERTIME). Finally, the pooled time series and cross-section equation results will include dummy variables for four of the five one-digit industry groups represented and three yearly dummy variables (1973 DUMMY, 1974 DUMMY, and 1975 DUMMY).

11.4 OSHA'S IMPACT ON INVESTMENT BEHAVIOR

Investment Regression Results

The functional form of the investment equation to be estimated was given by equation 11.10 above. Since the analysis will focus on pooled time series and cross-section data for INVEST from 1972 to 1975, it will be possible to analyze variations among both industries and years. Dummy variables were included for three of the four years and four of the five one-digit-level SIC codes represented.[28] The regression results are summarized in Table 11-3. At reasonable levels of significance, the hypothesis that the coefficients are identical for all years cannot be rejected.[29] This pooling test also serves as a test for an indirect effect of OSHA through its influence on the magnitudes of the other coefficients in the safety investment equation. There is no evidence of a change in enterprise investment behavior over the four-year period examined. It should be emphasized that this test is much stronger than is required, since even if the coefficients changed over time, one must still demonstrate that such changes in investment behavior are correlated with OSHA activities.

Table 11-3. Health and Safety Investment (INVEST)
Regression Results, 1972–1975[a]

Independent variables	Coefficients and standard errors		
	1	2	3
INSPECT$_t$	−1.093	—	—
	(1.804)		
INSPECT$_{t-1}$	−0.816	—	—
	(1.435)		
INSPECT$_{t-2}$	−0.019	—	—
	(1.437)		
INSPECT$_{t-3}$	1.297	—	—
	(2.821)		
PENALTY$_t$	—	−0.154	—
		(0.752)	
PENALTY$_{t-1}$	—	−0.149	—
		(0.552)	
PENALTY$_{t-2}$	—	−0.050	—
		(0.559)	
PENALTY$_{t-3}$	—	0.145	—
		(0.772)	
1973 DUMMY	0.017	0.010	0.0096
	(0.038)	(0.038)	(0.037)
1974 DUMMY	0.040	0.025	0.023
	(0.041)	(0.038)	(0.037)
1975 DUMMY	0.034	0.020	0.018
	(0.048)	(0.043)	(0.041)
FEMALE	−0.0057	−0.0057	−0.0050
	(0.0012)	(0.0012)	(0.0012)
PRODN	0.0050	0.0051	0.0057
	(0.0012)	(0.0012)	(0.0012)
BLACK	−0.014	−0.014	−0.014
	(0.003)	(0.003)	(0.003)
AGE45+	0.0027	0.0028	0.0028
	(0.0013)	(0.0013)	(0.0013)
OVERTIME	−0.021	−0.021	−0.021
	(0.016)	(0.015)	(0.015)
LOGIR$_{t-1}$	−0.116	−0.131	−0.133
	(0.032)	(0.028)	(0.027)
R^2	0.379	0.375	0.374
SSR	3.866	3.892	3.895

[a]Each equation also includes four industry group dummy variables,
Age24−, Hours, and PCNGEMP. The coefficients of the last three variables
were smaller than their standard errors.

The direct effect of OSHA on enterprise decisions is reflected in the coefficients
for the inspections per worker variables (INSPECT) and the expected OSHA penalties per worker variables (PENALTY), which appear in equations 11.1 and 11.2,
respectively. Each of these distributed lags was estimated using a second-order
polynomial distributed lag (or Almon lag) structure. None of the OSHA variables is

statistically significant individually and, using the results from equation 11.3, one can determine that jointly these coefficients also are not significantly different from zero.[30]

This finding combines with the pooling test result to suggest that there is no evidence of a direct or indirect effect of OSHA enforcement efforts on enterprise investment decisions. Given the negligible financial incentives created by the agency's regulatory efforts, this result is not unexpected.

The annual dummy variables may have had a direct effect on enterprise decisions. If there was an unexplained temporal increase in allocations for health and safety, OSHA might be credited with some impact not directly related to its enforcement efforts. However, none of the annual dummy variables in Table 11-3 is statistically significant, so that there is no evidence of any unexplained time trend. Safety investments also do not appear to be particularly sensitive to cyclical factors, since none of the three cyclical variables (HOURS, OVERTIME, PCNGEMP) is significant.

The five statistically significant determinants of investment behavior are characteristics of the technology and the work force.[31] Industries with a large percentage of physically demanding jobs (PRODN) will invest more in workplace safety, while those with predominantly white-collar and less hazardous types of jobs (FEMALE, AGE45+) will have lower levels of investment. Similarly, larger percentages of workers less averse to risk (BLACK) will reduce the incentives for investment.

Perhaps the coefficient of greatest interest is that of the lagged log-odds of the injury rate, $LOGIR_{t-1}$, which embodies two opposing influences discussed in the first part of Section 11.3. Its negative sign suggests that a high lagged injury rate reflects a technology in which high risks are optimal. This effect apparently swamps any role that a high $LOGIR_{t-1}$ might serve in indicating a level of health and safety capital that is below its optimal level.

Planned Investment Regressions

Particularly for regulatory efforts such as OSHA, which stress fundamental and diverse changes in the technology rather than minor modifications in operating procedures, there are likely to be substantial lags before the policy impact is produced. Organizational inertia and the time-consuming process of altering investment behavior may make the regulatory impact deferred rather than immediate. The INVEST regressions allowed for some decision and implementation lags, since a distributed lag of OSHA activities for the current and preceding three years was estimated. The empirical results did not suggest that inspection and penalty levels in earlier years were more influential than were current activities. The planned health and safety investment (PLANINV) data make it possible to ascertain whether there are such deferred effects since investment plans for the year $t + 4$ are sufficiently long-term to allow for reasonable response lags.

The pooled time series and cross-section results for PLANINV from 1973 to 1975, which are summarized in Table 11-4, reflect the same patterns of influence as did the INVEST results. Since one cannot reject the hypothesis that the coefficients differ over the period examined, there is no evidence of an indirect OSHA effect on planned investment behavior.[32] Moreover, neither the INSPECT nor the PENALTY

Table 11-4. Planned Health and Safety Investment
(PLANINV) Regression Results, 1972–1975[a]

Independent variables	Coefficients and standard errors		
	1	2	3
$INSPECT_t$	−2.431	—	—
	(2.633)		
$INSPECT_{t-1}$	−1.013	—	—
	(2.012)		
$INSPECT_{t-2}$	0.593	—	—
	(2.097)		
$INSPECT_{t-3}$	2.387	—	—
	(3.720)		
$PENALTY_t$	—	−1.693	—
		(2.070)	
$PENALTY_{t-1}$	—	−0.294	—
		(0.743)	
$PENALTY_{t-2}$	—	0.242	—
		(0.844)	
$PENALTY_{t-3}$	—	−0.083	—
		(1.015)	
1974 DUMMY	0.087	−0.0042	−0.0036
	(0.040)	(0.037)	(0.036)
1975 DUMMY	−0.040	−0.039	−0.048
	(0.054)	(0.050)	(0.048)
FEMALE	−0.0069	−0.0074	−0.0071
	(0.0018)	(0.0018)	(0.0018)
PRODN	0.0074	0.0079	0.0075
	(0.0017)	(0.0018)	(0.0017)
BLACK	−0.026	−0.026	−0.025
	(0.005)	(0.005)	(0.005)
AGE45+	0.0058	0.0057	0.0057
	(0.0019)	(0.0019)	(0.0018)
OVERTIME	−0.032	−0.035	−0.034
	(0.021)	(0.021)	(0.021)
$LOGIR_{t-1}$	−0.155	−0.174	−0.186
	(0.051)	(0.045)	(0.042)
R^2	0.405	0.398	0.396
SSR	5.821	5.884	5.909

[a]Each equation also includes four industry group dummy variables, AGE24−, HOURS, and PCNGEMP. The coefficients of the last three variables were smaller than their standard errors.

coefficients in the (second-order polynomial) distributed lag differ significantly from zero either individually or jointly, so that there is also no evidence of any direct OSHA effect on safety investment plans.[33] As with the INVEST results, the time dummy variables also are not significant so that there is no evidence of an unexplained temporal shift in planned investment behavior that might be attributed to OSHA.

The principal determinants of planned investments are the same as for actual health and safety investments. Both the direction and relative magnitudes of the five significant determinants of PLANINV (FEMALE, PRODN, BLACK, AGE45+, and LOGIR$_{t-1}$) directly parallel the INVEST results.[34] For both planned and actual health and safety investments, it is the nature of the technology and the industry's work force, rather than government regulation that affect enterprise decisions.

11.5 OSHA'S IMPACT ON HEALTH AND SAFETY OUTCOMES

Most previous analyses of OSHA have focused on the ill-conceived nature of OSHA's enforcement strategy. Perhaps the most detailed investigation along these lines is that of Oi (1976), who documents the ineffectiveness of the allocation of OSHA's enforcement efforts, with particular emphasis on the inordinate number of standards and the ineffective allocation of OSHA's efforts by firm size and industry. The comprehensive survey and policy analysis by Zeckhauser and Nichols (1979) reiterates these themes and notes the absence of a definitive study of OSHA's impact on national injury rates.[35] One portion of OSHA's activities that has been scrutinized is the Target Industry Program. This component of OSHA's early efforts was found by R. S. Smith (1976) not to have a perceptible impact on injury rates. Research by R. S. Smith (1976) of firms investigated by OSHA suggests that injury rates for small, hazardous firms exhibited statistically significant declines after OSHA inspections in 1974. The analysis to be presented below is an effort to obtain a more aggregative perspective on OSHA's impact. On the basis of the conceptual analysis of OSHA's weak enforcement effort, one would predict that OSHA should diminish hazards, although the magnitude of the impact should not be large.[36]

Equation 11.11, which was derived in Section 11.3, was estimated for pooled time series and cross-section data from 1972 to 1975, yielding to the results reported in Table 11-5. The explanatory variables have the same definitions as before except for LOGIR$_{t-1}$. The lagged injury rate variable, which serves as a proxy for the lagged stock of health and safety capital and consequently should have a positive coefficient, raises potential econometric problems if the error terms are serially correlated, so that LOGIR$_{t-1}$ and u_t^* will also be correlated. To obtain consistent estimates of β_3^*, I followed the two-step procedure of first obtaining an instrumental variables estimator LOGIR$_{t-1}$ and then using this created variable as the explanatory variable in the analysis of injury rates.[37]

Since the hypothesis that these coefficients are identical over the four-year period cannot be rejected, there is no evidence that the functional relationship determining injury rates has changed since 1972.[38] This result serves as the first test of OSHA's effectiveness, as it reflects any indirect effect of OSHA on the influence of the technology and worker characteristics on injury rates.

The direct effect of OSHA is captured in the coefficients of the INSPECT and PENALTY coefficients reported at the top of Table 11-5. Equations (4) and (5) in Table 11-5 omit the INVEST variable, so the coefficients for the OSHA variables in these equations also reflect any indirect OSHA effect through its impact on enterprise investment decisions. The coefficients of the OSHA variables in each equation

Table 11-5. Injury Rate Regression Results, 1972–1975[a]

Independent variables	Coefficients and standard errors					
	1	2	3	4	5	6
INSPECT$_t$	−1.415	—	—	−1.345	—	—
	(1.374)			(1.378)		
INSPECT$_{t-1}$	−0.288	—	—	−0.239	—	—
	(1.089)			(1.092)		
INSPECT$_{t-2}$	0.735	—	—	0.719	—	—
	(1.088)			(1.091)		
INSPECT$_{t-3}$	1.652	—	—	1.529	—	—
	(2.137)			(2.142)		
PENALTY$_t$	—	−0.059	—	—	−0.361	—
		(0.562)			(0.543)	
PENALTY$_{t-1}$	—	−.555	—	—	−0.491	—
		(0.418)			(0.413)	
PENALTY$_{t-2}$	—	−0.435	—	—	−0.422	—
		(0.423)			(0.422)	
PENALTY$_{t-3}$	—	−0.149	—	—	−0.154	—
		(0.582)			(0.583)	
1973 DUMMY	−0.106	−0.109	−0.112	−0.107	−0.110	−0.112
	(0.029)	(0.028)	(0.028)	(0.029)	(0.028)	(0.028)
1974 DUMMY	−0.120	−0.122	−0.130	−0.123	−0.123	−0.132
	(0.031)	(0.029)	(0.028)	(0.031)	(0.029)	(0.028)
1975 DUMMY	−0.180	−0.170	−0.184	−0.183	−0.171	−0.185
	(0.036)	(0.033)	(0.032)	(0.363)	(0.033)	(0.032)
INVEST	−0.082	−0.078	−0.077	—	—	—
	(0.056)	(0.056)	(0.056)			
FEMALE	−0.0027	−0.0028	−0.0027	−0.0022	−0.0023	−0.0022
	(0.0010)	(0.0010)	(0.0010)	(0.0010)	(0.0010)	(0.0010)
PRODN	0.0030	0.0033	0.0030	0.0026	0.0028	0.0026
	(0.0010)	(0.0010)	(0.0010)	(0.0010)	(0.0010)	(0.0009)
AGE 45+	−0.0011	−0.0010	−0.0011	−0.0013	−0.0013	−0.0013
	(0.0011)	(0.0010)	(0.0010)	(0.0010)	(0.0010)	(0.0010)
HOURS	0.0063	0.0060	0.0056	0.0062	0.0059	0.0055
	(0.0036)	(0.0035)	(0.0035)	(0.0036)	(0.0035)	(0.0035)
LOGIR$_{t-1}$	0.899	0.896	0.887	0.911	0.907	0.898
	(0.029)	(0.024)	(0.024)	(0.028)	(0.023)	(0.022)
R^2	0.962	0.963	0.962	0.962	0.962	0.962
SSR	2.195	2.195	2.225	2.221	2.224	2.248

[a]Each equation also includes a constant term, four industry group dummy variables, and the following variables with coefficients smaller than their standard errors: AGE24−, BLACK, OVERTIME, and PCNGEMP.

are not significant either individually or jointly.[39] The absence of any perceptible OSHA effect accords with one's expectations based on the nature of this regulatory policy.

A pattern of influence quite different from the health and safety investment regressions is the role of the yearly dummy variables. Each of the variables is consistently negative and statistically significant. Moreover, the size of these coefficients increases somewhat with time, suggesting a decreasing trend in injury rates that is not explained by other factors in the analysis. The magnitudes of these time effects are also not negligible, as the results imply a temporal effect on the injury frequency rate of 0.014 for 1973 and 0.024 for 1975.[40]

Although the exact cause of the time effects cannot be ascertained, four explanations appear most plausible. First, 60 percent of the overall time effect occurs between 1972 and 1973. A shift in the constant term for that year is to be expected since the sample is substantially altered in 1973 and the $LOGIR_{t-1}$ variable for the 1972 cross-section is subject to substantial error, biasing the constant term for that year.[41] Second, if enterprises became more lax in reporting injuries after the advent of OSHA, an unexplained decline in injuries would be observed. Third, the time effects may simply reflect continuation of the long-run temporal decline in accidents.[42] The fourth and final possibility might best be termed a placebo effect. Even though OSHA's enforcement activities do not create effective financial incentives, the widespread publicity given to the agency's efforts may have created the perception that OSHA is rigorously enforcing its regulations. The principal limitation of this explanation is that no similar temporal effect was observed for INVEST or PLANINV, so that the mechanism of influence is unclear.

The role of the other variables is quite similar to their influence on enterprise decisions. Variables reflecting a mix of light, white-collar jobs (FEMALE, AGE45+) have a negative effect on injury rates, while a larger percentage of production work activities (PRODN) results in greater injury rates.[43] The only statistically significant cyclical variable is HOURS, which indicates that the injury frequency rate rises as the workweek is lengthened. This variable, which may reflect changes in the speed of production, is consistent with the hypothesis that injury rates move procyclically.[44]

The instrumental variables estimator for $LOGIR_{t-1}$ is a powerful determinant of injury rates, which is to be expected since this variable serves as a proxy for the previous period's health and safety capital and other aspects of the technology. The enterprise INVEST level is also negatively related to $LOGIR_t$, though its statistical significance is marginal.[45] The weakness of the INVEST effect may be attributable to difficulties with the health and safety investment data, which are based on somewhat arbitrary categorizations that undoubtedly involve substantial measurement errors.[46]

11.6 CONCLUSION

The effectiveness of job hazard regulations hinges critically on the economic incentives created. Enterprise investments in work quality will increase if such allocations will diminish the expected penalties associated with noncompliance with OSHA standards. Although the provision of a safer work environment will be offset in part by diminished safety-enhancing actions by workers, only in the exceptional instance of very severe penalties will regulation be potentially counterproductive.

The weak financial incentives associated with the present enforcement effort combine with the ill-conceived nature of the enforcement strategy to provide at best only very weak incentives for enterprises to alter their actions. No significant effect of OSHA was found in an examination of pooled time series and cross-section data pertaining to health and safety investment, planned health and safety investments, and worker injuries from 1972 to 1975. Although there has been an unexplained downward temporal trend in injuries that may be attributable in part to the existence of the agency and misperceptions regarding the effectiveness of its enforcement activities, a variety of other factors, such as continuation of the temporal decline in injuries, may also be responsible.

What is clear is that the agency's enforcement policies have not had any direct impact on job hazards. Moreover, even if these efforts were effective, their desirability would be doubtful since the preponderance of violations are not for dimly understood health hazards but for readily monitorable safety hazards, the type that market forces are well equipped to handle through compensating wage differentials. In short, policymakers have paid too little attention both to the potential desirability of the present intervention and to the economic mechanisms through which the enforcement activities will exert their influence.

Appendix 11A
Model of Worker Response to Regulation

The discussion of Figure 11-1 in Section 11.2 indicated that workers would respond to a safer work environment by diminishing their safety-enhancing efforts. The spirit of this result is similar to the effect of auto safety regulations on driver behavior. Peltzman (1975) has demonstrated, for a model in which individuals maximize expected income, that safety measures that decrease the loss to the driver from accidents (e.g., seat belts) would increase driving speed, thus diminishing and perhaps offsetting any beneficial effect of regulation. The structure of the analysis of worker actions is somewhat different in that enterprise safety levels affect the wage rates paid by the firm, and workers are not assumed to have utility functions that are linear in money. Moreover, the possible mechanism by which the work environment and worker actions affect safety is through either the probability of an accident, the size of the loss, or both.

Let there be two possible states of the world. In state 1, the individual is in good health and has a utility function u^1, while in the ill health (state 2), the worker's utility function is u^2. For any given level of consumption, the level of the individual's utility and the marginal utility of consuming the composite consumption good x is greater in the healthy state, that is,

$$u^1(x) > u^2(x),$$

and

$$u_x^1 > u_x^2 > 0,$$

where letter subscripts indicate derivatives. The health state approach offers additional flexibility, since the shape of the utility function, not simply its arguments, can be influenced by accidents.[47] The qualitative nature of the analytic results would not be affected if all of the inequality signs above except those assuming positive marginal utilities were replaced by equal signs. The final assumption about worker preferences is that individuals are either risk-averse or risk-neutral, that is,

$$u_{xx}^1 \leq 0 \text{ and } u_{xx}^2 \leq 0.$$

The first mechanism by which employment hazards can be influenced is through the probability of an adverse outcome p. This probability is a function of both the work quality input q provided by the firm and a work effort variable e that is intended to capture the safety-enhancing actions that the individual might undertake. Each of these safety inputs has a diminishing effect on the probability of an accident, that is,

$$p_q < 0, \ p_{qq} > 0, \ p_e < 0, \text{ and } p_{ee} > 0.$$

Moreover, increasing the level of one safety input is assumed to have a nonincreasing effect on the marginal productivity of the other safety input, or

$$p_{eq} \geq 0.$$

The influence of individual and enterprise actions may not be through the probability of an accident but rather via the size of the loss of C it entails. The assumptions pertaining to the influence of q and e on C are analogous to those made for the probability of an accident:

$$C_q < 0, \; C_{qq} > 0, \; C_e < 0, \; C_{ee} > 0, \; \text{and } C_{qe} \geq 0.$$

If q and e do not influence the size of the loss from an accident, C can be set equal to 0, since the unattractiveness of the accident state will be captured in the shape of u^2. For simplicity, the effort e, loss C, and wage rate for the job w are scaled in comparable monetary units.

Individuals working at firms with lower work quality inputs receive compensating wage differentials, or

$$w_q < 0,$$

where the equilibrium level of the differential is assumed to be predetermined.[48] Consequently, actions taken by a hypothetical individual do not alter the wage rate paid by the firm. Except in instances in which safety-enhancing actions influence only the probability of an accident and not the size of the loss, the magnitude of the effect of q on the wage rate is assumed to be no greater than q's influence on the loss term, or

$$w_q - C_q \geq 0.\text{[49]}$$

The individual's consumption level in each state is given by

$$x_1 = w(q) - e,$$

and

$$x_2 = w(q) - e - C(q,e).$$

The role of worker assets (which affect x_1 and x_2 equally) and workers' compensation (which affects only x_2) are subsumed into the general functional forms of the state-dependent utility functions and will not be considered explicitly.

The worker at the firm with work quality q selects the effort variable e to maximize his or her expected utility V which is given by

$$V = [1 - p(q,e)]u^1(w(q) - e) + p(q,e)u^2(w(q) - e - C(q,e)).$$

The first-order condition for a relative optimum is

$$\frac{dV}{de} = 0 = \{-p_e[u^1 - u^2] - pC_e u_x^2\} - \{(1 - p)u_x^1 + pu_x^2\}, \quad (11.A1)$$

where the two bracketed terms on the right-hand side of equation 11.A1 are the marginal benefits (MB) and marginal costs (MC) of increased safety effort, as sketched in Figure 11-1. The positive MB term reflects the effect of increased e in both reducing the probability p of an accident and reducing the size of the loss C, while the MC term corresponds to the drop in expected marginal utility due to the increase in e.

Assuming that the marginal utility of income is greater when the worker is healthy than when he or she is not, an increase in q diminishes the magnitude of the MB term and increases the size of the MC term if q influences safety only through its effect on the probability of an accident. For the equilibrium wage structure, it can be shown that if an increase in q reduces the cost of an accident sufficiently, MC may be reduced by an increase in q, provided that the worker's absolute risk aversion is greater in state 1. As will be shown below, an increase in q lowers the optimal effort level irrespective of the direction in which the MC curve shifts in Figure 11-1.

To ensure that an interior solution may exist when safety-enhancing actions affect C and not p, $(-1 - C_e)$ will be assumed to be always positive unless safety inputs and actions only influence the probability of an accident, not the size of the loss. The second-order condition for a maximum is that

$$\frac{d^2V}{de^2} = -p_{ee}u^1 + 2p_e u_x^1 + (1 - p)u_{xx}^1 + p_{ee}u^2$$

$$+ 2p_e(-1 - C_e)u_x^2 + pu_{xx}^2(-1 - C_e)^2 - pu_x^2 C_{ee} < 0, \qquad (11.A2)$$

which is clearly satisfied given the earlier assumptions since all terms in equation 11.A2 are negative.

Letting D equal the left-hand side of equation 11.A2, one can totally differentiate equation 11.A1 and solve for de/dq;

$$\frac{de}{dq} = \left\{-\frac{1}{D}\right\} \{p_{eq}[-u^1 + u^2] + C_{eq}[-pu_x^2] + p_e[u_x^2(w_q - C_q) - u_x^1 w_q]$$

$$+ p_q[u_x^1 + u_x^2](-1 - C_e) - (1 - p)u_{xx}^1 w_q + p(-1 - C_e)u_{xx}^2(w_q - C_q)\} < 0,$$

since the first expression in brackets is positive and the second bracketed term consists of six separate terms, each of which is either negative or zero. Increases in the enterprise's safety inputs reduce workers' safety-enhancing efforts whether the influence of these efforts is through the probability of an accident, the size of the loss, or a combination of the two mechanisms. Enterprise efforts to increase work-quality outcomes consequently will be mitigated at least in part by diminished worker inputs in the production of health and safety.

NOTES

1. Analyses in this vein include the works by Oi (1975), R. S. Smith (1976), Nelson and Neumann (1975), and Viscusi (1979a).

2. This 1971 study by the Wisconsin State Department of Labor, Industry, and Human Relations was cited by Oi (1974). Although such allocations of responsibility for accidents are somewhat arbitrary, they are at least suggestive of the importance of worker behavior to health and safety outcomes.

3. The level of e* may equal zero. If such a corner solution occurs, there will be no effect on e resulting from an increase in q.

4. See Viscusi (1979a) for an analysis of the job hazard-quit relationship and for a more detailed formulation of the role of health and safety in the form of the production function.

5. There may, of course, be costs imposed by regulation that serve primarily as lump sum impositions. For example, OSHA-related paperwork and inspections of firms in compliance impose real costs to the firm. Inclusion of a lump sum payment would not alter the analysis.

6. This format in effect assumes that firms are risk-neutral. This assumption appears reasonable for the low level of penalties now employed. For very high penalties, it may be appropriate to incorporate an element of risk aversion into the firm's objective function.

7. Similarly, $\partial q/\partial q^* > 0$ if $G_{qq^*} < 0$.

8. If q increases to equal or exceed q*, no such result need occur since G_q will equal zero. Similarly, if e equals zero, q must necessarily increase until compliance is achieved so long as $c < -G_q$.

9. The capital stock and investment variables are on a per worker basis to adjust for differences in industry size.

10. For example, S may be either the probability 1-p that the worker is not injured or the log-odds of the probability of no injury, i.e., $\ln((1-p)/p)$.

11. The replacement portion of the investment could be treated somewhat differently from new investments that are additions to the capital stock by, for example, letting $\lambda = 1$ for this portion of the investment. This modification would not alter the functional form of the equation to be estimated but would alter the interpretation of the coefficients somewhat.

12. This assumption does not appear to be at variance with OSHA practices, which, while not capricious, are not determined by current industry injury rate levels. Most inspections are either random or determined on the basis of predetermined variables, such as the industry size, the presence of particular types of hazards (e.g., the Target Health Hazards Program), prior OSHA inspections (i.e., follow-up inspections), or the industry injury rate, which is provided to OSHA by the BLS with a time lag of over a year. The most deliberate inspection strategy that one might think would be jointly determined with the hazard level is the Target Industry Program, which accounted for only 10 percent of all inspections by 1974. That program, which was designed in 1971 based on injury trends through 1970, singled out several industries with high injury rates (SIC Codes 4463, 176, 201, 379, and 24) for more intensive inspection rates. Such activities clearly can be treated as predetermined variables for the purposes of estimation.

13. Elaboration of the components of α_1 for this empirical model would yield an investment function that included current and lagged values of all variables describing the technology and worker characteristics. The data available are not sufficiently rich to be able to estimate all of these relationships, which are of subsidiary interest.

14. These equations are part of a larger recursive system in which current hazard levels and other factors, such as worker education, determine the wage rate for the job. Such a recursive structure is implicit in all compensating wage differential equations, such as those in Thaler and Rosen (1976), R. S. Smith (1976), and Viscusi (1978a,b). In Viscusi (1979a), I test for the potential simultaneity of earnings and job risks, leading to results consistent with the recursive formulation.

15. Other costs, such as legal fees, also may be important, but data for these magnitudes are not available.

16. This figure is the number of establishments listed for 1973 in the U.S. Department of Commerce (1974). Excluded from this listing are government agencies, railroads, and the self-employed. In addition, I excluded mine workers, since they are covered by separate health and safety regulations.

17. See Thaler and Rosen (1976), R. S. Smith (1976), and Viscusi (1978a,b).

18. The price index used was that for producers' durable equipment. See the Council of Economic Advisors (1976), p. 175.

19. The 84 percent figure is for 1973.

20. The source of this variable is the U.S. Department of Labor, *Occupational Injuries and Illnesses in*

the United States by Industry, various issues. Unpublished figures for 1971 were provided by the U.S. Department of Labor.

21. The employment variable is from the U.S. Department of Labor, *Employment and Earnings*, various issues.

22. In addition, records of OSHA enforcement efforts for the first half of 1972 were not kept by the agency. I assumed that OSHA inspections and penalty levels were at a uniform rate for the entire year in constructing the INSPECT and PENALTY variables for 1972.

23. These variables are based on published data in *Employment and Earnings*, various issues.

24. The rate effect is undoubtedly quite complicated, since there also may be racial differences in accident propensities within particular activities. Overall, blacks have higher rates of accidents of all types than do whites. See Iskrant and Joliet (1968), p. 139. Racial discrimination could also be a factor, but there is no evidence of discrimination in terms of job characteristics. See Viscusi (1979a) for a discussion of this result and the wealth effect.

25. The percentage of workers in the middle-aged group was omitted since an intercept was included in the equation.

26. See Iskrant and Joliet (1968), p. 194.

27. Age-related effects include differences in willingness to accept job risks, accident propensities within job types, types of job, levels of specific training, and expected time horizons over which the employer can reap the benefits of the firm's training investment. Disentangling these many and often conflicting influences is not feasible given our limited understanding of the relation of age to each of these factors.

28. This ordinary least squares with individual constant terms approach yields results quite similar to more complicated variance components techniques. See Houthakker, Verleger, and Sheehan (1974).

29. Consider, for example, the results for the INSPECT equations, which yielded higher F-values. The F-statistic for the pooling test was 0.609, far below the critical $F(45,140)$ of approximately 1.45 at the 5 percent level.

30. In particular, one cannot reject the hypothesis that each group of coefficients equals zero at reasonable levels of significance. In particular, the F-statistic is 0.92 for the four INSPECT variables and 0.25 for the PENALTY variables, each of which is far below the critical $F(3,185)$ of 2.65 at the 5 percent level. The four OSHA variables utilize only three degrees of freedom due to the second-order polynomial lag structure.

31. All variables other than those five discussed below were not statistically significant at the usual confidence levels, except for the constant term and several industry dummy variables.

32. The F-statistic for pooling the INSPECT regressions (which is larger than for PENALTY) is 0.472, as compared with a critical $F(34,133)$ of about 1.53 at the 5 percent level.

33. The F-statistic is 0.825 for the four INSPECT variables and 0.234 for the PENALTY variables. The critical $F(3,164)$ value to test the joint significance of these variables at the 5 percent level is approximately 2.67.

34. The other significant variables include only the constant term and industry group dummy variables.

35. Moreover, their analysis suggest that previous studies of OSHA's impact in particular geographical areas should be regarded with great skepticism. For additional review of prior studies in this area, see R. S. Smith (1976).

36. The results below fail to suggest any statistically significant impact of OSHA. These findings are not inconsistent with Smith's (1978) results since the number of employees in small, high hazard firms is a negligible portion of the population under OSHA's jurisdiction.

37. The instrumental variables estimate was obtained by regressing $LOGIR_{t-1}$ on the current and lagged values of the other independent variables in the injury rate equation. This procedure is described by Griliches (1967).

38. For example, the F-value for the hypothesis that the coefficients in equation 4 in Table 11.5 are identical from 1972 to 1975 is 0.72, far below the critical $F_{0.95}(45,140)$ of approximately 1.50.

39. The critical $F_{0.95}(3,185)$ for equations 4 and 5 in Table 11.5 is 2.65, as compared with the F-value for the group of INSPECT variables of 0.75 and and F of 0.67 for the PENALTY variables. The calculated $F(3,184)$ values for equations 1 and 2 in Table 11.5 are both equal to 0.84.

40. These representative estimates were calculated for equation 4 in Table 11.5.

41. The use of an instrument variables estimator can be viewed as a partial correction for the latter problem. Injury rate data for 1971 are too unreliable to be released publicly. The data used are unpublished data available only on a two-digit basis.

42. The total number of disabling injuries in the U.S. declined by 3 percent from 1942 to 1970, but the injury frequency rate declined by 45 percent due to the growth in employment. While it is often noted that manufacturing injury rates rose prior to OSHA, the composition of the manufacturing industries also changed. Moreover, the nonmanufacturing injury rates dropped, so that overall the injury frequency rate decreased by 12 percent from 1960 to 1970. For supporting data, see the *Compendium on Workmen's Compensation* (1973), p. 3.

43. It should be noted that while the coefficient of AGE45+ is larger than its standard error, it is not significant at the usual levels.

44. The principal empirical analysis of cyclical effects to date is that of R. S. Smith (1976), who regressed the manufacturing injury rate on a single explanatory variable—the unemployment rate—and found the expected positive relationship for the 1948–1969 period.

45. The INVEST variable is significant at the 10 percent level but not at the 5 percent level. A distributed lag on $INVEST_t$ and the two preceding years was estimated for the 1975 LOGIR cross-section, but these variables were also not jointly significant.

46. While this measurement error may bias its coefficient in the LOGIR equation, the results for the INVEST equations will not be biased, since it is a dependent variable in the latter situation.

47. The state-dependent utility function approach to employment choice was introduced in Viscusi (1978b). The two principal empirical predictions—that there should be compensating wage differentials and that job risks should decline with worker wealth—were borne out empirically. See Viscusi (1979a) for a more detailed exposition of worker behavior. Viscusi and Evans (1990) estimate state-dependent utility functions for the job risk cases that are consistent with this formulation.

48. See Thaler and Rosen (1976), Oi (1974), and Viscusi (1979a) for a discussion of the determination of the equilibrium wage distribution.

49. This condition is required for the second-order condition to be satisfied. The analysis below focuses on the selection of e by workers at firms with work quality q. However, if the above conditions were violated, it can be shown that if q influences C and not p, then no interior solution for the level of q selected by the worker will ever exist.

12

The Impact of Occupational Safety and Health Regulation, 1973–1983

12.1 INTRODUCTION

The Occupational Safety and Health Administration began operations in 1971 as the most extensive effort to influence workplace conditions. This regulatory program also assumed broader significance as OSHA became a principal target of opponents of the new risk and environmental regulations. The popular consensus that early OSHA operations epitomized ineffective governmental regulation was borne out in the academic studies as well (Oi [1975]; Mendeloff [1979]; R. S. Smith [1976, 1979b]; Viscusi [1979b, 1983]; Zeckhauser and Nichols [1979]). Econometric studies, such as that in Chapter 11, found little or no impact of OSHA regulation on workplace safety, and this view continues to prevail in the literature.

None of these analyses, however, considered the performance of OSHA after the mid-1970s. This failure to address the more recent OSHA experience is of fundamental importance because there was a major overhaul of OSHA's enforcement effort during the Carter and Reagan administrations. This chapter updates the analysis in Chapter 11 to ascertain whether there has been a shift in OSHA's effectiveness or whether the additional information on more recent risk levels and OSHA activity enables us to estimate reliably a small effect that OSHA may have had since its inception. Although the evidence is mixed, some of the results are more favorable to OSHA than those found in earlier studies. OSHA inspections may have a significant effect on workplace safety that occurs with a one-year lag. This effect is not, however, robust across risk measures or time periods of analysis, so that this chapter does not provide unqualified support of the agency's efficacy.

Section 12.2 provides a brief review of past studies of OSHA's efficacy, none of which has considered data more recent than those of 1978. In Section 12.3, I introduce the empirical framework to be used in my examination of a pooled sample of 20 two-digit manufacturing industries over an eleven-year period. The analysis focuses on a safety equation that related the injury rate to a variety of variables, including current and lagged OSHA enforcement variables. The empirical results that appear in Section 12.4, and Section 12.5 contains both conclusions and an update on subsequent studies of OSHA's effectiveness.

12.2. PREVIOUS ECONOMETRIC STUDIES
OF OSHA'S EFFECTIVENESS

OSHA's general approach to regulation has remained unchanged since its inception. OSHA sets standards for workplace design and conditions (e.g., radiation exposure levels) that are rigid guidelines for industry behavior. To ascertain whether firms are in compliance, OSHA conducts inspections and can issue penalties for existing violations and continued noncompliance. From an economic standpoint, firms will find compliance in their self-interest if the costs of compliance, which are often considerable, are below the expected costs of noncompliance.

Chapter 11 assessed the impact of OSHA inspection and penalty variables on overall injury and illness rates and on enterprise investments in health and safety. For the 1972–1975 period analyzed, there was no significant effect of OSHA on workplace safety. Similarly, the analysis of the 1974–1978 experience by Bartel and Thomas (1985) failed to yield any statistically significant effect of OSHA on the lost workday accident rate. Because of the nature of the data on industry averages used in these studies, there may nevertheless be a small effect that could not be distinguished with available data.

An alternative to investigating data on industry averages is to use data on accident experiences at firms before and after an OSHA inspection. Examining firm-specific accident rates reduces the degree to which detailed information is lost in the aggregation process, but the focus on only inspected firms makes such analyses both more partial in scope and more susceptible to regression-to-the-mean effects if firms with temporarily high injury rates are the ones inspected.[1] R. S. Smith (1979b) found that small firms inspected in 1973 exhibited a subsequent drop in the lost workday rate, whereas firms inspected in 1974 did not. An update of this analysis by McCaffrey (1983) failed to yield any significant OSHA effects on manufacturing firms inspected in the 1976–1978 period. A possible explanation for this pattern is that the apparent 1973 effects of OSHA reflect either the overreporting of injuries in the initial years of OSHA or a remaining regression-to-the-mean effect that is more likely to be evident for smaller firms than for larger firms.

The strongest support of OSHA's effectiveness to date is Cooke and Gautschi's (1981) study of Maine manufacturing firms from 1970 to 1976. Their analysis of the relationship between the average days lost from injuries and OSHA citations produced evidence of a significant effect of OSHA on total lost workdays. There is the possibility, however, that the result is a spurious consequence of some regression-to-the-mean effect for firms that receive citations.

The size of the OSHA impacts in Cooke and Gautschi's analysis is consistent with the presence of such a bias. Their estimates imply that OSHA reduced lost workdays due to injury by 29 per 100 workers for firms with 200 or more employees and by 51 per 100 workers for firms with 300 or more workers. Since the average rate of total lost workdays in the manufacturing industry was 79.5 per 100 workers in 1976, estimates of this magnitude imply that the rate of lost workdays would have been 50 percent greater in 1976 in the absence of OSHA enforcement. The 1976 rate was already above the rate of lost workdays in 1972, which was only 62.6 per 100 workers, so that for these estimates to be reasonable an explosion in the level of workplace hazards would have had to occur in the absence of OSHA. The implausibly high level of effects may stem from the biases involved in analyzing inspected firms only.

The final empirical approach is to analyze workers' compensation records. In Mendeloff's (1979) analysis of the California workers' compensation experience in 1947–1974, some injury categories exhibited increases after OSHA, and others declined.[2] The net effect is unclear. As in the other studies, there was no clear-cut evidence in support of the agency's effectiveness.

12.3. SPECIFICATION OF THE SAFETY EQUATION

The basic empirical framework used here follows that in Chapter 11. The analysis here focuses on a sample of two-digit manufacturing industries from 1973 to 1983. The sample size is 220. Although OSHA began operations in 1971 and was fully operational in 1972, there was a change in the reporting system for injuries that led to a break in the risk series in 1971 and to a new injury definition beginning in 1972. Because of the inclusion of a lagged risk variable in the analysis, 1973 will be the starting year.[3] Focusing on two-digit manufacturing data avoids the problems of industry reclassification and missing data present in the three-digit series as well as the severe comparability problems with the OSHA statistics for the construction industry.[4]

The dependent variable for the subsequent analysis will be some measure of the risk level for industry i in year t, which I shall denote by $RISK_{it}$ for purposes of the general equation given below. Three different risk data series will be used. The first series, which is the only measure analyzed in Chapter 11, is the most comprehensive as it pertains to the annual frequency of all injuries and illnesses recorded by the firm. As a rough rule, this series includes all accidents and work-related illnesses severe enough to restrict one's work or to require medical treatment (other than first aid). The comprehensiveness of this measure is consequently coupled with considerable ambiguity regarding the classification of minor accidents, so that there are substantial reporting difficulties.

The overall injury and illness rate per 100 workers will be denoted by IR. The second measure is the annual frequency of cases that are severe enough to lead to at least one lost day of work or restricted workdays. This accident category is consequently more precisely defined than is IR. The incidence per 100 workers of cases involving lost workday injuries or illnesses will be indicated by LW. The final risk measure is the total number of days of work lost per 100 workers due to injury and illness, LWDAYS. Unlike LW, which measures only the incidence of particular cases, this measure weights their severity by the amount of work the employee loses.

The bounded nature of the risk variables must be taken into account when they are used as dependent variables. In each case, the value of the variable is nonnegative. Moreover, IR and LW represent the annual probabilities of occurrence of particular accident types, scaled up by a factor of 100. If we assume as a rough approximation that the chance of multiple accidents for a particular worker is small, then we can treat IR and LW as being in the range [0,100]. Following the approach in Chapter 11, we can then use the logistic transformation of the variables as the dependent variable. The log-odds of the risk variables used will be $\ln(IR/(100 - IR))$ and $\ln(LW/(100 - LW))$. The effects of OSHA were similarly weak for other transformations. In the case of the rate of total lost workday LWDAYS, I shall use the natural logarithm of this variable to avoid the variable's otherwise constrained nature.

The mean risk levels for the sample of two-digit manufacturing industries analyzed appear in Table 12-1. From 1975 on, all three measures performed in similar fashion. The overall injury rate rose until 1977, was somewhat lower in 1978 and 1979, and dropped significantly in the 1980s. The changes for LW and LWDAYS are comparable, as they rose until 1979 and declined thereafter. The decline in the 1980s is due at least in part to the cyclical downturn over much of that period, which tends to lower the accident rate. The principal puzzle is why the overall injury and illness rate declined from 1972 to 1975, while the other two measures did not. Government officials generally believe that a principal contributor to this trend was overzealous reporting under the new injury recording system. The two lost workday measures are less subject to errors in classification and consequently did not reflect this bias in the early reports.

In the empirical work below, I use an injury rate equation of the general form

$$RISK_{it} = \beta_0 + \sum_{k=1}^{n} \beta_k x_{kit} + u_i + \lambda_t + e_{it}, \qquad (12.1)$$

where x_{kit} values pertain to a series of variables dependent on the industry i and year t, μ_i reflects omitted effects pertaining to the industry, λ_t reflects omitted influences that vary across time but not across industries, and e_{it} is an independent and identically distributed random error term. If one estimates equation 12.1 by ordinary least squares by including only an intercept and the x_{kit} variables, then the estimates of β_k will be biased.

Table 12-1. Means of Risk Levels and OSHA Policy Variables for the Two-Digit Manufacturing Industry Sample, 1973–1983

Year	IR	LW	LWDAYS	INSPECT	PENALTY
1973	14.6	4.3	67.5	.0020	.19
1974	13.9	4.5	72.1	.0025	.20
1975	12.6	4.4	75.0	.0031	.35
1976	12.8	4.8	79.5	.0025	.41
1977	12.8	5.0	81.9	.0022	.50
1978	12.4	5.3	81.8	.0020	.65
1979	12.4	5.5	88.6	.0019	.64
1980	11.5	5.1	86.0	.0019	.54
1981	10.9	4.9	82.2	.0016	.22
1982	9.8	4.3	73.5	.0027	.25
1983	9.7	4.2	72.1	.0034	.35
1973–1983	12.1	4.8	78.2	.0023	.39

To account for the influence of the omitted industry-specific and time-specific influences, I shall adopt a fixed-effects model. Thus, the underlying assumption in formulating this model is that the constant term for the $RISK_{it}$ equation is given by $\beta_o + \mu_i + \lambda_t$, where μ_i is a constant industry-specific effect and λ_t is the constant time-specific effect common to all industries. The μ_is and λ_ts are each assumed to be parameters that vary across industry and across time, respectively, but do not vary randomly. If these assumptions hold, the fixed-effects model will yield consistent estimates of OSHA's effect on safety.

If, however, the μ_i and λ_t values are not fixed, but instead are random and correlated with the x_{kit} values, then the fixed-effects assumption underlying the model does not hold. Even in this situation, however, the fixed-effects estimator will yield best linear unbiased estimates conditional upon the μ_i and λ_t values for the sample.

The specific equation to be estimated is of the form

$$
\begin{aligned}
RISK_{it} = {} & \beta_o + \beta_1 OSHA_{it} + \beta_2 OSHA_{it-1} + \beta_3 RISK_{it-1} \\
& + \beta_4 PRODUCTION_{it} + \beta_5 FEMALE_{it} \\
& + \beta_6 \%CNGEMPLOYMENT_{it} + \beta_7 HOURS_{it} \\
& + \beta_8 OVERTIME_{it} + \beta_9 DUMMY{-}SIC_i \\
& + \beta_{10} DUMMY{-}YR_t + e_{it}, \qquad\qquad (12.2)
\end{aligned}
$$

where equation 12.2 includes a current and lagged OSHA enforcement variable ($OSHA_{it}$, $OSHA_{it-1}$), a lagged dependent variable, the fraction of production workers in the industry ($PRODUCTION_{it}$), the fraction of female workers in the industry ($FEMALE_{it}$), the percentage change in industry employment over the past year ($\%CNGEMPLOYMENT_{it}$), average weekly work hours ($HOURS_{it}$), average weekly overtime hours ($OVERTIME_{it}$), dummy variables for the industry ($DUMMY{-}SIC_i$) to capture the fixed industry effects μ_i, and dummy variables for each year ($DUMMY{-}YEAR_{it}$) to capture the fixed time-specific effects λ_t. In this fixed-effects model there are dummy variables for nineteen of the twenty SIC codes and ten of the eleven years to control for omitted industry-specific and year-specific effects. To prevent singularities, one dummy variable has been omitted in each case.

The use of the fixed-effects model makes possible a fairly parsimonious equation in terms of the number of substantive variables included. Measures of most safety-related variables are available only on an industry-specific basis rather than on an annual one. Inclusion of industry characteristic variables, such as unionization or census-based measures of the worker mix, does not affect the magnitudes of the other coefficients estimated, since these variables are simply linear combinations of the industry group dummy variables. Thus, inclusion of the age and race mix variables, as in Chapter 11, instead of some of the industry dummy variables would not alter the estimates of OSHA's effect on safety. Similarly, the year dummy variables are intended to capture any time-specific influences in changes in injury reporting practices, changes in the nature of OSHA standards, and other temporal influences. Aspects of the design and enforcement of OSHA regulations that are not captured in the OSHA variables used here, but which are time-dependent, will consequently be reflected in the year dummy variables. Each equation also includes a set of variables that is available by industry for each year.

The variables of primary interest are the regulatory enforcement variables, $OSHA_{it}$ and $OSHA_{it-1}$. Unfortunately, there is no ideal OSHA variable available that measures the expected costs of noncompliance. One can, however, construct proxies for the enforcement stringency. Table 12-1 presents the mean levels of these OSHA variables on an annual basis for the industries in this sample.

The first of these is $INSPECT_{it}$, which is the frequency of OSHA inspections per production worker in industry i and t. This expected inspection rate variable is an employment-adjusted measure of the firm's anticipated likelihood of an OSHA inspection. The main cost to the firm is the inspection event itself, since severe penalties are seldom assessed and, if the firm makes the mandated changes, penalties may be waived altogether. The firm may, however, incur substantial compliance costs as a consequence of the inspection, and it may face the threat of considerable penalties if it does not make the required changes. The INSPECT trends in Table 12-1 reflect the changes in the OSHA enforcement effort. Inspections began to decline in 1977, as OSHA eliminated inspections for trivial violations and shifted the emphasis toward more thorough inspections targeted at serious hazards. The rise in inspection rates in 1982 and 1983 is a consequence of the introduction of "records-check inspections," which involve inspection at the work site of accident reports the firm prepared for the U.S. Bureau of Labor Statistics (BLS). Record checks count as inspections even though the OSHA official does not determine whether any particular physical characteristics at the workplace meet OSHA standards. The addition of these inspections increased the absolute number of inspections undertaken.

The second OSHA policy measure is the assessed penalties per production worker, $PENALTY_{it}$. This variable accurately reflects the expected penalties incurred, but it does not reflect the ultimate financial impact an inspection might have, since a firm will face an ever escalating scale of fines for continued noncompliance. OSHA penalties have never exceeded $25 million and have dropped to $6 million annually in recent years. The PENALTY values for the sample summarized in Table 12-1 reflect a similar change in policy emphasis. Penalties per worker rose to a peak of $.65 in 1978 and had declined to $.35 by 1983. Punitive penalties for noncomplying firms have been deemphasized; OSHA focuses its efforts on negotiating compliance schedules, which, if not met, will lead to more substantial penalties. The penalty threat for continued noncompliance and the cost of the mandated changes in workplace conditions are the principal costs of an OSHA inspection. The low level of penalties suggests that the threat of a random inspection imposes few immediate costs, but, if inspected and found out of compliance, a firm will face considerably greater financial incentives for compliance.

For each equation estimated, I included both the current and lagged OSHA policy measures, $OSHA_{it}$ and $OSHA_{it-1}$, since firms may not respond immediately to the level of OSHA inspections in their industry—because of both the lag involved in making capital investment decisions and the nature of the compliance schedules negotiated by noncomplying firms. Longer lag structures were also explored, but no significant effects were found beyond a one-year lag.

If OSHA inspections are targeted strategically on a contemporaneous basis with the risk level, one might encounter some simultaneity between $OSHA_{it}$ and $RISK_{it}$. In practice, the risk level affects the inspection targeting with a lag. Overall, 86 percent of all OSHA inspections are general programmed inspections. To the extent that OSHA uses the industry injury rate to target the inspection, it does so with the lag of over one year that is involved in the generation of the pertinent BLS statistics. Even in the Reagan administration's ambitious targeting effort based on firms' accident reports—the records-check inspections—a lag is involved. A firm subject to a records check in 1986 will be given a detailed inspection then if its average lost workday rate for 1984–1985 (or 1983–1985 for small firms) exceeds the 1984 lost workday rate for manufacturing. This procedure necessarily involves a lagged effect of past injury experiences on enforcement and leads to a recursive rather than a simultaneous formulation.

The second leading inspection category is inspections stemming from worker complaints, which constitute 9 percent of all inspections. These inspections are generally ineffective and lead to few violations, perhaps because workers use these inspections to express other work related grievances (U.S. Department of Labor, 1982). Follow-up inspections of previously inspected workplaces are also not affected by $RISK_{it}$. The only inspection category jointly determined with the current risk level is investigations of fatalities, but these fatality risks are so small that they do not affect the published overall risk measures and constitute only a negligible part of the enforcement effort.[5] As a result, there is not likely to be any perceptible bias stemming from the influence of current risk levels on the enforcement strategy.

The possible presence of a simultaneity problem has been discussed by several authors, including myself, and, in one case—Bartel and Thomas (1985)—the authors explicitly assume a simultaneous relationship between OSHA enforcement and job risks. There has not, however, been any formal test of whether there is, in fact, evidence of a significant simultaneous relationship between these variables. To resolve the simultaneity issue, I carried out a series of Hausman (1978) tests to see whether the $OSHA_{it}$ variable was endogenous. The results, which are detailed in the appendix to this chapter, indicate that in all cases one can reject the hypothesis that OSHA enforcement efforts and the industry risk levels are simultaneously determined. The empirical properties of the equation consequently accord with our expectations based on the nature of OSHA enforcement efforts.

The other variables included in equation 12.2 are of subsidiary interest. The lagged dependent variable $RISK_{it-1}$ is included as a proxy for the firm's previous level of health and safety capital. OSHA enforcement efforts influence additions to this stock in any year so that the combined influence of new safety-related investments and the previous safety stock will determine the risk level. On the basis of theoretical considerations, one would expect the previous stock of health and safety capital to be positively correlated with the present risk level, so that $RISK_{it-1}$ should have a positive sign.

The remaining variables are BLS measures of worker mix and cyclical factors. The fraction of production workers in the industry ($PRODUCTION_{it}$) is intended to capture changes in the mix of jobs in the industry, where production jobs tend to be more risky on average than white-collar positions. Similarly, jobs with a higher fraction of female workers ($FEMALE_{it}$) should involve less physical effort and pose lower risk. Finally, one would expect accidents to be procyclical, because of the increased intensity of operations (in terms of work pace, use of night shifts, etc.)

and the introduction of more inexperienced workers into new work situations. The three variables capturing this influence were the percentage change in the industry's employment (%CNGEMPLOYMENT), average weekly work hours (HOURS$_{it}$), and average overtime hours (OVERTIME$_{it}$).

It is noteworthy that the mechanism by which OSHA enforcement influences safety—safety-related investments in the workplace—is not included in the equation. Such data are not particularly reliable because of the difficulty involved in identifying the safety-related component of capital investments and changes in the reporting of such data. The analysis in Chapter 11 failed to identify a significant role for this variable. With this variable omitted, the OSHA coefficients will reflect the direct effect of enforcement on safety as well as the indirect effect through enterprise decisions. These semi-reduced-form estimates consequently will capture the full effect of OSHA enforcement, which is the principal concern in the analysis.

12.4. EMPIRICAL RESULTS

Risk Equations

Table 12-2 summarizes the estimates of the various RISK$_{it}$ equations by using the INSPECT$_{it}$ variable as the measure of OSHA regulatory enforcement. The results for the non-OSHA coefficients are similar for equations using the other OSHA variables. The equations in Table 12-2 will consequently serve as the general reference point for discussion, and later we shall consider the role of the OSHA variables in more detail. In each case, 220 observations were included in the regression.

I shall begin by focusing on the general character of the results for variables other than OSHA enforcement, as the OSHA variables' effects will be discussed subsequently with respect to a broader set of regression findings. Since the results parallel those in Chapter 11, we shall discuss them only briefly. The most powerful variable overall is the lagged dependent variable, which has a consistent impact across all three equations. Roughly two-thirds of the risk level in any year will be transmitted to the subsequent year. Because of the capital-intensive nature of health and safety investments, firms that are risky are likely to remain so.

The cyclical variable that is consistently statistically significant is %CNG-EMPLOYMENT. As expected, there is a positive relationship between increases in the employment level in the industry and the observed risk level. This effect reflects the procyclical nature of job accidents.

The year dummy variables are of potential policy interest to the extent that they reflect omitted aspects of the OSHA enforcement effort. No consistent pattern is evident, however. The year dummy variables differ in sign depending on the risk variable, as they are usually negative for the overall injury and illness rate and positive otherwise. Much of this difference may be due to initial overreporting of total job injuries, which is more of a problem for the IR variable since it is more susceptible to classification problems.

The 1982 and 1983 dummy variables have particular policy significance, since there is the possibility that some firms may have begun to misrepresent their lost

Table 12-2. Job Risk Regression Results, 1973–1983

Independent variables[a]	Coefficients (*standard errors*)		
	$\ln[IR_{it}/(100 - IR_{it})]$	$\ln[LW_{it}/(100 - LW_{it})]$	$\ln(LWDAYS_{it})$
Intercept	−.404	−1.122	1.749
	(.542)	(.631)	(.897)
INSPECT$_{it}$	12.400	9.610	6.069
	(6.682)	(7.612)	(9.715)
INSPECT$_{it-1}$	−12.800	−16.637	−25.862
	(7.347)	(8.325)	(10.736)
Lagged dependent variable	.701	.618	.598
	(.050)	(.060)	(.068)
PRODUCTION	.0021	.0083	.0096
	(.0130)	(.0038)	(.0048)
FEMALE	−.0011	−.0060	−.0076
	(.0033)	(.0037)	(.0047)
%CNGEMPLOYMENT	.0071	.0071	.0046
	(.0012)	(.0013)	(.0017)
HOURS	−.0090	−.015	−.013
	(.0115)	(.013)	(.017)
OVERTIME	.013	.031	−.0037
	(.018)	(.020)	(.0262)
1974 DUMMY	.0096	.077	.079
	(.0165)	(.019)	(.024)
1975 DUMMY	−.0069	.106	.138
	(.0216)	(.025)	(.032)
1976 DUMMY	.015	.123	.135
	(.024)	(.025)	(.035)
1977 DUMMY	−.0012	.115	.123
	(.0201)	(.024)	(.033)
1978 DUMMY	−.039	.144	.101
	(.019)	(.025)	(.035)
1979 DUMMY	.0050	.181	.196
	(.0199)	(.027)	(.034)
1980 DUMMY	−.042	.128	.143
	(.021)	(.031)	(.040)
1981 DUMMY	−.059	.112	.117
	(.025)	(.030)	(.041)
1982 DUMMY	−.113	.042	.036
	(.026)	(.029)	(.039)
1983 DUMMY	−.074	.077	.100
	(.028)	(.027)	(.038)
$\bar{R}^2$	.99	.99	.98

[a]Each equation also includes a set of nineteen industry dummy variables.

workday incidence statistics once records checks began to target inspections by using this risk measure in October 1981. No evidence of any such time-related downward shift in reported values of LW is observed, however. The coefficients of the time dummy variables for 1982 and 1983 are smaller than those for previous years but not out of line with their trend since 1979.

OSHA Impacts

The effect of the OSHA enforcement variables is summarized for different time periods of estimation in Tables 12-3(a)–12-3(c). Table 12-3(a) presents the results for the log-odds injury rate equations, Table 12-3(b) presents the findings for the log-odds of the incidence of lost workday injuries and illnesses, and Table 12-3(c) presents the findings for the natural logarithm of the rate of total lost workdays.

In each case, the results are presented for several time periods of particular policy interest. I shall consider each of these time periods in succession. The 1973–1975 estimation period is similar to that in Chapter 11 and in other studies of the effectiveness of early OSHA operations.[6] For none of the specifications estimated in Tables 12-3(a)–12-3(c) is any significant OSHA effect on risk apparent during 1973–1975. This result is consistent with the literature.

The principal time period of interest for this study is from 1973 to 1983. For the results pertaining to the overall injury and illness rate in Table 12-3(a), the PENALTY variables are never statistically significant at the 5 percent level. The only statistically significant coefficient with a negative sign is that of $INSPECT_{it-1}$. Because the contemporaneous $INSPECT_{it}$ variable has a positive sign, the combined influence of the INSPECT variables is less than that of the lagged value of $INSPECT_{it-1}$ alone, and the net effect is that the two influences nearly cancel out each other. Even when considered individually, the lagged effect of inspections is

Table 12-3(a). Summary of Results for Injury Rate, Lost-Workday Case Rate, and Rate of Lost-Workdays Equations

		(a) Injury rate (IR) equations					
		Coefficients (standard errors)		Combined mean reduction in risk level		$OSHA_{it-1}$ mean reduction in risk level	
Estimation time period	OSHA variable	$OSHA_{it}$	$OSHA_{it-1}$	Absolute	Percentage	Absolute	Percentage
1973–1975	INSPECT	14.281 (21.845)	−17.349 (22.466)	a	a	a	a
	PENALTY	−.019 (.120)	−0.128 (.165)	a	a	a	a
1973–1983	INSPECT	12.400 (6.682)	−12.800 (7.347)	−.01	−.04	−.3	−2.6
	PENALTY	.024 (.015)	−.018 (.015)	a	a	a	a
1973–1979	INSPECT	−3.061 (11.280)	−6.104 (9.833)	a	a	a	a
	PENALTY	.009 (.018)	−.010 (.020)	a	a	a	a
1980–1983	INSPECT	10.771 (9.818)	9.084 (12.633)	a	a	a	a
	PENALTY	.066 (.034)	−.008 (.026)	a	a	a	a

aEffects are not reported in cases where no OSHA coefficients are negative and statistically signficant at the 5 percent level, one-tailed test.

Table 12-3(b)

		(b) Lost-workday case rate (LW) equations					
		Coefficients (standard errors)		Combined mean reduction in risk level		$OSHA_{it-1}$ mean reduction in risk level	
Estimation time period	OSHA variable	$OSHA_{it}$	$OSHA_{it-1}$	Absolute	Percentage	Absolute	Percentage
1973–1975	INSPECT	7.079 (23.289)	−17.265 (23.536)	a	a	a	a
	PENALTY	−.050 (.132)	−.056 (.180)	a	a	a	a
1973–1983	INSPECT	9.610 (7.612)	−16.637 (8.325)	−.1	−1.5	−.2	−3.6
	PENALTY	.016 (.017)	−.026 (.017)	a	a	a	a
1973–1979	INSPECT	−.678 (12.063)	−10.112 (10.613)	a	a	a	a
	PENALTY	−.006 (.019)	−.014 (.021)	a	a	a	a
1980–1983	INSPECT	13.047 (12.444)	6.055 (15.980)	a	a	a	a
	PENALTY	.100 (.041)	−.008 (.033)	a	a	a	a

a Effects are not reported in cases where no OSHA coefficients are negative and statistically signficant at the 5 percent level, one-tailed test.

small in absolute terms; it reduces the rate of injuries and illnesses by an average of .3 per 100 workers. Because the level of the IR variable itself is not high, the percentage reduction in injuries generated by $INSPECT_{it-1}$ is somewhat greater— on the order of 2 to 3 percent. Owing to the mixed signs of the OSHA coefficients, however, any evidence of OSHA's effect on the total injury rate measure is, at best, questionable.

The results in Table 12-3(b) for the log-odds of the lost workday rate equations show a significant effect for the 1973–1983 time period. The $INSPECT_{it-1}$ variable is the mechanism of influence. On a percentage basis, the overall effect of the two INSPECT variables combined is about 1.5 percent and for $INSPECT_{it-1}$ alone about 3.5 percent. Once again, the PENALTY variables are never statistically significant.

The 1973–1983 results for the rate of total lost workdays in Table 12-3(c) provide by far the strongest evidence of OSHA's effectiveness in promoting worker safety. The lagged $INSPECT_{it-1}$ effect in the 1973–1983 equation is significant, as before. It indicates an effect of 6 percent on injuries, or 5 percent after netting out the influence of $INSPECT_{it}$. In percentage terms, this is a much larger effect than on the incidence of lost workdays. These results consequently suggest that OSHA's efforts have yielded the greatest dividends for the most severe classes of risk, injuries of long duration, a result consistent with the increased emphasis placed on serious violations in the enforcement effort.[7] In addition, although the size of the effects is almost an order of magnitude below that in Cooke and Gautschi (1981), the pres-

Table 12-3(c)

		(c) Rate of Lost Workdays (LW DAYS) equations					
		Coefficients (standard errors)		Combined mean reduction in risk level		$OSHA_{it-1}$ mean reduction in risk level	
Estimation time period	OSHA variable	$OSHA_{it}$	$OSHA_{it-1}$	Absolute	Percentage	Absolute	Percentage
1973–1975	INSPECT	18.659 (29.128)	−16.818 (28.597)	a	a	a	a
	PENALTY	−.153 (.156)	−.132 (.213)	a	a	a	a
1973–1983	INSPECT	6.069 (9.715)	−25.862 (10.736)	−3.0	−4.7	−4.3	−6.1
	PENALTY	.015 (.023)	−.025 (.022)	a	a	a	a
1973–1979	INSPECT	−8.353 (14.091)	−18.298 (12.373)	a	a	a	a
	PENALTY	−.012 (.023)	−.013 (.026)	a	a	a	a
1980–1983	INSPECT	7.281 (16.241)	.498 (21.244)	a	a	a	a
	PENALTY	.092 (.054)	.023 (.041)	a	a	a	a

aEffects are not reported in cases where no OSHA coefficients are negative and statistically signficant at the 5 percent level, one-tailed test.

ence of a particularly large impact on the rate of total lost workdays is consistent with their finding that at the firm level OSHA has a major effect on severe risks.

The apparent evidence of a significant effect of the lagged OSHA inspection variable on both the lost workday incidence rate and the rate of total lost workdays raises the broader issue of why Tables 12–3(b) and 12–3(c) imply relatively strong OSHA effects compared with most findings in the literature. One possibility is that OSHA may always have been effective, but only with more years of data is it possible to estimate the relationship precisely. Alternatively, there may have been a shift in OSHA's effectiveness over time so that more recent OSHA inspections have a stronger effect on safety. A third, and not unrelated, possibility is that there has been a shift in the underlying structure of the equations so that the pooled results are not valid.

To examine these possibilities, Tables 12-3(a)–12-3(c) report results for two different subperiods, 1973–1979 and 1980–1983. The 1980 break point in the risk data corresponds to a break point of 1979 in the lagged OSHA variable, which is the primary mechanism of influence. The year 1979 was selected as the policy shift point for OSHA because it represented the first full year of the recent change in OSHA's emphasis. In October 1978, Assistant Secretary of Labor Eula Bingham eliminated 928 "nit-picking" regulations to enable OSHA inspectors to focus on a more streamlined set of regulations. Explicit targeting of OSHA inspections by the OSHA policy office also began in the 1978–1980 period and has been furthered by the Reagan administration's introduction of records-check inspections in October

1981. To isolate any specific effects of records-check inspections, I also estimated exploratory regressions that included an interaction of the OSHA variables with 1982–1983 dummy variables. No significant shift in OSHA's effectiveness was observed. Since the case hours per inspection have dropped, the absence of a drop in the estimated impact of the OSHA variable is consistent with a possible increase in the efficacy per hour of inspection time, which one would expect if inspections are targeted more efficiently.

For the overall injury results in Table 12-3(a), one can reject the hypothesis that the regression coefficients are stable across the 1973–1979 and 1980–1983 sub-periods.[8] Thus, the effect of the OSHA variables in the 1973–1983 equations, which on balance was roughly zero, may not be a reliable measure of the agency's impact. Examining the OSHA effects for the two subperiods does not, however, alter the spirit of these results. There are no significant OSHA coefficients in either of the two subperiods, so that the overall injury rate variable provides no strong evidence of OSHA's efficacy for any of the time periods considered. Since this risk measure is the one most susceptible to reporting problems, as noted earlier, these results do not, however, serve as a very reliable test of the agency's effectiveness.

In the case of the lost workday incidence rate results reported in Table 12-3(b), one cannot reject the hypothesis that the coefficients are stable across the two subperiods.[9] Thus, because of its larger sample size, the 1973–1983 results, which yielded a statistically significant effect of the $INSPECT_{it-1}$ variable, are the most meaningful findings. Nevertheless, it is noteworthy that there is no apparent shift of the OSHA coefficients in the negative direction between 1973–1979 and 1980–1983, as one would expect if OSHA were becoming increasingly effective. Indeed, the coefficients for the inspection variables are both positive, but not statistically significant in 1980–1983. Thus, the evidence of OSHA's efficacy in the lost work-day incidence results appears to be the consequence of a larger sample rather than any evident improvement in OSHA's efficacy over time.

For the results pertaining to the rate of total lost workdays in Table 12-3(c), one can reject the hypothesis that the coefficients are stable across the two subperiods.[10] In this instance, as for Table 12-3(a), coefficients other than the OSHA variables were also shifting over time. As a result, the strong OSHA effects found for 1973–1983 may be attributable, at least in part, to structural shifts other than those stemming from regulatory influences. Moreover, the temporal pattern of the coefficients is almost the opposite of what one would expect if OSHA inspections were becoming increasingly effective. The inspection variables' coefficients for 1980–1983 are positive and statistically insignificant at the usual levels, whereas the 1973–1979 coefficients are both negative and jointly significant at the 5 percent level, with the $INSPECT_{it-1}$ variable's being individually significant at the 10 percent level for a one-tailed test. The results for the rate of total lost workdays provide mixed overall support of OSHA's efficacy but do not provide any support for the hypothesis that OSHA has been increasingly effective in recent years.

The following general patterns emerge. First, the evidence presented here regarding the agency's effectiveness is more favorable than the prevailing view in the literature, but it is still very mixed. Only the two lost workday accident risk measures yield any significant negative influences, and these effects are modest in terms of their size and are of questionable validity in the case of the rate of total lost workdays.

Second, when there is a significant effect, it is the INSPECT variable rather than PENALTY that is instrumental. The presence of OSHA and the threat of fines for continued noncompliance are more important than the modest financial incentives created by fines for violations discovered in a random inspection. The recent reduction in penalties for initial violations consequently may not have a major effect on safety, provided that there are major penalties for continued noncompliance.

12.5. CONCLUSION

Although OSHA's initial efforts are widely regarded as having been ineffective, the substantial reforms in OSHA's enforcement strategy during the Carter and Reagan administrations raise the question of whether this conclusion remains valid. Furthermore, the additional data now available on OSHA's performance make it possible to get a broader perspective on the agency's impact than was afforded by the more limited studies of the 1970s. It appears that having a longer time period to assess the agency's impact is the more influential of these two considerations since there is no evident shift in the OSHA regulation coefficients in recent years.

Based on the results presented here, any conclusion regarding the efficacy of OSHA's regulatory policy must necessarily be guarded. It clearly is not correct to conclude that the agency has no effect on safety whatsoever. Although this result is not strong support for OSHA, the likelihood that the agency has a nonzero risk-reducing impact does represent an improvement over OSHA's traditional standing in the literature.

The significant influences of OSHA on safety that were observed are neither dramatic in terms of their magnitude nor robust across different measures or risk. The overall injury rate series provides no support of a positive net effect. The lost workday incidence rate data suggest a significant effect for 1973–1983 for an equation that is stable over time. On the basis of these results, OSHA's effect appears to be in the range of 1.5 to 3.6 percent of the current lost workday incidence rate. Viewed somewhat differently, OSHA prevents from 1 to 2 injuries involving at least one lost day of work per 1,000 workers annually. Analysis of subperiods of data for this risk measure provides no evidence of increased efficacy, however. Finally, the rate of total lost workdays measure provided the strongest support over the 1973–1983 period, but this equation shifted structurally over time. Further research is needed to ascertain whether the changes in the accident equation structure are due to OSHA or to other economic factors.

Since these results were first published, two other studies of OSHA's impact have corroborated the finding in this chapter of a small but significant effect of OSHA on safety. Ruser and Smith (1988) estimate that records check inspections led to a 5 to 14 percent decline in reported accident rates, but the extent to which this result is due to underreporting of injuries is not clear. Scholz and Gray (1990) found a modest but significant effect of enforcement on firm-specific accident rates.

The existence of some beneficial effect on worker safety is expected on economic grounds. If the standards are related to worker safety, enforcement that increases firms' efforts to meet those standards will improve worker well-being. Although the actual penalties levied are inconsequential, the threat of additional penalties for continued noncompliance coupled with the role of workplace inspections has had a safety-enhancing effect. Firms' investments in health and safety should respond in this direction, although the magnitude of the impact has long been a matter of dispute.

Since the safety gains have fallen far short of the expectations at the time the agency was established, there is a need for greater realism when projecting the benefits of future regulations. For example, the usual assumption in regulatory analyses that regulations will completely eliminate particular risks is at sharp variance with reality.

Whether OSHA regulations are on balance beneficial is difficult to ascertain. The costs associated with compliance run in the billions, and there has never been a precise tally of the costs actually incurred, as opposed to the prospective costs calculated at the time of promulgation of the regulation. Most available cost studies fail to show examples where the benefits of OSHA standards exceed the costs, although the recent OSHA hazard communication standard is a prominent exception.

The existence of some significant beneficial effect should, however, suggest that the regulatory strategy is not so intrinsically flawed that OSHA can never play a constructive role. The remaining task for policy is to structure the regulatory approach and the enforcement strategy to ensure that the overall impact of the policies is in society's best interests.

Appendix 12A

To test for the simultaneity of $OSHA_{it}$ and $RISK_{it}$ in equation 11.2, I use a Hausman (1978) specification test for simultaneity. The procedure involves developing an instrumental variables estimator for $OSHA_{it}$, which I shall denote by $OSHA_{it}^*$. Including this as an additional variable in equation 12.2 yields an associated coefficient β_i^*. If the coefficient of β_i^* is statistically significant, then we cannot reject the hypothesis that the $OSHA_{it}$ variable is endogenous, and thus we must use an estimation procedure to address the simultaneity problem.

There is some flexibility in the choice of instruments that will be used to create $OSHA_{it}^*$. We must select which additional exogenous variables not in equation 12.2 we shall use as instruments. Since multicollinearity may be a problem, some or all of the exogenous variables may not be good instruments, as noted by Spencer and Berk (1981). The procedure we adopted was to use all other variables in equation 12.1 except for $OSHA_{it-1}$ and to augment this set with the fraction of firms in the industry that were found to be in compliance with OSHA regulations and the employee coverage per inspection (current and lagged one and two periods). The simultaneity tests were quite robust with respect to the choice of instruments.[11]

Table 12-A1 reports the specification test results for the risk equations using the OSHA inspection variables (INSPECT) for the time periods 1973–1983, 1973–1979, and 1980–1983. Similar results were obtained with the PENALTY variable, but these findings are of subsidiary interest, since none of the PENALTY variables is statistically significant in the equations estimated. The reported results are for equations using each of three risk measures. In each case we can reject the hypothesis of simultaneity at all reasonable significance levels.

Table 12-A1. Specification Test Results

	Coefficients and standard errors for $OSHA_{it}^*$		
Dependent variable	1973–1983	1973–1979	1980–1983
$\ln((IR_{it})/(100-IR_{it}))$	−6.639	−38.884	−15.853
	(11.903)	(30.622)	(16.041)
$\ln((LW_{it})/(100-LW_{it}))$	−5.401	−42.460	−14.674
	(13.458)	(32.619)	(20.566)
$\ln(LWDAYS_{it})$	−9.183	−48.916	−39.913
	(17.735)	(38.871)	(26.227)

NOTES

1. These studies attempted to control for such influences and thus made the importance of this factor less than it might be in a less careful analysis.

2. In an update of his work to more recent years, Mendeloff has also found that some of the earlier effects were not robust (oral communication with the author).

3. The 1971 risk figures using fragmentary, unpublished data were included in Viscusi (1979b) because the absence of a long time series for analyzing OSHA's impact made inclusion of even a highly imperfect set of data more attractive than it would be now, when additional data are available.

4. In particular, OSHA's counting of construction inspections is different from that of manufacturing inspections. For a construction inspection where there are multiple contractors at a particular site, an inspection is counted for each of the contractors; data for these multiple counted inspections are not comparable to manufacturing inspection data.

5. Overall, under 2 percent of all inspections involve investigations of fatalities.

6. As noted above, the year 1972 was not included because of problems with the 1971 BLS risk data, which are so unreliable that they have not been publicly released.

7. More specifically, the proportion of OSHA violations that were designated as being "serious" by the OSHA inspector rose from .02 in FY1976 to .11 in FY1977, .25 in FY1978, .34 in FY1980, and .38 in FY1983 (on the basis of data generated by OSHA for this study). These data are consistent with a general reorientation of inspections toward more serious violations, but they do not provide conclusive evidence of such a linkage. For example, a deterioration in work safety could have led to more serious violations being discovered.

8. The calculated F-statistic of 1.85 is above the critical F-values of approximately 1.54 (5 percent probability) and 1.83 (1 percent probability).

9. The calculated F-statistic of 1.39 is well below the 5 percent F-value of approximately 1.54.

10. The calculated F-statistic of 2.34 leads to rejection, at all reasonable significance levels, of the hypothesis that the coefficients are stable.

11. The exogenous variables not in the equation (the compliance rate and the three employee coverage per inspection variables) were also used separately as instruments, in conjunction with the SIC code dummy variables, and yielded similar results.

13

Consumer Behavior and the Safety Effects of Consumer Product Safety Regulation

13.1 INTRODUCTION

A recurring issue in the economic analysis of risk regulation agencies is whether these efforts have had any significant favorable effect on safety. Although the existence of such an effect would not necessarily imply that these efforts were worthwhile, without an enhancement in safety there is no potential rationale for these regulations.

Most of the research on this issue to date has focused on auto accidents and job risks. Motor vehicle accidents pose the chief safety risk, accounting for one-half of all accidental fatalities.[1] Studies of the safety-enhancing effects of seat belts have, however, failed to indicate any clear-cut beneficial effect of this safety measure on auto fatality rates.[2] One contributor to their ineffectiveness is that drivers will reduce the degree to which they exercise care as their safety protection from seat belts and other protective features increases, thus dampening and possibly even offsetting the safety improvements from seat belts.

The studies of job safety have placed less emphasis on the role of individual behavior, not because worker actions are unimportant but because Occupational Safety and Health Administration regulations have not been particularly effective in altering firms' incentives to invest in safety. Noncompliance with OSHA regulations is quite frequent, in large part because the expected penalties for noncompliance are negligible and the costs that must be incurred to achieve compliance are considerable. The net effect shown in Chapters 10 through 12 is that there is little evidence of a significant effect on safety.

The Consumer Product Safety Commission (CPSC) represents an intermediate case in terms of the level of the risks possibly affected by agency actions. Roughly 30 percent of all home accident deaths are product-related, which is almost double the risk level from work accidents and just over half that of motor vehicle accidents.[3] Although some products (for example, boats) have been specifically excluded from the CPSC's jurisdiction, the agency has broad authority over a wide range of consumer products.

This scope derives from the historical role of the CPSC, an independent regulatory commission established in 1972 (and first operating in 1973) in order to consolidate the product safety functions scattered throughout the federal government. The CPSC inherited the functions of the Federal Hazardous Substances Act (formerly administered by the U.S. Department of Health, Education, and Welfare, the U.S. Department of Commerce, and the Federal Trade Commission), the Poison Prevention Packaging Act of 1970 (formerly administered by the U.S. Department of Health, Education, and Welfare), and the Refrigerator Safety Act (formerly administered by the U.S. Department of Commerce and the Federal Trade Commission). Congress also gave the CPSC broad authority to set standards to eliminate "unreasonable" risks and to issue bans and recalls of products that violate CPSC standards or that create "a substantial risk of injury to the consumer."[4]

Notwithstanding the potential importance of the CPSC, there has been very little systematic scrutiny of its efforts. Published studies have addressed the limitations of its product safety data base and one particular standard—the mattress flammability standard—but there has been no comprehensive empirical assessment of the agency.[5] This chapter is intended to provide a detailed empirical assessment of the effect of CPSC regulations on product safety.[6]

The effect of product safety regulations depends not only on the engineering standards mandated by the CPSC but also on the interaction of product characteristics with consumers' precautionary behavior. As the conceptual analysis in Section 13.2 indicates, the net effect of these influences may be counterproductive.

Section 13.3 begins the empirical analysis with a review of the principal home accident data series, for which I will test whether there has been any shift in accident trends as a result of the CPSC's efforts. These aggregative statistics do not suggest any statistically significant effects, a finding that is similar to the results of analyses of other risk-regulation agencies. Section 13.4 presents the principal case study—the effect of protective bottle caps on poisonings. The implications of this regulation are strongly related to consumers' behavioral response to safety caps. The strength of this behavioral response and the detailed information available regarding poisonings make this a particularly instructive case study of consumers' response to regulatory protection. A series of other CPSC regulations are reviewed in Section 13.5 in order to ascertain whether there may be some beneficial product-specific effects that are not apparent in the aggregative data or in the poisoning trends. These data provide no evidence of any significant beneficial impacts on product safety.

13.2 THE LULLING EFFECT: A CONCEPTUAL MODEL OF CONSUMER RESPONSE TO SAFETY STANDARDS

In 1972 the Food and Drug Administration imposed a protective bottle cap requirement on aspirin and other selected drugs. This regulation epitomizes the technological approach to social regulation. The strategy for reducing children's poisoning risks was to design caps that would make opening containers of hazardous substances more difficult. This engineering approach will be effective provided that children's exposure to hazardous products does not increase. If, however, parents leave protective caps off bottles because they are difficult to open, or increase children's access to these bottles because they are supposedly "childproof," the regulation may not have a beneficial effect.

This safety cap requirement will be the focal point of my model of consumer responses to safety regulations, but the results generalize to any product safety situation where consumer actions and product characteristics interact. Subsequent sections will document the behavioral linkages in the model.

One can distinguish three different mechanisms by which protective packaging requirements or other safety standards may alter precautionary behavior and consequently the level of safety ultimately produced by the regulation. First, regulations will lead to a reduction in safety-related efforts for the affected product. Second, the regulation may produce misperceptions that lead consumers to reduce their safety precautions because they overestimate the product's safety. Finally, if there are indivisibilities in one's actions (for example, choosing whether to keep medicines in a bathroom cabinet or in the kitchen), regulating one product may affect the safety of other products. These effects are quite general and are not restricted to the case of protective bottle caps.

The existing theoretical literature on individual responses to regulatory protection began with the analysis by Peltzman (1975), who showed that seat belts would lead to increased driving intensity (for example, less caution or higher speeds). The economic mechanism generating this effect is similar to that which produces adverse incentives or moral hazard problems in the insurance context. As one reduces either the probability of a loss or the size of the loss, individual incentives to take precautionary actions will be reduced. Regulations function much like insurance in this regard, with the only difference being that one need not pay an insurance premium. There may, however, be an effect of the regulation on the product price.

The results in Chapter 11 indicated that for the case of worker safety the effect of regulations on safety will seldom be counterproductive. Except in the case of very stringently enforced government regulations, firms would not make technological changes in the workplace that decreased safety. Compliance with policies such as seat belt and bottle cap requirements is less discretionary, however, so one cannot rule out counterproductive regulatory effects in these instances.

To investigate these effects more formally, consider a simple model that captures the essential features of these analyses. Let s be the stringency of the government policy and e be the precautionary effort, where each of these reduces the probability $p(e,s)$ of an accident at a diminishing rate. Alternatively, one can make the mechanism of influence the size of the accident loss L, as in Peltzman, but for purposes of this model I will make L a constant. The individual's effort e generates a disutility $V(e)$, where V', $V'' > 0$. Finally, let the person have an income level I.

The payoff in the case of an accident is $I - V(e) - L$, and the payoff if there is not an accident is $I - V(e)$. The individual's expected utility (assuming risk neutrality) is $I - V(e) - p(e,s)L$. In setting the optimal level of e, one equates the marginal reduction in the loss $p_e L$ to the marginal value of the effort $-V_e$, leading to the optimal point A in Figure 13-1.

The effect of the regulation on safety effort will be negative, or

$$\frac{de}{ds} = \frac{-p_{es}L}{p_{ee}L + V_{ee}} < 0,$$

provided that $p_{es} > 0$ (or $L_{es} > 0$ in Peltzman's loss model). For safety efforts to decline, the safety regulation must reduce the marginal safety benefits from precautionary efforts, that is, the reduction in the expected loss from higher levels of effort

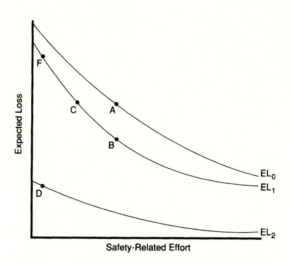

Figure 13.1 Precautionary behavior and expected losses

is less negative than before. One will then choose a point to the left of point B on the EL_1 curve in Figure 13-1. This effect should not be particularly controversial. Few would question the opposite relationship where individuals increase their precautions when moving from EL_1 to EL_0. For example, one will drive more carefully on icy streets and reduce smoking if exposed to synergistic asbestos risks.

What is more problematic is whether the reduction in precautions will be so great that there will be a reduction in safety to a point to the left of point C on EL_1. The conditions for this to occur have never been investigated and are quite stringent. It is not sufficient that the marginal expected loss reduction at point C can be no greater than at A. The requirement is stronger since the marginal disutility of effort V_e will be lower at lower effort levels. To equate the marginal expected loss reduction p_eL to the marginal effort cost $-V_e$, the loss curve EL_1 must be flatter at point C than EL_0 was at point A. Since there is the additional restriction that EL_1 lie below EL_0, it will be difficult to meet these requirements.

The chance that the impact of protective regulations may be counterproductive may be enhanced if individuals either do not perceive accurately the accident probabilities or do not fully bear the accident costs. Parents assume "child-resistant" caps are childproof. Indeed, commissioners of the CPSC have referred to safety caps as making products "childproof." Parents may consequently overestimate the safety associated with these products. Safety precautions will decline, perhaps to so great an extent that overall safety is reduced. For example, parents may select point D off of their perceived loss curve EL_2 in a situation where the true loss curve is EL_1 and the actual outcome is point F.

A similar effect could occur if parents do not fully value the welfare of their children, or if drivers do not fully internalize the accident costs to pedestrians and other parties. Unlike the case of biased probabilistic beliefs, this modification in the problem need not entail a shift in the relative values of the accident loss in the regulated and unregulated situations. Thus, the EL_0 and EL_1 curves may both simply shift proportionally. In contrast, misperceptions such as those discussed above necessarily lead to a comparatively greater downward shift in the perceived expected loss, increasing the chance of a counterproductive effect.

One's precautionary actions may affect the safety of unregulated products as well as those that are regulated. In the case of child-resistant bottle caps, parents may make overall decisions regarding the storage of medicines. Should they keep all of the medicines in the bathroom cabinet, on a kitchen shelf, or in a safety-latched drawer? More generally, should they worry about access to medicines or undertake only a mild level of precautions, since the most hazardous products are presumably protected by child-resistant containers?

The analytics of this effort decision parallel that given above, where the only difference is that the EL_0 and EL_1 curves are a weighted average of the component risks, where some products are protected and others are not. A joint risk curve EL_1 will tend to shift downward less in response to a regulation than a comparable curve for a particular regulated product, since the presence of the unregulated product will dampen the response.

There is a clear-cut empirical test of whether indivisible actions such as this play a role. If there are such spillover effects, the reduction in safety-enhancing efforts induced by the regulation should increase the risk posed by the unregulated product. In addition, the safety improvement of the regulated product will be reduced at least in part by the reduction in individual precautions. The net effect on safety could be adverse for the regulated product or for both products combined, but one must satisfy fairly stringent conditions for the net effect to be adverse unless misperceptions of the risk play a major role.

13.3 AN OVERVIEW OF THE IMPACT OF THE CPSC

The two principal policy mechanisms the CPSC has for influencing product safety are issuing standards and banning or recalling hazardous products. The standard-setting activities have been comparatively modest. The CPSC has issued just over twenty standards pertaining to a variety of products: lawn mowers, matchbooks, baby cribs, bicycles, and children's sleepwear. Many of its efforts have focused on banning or recalling hazardous products, in part because this policy approach does not require that the CPSC go through the rulemaking process. Recent CPSC ban and recall actions have addressed a wide variety of products, including refuse bins, asbestos-containing hair dryers, roller skates, electric drills, motorcycles, scuba diving equipment, and thermostats.

In each case, the CPSC does not encounter the same types of enforcement problems as does OSHA since it can typically monitor a small number of units in a standardized product line to ascertain whether firms are in compliance. For example, a single trip to a drugstore will provide very detailed information about whether drug companies are in compliance with CPSC safety cap requirements, whereas ascertaining compliance with an OSHA chemical exposure standard will require visits to possibly thousands of workplaces using the chemical. The general consensus, including the opinion of the CPSC, is that there is a high degree of compliance with CPSC requirements.[7]

Even if fully effective, however, the CPSC regulations may not have a major effect on safety. The scope of the CPSC actions is quite modest; OSHA, for example, has promulgated over 200 times as many standards as has the CPSC. In addition, the bulk of the product risk problem cannot be eliminated without major changes in our lifestyles. Table 13-1 lists the ten most hazardous product groups, based on the CPSC's hospital emergency room admission data. Falls down various types of stairs and ramps head the list but are not covered by CPSC policies because of the decentralized nature of the use of this product. The CPSC could, however, establish a stair width and handrail requirement if it chose to do so. The second leading cause of accidents—riding bicycles—is already the subject of CPSC regulations, which, except for a reflector requirement, seem to bear a tenuous relationship to bike safety. Four of the other ten riskiest "products" are also sports-related activities—baseball, football, basketball, and skating. The potential impact of any CPSC regulation on these risks is likely to be negligible. The risk of being cut by a nail or a thumbtack likewise will remain so as long as such products are in use.

The three remaining product risk categories are potentially more subject to the influence of CPSC policies. The CPSC has in place flammability requirements for chairs and sofas. Similarly, glass doors and windows are at least partially regulated through architectural glazing requirements. Finally, nonglass tables could conceivably be regulated by, for example, prohibiting the presence of sharp corners and requiring rounded edges on furniture, but no such regulation now exists and would be of questionable merit. The impact of current CPSC regulations is likely to be quite small, and even if the agency were much more active than it now is, it is doubtful whether there would be a dramatic impact on product safety.

The absence of any stark shift in product safety after the advent of the CPSC is borne out by the accident trend data in Table 13-2. Fatal home accident rates dropped from 13.2 per 100,000 to 10.1 per 100,000 during the 1970s, but this

Table 13-1. The Ten Products Most Involved in Injuries, 1981

Product group	Injuries (*in thousands*)
Stairs, steps, ramps, and buildings	763
Bicycles and bicycle accessories	518
Baseball	478
Football	470
Basketball	434
Nails, carpet tacks, screws, and thumbtacks	244
Chairs, sofas, and sofa beds	236
Skating	225
Nonglass tables	225
Glass doors, windows, and panels	208

Source: U.S. Consumer Product Safety Commission, Annual Report (1982), p. 22.

Table 13-2. Accidental Death Rates (Rates per 100,000 Population)

Year	Home	Poisonings (*under age five*)	Fires and burns (*under age five*)	Ingestions (*under age five*)
1935	25.2	5.4	17.9	—
1940	23.9	5.0	14.8	—
1950	19.2	2.5	8.1	6.6
1960	15.6	2.2	7.3	7.0
1970	13.2	1.3	4.8	5.2
1980	10.1	.4	4.2	2.7

Source: National Safety Council, *Accident Facts* (1982).

change appears to represent a continuation in the downward trend that has prevailed throughout this century. As society has become richer, safety levels of all kinds have increased because of the positive income elasticity of demand for good health. The three specific accident rate series listed—poisonings, fires and burns, and ingestions—likewise have been affected by a downward trend from increasing social wealth. Since some of these component risks are strongly related to age, each of the specific risk series is for the population under five years of age, which is a high risk group.

The first risk series I will analyze is the overall home accident rate (HR). These statistics are based on National Center for Health Statistics accident reports. Although data have been collected by this organization on a continuous basis for over fifty years, there have been some changes over time because of periodic modifications in the international classification of diseases. These changes in disease categorization primarily affect illnesses rather than accidents.[8] Previous classification periods will be captured through a series of dummy variables (D1, D2, D3, and D4) that take on a value of one during a particular classification period and zero otherwise.

The two time periods to be analyzed will be 1933–1981 and 1949–1981. The 1933 starting period was selected both to avoid the complicating influence of the depression and to have a comparable starting date of all major accident series, some of which are unavailable before that date. The 1949 starting date is for a post–World War II analysis, which may better reflect current behavior to the extent that the home accident rate relationships have not been stable over the past fifty years. I selected 1949 as the starting point since a new revision in the classification system began in that year.

The first substantive explanatory variable included was the lagged value of the home accident rate (HR_{t-1}). The linear form of the accident probability was used largely to provide greater ease in interpreting the results. To take into account the constrained nature of the dependent variable, one could use the logarithm of the accident rate as in Peltzman (1975) or the log-odds of the accident rate as in Chapters 11 and 13. The regression results with respect to the impact of CPSC were quite robust with respect to such changes in specification.[9]

Since consumer safety will be affected not only by current products but also by the stock of existing products and their manner of use, HR_{t-1} should have a positive effect on HR_t. Lagged dependent variables play a fundamental role in most accident rate equations in the literature, and in this instance omission of the HR_{t-1} variable will generate serial correlation problems.

The second principal variable is the value of real per capita consumption (PCC). This variable is intended to capture the effect of rising consumer wealth, which should have a negative effect on accidents to the extent that rising wealth leads to a greater demand for safety. There may, however, be other effects of PCC other than a pure income effect. Increased wealth may increase the volume of consumer product purchases and the nature of the product mix. For example, it may lead to increased use of pharmaceutical products, which will then increase the risk of poisoning to one's children. From a theoretical standpoint, the predicted sign of PCC is not clear.

The fundamental variable of interest is the CPSC, which is a regulatory dummy variable that takes on a value of one during the 1973–1981 period and zero otherwise. This variable is intended to capture any shift in the intercept term as a result of the CPSC. Finally, the equations for the entire sample included a variable that would reflect the demographic composition, in particular, the percentage of children in the population who are under age five (%UNDER5). This group is a particularly high risk segment of the population for poisonings, ingestions, and fire and burn deaths.

Since it is not feasible to include all the diverse factors affecting product safety, the empirical analysis focuses on what might best be viewed as a reduced-form model of a complex accident generating process. For the full sample, the equation to be estimated is

$$HR_t = \alpha + \beta_1 HR_{t-1} + \beta_2 PCC + \beta_3 CPSC$$
$$+ \beta_4 \%UNDER\ 5 + \beta_5 D1 + \beta_6 D2$$
$$+ \beta_7 D3 + \beta_8 D4 + u_t. \tag{13.1}$$

The D1 and D2 terms are omitted for regressions over time periods in which these periods of illness classification are not relevant. The expected signs of the key variables are positive for β_1, negative or conceivably positive for β_2, negative for β_3, and positive for β_4.

Table 13-3 summarizes the home accident rate regression results for both time periods. For each equation, I also report the Durbin-Watson statistics.[10] Here and throughout the rest of the paper, there is no firm evidence of serial correlation.

The lagged home accident rate has a consistently positive effect on accidents, as we would expect. The effect is especially pronounced during the post–World War II period. Over the past few decades, over half the value of HR_{t-1} is transmitted in the subsequent year to influence HR_t. There is consequently a strong intertemporal linkage in the accident-generating process.

Real per capita consumption has a significant negative effect on home accident rates, which suggests that the wealth effect dominates any possible increase in risk from the greater level of consumption by wealthier consumers. The importance of this time trend was not sensitive to the particular measure used. Similar results were obtained using either a simple time trend variable or real per capita income instead of PCC.

Table 13-3. Home Accident Rate
Regression Results

Independent variable	Coefficients and standard errors	
	1933–1981	1949–1981
Intercept	17.49	17.79
	(4.17)	(9.96)
HR_{t-1}	.277	.548
	(.104)	(.174)
PCC	−.003	−.002
	(.001)	(.001)
CPSC	.087	−.333
	(.684)	(.370)
%UNDER5	14.66	−53.80
	(25.53)	(41.94)
D1	4.26	—
	(1.72)	—
D2	3.90	—
	(1.36)	—
D3	.428	1.309
	(1.097)	(.734)
D4	−.631	.777
	(.825)	(.525)
R^2	.97	.97
D − W	1.85	1.97

The CPSC regulation variable is never statistically significant and never has a t-statistic above 0.9. In the home accident data there is no evidence of a post-CPSC downward shift in the intercept term. The largest point estimate of an impact of the CPSC is in the equation for 1949–1981. Taken at face value this coefficient implies a mean effect that is almost 4 percent of the 1981 home accident rate, which would have been 9.5 deaths per 100,000 rather than 9.2 if the CPSC had not been in existence. Since we cannot reject the hypothesis that the coefficient is significantly different from zero, what this result suggests is that if there is a nonzero effect, it is likely to be small. Indeed, the upper bound of the 95 percent confidence interval suggests an impact of just under 1.0 deaths per 100,000, or less than a 10 percent reduction in the home accident rate.

The principal variables influencing consumer safety are not CPSC but HR_{t-1} and PCC. The age composition variable (%UNDER5) and the disease classification dummy variables were not statistically significant except in the pre–World War II data (D1 and D2).

One obtains similar results in an analysis of the principal accident categories that make up the overall accident rate, as reported in Table 13-4. Here I will focus on the three accident classes most directly affected by CPSC regulations—poisonings, fires and burns, and ingestions. In each case the equations estimated were of the same general form as equation 13.1. The only difference was with respect to the

Table 13-4. Summary of CPSC Effects on Poisoning, Burn, and Ingestion Death Rates

| Accident type | Coefficients and standard errors for CPSC variables | | | |
| | 1933–1981 and 1941–1981 (ingestions) | | 1949–1981 | |
	Entire population	Population under age five	Entire population	Population under age five
Poisonings	.054	.209	.191	−.054
	(.155)	(.201)	(.181	(.107)
Burns	−.136	1.286	−.193	.171
	(.414)	(.744)	(.463)	(.467)
Ingestions	.074	.340	.052	.988
	(.082)	(.604)	(.107)	(.614)

starting point of the CPSC dummy variable, which was adjusted so as to pertain to the regulations likely to affect that risk class.

A leading target of CPSC actions has been poisonings of children. In order to reduce these hazards, Congress passed the Poison Prevention Packaging Act of 1970. Beginning in 1972, aspirin, controlled drugs, and furniture polishes were subject to a protective packaging requirement. Additional products were added to this list in the subsequent decade.

Since these packaging requirements are among the most extensive and well-known CPSC regulations, it is instructive to ascertain whether they had any effect on the poisoning death rate. The particular CPSC variable used took a value of one beginning in 1972. As the CPSC coefficients in Table 13-4 indicate, there was no downward shift in poisoning deaths in the 1972–1981 period. Even more disturbing is that in the two cases in which the coefficients exceeded the standard errors, the effects are positive. While not statistically significant at the usual levels, these effects may be a signal of a possible positive upward shift in subcategories of poisoning rates. This possibility will be explored in Section 13.4.

The next accident category, fire and burn deaths, has been the target of a wide variety of CPSC standards. Most of these efforts have been concerned with flammability requirements instituted in response to the Flammable Fabrics Act of 1953. The pivotal year in the CPSC's regulation of these hazards was 1975, in which it instituted regulations for carpets and rugs, children's sleepwear, and clothing textiles, and set final mattress flammability requirements (for which regulation began in 1973).[11] Some of these regulations have been major sources of controversy. The flammability requirements for children's sleepwear led to use of the flame-retardant Tris, which was subsequently found to be potentially carcinogenic. The beneficial safety effects of these regulations have also come under question; Linneman (1980), for one, was unable to find any significant effect of the CPSC mattress standard on mattress-related burns.

The results on the second line of Table 13-4 also fail to suggest any downward shift in fire and burn deaths over the primary period for which the CPSC regulated such risks. The most pertinent results are for the population under age five, where these coefficients are positive. The positive CPSC variable is only significant (at the 5 percent level, one-tailed test) in the case of the 1933–1981 data, a result that may be due to the inability of this equation adequately to capture the nature of more recent experience. The positive CPSC effect is much smaller in magnitude and not significantly different from zero in the more recent results, which suggests that the burn-related regulations had no significant effect.

Similar results for fire and burn deaths (BR$_t$) are borne out by the data gathered through the CPSC's National Electronic Injury Surveillance System (NEISS) based on reports from selected hospitals. The actual level of fire-related deaths per 100,000 persons decline somewhat from the 1974–1978 period, as shown in Table 13-5. Using the overall NSC fire and burn death equation estimated in Table 13-4 for the 1950–1981 period, one can calculate the predicted death rate level by adjusting the NSC equation by the ratio of the NEISS burn rate in 1974 to the NSC 1974 burn rate to put them on a comparable basis. More specifically, if we let

$$\xi = \frac{BR_{74}(\text{NEISS})}{BR_{74}(\text{NSC})},$$

the estimated level of NEISS burn rates is $\xi BR_t(\text{NSC})$, where BR$_t$ is the estimated burn rate from the burn rate analog of equation 13.1. Actual NEISS burn rates after the regulation average slightly above their predicted levels, but by an insignificant amount (under half the standard error of the predicted value).

The final accident category considered was ingestions of objects. The CPSC has attempted to address this risk by imposing minimum size requirements on pacifiers (1977), rattles (1978), and toys (1979). All toys intended for use by children under the age of three must be sufficiently large so as not to fit within a cylinder that is 1.24 inches in diameter and 2.25 inches high.[12] The initial year 1977 was selected as the starting point for the regulatory shift variable, but similar results were obtained using 1978 and 1979. In all cases the CPSC variable is not significantly different from zero.

In terms of overall impact, there is no evidence in the aggregative data of any

Table 13-5. Actual and Predicted Fire-Related Deaths, 1974–1978

Year	Fire-related death rate per 100,000		
	Actual	Predicted	Difference
1974	.65	—	—
1975	.63	.65	−.02
1976	.65	.61	.04
1977	.63	.59	.04
1978	.58	.56	.02
Average for regulated period	.62	.60	.02

Source: CPSC's NEISS data and calculations by the author.

beneficial effect on product safety. In the case of poisonings, the results suggest that there may even be a possible adverse effect. Whether or not this is the case is the focus of the next section.

13.4. SAFETY CAPS AND POISONINGS

One CPSC regulation familiar to all consumers is the protective bottle cap requirement. Congress passed the Poison Prevention Packaging Act of 1970 to address the problem of accidental poisonings that primarily involved young children under the age of five. This cause of accidents had gained increasing attention throughout the 1960s, in large part because increases in the percentage of the population in this group boosted the total number of poisonings. Although the poisoning rate occasionally increased as well, the dominant long-run trend in the frequency of poisonings was in the downward direction, as the fatal poisoning rate for children under five dropped from 2.52 per million in 1950 to 2.19 per million in 1960, and to 1.32 per million in 1970.[13]

The poisoning problem, which typically involves nonfatal outcomes, had shown signs of diminishing even more rapidly than before. This improvement may be attributable in part to a series of efforts directed at reducing poisonings. In the mid-1960s firms limited the number of tablets per bottle, placed warning labels on the bottles, replaced screw caps with snap caps, and in some cases voluntarily introduced safety caps. Perhaps even more important, there was a widespread educational campaign to urge parents to limit their children's access to drugs. The regulation variable used below will not capture these influences, some of which may have been undertaken in anticipation of regulation.

These efforts were augmented by explicit government regulation beginning in 1972 when the FDA required protective bottle caps on aspirin, furniture polishes, methyl salicylate, and several controlled drugs. The scope of product coverage was subsequently expanded to include turpentine (1973), oral prescription drugs (1974), iron preparations (1977), acetaminophen (1980), and several other products. Each of these regulations is now administered by the CPSC.

These measures have aroused some controversy because individuals without children—particularly many elderly with arthritis who find the caps difficult to open—are forced to incur the inconvenience of safety caps without reaping any benefits. Although such costs (plus those of the caps themselves) may exceed any prospective benefits, one would expect that the impact on safety should be favorable if consumer behavior remains unchanged.

In practice, consumer behavior will not remain the same. In the case of seat belts, for example, Peltzman (1975) showed that added seat belt protection diminished drivers' incentive to exercise care. As indicated in the recent critical review by Blomquist (1988), the available empirical evidence on auto safety remains consistent with this hypothesis.

Section 13.2 hypothesized that safety caps and similar safety devices will induce a "lulling effect" on consumer behavior that comprises three components. First, the presence of safety caps will diminish the expected safety gains to be achieved by decreasing parental precautions regarding drugs. As a result, parents will have less incentive to reduce children's access to drugs for much the same reason that drivers protected by seat belts have less incentive to exercise care. This diminished responsibility could lead to a net reduction in the safety level after the advent of protective caps, but the conditions required for this to occur are quite stringent.[14]

A second type of influence arises because of the indivisibility of individuals' safety-related actions. Many safety precautions relating to pharmaceuticals affect a variety of products, not simply those with protective caps. Parents may choose to keep drugs in a medicine chest, a kitchen cabinet, on a bathroom shelf, in a safety-latched drawer, or in a purse. To the extent that there is a spillover effect of the diminished responsibility on other products, safety caps will increase poisoning rates for these unprotected products. The net effect on safety will continue to tend to be favorable, but the effect will be dampened by the consumer response. One cannot, however, rule out a potentially counterproductive impact.

Finally, the regulation may induce consumer misperceptions regarding the importance of precautions. Safety caps are routinely called "childproof" caps rather than "child-resistant" caps even by leading CPSC officials.[15]

The Impact on Aspirin Poisonings

To test the lulling effect hypothesis, consider the first major target of the protective packaging requirements—aspirin. Aspirin accounted for 8 percent of all accidental poisonings in 1972 and 17 percent of all poisonings from medicines. Manufacturers were not required to use safety caps for all aspirin sold. The FDA exempted one size from the regulation, and firms typically selected their best selling size (usually the 100 tablet bottle) to be free of a safety cap.

The CPSC's statistical defense of the effectiveness of its safety cap requirements focuses on total poisonings rather than the poisoning rate, thus ignoring the decline in the high risk population group of children during the 1970s.[16] Nevertheless, even the poisoning rate trend followed the pattern one would expect from an effective regulation. The fatal poisoning rate declined from 2.6 per million children under age five in 1971 to a rate of 0.6 by 1980. Similarly, overall aspirin poisonings leading to hospital emergency room treatment dropped from 5.0 to 1.7 per thousand children under the age of five.

These declines need not imply that the regulation was effective. Aspirin's share of the pain reliever market has diminished as acetaminophen products, such as Tylenol, have assumed a greater role. In addition, almost all accident trends have declined throughout this century as society has become richer.

To isolate the influence of the protective packaging requirements, I will use a regression in the same spirit as equation 13.1, but with some modifications. The aspirin poisoning rate for children under five ($PR5_t$) is the dependent variable (CPSC), which takes on a value of one beginning in 1972. In addition, I will include an alternative measure of regulatory effectiveness—the fraction of aspirin sold with safety caps (SAFETYCAPS)—in some of the regressions. Because of the rise of acetaminophen products in the 1970s, there was a downward shift in the trend in aspirin sales. To control for changes in the exposure to aspirin, each regression will include one of three measures: the deflated or real value per capita of aspirin sales

(RSALES), total aspirin tablets produced per capita (PROD), and total aspirin tablets sold per capita (SALES).[17] In all, there were six different equations to be estimated.

Table 13-6 reports the death rate results for the 1963–1980 period, and Table 13-7 reports the overall poisoning rate results for the same period. The results are consistently similar in each case. There is the expected positive lagged influence of $PR5_{t-1}$ on the current poisoning rate. Moreover, as society's wealth has risen, the poisoning rate has exhibited the expected decline. Except in the case of the RSALES variable, in the death rate equation the aspirin use variable did not play a significant role. In that case the variable had a negative sign, which is the opposite of what one would expect. Since the tablet-based measures (PROD and SALES) fail to show a similar negative effect and appear preferable, in that they avoid the distorting effect of changes in the price level, this negative result appears to be an aberration.

The choice of the regulation variable is not consequential, since there is no evidence of any significant shift in poisoning rates after the advent of the safety cap requirement. These results are also not sensitive to the aspirin use variable that is employed. The regression results consequently offer no support for the hypothesis that CPSC safety cap regulations had a statistically significant favorable effect on poisonings.

In the case of the aspirin death results, four of the six regulation coefficients are positive. More favorable results for safety caps appear in Table 13-7, where the largest mean impact of the regulation is for equation 5 in Table 13-7, where the

Table 13-6. Aspirin Poisoning Death Rate (under Five Years), Regression Results, 1963–1980

Independent variable	Coefficients and standard errors					
	1	2	3	4	5	6
Intercept	16.92	9.58	9.68	17.67	9.50	9.31
	(5.65)	(4.36)	(4.28)	(5.69)	(4.38)	(4.23)
$PR5_{t-1}$	.408	.489	.450	.382	.483	.456
	(.204)	(.221)	(.249)	(.205)	(.225)	(.251)
PCC	−.003	−.002	−.003	−.003	−.002	−.002
	(.001)	(.001)	(.001)	(.001)	(.001)	(.001)
CPSC	−.224	.191	.305	—	—	—
	(.524)	(.553)	(.538)	—	—	—
SAFETYCAPS	—	—	—	−.677	.100	.314
	—	—	—	(.907)	(.979)	(.938)
RSALES	−.016	—	—	−.017	—	—
	(.009)	—	—	(.008)	—	—
PROD	—	−.023	—	—	−.032	—
	—	(.101)	—	—	(.102)	—
SALES	—	—	.037	—	—	.028
	—	—	(.102)	—	—	(.103)
R^2	.96	.95	.95	.96	.95	.95
D − W	2.49	1.91	1.83	2.58	1.95	1.84

Table 13-7. Aspirin Poisoning Rate (under Five Years),
Regression Results, 1963–1980

Independent variable	Coefficients and standard errors					
	1	2	3	4	5	6
Intercept	897.5	819.6	627.5	861.1	810.6	618.5
	(1,157.5)	(335.9)	(292.4)	(1,133.9)	(326.7)	(289.2)
$PR5_{t-1}$	.732	.734	.707	.713	.723	.694
	(.330)	(.180)	(.140)	(.322)	(.176)	(.139)
PCC	−.194	−.167	−.195	−.183	−.158	−.185
	(.176)	(.088)	(.085)	(.169)	(.084)	(.081)
CPSC	−25.3	−28.3	9.7	—	—	—
	(99.5)	(96.3)	(98.6)	—	—	—
SAFETYCAPS	—	—	—	−71.0	−78.1	−9.74
	—	—	—	(167.0)	(163.1)	(169.0)
RSALES	−.435	—	—	−.364	—	—
	(3.321)	—	—	(3.277)	—	—
PROD	—	−7.33	—	—	−7.83	—
	—	(19.35)	—	—	(19.28)	—
SALES	—	—	15.1	—	—	14.4
	—	—	(13.6)	—	—	(13.7)
R^2	.92	.92	.92	.92	.89	.92
D − W	1.65	1.63	1.87	1.66	1.66	1.87

safety cap effect represents roughly 9 percent of the average home accident rate over the sample period. This impact cannot be distinguished statistically from the no effect hypothesis, and the overall magnitude of any potential impact of safety caps appears to be modest.

One possible explanation for the lack of effectiveness is that consumers may have purchased those bottle sizes that did not have safety caps so that it is conceivable that almost all poisonings were from unprotected bottles. This possibility can be ruled out on inspection of the data in Table 13-8 for aspirin and aspirin and analgesics combined. Just over half of all aspirin sold was in safety cap bottles.[18] This figure did not change substantially during the 1970–1978 period for which detailed poisoning data are available. In contrast, the safety cap share of poisonings rose from 40 percent in 1972 to 73 percent in 1978. Not only are safety cap bottles not risk free, but they account for a majority of all aspirin poisonings. Indeed, a disproportionate share of poisonings are linked to safety caps. This result may not imply that safety cap bottles are more risky since parents with children may buy the safety capped containers more often than consumers not in the high risk group. Safety cap bottles may be better matched to parents with children, but this event has not had a beneficial effect on safety.

Of particular interest is the data series on the share of open bottles involved in the poisonings. Although these data are not available for bottle types (that is, for whether it was a safety cap bottle), it is noteworthy that over two-fifths of all aspirin poisonings are from open bottles. In the case of an open container, a safety cap will serve no useful function. Some open bottle poisonings occur while the parent is

Table 13-8. Characteristics of Poisoning Incidents

	1971	1972	1973	1974	1975	1976	1977	1978
Aspirin:								
Sold with safety caps (%)	—	53	56	59	56	56	55	52
Poisonings from safety cap bottles (%)	—	40	52	60	59	67	71	73
Open bottle share of poisonings (%)	—	41	43	44	48	46	44	49
Aspirin and analgesics:								
Poisonings from safety cap bottles (%)	—	34	44	53	54	63	67	66
Open bottle share of poisonings (%)	—	43	43	44	47	44	39	47
Total poisonings	168,930	167,270	153,670	126,520	137,010	112,860	112,840	111,420

Source: Based on unpublished Poison Control Center computer printouts and pharmaceutical industry data on aspirin sales.

administering the aspirin to the child and leaves the bottle unattended. The presence of open aspirin bottles also may be related to the difficulties consumers have in opening these protective caps. Consumers may leave the bottles open rather than grapple with caps that they find difficult to open. There is some evidence in support of this possibility since the rise in safety cap poisonings has been accompanied by an increase in the role of open bottles.

The evidence on aspirin poisonings is consistent with a lulling effect on consumer behavior. Safety cap bottles accounted for a sizable share of poisonings, and many of these bottles were left open. The net effect was that there is no evidence of a favorable impact on aspirin poisonings. If this were the full effect of the regulation, the outcome would not be greatly different from what has been observed in the seat belt case. The principal difference is that the data on the role of safety caps and open bottles enable us to address the mechanisms of influence more directly.

The Effect on Analgesic Poisonings

The distinctive feature of these safety effects is the presence of a spillover effect on analgesic poisonings. Analgesic poisonings from products such as Tylenol rose from 1.1 per 1,000 children under five in 1971 to a rate of 1.5 per 1,000 in 1980. Since this upward shift may be attributable to other factors, such as increased sales, once again it is desirable to isolate such influences statistically. The variables included in the analgesic poisoning rate equations reported in Table 13-9 are similar to those in the aspirin regression equations. One principal difference is that the CPSC variable takes on a value of one only in 1980, the year in which the safety cap requirement was extended to acetaminophen products. The hypothesis that the

Table 13-9. Analgesic Poisoning Rate (under Five Years), Regression Results, 1963–1980

Independent variables	Coefficients and standard errors			
	1	2	3	4
Intercept	−160.6	−162.4	−146.0	−154.7
	(59.8)	(62.7)	(58.7)	(58.2)
$PR5_{t-1}$	.388	−.003	.002	−.025
	(.293)	(.356)	(.283)	(.288)
PCC	.076	.077	.069	.073
	(.025)	(.027)	(.025)	(.025)
CPSC	−2.16	−1.97	−5.73	−4.66
	(15.43)	(16.05)	(15.13)	(15.07)
UNREG	22.33	23.70	21.46	23.56
	(9.70)	(11.75)	(9.39)	(9.45)
RSALES	—	.041	—	—
	—	(.182)	—	—
PROD	—	—	2.61	—
	—	—	(1.88)	—
SALES	—	—	—	2.73
	—	—	—	(2.02)
R^2	.97	.97	.97	.97
D − W	1.84	1.86	2.10	2.00

lulling effect from protective bottle caps on aspirin had a spillover effect on analgesics will be captured by the dummy variable UNREG, which takes on a value of one during the 1972–1979 period. If bottle caps had such a spillover effect, this variable should have a positive sign.

The overall fit of the equation is quite good, but the nonregulatory variables do not perform as well as in the aspirin equation. The lagged poisoning rate has the expected positive effect on current poisonings, but this variable is not statistically significant once the sales variables are included. The difficulty is that PR_{t-1} is strongly correlated with RSALES, PROD, and SALES. Real per capita consumption also has a positive effect, which is not what one would expect if PCC captured the wealth effect on safety alone.[19] This trend variable also may reflect any temporally related diminution in consumer responsibility toward access to such medicines.

The two central variables of interest are the regulatory variables. As in the aspirin case, the CPSC variable does not pass the usual tests of statistical significance. The magnitude of the coefficient is also not great, as it never exceeds a 5 percent drop in the mean poisoning rate over the sample period. The UNREG variable, however, reflects a powerful upward shift in the poisoning rate by almost one-fifth, which easily passes the usual tests of statistical significance. This effect is remarkably robust and is not greatly altered by the inclusion of analgesic sales variables. After the advent of protective caps on aspirin there was an upward shift in analgesic poisoning rates for children under five that cannot be explained by poisoning rate trends, changes in wealth, or increases in analgesic sales.

The absolute magnitude of the post–safety cap shift is quite substantial. These results imply that 47 percent of the increase in analgesic poisoning between 1971 and 1980 was due to the role of UNREG. Overall, this effect represents 3,500 additional analgesic poisonings of children under five annually. As in all such assessments of the impact of risk regulation, it cannot be ascertained whether this shift arose because of safety caps or some other factor correlated with this policy and not included in the equation. One such possibility is that parents with young children shifted from aspirin to Tylenol and other acetaminophen products, thus generating a higher risk consumer group than before. Consumer self selection of this type should, however, lower the risk from aspirin poisonings, and no such decline was observed.

The net effect of the shifts in aspirin and analgesic poisoning rates after the advent of safety caps is adverse. The overall behavior pattern is consistent with what would occur if safety caps led to a decrease in parental caution with respect to access to drugs. Because of the indivisibility of certain types of safety precautions, there was an adverse effect on analgesic poisonings, since these products were not initially covered by the safety cap requirements.

Overall Effect on Poisonings

If safety caps reduced other types of poisonings so that these adverse effects were restricted to aspirin and analgesics, one might question whether these findings were the result of some factor other than changes in consumer behavior. To explore this possibility more fully, we will analyze poisoning data for a wide variety of regulated products. These product groups are listed in Table 13-10. In each case, a CPSC

Table 13-10. Poisoning Rate Regression Results for Product Groups, 1968–1980

Product category	Coefficients and standard errors	
	CPSC	UNREG
Pooled product groups:		
Prescription drugs	−.083	.987
	(.621)	(.550)
Unregulated internal medicines	—	35.52
	—	(17.07)
Single products:		
Baby aspirin	−.398	—
	(8.560)	—
Adult aspirin	.932	—
	(1.310)	—
Aspirin, unspecified	.401	—
	(1.210	—
Analgesics	−.391	2.247
	(1.878)	(1.251)
Barbiturate sedatives	−.308	−.135
	(.238)	(.337)
Nonbarbiturate sedatives	.571	.522
	(.400)	(.345)
Internal antibiotics	1.501	2.345
	(1.105)	(.770)
Psychopharmocological agents	.350	4.154
	(3.000)	(2.849)
Iron preparations	−1.123	−.205
	(.783)	(.397)
Hormones	1.424	2.540
	(1.996)	(1.571)
Cardiovascular	−.184	.076
	(.763)	(1.484)
Amphetamines	−.814	.468
	(.702)	(1.125)
Miscellaneous internal medicines	4.437	5.576
	(3.139)	(2.674)
Liquid polish or wax	4.510	—
	(1.729)	—
Turpentine	−.495	—
	(.596)	—
Solvents and thinners	.273	—
	(1.803)	—
Unregulated cleaning and polish-	—	33.15
ing products	—	(11.95)

dummy variable was created to match the particular year in which this product came under a protective packaging requirement. (These years were summarized at the start of Section 13.4.) The UNREG variable for a product took on a value of one for all years after which part of the general product class came under regulation before the particular product became subject to a safety cap requirement. This starting point was always 1972, since internal medicines and cleaning and polishing agents both came under regulation in that year.

The first two sets of results are for product groups. These results were based on pooled time series and cross section regression of the general form as for aspirin and analgesics except that category-specific intercepts for particular products within the group were included, and data shift terms were omitted because they were not pertinent to Poison Control Center data. In the case of prescription drugs, for which the total sample included 336 observations, the advent of the caps had no significant effect on the poisoning trend; but there had been an earlier increase in 1972 and 1973 as reflected in the positive UNREG variable. The poisoning rate of internal medicines that were not subject to safety caps exhibited an alarming increase. These products include cough medicines and other nonprescription drugs.

The bottom portion of Table 13-10 presents similar results for narrowly defined product groups. In the case of aspirin, for which I found no significant CPSC effect overall, there is also no evidence of effectiveness for particular product groups such as baby aspirin. The only CPSC coefficient that passes the usual tests of statistical significance is that for liquid polish or wax, which reflected a small positive shift in the poisoning rate trend. The UNREG variables for three drugs were both positive and statistically significant: analgesics, internal antibiotics, and miscellaneous internal medicines. There was an increase in poisonings for unregulated cleaning and polishing agents of roughly the same magnitude as for unregulated internal medicines.

The general pattern is consistent with the more aggregative results. There is no evidence of a downward shift in poisonings from regulated products, but poisonings from several products escalated during the periods in which they were not covered by safety caps. Those products with significant UNREG coefficients include analgesics, internal antibiotics, psychopharmacological agents, miscellaneous internal medicines, and unregulated cleaning and polishing agents.

The net effect was adverse. This evidence is broadly consistent with a model in which there are indivisibilities in consumers' safety precautions, so that the reduction in consumer precautions increased the risk from unprotected bottles. Diminished parental responsibility included leaving bottles uncapped. The strength of these effects suggests that there may also have been some consumer misperception regarding the effectiveness of the caps. Consumers may have dismissed the importance of the safety problem because of the false assumption that these caps were "childproof."

13.5 ANALYSIS OF CPSC RISK DATA

Although the safety cap requirements were not effective in promoting safety, other CPSC regulations may have had a beneficial effect that was too small to be reflected in the aggregative data analyzed in Section 13.3. To address this possibility, I will focus on the CPSC's NEISS data, which was used in Section 13.3 with respect to fire-related accidents. The CPSC uses a sample of selected hospital emergency room admissions to generate national injury estimates for 1,000 specific product groups (for example, power sanders). Since the first complete calendar year for which such data are available is 1973, and in some cases later, this information provides insight only into recent product safety trends.

Unlike most risk data series, the NEISS data have been the object of considerable controversy.[20] The disputes have not focused on the validity of the injury numbers but on their use. The fundamental objection is that the CPSC bases its policies on trends in the total number of injuries provided through the NEISS system rather than on a use-adjusted risk level or, what is even more pertinent, on the overall merits of the regulation. This deficiency in the nature of the risk measure can be remedied by putting the risk data in per capita terms, as are other leading risk data series. In some cases I will adjust even more specifically for the extent of use by, for example, calculating the number of bicycle injuries per bicycle in use.

A second shortcoming is that narrowly defined product categories (such as stepladders) pose small sample problems and categorization problems (for example, one can record a ladder-related accident under any one of several product-related categories, such as ladders not specified or stepladders). I will avoid each of these difficulties by analyzing only broad product groups.

I will begin with an analysis of three fire-related regulations promulgated under the Flammable Fabrics Act, which is now administered by the CPSC. Although the analysis of two data series on fire-related deaths in Section 13.3 failed to indicate any significant shift, specific product groups may have had a more favorable response. The first product safety standard I will analyze is the CPSC mattress standard, for which Linneman (1980) failed to find any evidence of a downward shift in the risk level during the 1974–1977 period.

The CPSC promulgated an early version of the standard in 1973 and the current version in 1975.[21] This flammability standard was performance-oriented in that it imposed, for example, maximum char length limits on mattresses exposed to a lit cigarette. The per capita death risk from mattresses and bedding dropped by 30 percent since 1974.[22] Table 13.11 summarizes average actual and predicted levels of the NEISS-based measure of mattress-related death rates per 100,000 persons for the 1974–1978 period for which CPSC data are available. There was a 30 percent drop in the death rate over this period, but at least some of this decline should be expected because of the general increase in safety over time.

Table 13-11. Summary of Effects of CPSC Regulations

Risk category	Regulated period averages		
	Actual	Predicted	Difference
Mattress/bedding (deaths per 100,000)	.89	1.02	−.13
Matches (injuries per 100,000)	2.98	2.91	.07
Carpets and rugs (injuries per 100,000)	14.69	7.39	7.30
Cribs (injuries per 1,000 births)	2.81	2.66	.15
Bicycles (injuries per bicycles in use)	7.88	6.05	1.83

Source: Calculations by the author using unpublished NEISS data and data from the Bicycle Manufacturers Association and U.S. Bureau of the Census.

Using the equation for the NSC fire and burn death rates from Section 13.3 and adjusting the scale appropriately,[23] we can forecast the predicted rate of mattress deaths beginning in 1975, the year of the final standard. The difference between actual and predicted mattress deaths is consistently negative, and the average difference represents about 12 percent of initial death rates. One cannot rule out the possibility that a small shift has occurred, particularly in view of the consistent negative signs involved.[24] An alternative possibility is that the causal factor is not improved mattresses but a decline in cigarette smoking by adults in the mid-1970s, which has reduced the major cause of mattress fires.[25]

The risk pattern displayed in the period after the imposition of the CPSC matchbook safety standard displays a similar downward trend. This standard required that the friction be on the outside back cover or at the bottom of the matchbook, that the matchbook remained closed without external force, and that firms undertake adequate control. One would not expect these measures to have a major effect on hospital emergency admissions for matchbook-related injuries. The poststandard decline parallels the pattern one would expect on the basis of the overall firm and burn trend and is in fact insignificantly higher than the predicted level. In addition, the rising market share of butane lighters also should have contributed to a decline in match-related risks.

The most surprising of the fire-related product risk trends is that for carpets and rugs. On December 30, 1975, the CPSC issued flammability performance criteria for carpets that were intended to reduce fire-related accidents associated with these products.[26] Although most carpet-related accidents, such as falls, do not stem from flammability risks and are not directly affected by the regulation, there is no reason a priori to believe that these accidents will be influenced adversely by the standard.

The carpet-related injury rate has doubled from its preregulation level, and the increase is more than double when compared with the trend one could have expected based on home accident rate trends. An increase in carpet sales is not the explanation, since annual sales declined in real terms over that period.[27] The principal nonfire source of carpet accidents—falls—also does not appear to be responsible, since total deaths from falls dropped by 16 percent from 1975–1981.[28]

At least some of the upward shift may be due to changes in the NEISS data base. In 1978, the year in which the carpet injury rate rose by one-fourth, the CPSC changed its sample of hospitals and altered its method of risk classification.[29] The explanation appears to account for only part of the shift. A more disturbing possibility is that the nature of the carpet materials now in use may pose greater risks. Since carpet components are selected in part to comply with CPSC standards, it is surprising that the CPSC has not addressed this emerging risk problem other than to note that it merits "continuing attention."[30]

The difference between actual and predicted risk levels for two well-known safety-related standards also provides little evidence of CPSC's effectiveness. Along with safety caps, the CPSC crib standard ranks as the most prominent CPSC regulation in terms of its perceived effectiveness by CPSC officials. Beginning in 1973, the CPSC required that crib bars on full-sized cribs be spaced no farther than $2^3/_8$ inches apart.[31] This spacing requirement, which is a desirable regulation intended to prevent babies' heads from becoming lodged between the bars, was accompanied by more questionable provisions that were tantamount to a complete crib design standard. For example, the CPSC required that cribs be 28 ± $^5/_8$ inches wide and 52$^3/_8$ ± $^5/_8$ inches long.

The frequency rate I constructed for crib injuries pertained to the risk per 1,000 births, since these risks are most pertinent for very young children. The average crib injury risk during the postregulation period is about 10 percent lower than in 1973. This decline is, however, slightly less than one would expect on the basis of the home accident rate trends that were used to calculate the predicted risk level.[32]

The final CPSC standard I will consider is the CPSC bicycle standard issued in 1978.[33] Although some features of the standard, such as the reflector requirement, clearly may affect safety, this regulation also imposes meticulous design and road test requirements that run to twenty-four pages in the Code of Federal Regulations. For example, the CPSC requires that "control cables are greater than 6.4mm ($^1/_4$ inch) in diameter and cable clamps made from material not thicker than 4.8mm ($^3/_{16}$ inch) may be attached to the top tube." The genesis of these meticulous requirements and the bicycle standard itself can be traced not to safety concerns but to the bicycle industry's efforts to keep out cheap foreign imports that were making inroads in U.S. markets.[34]

Since bicycle use has been increasing in the past decade, ideally the risk measure should reflect this change. The variable I constructed was the number of bicycle injuries per bicycle in use. This variable does not, however, take into account increased intensity of use. This greater intensity is apparently responsible both for the increase in bicycle accident rates and for an excess of actual risk levels over those predicted on the basis of home accident rate trends. If there has been any beneficial effect of the CPSC standard, it is being obscured by these factors that boost injury rates.

13.6 CONCLUSION

Neither the aggregative data nor the CPSC's NEISS data on particular products provide any clear-cut evidence of a significant beneficial effect on product safety from CPSC actions. If there is a beneficial effect of these regulations, then it is too small to estimate reliably. Since the CPSC's regulatory efforts address a small portion of the product safety problem and in some cases bear only a tangential relationship to product safely, this type of result accords with what one might expect.

The evidence pertaining to the lulling effect is not restricted to poisoning risks alone. An interesting application of this phenomenon occurred within the context of auto safety. Beginning in 1984, many firms began installing a safety belt system in cars for which a motorized belt automatically crossed over the chests of the front seat passengers after the car doors were closed and the ignition was turned on. Passengers would still have to buckle the lap belt manually. But what safety officials found is that the presence of the automatic safety mechanism may have discouraged the taking of protective behavior on the part of automobile passengers. In particular, "70 percent of drivers and riders, lulled by the automatic shoulder strap into a false sense of security, do not fasten their lap belts."[35] Since failure to buckle the lap belt may lead to the ejection of the occupant upon impact or "submarining" under the shoulder belt during a collision, automobile passenger safety may have been reduced as compared with the situation in which all belts are fastened manually.

A much more surprising result was the pattern displayed by poisoning rates after the advent of safety caps. For those products covered by safety caps, there was no downward shift in poisoning rates. This ineffectiveness appears to be attributable in part to increased parental irresponsibility, such as leaving the caps off bottles. This lulling effect in turn led to a higher level of poisonings for related products not protected by the caps.

The more general ramification of these results is that technological solutions to safety problems may induce a lulling effect on consumer behavior. The safety benefits will be muted and perhaps more than offset by the effect of the decreased efficacy of safety precautions, misperceptions regarding the risk-reducing impact of the regulation, and spillover effects of reduced precautions with other products. Although the precise contribution of the regulation cannot be distinguished from other shifts in behavior that may have occurred in the 1970s, it is clear that individual actions are an important component of the accident-generating process. Failure to take such behavior into account will result in regulations that may not have the intended effect.

NOTES

1. National Safety Council (1989).

2. See, in particular, Peltzman (1975), Blomquist (1988), and Crandall and Graham (1984).

3. The 30 percent figure is based on the CPSC's estimate that 30,000 consumers are killed annually using consumer products, in conjunction with data on an overall accidental death level of 99,000 in 1981.

4. See the Consumer Product Safety Act, Pub. L. 92-573, § 2(a) and § 15(a), 86 *Stat.* 1207, 1221 (1972) (codified at 15 U.S.C. § 2064(a) (1982)).

5. Two principal published studies are Broussalian (1976) and Viscusi (1984).

6. See Viscusi (1984) for a more extensive and less technical assessment of the CPSC that complements the material presented here.

7. This evidence is reviewed in Viscusi (1984).

8. In particular, in the case of the ninth revision, which occurred in 1976, there was an effect of the coding system of less than 2 percent on all accidents other than those related to motor vehicles. The 1976 shift will be adjusted for explicitly using comparability ratios developed by the National Center for Health Statistics (1980).

9. Other specifications of the dependent variable included the log-odds, logarithm, and percentage change in the death risk (without a lagged dependent variable). The results were very similar. For example, the CPSC variable in the natural log specification of the analog of the equation for the entire population for 1950–1981 (see Table 13–3) had a t-statistic of −1.15, which is marginally different from the value of −0.90 for the linear probability version.

10. Although the Durbin h-statistic is more appropriate when a lagged dependent variable is included, it has similar small sample properties. In addition, this statistic was undefined for many regressions, including all of those in Table 13–9.

11. One obtains similar results using a 1973–1981 dummy variable for the CPSC rather than a 1975–1981 variable.

12. C.F.R. § 1501.4 (1979).

13. All overall poisoning rate data cited in this section are based on unpublished Poison Control Center computer printouts prepared for this study. Poisoning death data are based on unpublished National Center for Health Statistics data.

14. The principal condition is that for all levels of effort that lead to levels of risk above those in the pre-safety cap situation, the marginal reduction in expected poisoning costs in response to additional precautions must be sufficiently below the marginal effectiveness of precautions in the pre-safety cap situation.

15. See, for example, the statement by Sam Zagoria, CPSC Commissioner, *Washington Post*, November 14, 1983, p. A15.

16. See Alisone Clarke and William Walton, "The Effect of Safety Packaging on Children's Aspirin Ingestions (internal report, Consumer Product Safety Commission, 1978), and the U.S. Consumer Product Safety Commission, Poison Prevention Packaging Act, Summary Report (1983).

17. The data shift variables (for example, D4) were omitted for the Poison Control Center data since these nonfatal risk data are not subject to the international disease classifications. In the case of the fatal poisoning rate equations, the shift terms are not statistically significant. Sales of these drugs will be affected by the perceived risk of the product. Since there is a two-year lag in the compilation and release of CPSC accident statistics, in the absence of a major catastrophe (for example, toxic shock syndrome from tampons) the effect of the product risk on consumption is likely to be recursive rather than simultaneous.

18. These figures were based on sales data for five leading aspirin products: Bayer aspirin, St. Joseph's aspirin for children, Bufferin, Excedrin, and Anacin.

19. The PCC variable continues to have a positive sign even if the per capita sales variable is omitted from the equation.

20. Two discussions of these shortcomings are by Broussalian (1976) and Viscusi (1984).

21. C.F.R. § 1632 (1975).

22. These data are more comprehensive than Linneman's (1980), since burn and smoke-inhalation deaths are both included, whereas Linneman's data were restricted to burns only. If the mix of accidents is not changing, however, this difference should not be consequential except insofar as the sample size of mattress-related accidents is a bit larger. In the case of Linneman's study, 269 of the reported burns between 1965 and 1974 were mattress-related. The CPSC mattress death data I use pertain to an average of about 200 mattress or bedding deaths annually.

23. In particular, I used the fire and burn death rate equation estimated for the 1949–1981 period for the entire population using NSC data. The scale of the equation was adjusted by multiplying the predicted values by the ratio of the 1974 mattress-related death rate to the overall NSC fire and death rate.

24. The pattern of these discrepancies was a bit uneven, with 1976 and 1978 representing the largest difference. Presumably, the effect should be steadily increasing if the CPSC standard were effective.

25. There was a 6 percent decline in the adult smoking population from 1974 to 1979. See U.S. Department of Commerce (1984), p. 123.

26. C.F.R. § 1630 (1975).

27. See U.S. Department of Commerce (1984), pp. 774–775, for nominal sales data for floor coverings, which exhibited a rise of 5 percent from 1977 to 1980. The overall inflation rate over that period was 36 percent.

28. National Safety Council (1982), p. 84.

29. Multiple products could now be associated with any single accident. These changes may have contributed to a substantial part of the increased hazard, but they do not explain the jump that occurred in 1977, shortly after the standard took effect, or in 1980.

30. See the Flammable Fabrics Report included in the *Consumer Product Safety Commission, Annual Report*, Pt. 2 (1981).

31. C.F.R. § 1508 (1973).

32. More specifically, I used the overall home accident rate equation for the 1949–1981 period. The only years with risk levels below those predicted were 1975 and 1976. Presumably, such negative discrepancies should have occurred in more recent years if the standard was effective, since the fraction of CPSC-approved cribs in the stock of existing cribs will be rising over time.

33. C.F.R. § 1512 (1978).

34. See Cornell, Noll, and Weingast (1976).

35. See *The New York Times*, June 13, 1991, p. A1.

14

The Mis-Specified Agenda:
The 1980s Reforms of Health,
Safety, and Environmental Regulation

14.1 THE AGENDA FOR REGULATORY REFORM

The 1970s marked the advent of a new wave of regulation of health, safety, and the environment.[1] Congress created a series of new agencies with broad responsibilities, including the Occupational Safety and Health Administration (OSHA), the Environmental Protection Agency (EPA), the National Highway Traffic Safety Administration (NHTSA), the Consumer Product Safety Commission (CPSC), and the Nuclear Regulatory Commission (NRC). Although some of these agencies consolidated the functions previously dispersed among other smaller agencies, the sweeping legislative mandates given to these agencies marked a dramatic increase in the level of regulation of the American economy. Congress directed these agencies to promote health, safety, and environmental quality almost without compromise.

Expectations were high. One of the principal authors of OSHA's enabling legislation predicted that the agency would cut workplace injuries in half.[2] Engineering studies of traffic safety claimed automobile safety belts would dramatically reduce the carnage on the highways.[3]

This initial optimism was coupled with substantial resistance on the part of firms. These government regulations represented an intrusion into previously unregulated decisions. Enterprises no longer had the freedom to select the most profitable technology. Instead, they had to meet often quite explicit guidelines regarding the character and performance of these technologies. To make matters worse, there were also widespread suggestions that the regulations were ineffective in promoting their intended objectives.

It quickly became clear that these efforts were quite costly and that their economic impacts had to be monitored. These concerns provided the impetus for establishing White House regulatory oversight efforts.

The second general reaction to the new wave of regulation was that of dissatisfaction. The findings in Chapters 10–13 documented this weak performance. Supporters of regulation demanded greater achievements that were commensurate with these agencies' responsibilities, and critics placed great emphasis on the low benefits relative to the dollars being expended. Reform for health, safety, and environmental regulation had become a prominent political issue less than one decade after the establishment of these agencies.

Although there was not unanimous agreement on the direction these agencies should take, there were a number of central themes to these calls for reform.[4] Here I will review the guidelines for reform that emerged in the economic literature and policy debates of the 1970s. These guidelines will serve as the reference point for assessing the regulatory reforms of the 1980s.

First, economists recognized that there were often legitimate market failures that needed to be addressed. Environmental problems involve a classic case of externalities. Moreover, imperfect consumer and worker information may impede market provision of safety. Market forces involving risk are not, however, completely absent. A series of studies reviewed in Chapter 4 documented labor market compensation for risk on the order of several hundred thousand dollars per statistical death for workers who had selected themselves into very high-risk jobs to as much as several million dollars per death for the more typical blue-collar worker.[5] Because of these constructive market forces, it is essential to ascertain that there is a legitimate market failure before determining that a regulation is warranted.

The second general principle is that one should obtain an assessment of the costs and benefits of the regulatory policy. Initially, the concern was with regulatory costs. The steel and automobile industries, for example, were hit particularly hard. Since these basic industries were in decline and threatened by foreign competition, ensuring that excessive government regulation was not the causal factor in their demise became a prominent concern.

Regulatory impacts should, however, be measured correctly. In assessing these costs and benefits, what matters is the value of the expected payoffs that will accrue to society. One should use the mean of the probability distribution rather than focusing on worst-case scenarios or, as many agencies do, the upper end of the 95 percent confidence interval for the risk level.[6]

Although assessing the impacts of policies is an essential prerequisite to sound policy choice, one must then utilize this information to select among policy alternatives. The third regulatory principle is that policy choices should be cost-effective. Available policy alternatives that can achieve the same benefits at less cost are preferable. Another example of an inefficient regulatory alternative was the imposition of a requirement for a technological solution to air pollution problems by mandating the installation of scrubbers, whereas a lower-cost method of achieving the same benefits by altering the type of coal used would have been sufficient.[7]

A class of regulatory options viewed as being superior to existing regulations on cost-effectiveness grounds is that of performance-oriented alternatives.[8] Performance standards for the guarding of machines, for example, would not only be less costly than OSHA specification standards but also would pertain to more types of machine designs, thus reducing machine guarding risks for a larger number of workers. Similarly, use of protective equipment to avert hearing loss resulting from excessive noise exposures would impose considerably lower compliance costs than changing the workplace environment. Although there are legitimate debates regarding the feasibility of such performance-oriented alternatives, due to the difficulties of monitoring compliance, the economic critics of regulatory agencies have urged these agencies to at least assess the merits of performance-oriented alternatives.

A fourth regulatory reform principle is that there should be an appropriate balancing of the benefits and costs of policies. Strict adherence to efficiency guidelines suggests that a benefit-cost test would be applicable, but the oversight process did not formally adopt this criterion until the 1980s. Even where a precise calculation of benefits and costs is not feasible, agencies should consider the overall merits of the policy and pursue only those policies that they judge to be in society's best interests.

Although the degree to which economists adhere to strict compliance with a benefit-cost test varies, the importance of addressing efficiency concerns is widely accepted as an important role for economists active in these policy debates.[9] As the Carter administration's chairman of the Council of Economic Advisors, Charles L. Schultze (1982), observed:

For this reason, I strongly believe that economists in government have a particular role to play in the area of micro policy, not merely as disinterested purveyors of technical advice, but as advocates. I am not merely offering the pious statement that the economists ought to favor efficiency. What I am saying is that in matters of specific micro policy, and within reasonable bounds, his role is to be the partisan advocate for efficiency *even when the result is significant income losses for particular groups*—which it almost always is.

Emphasis on the role of balancing of benefits and costs also leads to support for market-oriented alternatives. For example, one can achieve the efficient outcome with respect to environmental risks by appropriate pricing of pollution. Although there has been no effort to establish large-scale markets for pollution rights, under the Carter administration the EPA introduced a number of innovative market-oriented options,[10] such as the bubble policy introduced in December 1979.[11] The bubble policy was introduced on only a very limited basis just before the turn of the decade, but its originators hoped that this policy could be extended to enable firms to meet their pollution-control objectives at less cost.

Even if these regulations were well designed, effective enforcement would be needed to ensure compliance. OSHA promulgated thousands of standards for health and safety, but it coupled these detailed requirements with very weak enforcement. The prospect that a firm would see an OSHA inspector was remote, as these inspectors visited firms with roughly the same frequency as the passage of Halley's comet. If an inspector did arrive, the penalties assessed were very low. Greater financial penalties were needed if firms were to have the proper safety investment incentives.

The final and perhaps most important theme that emerged is that there was a need for broad-based reform. The legislative mandates established by Congress were overly restrictive and did not adequately recognize the economic tradeoffs. All of the enabling legislation for the risk and environmental agencies required that the agency promote the health or environmental objective, but none of them required that there be an explicit balancing of the costs and benefits of these efforts. Moreover, many of these pieces of legislation explicitly prohibited such tradeoffs. The U.S. Supreme Court's interpretation of the Occupational Safety and Health Act is that the agency could not base its regulations on a formal benefit-cost test. Moreover, the Clean Air Act even more explicity prohibits the consideration of costs of any kind in setting ambient air-quality standards, much less utilizing benefit-cost analysis.

By far the most important need was for fundamental legislative reform to incorporate the opportunity for such balancing of cost and benefit considerations in the design of regulatory policy. Such changes are fundamental to any reform effort, since the legislative mandates will limit the degree to which regulatory oversight activities will be able to influence the policies of the regulatory agencies. Short-term efforts to alter regulatory policies by slowing the pace of regulation or altering the enforcement effort will not yield long-run changes in the regulatory approach. Ultimately, the agency's enabling legislation will determine the shape of these policies.

A major failure of the Reagan regulatory reform effort is that not only were such reforms never achieved but they were never even attempted. The legislative energies of the Reagan administration were devoted to tax reform rather than rewriting the legislative mandates of regulatory agencies. Although regulatory reform was one of the four key pillars of the Reagan economic program, it was generally viewed as meriting the lowest priority of the four major areas of concern. As a result, the reform measures that were introduced would necessarily have a short-term impact. Indeed, the deregulation effort did not even last through the first Reagan term.

The analysis begins with a discussion of the changes in institutional structure, notably the budgetary and staffing allocations of the regulatory agencies and the strengthening of the regulatory oversight mechanism. I then turn to the performance of the regulatory reform effort in altering the structure of regulation, promoting the balancing of benefits and costs, revamping existing regulations, and modifying the structure of new regulatory initiatives. I then examine changes in regulatory enforcement policy and the overall impact of health, safety, and environmental regulation in the 1980s.

The principal theme of this assessment is that there were two quite distinctive regulatory agendas during the two Reagan administrations. The first period, which constituted most of the first Reagan term, was one of deregulation. There were a number of constructive changes, including the strengthening of the regulatory oversight mechanism, an improvement in the balancing of costs and benefits of regulatory policies, and selected new regulatory initiatives. These reform efforts failed to achieve their full potential because of the absence of fundamental legislative reform and, more generally, the absence of meaningful regulatory reform as contrasted with regulatory relief.

After the enthusiasm for the initial deregulation agenda waned, the regulatory approach came to resemble that of the pre-Reagan era. The pace of regulation and the implementation of these regulations became more vigorous, and there was little evidence that the character of the regulatory policies had undergone much more than a temporary interruption during the short-lived period of deregulation. The opportunity for sound regulatory reform through an appropriately specified reform agenda had been missed.

14.2 BUDGETARY AND STAFFING TRENDS

The Rationale for Cutbacks

For the usual economic process in which there are diminishing marginal benefits and rising marginal costs, economists would recommend a decrease in such activities once the incremental burdens exceed the benefits. This maxim also applies to regulatory policy if scaling back the degree of regulation will eliminate regulations whose net effects are adverse.

Straightforward application of this principle assumes that the policy mix is efficient. If we are not on the efficient frontier, then the main reform that is needed is to alter the character of the regulation. Although some regulations were excessively stringent, there is little evidence that the number and scope of safety and environmental regulations promulgated was too great. In contrast, for rate and entry regulation, there was a widespread consensus that regulatory restrictions of all kinds were unnecessary, as they impeded the efficient operation of markets. In these contexts, sound regulatory reform was synonymous with deregulation. Unfortunately, deregulation is not an appropriate objective for all classes of regulatory activity.

The need for better risk regulation rather than deregulation was also stressed by leading economists in Reagan's regulatory reform effort. Shortly after Reagan's election, the future chairman of the Council of Economic Advisors, Murray Weidenbaum (1980), observed:

In the case of the newer social regulation, which typically attempts to correct imperfections in the market (so-called externalities, meaning the costs imposed by one segment of the economy on another), the approach should be to seek out the most effective and the least burdensome methods of achieving the desired objectives.

The distinctions made by other administration spokesmen were less refined. Office of Management and Budget Director David Stockman called for a "substantial rescission of the regulatory burden," with a need for a major "regulatory ventilation" to assist American business.[12] President Reagan subsequently established the Presidential Task Force on Regulatory Relief headed by Vice-President Bush, with a notable emphasis on relief rather than reform. In reflecting on the regulatory achievements of the Reagan administration, President Reagan observed:

Over the last 7½ years, we have substantially reduced that burden, cutting red tape and slowing the pace of new regulation.

When I became President in 1981, I directed that Federal agencies, within the scope afforded by law, should reduce the excess burden of government regulation that is borne by every worker, consumer, business, and state and local government in this Nation. Under the guidance of the Presidential Task Force on Regulatory Relief, Federal agencies have eliminated unnecessary regulatory costs ranging in the tens of billions of dollars.[13]

Achieving a balance between regulatory costs and risk reductions had become a subsidiary concern. Deregulation had become the fundamental policy objective during the initial years of the Reagan administration.

Shifts in Budgets and Staffing

One mechanism for scaling back the role of government regulation is to cut back on the budget and staff of regulatory agencies. In the extreme case, one could eliminate an agency altogether.

A prominent target for elimination was the Consumer Product Safety Commission. This small-scale product safety agency had a disappointing performance record from the standpoint of both supporters and opponents of the overall function of the agency. Short of abolition, another possibility was to move this independent commission into the executive branch by making it an agency within an existing cabinet, thus increasing the potential for executive oversight. Although there were suggestions that such options were under consideration, no serious efforts were made to achieve a restructuring. The policy option chosen instead was to cut back on the agency's activities. From 1980 to 1989, the CPSC budget dropped by one-fourth (Table 14-1) and its staffing declined by over 40 percent.

These extreme cutbacks are not the only instance of increasing budgetary stringency. In terms of staffing, the summary statistics at the bottom of Table 14-2 indicate that there was an overall drop of personnel in all of the risk agencies listed. The fringe advisory groups—the Council on Environmental Quality and the Occupational Safety and Health Review Commission—experienced particularly dramatic declines in their staffs.

For most agencies, the general pattern from 1980 to 1985 was one of fairly stable nominal budgets but declining personnel. From 1985 to 1989, there was a stabilization and in some cases an expansion of the regulatory agencies. The case of OSHA is particularly noteworthy. OSHA's staff in 1980 was almost one and one-half times greater than in 1985. These cutbacks primarily affected the OSHA inspection per-

Table 14-1. Budgetary Trends for Principal Health, Safety, and Environmental Agencies

	Obligations (*$millions*) by fiscal year			
	1975	1980	1985	1989
Environmental Protection Agency	794	1,360	1,928	3,309
Council on Environmental Quality	4	8	1	1
Occupational Safety and Health Administration (DOL)	97	191	220	248
Mine Safety and Health Administration (DOL)	67	144	150	162
Food and Drug Administration (HHS)	207	334	437	530
National Highway Traffic Safety Administration (DOT)	104	136	114	133
Federal Aviation Administration (DOT)	196	281	294	424
Consumer Product Safety Commission	37	43	36	34
Nuclear Regulatory Commission	148	396	445	421
National Transportation Safety Board	10	17	22	25
Food Safety and Inspection Service (DOA)	—	381	405	457
Occupational Safety and Health Review Commission	5	7	6	6
TOTAL:	1,669	3,298	4,058	5,750

Source: Melinda Warren and Kenneth Chilton, "Regulation's Rebound: Bush Budget Gives Regulation a Boost," Center for Study of American Business, OP81 (April 1990), Table A-1. Agency selection and totals calculated by the author.

254 Risk Regulation

Table 14-2. Staffing Trends for Principal Health, Safety, and Environmental Agencies

	Permanent full-time positions by fiscal year			
	1975	1980	1985	1989
Environmental Protection Agency	11,004	11,615	13,978	15,321
Council on Environmental Quality	50	32	11	9
Occupational Safety and Health Administration (DOL)	2,435	3,015	2,176	2,415
Mine Safety and Health Administration (DOL)	2,940	3,857	2,829	2,671
Food and Drug Administration (HHS)	6,441	7,419	7,104	7,226
National Highway Traffic Safety Administration (DOT)	881	874	640	652
Federal Aviation Administration (DOT)	6,947	6,692	6,358	4,556
Consumer Product Safety Commission	884	871	502	487
Nuclear Regulatory Commission	2,006	3,041	3,318	3,078
National Transportation Safety Board	310	388	357	324
Food Safety and Inspection Service (DOA)	—	13,213	9,839	8,962
Occupational Safety and Health Review Commission	172	165	94	74
TOTAL:	34,070	51,182	47,206	45,775

Source: Melinda Warren and Kenneth Chilton, "Regulation's Rebound: Bush Budget Gives Regulation a Boost," Center for Study of American Business, OP81 (April 1990), Table A-2. Agency selection and totals calculated by the author.

sonnel, as there was a dramatic decrease in the OSHA enforcement staff. By decreasing the enforcement effort, the government could reduce the burden on business imposed by government regulation. Decreasing the enforcement stringency did not, however, address the long-term reform need, which was a restructuring of the standards that would be enforced. The extent of the decreased inspection effort may not have been of major consequence, however, since the probability of inspection was already quite low and this probability did not change much in the early 1980s. By 1989 the OSHA staff and budget had increased substantially from its 1985 level, but in terms of personnel OSHA remained below its 1980 level.

The principal exception to these adverse trends was EPA. Although there were cutbacks at EPA during the Gorsuch era in the early 1980s, these cuts were quickly reversed. Because of the increased responsibilities of EPA over an increasingly broad range of hazards including unconventional pollutants, such as hazardous wastes and toxic substances, both the budget and personnel of this agency rose considerably in the 1980s. Indeed, the total EPA budget in 1989 was more than double its 1980 level.

Altering budgetary allotments and personnel in the manner indicated in Tables 14-1 and 14-2 is much easier to achieve than a fundamental shift in the character of policy. Overhauling an agency's regulatory structure is a daunting task, as the performance record considered below will indicate. However, reducing an agency's expenditures and staffing within the context of broadly based cutbacks in taxes and government programs simultaneously achieves regulatory relief as well as economic savings.

In some cases, the loss in safety from these cutbacks was not great. The Occupational Safety and Health Review Commission, for example, plays only a minor advisory role. Moreover, the overall emphasis of the cutbacks was correct. EPA merited the greatest increases since it had the fastest-growing regulatory agenda. New classes of environmental risks emerged to augment the traditional concerns of the agency with air pollution, water pollution, and pesticides, as well as the increased concern with long-term hazards such as acid rain and global warming. Although the overall cutback strategy appears to have been ill chosen, the realignment of the relative degrees of responsibility among these agencies appears to have been correct.

14.3 THE REGULATORY OVERSIGHT PROCESS

Although appointments to regulatory agencies are an important mechanism for influencing policy, the incentives of the agencies' career staff and the pressures exerted by the traditional constituencies lead to the need for some form of executive branch oversight. Unlike legislative initiatives, regulations do not require congressional action. Judicial review will also not be sufficient, since the agency generally has broad leeway subject to its legislative mandate and provisions of the Constitution.

Regulatory Oversight in Previous Administrations

To address the costs imposed by regulations, President Nixon introduced informal quality-of-life reviews. This framework took on more structure within the Ford administration, as President Ford established a formal oversight process whereby regulatory agencies were required to prepare an inflationary impact statement assessing the effect of major regulations on productivity and costs.[14] In addition, the Ford administration established the Council on Wage and Price Stability in 1974 to oversee this effort. The council's legislation enabled it to "intervene and otherwise participate on its own behalf in rulemaking, ratemaking, licensing, and other proceedings before any of the departments and agencies of the United States, in order to present its views as to the inflationary impact that might result from the possible outcomes of such proceedings." The agency's authority was advisory in nature, and it covered independent and executive branch regulatory agencies.

President Carter bolstered the structure of this review process by requiring that regulatory analyses show that "alternative approaches have been considered and the least burdensome of the acceptable alternatives have been chosen."[15] This requirement was tantamount to a cost-effectiveness test. The Council on Wage and Price Stability remained the main oversight group responsible for overseeing this effort. Carter also established a regulatory council to track agencies' upcoming regulatory agendas in its regulatory calendar. These activities were supplemented by a new body within the Executive Office of the President—the Regulatory Analysis Review Group (RARG). RARG consisted of representatives from the Council of Economic Advisors, various branches of the White House (Domestic Policy Staff, Council on Wage and Price Stability, and Office of Management and Budget) and various executive branch agencies that served on a rotating basis. This interagency group prepared assessments of selected major regulatory activities that were then filed in the rule-making proceedings by the Council on Wage and Price Stability. These advisory efforts laid the substantive groundwork for lobbying by leading White House officials—the chairman of the Council of Economic Advisors and the Inflation Advisor to the President, Alfred E. Kahn.

Although these advisory efforts sometimes influenced the structure of regulations and, perhaps more importantly, educated the regulatory agencies concerning the appropriate perspective they should take in assessing prospective regulations, there was a general agreement that the process needed to be strengthened. So long as the oversight activities remained advisory in nature, their ultimate impact would be modest. Second, the economic tests applied to new regulations did not require that agencies strike any balance between the benefits and costs of regulations, only that they attempt to achieve a particular objective as cheaply as possible, however ill chosen that objective might be.

Reagan's Oversight Process

The Reagan administration quickly restructured the oversight process. First, it abolished the Council on Wage and Price Stability so as to eliminate the wage and price standards role of the council that had emerged during the Carter administration. The council's regulatory oversight staff then moved to the Office of Management and Budget. From an institutional standpoint, this change enhanced the leverage that the regulatory oversight process could exert since it was more closely involved with budgetary and staffing decisions. The only disadvantage is that the abolition of the council also eliminated the legislative authority to intervene in the rulemaking proceedings of independent agencies, such as the FTC and CPSC.

The leading economic participants in the development of the initial oversight effort were CEA chairman, Murray Weidenbaum, and James C. Miller, III as the administrator of the Office of Information and Regulatory Affairs (OIRA) at OMB. Miller was an experienced regulatory reformer, having served as an official at the Council on Wage and Price Stability during the Ford administration.[16] The day after his inauguration, President Reagan established the Presidential Task Force on Regulatory Relief chaired by Vice-President Bush, with Miller serving as the Executive Director. Shortly thereafter, President Reagan promulgated his Executive Order 12291, which established the major ingredients of the new regulatory oversight structure.[17]

This executive order instituted two major changes. First, agencies were required to show that the benefits of regulations exceeded their costs and that they had chosen the policy option that maximized the net benefits to society. Although agencies were exempted from this requirement when it violated their legislative mandate, even in these situations the agency was required to assess, but not necessarily compare, benefits and costs. Unfortunately, the exemption pertaining to conflicts with legislative mandates is the central provision, not a minor nuance. Since all health, safety, and environmental agencies are governed by restrictive legislative mandates that limit benefit-cost tradeoffs, in practice the OMB cannot require that these regulations satisfy a benefit-cost test.

The second component of Executive Order 12291 is that approval by the regulatory oversight group was no longer an advisory process. The agency was required to submit the proposal to OMB for approval before it could move forward. It could appeal any adverse decision to the President's Task Force on Regulatory Relief. This executive order continues to be regarded as "the backbone of executive regulatory oversight activities."[18]

The oversight process also added an earlier review procedure through the institution of regulatory planning provisions in 1985.[19] President Reagan issued Executive Order 12498, which required regulatory agencies to submit to OMB a draft regulatory program, thus expanding the regulatory calendar concept of the Carter administration. Oversight activities address regulations in their final stages. By that point, the agencies have already established a major commitment to a regulatory policy, making their positions difficult to alter. Moreover, agencies have also generated substantial political support for regulations soon to be issued, limiting the ability of OMB to alter the regulatory structure. By influencing the regulatory program of an agency at an earlier stage, OMB could better alter the direction of regulatory policy.

A controversial component of the regulatory oversight agenda was the principle of Federalism: "Federal regulation should not preempt state laws or regulations, except to guarantee rights of national citizenship or to avoid significant burdens on interstate commerce."[20] The economic rationale is that the costs and benefits of regulations may differ by area and that regulations should reflect this heterogeneity.

Rigid application of this approach, however, ignores some of the benefits of uniform national standards. If firms must invest in technologies to comply with a variety of different regulations, regulatory compliance costs may escalate.

One such situation is with respect to hazard warnings. Uniform national standards are desirable since they provide individuals with a common warnings vocabulary. Right-to-know movements with differing requirements have, however, proliferated at the local level. A chief example is California Proposition 65, passed in 1986, which requires firms selling products posing risks of cancer or birth defects (e.g., wine manufacturers) or which expose their workers or customers to carcinogens (e.g., gas stations) to provide appropriate warnings. Beginning in 1986, the food industry sought federal preemption of these local warning efforts, urging the FDA to adopt a uniform national warning standard. The worst-case outcome for industry involves packaging foods with different warnings for different states. Application of the Federalism principles suggested that there is no reason for the government to intervene, and the government did not. Although the national government should not attempt to establish uniform national regulations that adopt unattractive state regulations on a broader scale, national uniformity may benefit firms through reduced compliance costs.

The Regulatory Budget Alternative

Although the Reagan oversight mechanism included many of the ingredients needed to make oversight more effective, it did not undertake the radical transformation in the oversight process that some individuals had advocated. There had been several proposals in the late 1970s and early 1980s that the government establish a regulatory budget, not unlike its budget for actual allocations.[21] In its simplest version, the regulatory budget concept involves OMB establishing a budgetary limit for each regulatory agency, where this budget pertains to the total cost these regulations can impose on society. Imposing such limits clearly would provide regulatory discipline.

There are, however, several factors that limit the attractiveness and feasibility of this proposal. First, the regulatory budget proposal is responsive to the regulatory relief objective, but it does not directly alter the character of regulations. Second, whereas budgets for agencies have an automatic validating process in that we will know at the end of the year whether we have exceeded the budget, there is no such internal check for a regulatory budget. We must rely on cost estimates that may not accurately reflect the actual impacts. In some cases, even calculating costs will be a substantial object of controversy. What, for example, is the cost of affirmative action requirements?

Finally, establishing a regulatory budget requires that we know in advance what the appropriate budgetary levels should be. Moreover, that calculation requires a detailed assessment of the benefits and costs of regulations. For prospective regulations, assessing benefits and costs can be done most easily within the context of the type of oversight mechanism that OMB adopted. Since we would always wish to pursue an effort with a positive benefit-cost balance irrespective of our previous budgetary decision, there seems then to be no rationale for proceeding on other than a piecemeal basis for new regulations. If existing regulations were to count with respect to the budget, difficult problems arise in determining the cost of regulations promulgated many years earlier. Moreover, achieving changes in existing regulatory policies for which many firms have already invested billions of dollars in compliance expenditures will create substantial political opposition. One cannot simply replace a regulation from the 1970s with an unfavorable benefit-cost balance by a new regulation with a more favorable benefit-cost balance. The substantial vested interests in the earlier regulatory regime will resist such changes.

Overall, the regulatory budget does not appear to be compelling conceptually and, more importantly, it would impose a degree of discipline on the regulatory agencies that would far exceed what was achievable. In practice, OMB encountered substantial opposition in promoting a benefit-cost requirement for new regulatory policies. Implementing an overall regulatory budget concept would have required much more political support than the oversight group had.

Performance of the Reagan Oversight Effort

An assessment of the overall performance of the regulatory oversight process cannot be divorced from an evaluation of substantive changes in regulatory policy, which is the subject of the subsequent sections. However, it is useful to highlight a few of the most distinctive aspects of this process.

First, the change in the oversight test to include a benefit-cost requirement was consistent with most reform agendas. The regulatory analysis filings during the Ford and Carter administrations often advocated such balancing even though the executive orders empowering these efforts did not require a benefit-cost test.

The benefit-cost analysis requirement often led to exemplary studies of this type.

A prominent example of a well-executed benefit-cost assessment is the Department of Transportation's analysis of the merits of center-high-mounted stop lamps, which analyzed the comparative efficacy of different types of different stop lamps in reducing collision damage and compared these reduced damage savings with the lamps' costs. The EPA's assessment of the gasoline lead phasedown rule similarly was accompanied by an excellent regulatory analysis, as was the analysis of the construction fall-protection standard carried out by OSHA.[22] These improvements in the quality of regulatory analyses represented a substantial advance from earlier years.

What is less clear is the extent to which these improved analyses altered the policy choices or simply verified the good choices being made. Although many of the benefit-cost analyses carried out by the agencies were of high quality, it would be naive to assume that regulatory policies in the 1980s were dictated by strict adherence to a benefit-cost test.

The second major advance of the Reagan regulatory oversight process was the increased leverage given to the oversight effort. The requirement that the agency submit the regulatory proposal to OMB for prior approval gave the oversight group more binding authority than it had had in the past. Indeed, many supporters of the efforts of regulatory agencies feared that OMB would now dictate regulatory policy. The substantially increased authority of the regulatory oversight process was noted by James C. Miller III, whom the press designated the "regulatory czar": "If you are the toughest kid on the block, most kids most won't pick a fight with you. The Executive Order establishes things quite clearly."[23]

After the initial wave of regulatory reform efforts, the political support for deregulation began to wane. This shift was reflected in Vice-President Bush's decision to abolish the Presidential Task Force on Regulatory Relief in August 1983. Agencies also began to challenge this authority.

The extent of the decreased impetus for regulatory reform is reflected in several events. During the debate over the 1986 reauthorization of the oversight group, Representative Dingell led an effort to eliminate the OIRA group. The compromise ultimately reached provided for more disclosures of OMB's review efforts.

A 1986 court decision (*Environmental Defense Fund v. Lee Thomas*) required that OMB not delay rule makings if the agency faced a statutory deadline. EPA subsequently used this ruling to curtail OMB's review ability by delaying proposals until near the legislative deadline. Whereas the deadline was reached only once before 1986, after the court decision EPA ran up against the constraint six to seven times per year. Labor unions have also adopted this strategy on behalf of OSHA, as they have obtained court orders to force regulation of formaldehyde, ethylene oxide, asbestos, and lead. The courts required that OSHA examine these issues, not that it necessarily issue regulations. The OSHA health standards staff, however, used these orders to push for stringent regulations.

In the same vein, Representative Dingell wrote a letter to Lee Thomas in 1987 expressing concern with respect to OMB review before EPA had made its regulatory decision. This congressional concern has also been utilized by EPA to curtail the role of OMB. In 1990–1991, the U.S. Senate held up confirmation of the Bush administration's nominee to head the oversight group for more than a year in an effort to weaken the OMB process.

The result has been a substantial expansion of regulatory activity. Whereas EPA proposed an average of three to five major rules in the early 1980s, under Lee Thomas EPA's major rules proposals averaged twenty per year. The decrease in the regulatory initiatives in the early 1980s proved to be only temporary, as OMB had little ability to alter the structure of this expanded regulatory regime in a fundamental way. By the end of the 1980s and early 1990s, the OMB oversight group was no longer Miller's "biggest kid on the block." Instead, it was influential only on the margin.

The success of the components of the OMB effort had also differed. The basic Executive Order 12291 providing for benefit-cost analyses and establishing the character of regulatory reviews has proven to be most consequential. The subsequent Executive Order 12498 requiring OMB review of the regulatory agendas has proven to be less successful. The thumbnail sketches of regulatory options being considered provide OMB with some indication of future regulatory policies, but these projected agendas have been sufficiently fragmentary and OMB's leverage has been sufficiently weak that there has been little influence on the future direction of regulatory policies.

Although the strengthening of the regulatory oversight process represents a prominent but limited achievement, the transformation in the character of the oversight mechanism also has deficiencies. Whereas regulatory oversight in earlier administrations entailed comprehensive analyses of regulations that would be filed in the public record for the rule-making proceeding, OMB's review is an internal procedure. In situations in which oversight officials do not have to compile comprehensive analyses and make public the results of these analyses, the oversight mechanism may not serve as an advocate of the most attractive option from an economic standpoint. Moreover, until the benefit-cost assessment is undertaken, the optimal regulatory alternative may not be clear. The danger of mistaken decisions is particularly great when leading political actors in the White House believe that they know the answer in advance and do not feel the need to be guided by a precise analysis of the merits of the regulatory option.

The absence of a more public regulatory debate has other possible drawbacks as well. Although the secretive nature of the negotiation process with agencies has advantages in terms of enabling parties to modify their stance without incurring the costs of altering their positions in a public confrontation, disclosure of OMB's reasoning would foster public understanding and provide guidance to other agencies regarding proper criteria for policy design. In many situations, OMB was attacked, perhaps needlessly, for delaying regulations or blocking regulations.

OMB's record in reforming regulation suggests that in most cases the review process has little effect on the regulation (see Table 14-3). Almost three-fourths of all regulations in 1987 were approved by OMB in their initial form, and almost one-quarter were approved after revision. Only 3 percent of the proposals were rejected. In the absence of a public record of the manner in which the proposals were altered either in anticipation of the review or as part of the review, a more precise assessment of the impact of oversight is not possible.

Table 14-3. Nature of Regulatory Oversight Actions, 1987

	USDA	EPA	DOT	DOL	Total for all agencies	Percentage of total
Total reviews	420	205	202	64	2,314	100
Consistent without change	345	123	127	31	1,631	71
Consistent with change	58	60	64	31	549	24
Withdrawn by agency	5	9	7	0	59	3
Returned for consideration	2	0	4	0	10	0
Returned sent improperly	0	1	0	0	5	0
Emergency	6	0	0	1	15	1
Statutory or judicial dealine	4	12	0	1	45	2

Source: Office of Management and Budget (1988), p. 552.

14.4 ESTABLISHING AN APPROPRIATE PRICE FOR RISK

Agency Practices in Establishing Risk-Dollar Tradeoffs

The essential ingredient of benefit-cost tradeoffs in the context of risk and environmental regulations is to establish the risk-dollar tradeoff. Before the Reagan administration, agencies erred in two competing directions. First, in monetizing the benefits of health risks, agencies typically assessed the lost earnings and medical costs associated with the risk. Some agencies, such as the CPSC, had more detailed injury cost models, but these were not based on individuals' willingness to pay for risk reduction. Nonpecuniary health impacts and, more generally, society's willingness to pay to avoid small risks, were not recognized.

An opposite bias is that the legislative mandates of the risk-regulation agencies were absolute in character. The Clean Air Act requires EPA to set ambient air-quality standards independent of cost considerations. In other instances, tradeoffs are possible, but these tradeoffs must fall short of a full-blown benefit-cost test. Agencies such as OSHA and EPA consequently focused on affordability. Indeed, OSHA's legislative mandate requires that it follow this approach. The general consensus is that the net effect of these biases led most risk-regulation agencies to err on the side of excessive stringency, judged from the standpoint of economic efficiency.

The obvious solution is to rewrite the legislative mandates of these agencies. Ultimately, no meaningful regulatory reform can be achieved without some explicit attempt to balance the competing effects of regulation. Because legislative reform was not undertaken to achieve this end, the regulatory reform efforts could have only a modest and short-term impact.

Valuing Life: The Hazard Communication Debate

Perhaps the most noteworthy change in the nature of the regulatory debate is that the appropriate government expenditure per statistical life saved became an explicit object of concern. In earlier administrations, the regulatory oversight staff raised issues dealing with the value of life, with the principal reaction of agency economists being that such calculations were politically infeasible. Since lives were too sacred to value, agencies calculated the "costs of death." These costs consisted of the present value of the lost earnings and medical expenses. Although this concept may be appropriate from a tort liability compensation perspective, it abstracts from the value that individuals place on their welfare above and beyond their financial well-being. Moreover, it neglects the fact that attitudes toward risk-dollar tradeoffs involving small probabilities may entail quite different terms of trade than if one were faced with the prospect of certain death. In this as in other policy contexts, the appropriate benefits value is society's willingness to pay for the risk reduction.

Agencies ultimately adopted the value-of-life approach, but not because of its compelling intellectual foundation. In the 1980s OSHA undertook a regulatory analysis for its hazard communication standard, which would have required labeling and other forms of risk communication for all risky chemicals used in manufacturing. OSHA's regulatory analysis indicated that the benefits exceeded the costs. Armed with this favorable result, OSHA submitted the regulation to OMB for approval. OMB correctly observed that the risk effects had been misassessed by OSHA, leading to a substantial upward bias in the benefits. OMB concluded that a more accurate assessment implied that costs exceeded benefits. After OMB rejected the regulation in 1982, OSHA appealed its case to the Presidential Task Force on Regulatory Relief.

To see how value-of-life considerations entered this debate, consider the statistics in the summary Table 14-4. All figures in this table have been discounted to reflect the appropriate time lags involved for diseases such cancer, which have long latency periods. Although the hazard communication regulation would affect lives, it would also affect other health impacts, chiefly nonfatal job injuries and disabilities. At the time of the analysis, statistics were available on the implicit dollar value that workers attached to nonfatal injuries and fatalities, but there were no comparable values for disabling injuries. The approach I used to resolve this policy debate was to assess the sensitivity of the results, taking as fixed the estimated tradeoff between

Table 14-4. Summary of Benefit and Cost Effects of the OSHA Hazard Communication Regulation

	Lost workday equivalents			
	Weights—1,1,20[a]		Weights—1,5,20[a]	
	Effectiveness		Effectiveness	
	5%	10%	5%	10%
Net discounted costs less monetized benefits	$2.632 × 10^9$	$2.616 × 10^9$	$2.632 × 10^9$	$2.616 × 10^9$
Total lost workday case equivalents (discounted)	$9.5 × 10^4$	$18.9 × 10^4$	$24.7 × 10^4$	$49.7 × 10^4$
Net discounted cost/lost workday case equivalent	$27,900	$14,000	$10,700	$5,300

[a]These are the relative weights placed on lost workday cases (always 1), disabling illnesses (1 or 5), and cancers (always 20) in constructing a measure of lost workday case equivalents.

Source: W. Kip Viscusi, "Analysis of OMB and OSHA Evaluations of the Hazard Communication Proposal," Report Prepared for Secretary of Labor Raymond Donovan, March 15, 1982.

fatalities and lost workday injuries (estimated to be at a ratio of 20:1) and varying the rate of tradeoff between lost workday injuries and disabling injuries from a situation in which they receive equal value to one in which disabling injuries have a value five times as great as a lost workday injury. The other major assumption needed pertains to the efficacy of the regulation in reducing risk. OMB indicated that the risk reduction that would be experienced would be on the order of 5 percent, whereas OSHA estimated the impact of the regulation as reducing injuries by 10 percent.

Table 14-4 includes each of these benefit-weighting assumptions and provides calculations for both the OMB and the OSHA risk assessments. The first row of statistics in Table 14-4 consists of the net discounted costs minus all monetized benefits, thus providing a net financial impact figure that can be used in calculating the net cost per unit health impact. The second row provides the estimated discounted total lost workday case equivalents for the regulation using the weights given at the top of the table. The bottom row of Table 14-4 presents the estimated discounted cost per lost workday case equivalent injury prevented.

Whether the regulation should be pursued depends on whether this cost-effectiveness measure is greater than the estimated value of nonfatal injuries. My past estimates indicated an implicit value of injuries on the order of $23,000 to $35,000 (in 1982 dollars—the year of the analysis) so that for three of the four sets of assumptions listed the regulation clearly passes a benefit-cost test. In one instance the benefits exceed the cost except for the lowest end of the range of estimates of the implicit values workers attach to injuries.

Secretary of Labor Donovan indicated that he viewed this analysis as providing support of the regulation, but OMB regulation head Christopher DeMuth maintains that he was not fully persuaded.[24] The ultimate decision to issue the regulation may reflect in part the increased strength of the regulatory agencies after the initial period of deregulation. Moreover, the regulation had the strong support of labor as well as chemical industry groups, who sought to avoid the costs associated with a variety of state warnings regulations by having a uniform national regulation.

The policy outcome was not as consequential as the process that took place. The terms of the debate had changed dramatically since the 1970s. Regulatory agencies and the White House oversight group focused their attention on whether the benefits of the regulation exceeded the costs, whereas in earlier administrations such concerns were subsidiary. Agencies had viewed their role as being governed by a higher-level agenda in which formal tradeoffs of this type were not permitted.

The new enthusiasm of agencies for the value-of-life approach can be traced primarily to its effect on the attractiveness of policies. This methodology boosts the monetized value of health benefits by a factor of 10, which is approximately the ratio of the estimated implicit value of life to the present value of the earnings of workers for whom these values are estimated. Although agency decisions are seldom dictated solely by benefit-cost concerns, the preparation of proper benefit assessments represents a substantial dividend of the OMB oversight effort.

The Value-of-Life Regulatory Record

The net effect of the effort to strike a balance between benefits and costs is shown in the cost-per-life-saved statistics in Table 14-5.[25] Since these figures pertain to aver-

Table 14-5. The Cost of Various Risk-Reducing Regulations per Life Saved

Regulation	Year and status	Agency	Initial annual risk[a]	Annual lives saved	Cost per life saved (*millions of 1984 $*)
Pass benefit-cost test:					
Unvented space heaters	1980 F[b]	CPSC	2.7 in 10^5	63.000	$ .10
Oil and gas well service	1983 P	OSHA-S	1.1 in 10^3	50.000	.10
Cabin fire protection	1985 F	FAA	6.5 in 10^8	15.000	.20
Passive restraints/belts	1984 F	NHTSA	9.1 in 10^5	1,850.000	.30
Underground construction	1989 F	OSHA-S	1.6 in 10^3	8.100	.30
Alcohol and drug control	1985 F	FRA	1.8 in 10^6	4.200	.50
Servicing wheel rims	1984 F	OSHA-S	1.4 in 10^5	2.300	.50
Seat cushion flammability	1984 F	FAA	1.6 in 10^7	37.000	.60
Floor emergency lighting	1984 F	FAA	2.2 in 10^8	5.000	.70
Crane suspended personnel platform	1988 F	OSHA-S	1.8 in 10^3	5.000	1.20
Concrete and masonry construction	1988 F	OSHA-S	1.4 in 10^5	6.500	1.40
Hazard communication	1983 F	OSHA-S	4.0 in 10^5	200.000	1.80
Benzene/fugitive emissions	1984 F	EPA	2.1 in 10^5	0.310	2.80
Fail benefit-cost test:					
Grain Dust	1987 F	OSHA-S	2.1 in 10^4	4.000	5.30
Radionuclides/uranium mines	1984 F	EPA	1.4 in 10^4	1.100	6.90
Benzene	1987 F	OSHA-H	8.8 in 10^4	3.800	17.10
Arsenic/glass plant	1986 F	EPA	8.0 in 10^4	0.110	19.20
Ethylene oxide	1984 F	OSHA-H	4.4 in 10^5	2.800	25.60
Arsenic/copper smelter	1986 F	EPA	9.0 in 10^4	0.060	26.50
Uranium mill tailings, inactive	1983 F	EPA	4.3 in 10^4	2.100	27.60
Uranium mill tailings, active	1983 F	EPA	4.3 in 10^4	2.100	53.00
Asbestos	1986 F	OSHA-H	6.7 in 10^5	74.700	89.30
Asbestos	1989 F	EPA	2.9 in 10^5	10.000	104.20
Arsenic/glass manufacturing	1986 R	EPA	3.8 in 10^5	0.250	142.00
Benzene/storage	1984 R	EPA	6.0 in 10^7	0.043	202.00
Radionuclides/DOE facilities	1984 R	EPA	4.3 in 10^6	0.001	210.00
Radionuclides/elem. phosphorous	1984 R	EPA	1.4 in 10^5	0.046	270.00
Benzene/ethylbenzenol styrene	1984 R	EPA	2.0 in 10^6	0.006	483.00
Arsenic/low-arsenic copper	1986 R	EPA	2.6 in 10^4	0.090	764.00
Benzene/maleic anhydride	1984 R	EPA	1.1 in 10^6	0.029	820.00
Land disposal	1988 F	EPA	2.3 in 10^8	2.520	3,500.00
EDB	1989 R	OSHA-H	2.5 in 10^4	0.002	15,600.00
Formaldehyde	1987 F	OSHA-H	6.8 in 10^7	0.010	72,000.00

[a]Annual deaths per exposed population. An exposed population of 10^3 is 1,000, 10^4 is 10,000, etc.

[b]F, P, or R = Final, proposed, or rejected rule.

Source: John F. Morrall III (1986), p. 30. These statistics were updated by John F. Morrall III via unpublished communication with the author, July 10, 1990.

age costs per life saved rather than marginal costs, the tests indicate whether the regulation is preferable to no regulation, not whether the level of stringency is optimal. An appropriate reference point for assessing how far we should move down this table in terms of policy acceptability is the value-of-life estimates in the literature at that time.[26] The results in Chapter 4 indicated a broad range. Workers in high-risk jobs value each expected death at under $1 million; the value of life of workers in typical blue collar risk jobs was on the order of $3 million; and the value of life of individuals in very high-income positions may be $6 million or more, but these estimates are least precise.

Judged by these standards, many of the regulations in the 1980s clearly pass a benefit-cost test. The policies of the FAA appear to be outstanding bargains. Their low costs-per-life-saved figures should not, however, be viewed as a regulatory success. A main contributor to this low figure is that the FAA valued the lives saved in airplane crashes using the present value of the lost earnings of the accident victims. This approach underestimates the value of life of airplane passengers by more than an order of magnitude. In one case, the FAA dismissed repairs of the DC-10 as being not worthwhile because of the low level of the risk, whereas a proper benefit-cost calculation indicates that the risk reductions were clearly desirable.[27] Application of value-of-life principles and benefit-cost analysis would have led an agency to be more aggressive.

The cutoff in Table 14-5 for policies with benefits in excess of their costs is probably just below the regulation of benzene/fugitive emissions, with a cost per life saved of $2.8 million. Policies below that regulation in the table would not pass a benefit-cost test unless they protect populations with comparatively high values per life. OMB rejected none of the policies with lower costs per life, whereas they rejected eight policies with higher costs per life. OMB blocked some of the particularly inefficient regulations, although several regulations with very low efficacy were enacted. Indeed, the minimum tradeoff threshold for OMB to reject a regulation is quite high. None of the regulations in Table 14-5 with costs per life saved below $142 million were rejected. OMB's efficacy is apparently limited to the most extreme instances of regulatory excess.

Given the uncertainties involved with benefit-cost analysis, the character of the agency's legislative mandates, and the continued ability of regulatory agencies to wield substantial influence, the most that could have been hoped for is an elimination of the most unattractive policies from a benefit-cost standpoint. By that criterion, substantial progress was made.

14.5 SUNSET ACTIONS AND REGULATORY REFORMS

The Reform Record

The widespread dissatisfaction with the character of regulatory standards has long led regulatory reformers to urge modification of these regulations. President Ford's Task Force on Regulatory Reform proposed that OSHA's standards be replaced by more performance-oriented alternatives. More generally, since the original regulations had seldom been based on benefit-cost grounds, there was always a potential gain from altering previous policies.

The major sunset action of the Carter administration was the decision by OSHA director Eula Bingham to eliminate or modify 928 OSHA regulations in October 1978. Although many of the changes that she instituted were only editorial and did not alter the substantive focus of the regulation, this regulatory pruning eliminated the "nitpicking" aspects of OSHA regulation, which were the source of widespread ridicule of OSHA's efforts.

A potentially ambitious effort at deregulation occurred in 1980, as Carter administration economists developed an automobile industry relief package. The auto industry bore the brunt of a substantial body of regulatory costs, including emissions requirements, safety standards, and fuel-economy standards. Some regulatory critics believed these costs contributed to the economic decline of the automobile industry. However, the timing of the main cost increases—the late 1960s, early 1970s, and 1980–1981—does not coincide with the economic decline of the auto industry. A more influential factor was the rise in fuel prices in the 1970s and the shift to small cars. Substantive action to support a pivotal industry in an election year did, however, offer political benefits.

The Carter administration developed a reform package that provided only very limited relief. Its principal component was a proposal to reduce the stringency of high-altitude emissions requirements, which offered a payoff of $500 million over a three-year period. The rest of the package had little substance because policy changes were opposed by the EPA and NHTSA administrators.[28]

Reagan's Auto Industry Relief Package

The advent of the Reagan administration marked a change in the regulatory climate. Shortly after taking office, the Reagan administration suspended the "midnight regulations" issued by the Carter administration in its closing days and ordered a reexamination of their merits. This effort yielded some partial dividends. As Council of Economic Advisors member William Niskanen (1988) observed: "Of the 172 proposed rules that were suspended, for example, 112 were approved without change, and only eighteen were withdrawn. OIRA's batting average would never again be as high."

The Reagan administration's most comprehensive deregulation effort was its automobile industry relief package. The agenda for this reform effort was not a product of the Reagan administration efforts alone. Many of the regulations included in this group had previously been opposed at the time of their promulgation by the White House economists, many of whom were now at OMB. In addition, some of the components of the relief package had previously been advocated by the Carter administration economists for inclusion in the 1980 relief package but were not included because of opposition from the affected agencies.

The impetus for reform stemmed in part from the rise in regulatory costs in 1980 and 1981. The estimates by White (1982) indicate that the total costs of emission regulations per automobile mushroomed from $559 in 1979 to $906 in 1980, and then to $1,551 in 1981. Safety regulation costs were in addition to this amount. Estimates by Crandall et al. (1986) suggest that the additional equipment cost per automobile rose from $431–$641 in 1979 to $512–$822 in 1981; and the fuel penalty increased from $116 in 1979 to $159 in 1981. The Reagan package for relief of the automobile industry consequently had been developed in an environment of rapid cost escalation for automobiles that could be traced to the influence of government standards.

Table 14-6 summarizes the components of the package, their status as of

Table 14-6. The Reagan Administration's Auto Reform Package

Issue	Action (*date of completion*)	Five-year savings ($*millions*) Industry	Public
Rules acted on:			
Gas-tank vapors	Declined to order new controls on cars (April 1981)	$103	$1,300
Emissions tests	Streamlined certification of industry tests on vehicles (Oct. 1981, Nov. 1982)	5	—
	Raised allowable "failure rate" for test of light trucks and heavy-duty engines from 10 to 40 percent (Jan. 1983)	19	129
	Reduced spot checks of emissions of vehicles on assembly lines by 42 percent; delayed assembly-line tests of heavy-duty trucks until 1986 (Jan. 1983)	1	1
High-altitude autos	Ended assembly-line tests at high altitude, relying instead on industry data (April 1981)	0.2	—
	Allowed industry to self-certify vehicles as meeting high-altitude emissions standards (April 1981)	1	1
Pollution waivers	Consolidated industry applications for temporary exemptions from tougher emissions standards for nitrogen oxide and carbon monoxide (Sept. 1981)	—	—
Paint shops	Delayed until 1983 tougher hydrocarbon pollution standards for auto paint shops (Oct. 1981)	300	—
Test vehicles	Cut paperwork required to exempt prototype vehicles from environmental standards (July 1982)	—	—
Driver vision	Scrapped existing 1981 rule and second proposed rule-setting standards for driver's field of view (June 1982)	160	—
Fuel economy	Decided not to set stiffer fuel-economy standards to replace those expiring in 1985 (April 1981)	—	—
Speedometers	Revoked rule-setting standards for speedometers and tamper-resistant odometers (Feb. 1982)	—	20
Tire rims	Scrapped proposal to set safety standards for explosive multipiece tire rims (Feb. 1982)	300	75
Brake tests	Eased from 30 to 20 percent the steepness of grades on which post-1984 truck and bus brakes must hold (Dec. 1981)	—	1.8
Tire pressure	Scrapped proposal to equip vehicles with low–tire pressure indicators (Aug. 1981)	—	130
Battery safety	Scrapped proposal to set standards to prevent auto battery explosions (August 1981)	—	—
Tire safety	Revoked requirement that consumers be told of reserve load capacity of tires; eased tire makers' reporting requirements (June 1982)	—	—
Antitheft protection	Eased antitheft and locking steering wheel standards for open-body vehicles (June 1981)	—	—
Fuel economy	Streamlined semiannual reports of automakers on their progress in meeting fuel-economy goals (Aug. 1982)	—	0.1
Tire ratings	Suspended rule requiring industry to rate tires ac-	—	10

(*continued*)

Table 14-6. (*Continued*)

Issue	Action (*date of completion*)	Five-year savings ($millions)	
		Industry	Public
	cording to tread wear, traction, and heat resistance (Feb. 1983)		
Vehicle IDs	Downgraded from standard to administrative rule the requirement that all vehicles have ID numbers as an aid to police (May 1983)	—	—
Seat belt comfort	Scrapped proposal to set standards for seat belt comfort and convenience (June 1983)	—	—
Rules with uncertain futures:			
High-altitude emissions	Failed to revise Clean Air Act order ending weaker high-altitude emissions standards in 1984; eased through regulatory changes	38	1,300
Emissions reductions	Failed to revise Clean Air Act order to cut large trucks' hydrocarbon and carbon monoxide emissions by 90 percent by 1984; standard was delayed until 1985	105	536
	Failed to ease Clean Air Act order reducing nitrogen oxide emissions from light trucks and heavy-duty engines by 75 percent by 1984; regulatory changes under study	150	563
Particulate pollution	Delayed a proposal to scrap specific particulate standards for some diesels in favor of an average standard for all diesels; stiffer standards delayed from 1985 to 1987	40	523
Methane standards	Shelved because of "serious" costs; questions a plan to drop methane as a regulated hydrocarbon	—	—
Passive restraints	Delayed and then revoked requirement that post-1982 autos be equipped with passive restraints; revocation overturned by Supreme Court in June 1983	428	981
Bumper damage	Cut from 5 to 2.5 mph the speed at which bumpers must resist damage; change is on appeal	—	308

Source: Michael Wines, "Reagan Plan to Relieve Auto Industry of Regulatory Burden Gets Mixed Grades," *National Journal*, July 23, 1983, pp. 1534–1535.

mid-1983, and the cost savings that the administration claimed for them.[29] The measures with the greatest savings for industry included the delay of the paint shop standard, the elimination of the driver vision standard, the delay of the tougher hydrocarbon solution standards, the scrapping of the safety standards for explosive multipiece tire rims, and the delay of the passenger restraint requirements. Overall, this reform package provides a very comprehensive program of regulatory relief.

The success of this reform effort stemmed not only from the White House regulatory reformers' zeal but also from the nature of the Reagan appointments to regulatory agencies. The NHTSA head, Raymond Peck, has been justifiably termed "an expert deregulator,"[30] and EPA administrator Anne Gorsuch developed a well-deserved reputation for scaling back the efforts of her agency.

Although some of the items in Table 14-6 represent attractive reforms, others may not pass the usual economic tests. The paint shop requirement, for example, may represent the most cost-effective way of meeting hydrocarbon emissions standards. Abolition of this regulation would lead to more costly controls being required for other establishments near automobile paint shops, such as gasoline stations.[31] The costs of the regulation were, however, quite high, particularly in the short run. By delaying the regulation, OMB gave firms additional opportunity to change over to the new technologies required, greatly reducing the ultimate costs of the regulation. The merits of passive restraints are also much debated, even by economists.

Some of these deregulation efforts ultimately were viewed as constituting regulatory relief rather than regulatory reform. The Supreme Court eventually overturned NHTSA's rescission of the air bag rule.

There are likely to be some disagreements regarding the particular components of the program as well as the permanence of the regulatory reforms. On balance, however, these auto industry relief measures primarily delayed regulatory costs. They did not alter the long-term structure of auto regulations in any fundamental manner.

Perhaps the main reason that there was a failure to restructure the regulations rather than simply reduce their cost is that the overriding objective was not regulatory reform but auto industry relief. OMB Director Stockman (1986) viewed these policies with some disapproval, as he considered them to be a thinly veiled policy of protectionism.[32] The overriding objective of cost reduction rather than meaningful reform limited the degree to which this political success was also a beneficial reform measure.

Other Reforms and Sunset Actions

Other reform efforts met with less success. Chapter 10 focused on a major reform effort at OSHA—its reexamination of the cotton dust regulation that had been bitterly opposed by both the textile industry and Carter administration economists in a dispute that ultimately led to a battle in the U.S. Supreme Court. OSHA's reassessment of the regulation indicated that the original regulatory analysis was wildly inaccurate and that the standard could be profitably altered in several ways. For example, a policy of low-cost environmental controls (e.g., taping leaks in ductwork) coupled with testing and rotating workers would achieve most of the health gains of the original standard. One could also question whether the risk-dollar tradeoff for each case of partial or total disability prevented was reasonable. The Supreme Court's decision to explicitly rule out a benefit-cost test in the cotton dust case and to require that the agencies set the lowest "feasible" standard did not preclude performance-oriented alternatives or some balancing of competing interests. However, by the time of the Reagan administration review, the largest textile manufacturers were already in compliance with the cotton dust regulation, leading them to join with labor in advocating retention of the status quo.

The lack of enthusiasm for altering a regulatory regime that was once bitterly opposed is likely to be a more general phenomenon whenever firms incur fixed costs of compliance. The regulatory reforms OSHA did undertake were largely of a piecemeal variety. For example, OSHA revised its electrical standards for the construction industry to be in conformance with new industry standards.[33]

The overall performance of the Reagan administration's deregulation and sunset actions was mixed. Of 119 regulations reviewed by the Presidential Task Force on Regulatory Relief, 76 regulations were revised, in 27 cases revisions were proposed, and in 16 cases revisions by the task force were still under way when this group issued its final regulatory report.[34]

The extent of the various revisions cited in the report card that the Presidential Task Force issued on its performance is not indicated, but particularly in the early years it is evident that some progress was made. The fact that the task force was disbanded in 1983 is a reflection of the decreasing prospects over time for altering the structure of regulation. The climate for regulatory reform had clearly changed, and there would soon be a return to the previous regulatory environment.

Sunset actions and other changes in the structure of existing regulation are difficult to achieve. With regulations already in place, industry's interest in altering these regulations is divided. Moreover, shifting the character of regulations over time may impose additional adjustment costs. The initial wave of deregulation efforts under the Reagan administration isolated some promising candidates for change. The greatest subsequent gains could be achieved by focusing on new regulatory proposals.

4.6 NEW REGULATORY INITIATIVES

Environmental Policy

The major regulatory innovation sought by economists in the environmental area has been the greater utilization of market-based policies. Notwithstanding the widespread enthusiasm of economists and reformers for various forms of emissions trading options, such measures remain the exception rather than the rule.

Table 14-7 summarizes the performance of these policies through 1984. The most popular market-oriented trading system is that of netting, whereby a firm can modify its existing plant and equipment in a manner that increases the level of pollution from one source, provided that it also decreases pollution emissions from other sources in a manner so that the *net* increase does equal that of a major source. The netting policy is restricted to internal trading for a particular firm. By its very design this effort should have little effect on environmental quality. Table 14-7 indicates that the emission-control cost savings from netting are substantial.

The second most frequent emissions trading option is that of offsets. This option introduced in 1976 permits construction of new facilities that will create pollution in areas of the country that exceed maximum allowable concentrations for pollutants. Companies must, however, purchase offsets from existing facilities that provide for more than equivalent reduction of the same pollutant from pollution sources that are already in compliance. By 1984, most of the offset transactions were internal rather than involving external trades, and the cost savings are not believed to be substantial.

The third trading concept in Table 14-7 is the bubble policy, which was introduced by the Carter administration in December 1979. By envisioning an artificial bubble around a firm for which the firm must be in compliance in terms of its total

Table 14-7. Summary of Emissions Trading Activity

Activity	Estimated number of internal transactions	Estimated number of external transactions	Estimated cost savings (*millions*)	Environmental-quality impact
Netting	5,000 to 12,000	None	$25 to $300 in permitting costs; $500 to $12,000 in emissions-control costs	Insignificant in individual cases; probably insignificant in aggregate
Offsets	1,800	200	Probably large, but not easily measured	Probably insignificant
Bubbles:				
Federally	40	2	$300	Insignificant
approved	89	0	$135	Insignificant
State approved				
Banking:	<100	<20	Small	Insignificant

Source: R. W. Hahn and G. L. Hester (1989), p. 138.

level of pollution rather than having to meet a particular requirement for each pollution source, a firm can establish the most cost-effective mechanism for achieving the pollution reduction within its "bubble." By 1984, bubbles had been adopted in fewer than 200 instances, with cost savings believed to be under $500 million.

The final trading option—banking—enables firms to store rights to pollution over time if they are in compliance with their standards and then use these compliance rights as offsets against pollution. This policy enables firms to avoid sacrificing pollution rights should they choose to replace their current high-polluting plant and equipment with a more efficient lower-pollution technology. The use of banking policies has, however, been infrequent.

These market-oriented systems have generated nontrivial financial benefits, without any substantially detrimental environmental consequences. The small scale of these efforts reflects the extent to which the EPA has viewed these market systems as experimental options rather than as an integral part of agency policy.

Firms must obtain EPA approval to utilize these trading options, and the costs of this approval are often substantial. Approval of the applications is not always forthcoming, as there has been long-term suspicion by most EPA officials and environmentalists more generally of market options. Pollution rights trading policies involve costs in locating a seller of emissions credits and in establishing the terms of trade. Firms also face substantial uncertainties when they embark on the emissions-trading path, since there is no guarantee that these experimental EPA policies will continue for the duration of the investment that they must make.

Although economists in the Carter and Reagan administrations had long advocated such market approaches, it was not until the Bush administration that such efforts became a prominent part of the nation's declared economic agenda.[35] The degree to which these efforts will become a central component of EPA policy is not yet apparent.

Although EPA expanded the role of market-oriented systems very little in the 1980s, it did undertake other initiatives. Its air pollution efforts were particularly active, especially with respect to the continuing phasedown of the use of lead in gasoline. In 1985 the permissible lead content in gasoline was reduced from 1.0 to 0.5 grams/gallon, and in 1986 the permissible level dropped to 0.1 grams/gallon. What was particularly noteworthy about this increasing stringency of the lead standard is that it was also supported by sound regulatory analysis demonstrating the excess of benefits over costs.[36] EPA also expanded its efforts against airborne toxins in the 1980s, and it undertook substantial efforts to reduce indoor air pollution stemming from asbestos and radon.

As will be discussed subsequently within the context of enforcement, implementation of the Superfund legislation (CERCLA, 1980) also was a new concern of the agency in the 1980s. The 1984 RCRA amendments also were a major legislative initiative through which Congress imposed a series of deadlines for EPA actions, thus limiting the agency's discretion.

Two other major additions to EPA's agenda were the long-range problems of acid rain and the greenhouse effect. In each case, EPA identified major problems meriting national attention, but it failed to justify the economic merits of these efforts. The result has been a delay for greater study of these problems and symbolic efforts as part of the international dialogue on these issues.[37] With respect to the global environmental problems, the United States participated in the 1985 Vienna Convention and the 1987 Montreal Protocol, which led to the freezing of chlorofluorocarbon production levels, and in 1989 the United States participated in the Paris Summit focusing on global environmental concerns. To the extent that the United States has been an activist member of these groups, it has been through fostering recognition of the economic costs involved.

The desirability of particular global warming and acid rain policies remains in doubt. Portney (1990) estimates that the acid rain provisions of the 1990 Clean Air Act amendments will provide $5 billion in benefits with costs in the $2 to $9 billion range. These acid rain provisions are desirable only if the costs are not much above the midpoint of the cost range. The exploratory analysis of global warming policies by Nordhaus (1990) likewise indicates mixed results regarding the attractiveness of the policy measures that have been proposed. Actions such as control of chlorofluorocarbons are economically desirable, but very ambitious policies may not be worthwhile. The main shortcoming of EPA policies with respect to these long-run environmental issues is the continuing need to identify the specific policies that merit adoption in terms of the net benefits they offer society.

Although EPA was not successful in winning approval for these policies, overall the late 1980s marked a dramatic resurgence in EPA regulatory activity. Table 14-8 summarizes the present value of costs for major EPA rules proposed or finalized from 1987 to 1990. These cost levels are quite impressive, including proposed regulations with costs of $70 billion in 1987 and $250 billion in 1990 and final regulations with costs of $84 billion in 1988 and $95 billion in 1990. To put these levels in perspective, note that during the expansionary period of EPA regulation before Reagan, the costs associated with proposed EPA regulations were $26 to $29

Table 14-8. Trends in EPA Regulation Costs

| Year | Present value of costs (*$billions*) of EPA regulations | |
	Proposed rules	Final rules
1987	70	14
1988	21	84
1989	17	6
1990	250	95

Source: Estimates prepared by U.S. Office of Management and Budget, August 1990. Figures for 1989 and 1990 are preliminary.

billion in 1979, and for the entire 1975–1980 period were only $218 to $296 billion.[38]

EPA had not simply returned to its earlier degree of regulatory activity; by the late 1980s and 1990s EPA was undertaking more costly regulatory initiatives than at any time in its history.

Pharmaceutical Regulation

One of the most highly publicized areas of successful new regulatory initiatives was for pharmaceuticals. Critics of the FDA had long charged that the agency erred on the side of preventing adverse effects of newly approved drugs as opposed to taking into consideration the benefits that new drugs may offer.[39] One FDA official remarked that no one was going to blame him for slow approval of a beneficial drug, but he would be blamed for approving the next thalidomide.[40]

Throughout the 1980s, the OMB regulatory oversight group sought to expedite the FDA drug-approval process. The political leverage for achieving an accelerated approval time for new drugs was increased by the AIDS constituency. Since the prospects of patients suffering from life-threatening diseases such as AIDS were quite low, a policy of giving expedited approval to these drugs offered potential benefits with little apparent mortality risk.

FDA adopted a general regulatory commitment to trying to accelerate the drug-approval process without compromising its quality, and it established a special commitment to expediting the approval of drugs for diseases such as AIDS.

The statistics in Table 14-9 present the total number of new chemical entities approved and their approval time. Drugs that are ranked 1A are believed to be of substantial importance, and the 1AA drugs are generally drugs for diseases such as AIDS. If we contrast the patterns before and after the FDA policy change in 1987, there is no striking departure from earlier trends. The number of new drug approvals increased somewhat from the earlier years, particularly given the low drug approval rates in 1980 and 1983. The number of approvals given to the 1A and 1AA drugs increased in 1988 and 1989 from the level in the mid-1980s, but the total number of such approvals was almost identical to the rate of approval in 1982–1983. The speed of the drug approvals also did not change markedly. The average drug ap-

Table 14-9. New Drug Approvals and Time to Approval

Year	Number of NCE approvals		Average lag time (*months*) from submission to approval	
	All drugs	1AA/1A drugs	All drugs	1AA/1A drugs
1980	11	2	35.18	26.38
1981	23	2	31.03	14.25
1982	22	4	26.02	9.81
1983	12	4	28.67	21.44
1984	21	2	43.44	27.75
1985	26	3	32.08	32.67
1986	18	1	34.19	17.50
1987	18	2	32.76	12.00
1988	16	4	36.39	41.00
1989	21	5	35.61	22.05

Source: All figures based on calculations by the author using chronology of new chemical entities developed by the University of Rochester Center for Study of Drug Development, July 10, 1990 (computer printout).

proval time in the late 1980s is not substantially different from that in earlier years. The rate of approval for the 1A and 1AA drugs was particularly rapid in 1987 and 1989, but was comparatively slow in 1988.

The most that can be concluded from this evidence is that there has been some modest effort to target more drugs as being 1A or 1AA and to avoid the long lag time of over three and one-half years that was present in 1984. Since many of the drugs involved in this approval process have been in the FDA pipeline for several years, the ultimate effects of a shift in FDA drug-approval policy will not be fully apparent until the 1990s. The changes that have been made are consistent with the principles being advocated by most economists, and the extent of the changes evidenced in FDA activities has been modest.

Occupational Safety Regulation

The literature on OSHA has long stressed the need to go beyond the technology-forcing nature of the initial era of OSHA regulation. One such performance-oriented mechanism is the 1980 OSHA proposed hazard communication regulation included as part of Carter's "midnight regulations" package. This regulation established chemical labeling in the manufacturing industry.

The ultimate regulation issued by the Reagan administration expanded on the original Carter proposal by adding material safety data sheets. Chemical suppliers were required to provide downstream firms with information regarding chemical ingredients. Although potentially attractive in theory, the material safety data component of the regulation has been of little benefit because of the overly technical nature of the information provided. In addition to being the most costly new regulatory initiative in the risk area during the first Reagan term, this regulation also was innovative in many respects. This informational regulation represented a shift in the domain of regulatory activity that occurred throughout the 1980s. Right-to-know measures at the federal and local level proliferated in an effort to inform individuals of the risks from exposures on the job, exposures from the environment, and exposures from products.

The other major innovation in OSHA's regulatory structure was the adoption of the permissible exposure limits of the Amercian Conference of Governmental Industrial Hygienists (ACGIH). OSHA's original standards for health risk exposures were based on approximately 400 exposure limits that had been recommended by the ACGIH, which is an industry advisory group. Each year a committee of fifteen individuals, composed chiefly of hygienists and toxicologists from industry, meets to set threshold limit values for chemical exposures, where the objective is to achieve levels for which "no injurious effect will result no matter how often the exposure is repeated."[41] Although a zero risk exposure is not necessarily optimal, this industry group informally incorporates concerns of feasibility.[42] The ACGIH had developed 200 standards for new health hazard exposures as well as 100 revisions of the exposure limits for existing OSHA standards that had been based on the earlier ACGIH exposure limits. Adopting all of these revisions through a generic regulation rather than through a substance-by-substance rule-making approach enabled OSHA to expand its efforts in the health area, which had been given insufficient attention compared to safety concerns.

Although this regulation appears to be attractive on balance, its main shortcoming is that the process for generating such broadly based standards did not originate within the agency but was instead devised by an industry group. This process raises the long-term possibility that the function of such industry-designed standards will be to restrain competition and to promote the vested interests of the particular firms represented in the industry organization rather than to advance the interests of society at large. This type of capture theory has been offered by Stigler (1971) in the case of economic regulation. If OSHA were to continue to base its regulations on guidelines recommended by industry, then this procedure would all but ensure the long-run capture of OSHA. These dangers are also apparent in other areas of OSHA regulation, as the lobbying of the large textile firms in support of the retention of the cotton dust standard illustrated.

The other innovations in OSHA's regulatory agenda were more incremental. A collaborative effort of OSHA and the OMB regulatory oversight group led to an innovative OSHA grain-handling standard.[43] Grain dust levels in grain-handling facilities often led to explosions involving the deaths of dozens of workers. In 1984, OSHA proposed to reduce the risks posed by such exposures by decreasing the permissible grain dust level. The outcome that resulted from the collaboration by OSHA and OMB offered firms a series of several performance-oriented alternatives that they could choose in order to achieve compliance:

(i) To clean up the dust whenever it exceeds $\frac{1}{8}$ of an inch;
(ii) To clean up the dust at least once per shift; or
(iii) To use pneumatic dust control equipment.[44]

The flexibility offered by these various alternatives enables firms to choose the most cost-effective mechanism for achieving the desired safety objective. Although the introduction of flexibility of this type did not become a prevalent characteristic of new OSHA standards, it did mark the introduction of a greater degree of diversity in the regulatory approach than had been reflected in previous OSHA efforts.

Perhaps most important is the trend in the level of OSHA regulation. As in the case of EPA, there was a resurgence of regulation in the late 1980s. As indicated by the present value of the costs of proposed and final rules summarized in Table 14-10, new OSHA regulations were generating substantial costs. Major regulations proposed in 1988 and 1989 would impose costs of $12 billion and $10.5 billion. If we exclude the OSHA carcinogen policy that was proposed in 1978 but never adopted, proposed OSHA standards imposed costs of only $35 to $44 billion for the entire 1975–1980 period.[45] The level of OSHA policy initiatives at the end of the Reagan term had surpassed that of the pre-Reagan era.

Traffic Safety Regulation

One of NHTSA's early success stories in the 1980s that promoted safety in an effective manner was the promulgation of the regulation for rear-window brake lights.[46] The installation of such brake lights reduces the reaction time of drivers of following vehicles because of the greater visibility of the single center-high-mounted stop lamp.

The Department of Transportation regulations with the broadest potential impact on fatalities were its safety belt standards. The Department of Transportation issued regulations requiring that states comprising two-thirds of the United States population enact safety belt laws. If this condition was not met, the federal government would require phased installation of passive restraint systems.

This compromise measure was a response to the U.S. Supreme Court decision to overturn the automobile industry relief package's rescission of the passive-restraint requirements. Since many of the benefits of passive restraints could be achieved through use of seat belts, this measure represents an effort to utilize the ability of the individual to reduce his or her own risk rather than always relying upon a technological solution. The decision to leave the ultimate decision of whether mandatory safety belt laws would be enacted to the states is consistent with the Reagan administration's principle of Federalism.

In this case, there is no apparent heterogeneity in the benefits or the costs of a mandatory seat belt requirement to warrant leaving this matter up to the states. Since

Table 14-10. Trends in OSHA
Regulation Costs

| Year | Present value of costs (*$billions*) of OSHA regulations | |
	Proposed rules	Final rules
1987	2.8	2.7
1988	12	0.2
1989	10.5	12.7

Source: Estimates prepared by U.S. Office of Management and Budget, August 1990.

most economic studies indicate that the benefits of seat belt use far exceed the costs, the case for making the standard nationwide seems quite strong, if a mandatory requirement overruling individual choice is sensible.[47]

Smoking and Individual Responsibility for Risk

Perhaps the most aggressive new area of risk regulation in the 1980s was with respect to smoking behavior. The Surgeon General C. Everett Koop issued increasingly strident attacks against cigarette smoking, designating cigarettes as more addictive than heroin and calling for a smoke-free society by the year 2000. Even the Council of Economic Advisors joined in the chorus of attacks against smoking, calling it the "greatest avoidable risk."[48]

The governmental policy efforts against smoking took two forms. The first consisted of public attacks against cigarettes that usually accompanied the issuance of the Annual Report of the Surgeon General on smoking. Such reports ideally inform individuals regarding the risks of smoking, thus promoting a greater balancing of risks and benefits in individuals' decision making. The Surgeon General's reports, however, went beyond providing information; they became advocacy documents against smoking behavior.

The second form of policy action consisted of a change in the warnings accompanying cigarettes. In 1984 Congress mandated a series of rotating cigarette warnings alerting consumers to a diverse set of risks pertaining to cigarettes. These warnings replaced the single warning in place since 1969 that indicated that "cigarette smoking is dangerous to your health."

Changes in hazard warning programs and public information campaigns can be easily undertaken by a policymaker wishing to pursue antismoking policies. These measures are more feasible than changes in the cigarette tax or national regulations pertaining to smoking behavior. However, as the percentage of smokers in society declined in the 1980s, the pressures against smoking increased.

Table 14-11 summarizes several key smoking trends. The total cigarette consumption per capita dropped considerably in the 1980s. As cigarette companies began to market their product to an increasingly smaller group, the price of cigarettes rose, which in turn also influences the number of people who will purchase the product. Cigarette taxes as a percentage of the retail price have dropped over the

Table 14-11. Principal Aspects of Smoking Behavior

	Cigarettes per capita	Cigarette price per package (*$average*)	Cigarette taxes as a percent of retail price (*median*)	Present smoker percentage	Former smoker percentage
1970	2,534	.39	46.8	36.7	17.9
1980	2,821	.63	33.1	32.6	20.6
1985	2,501	1.05	30.8	29.8	24.4
1989	2,156	1.44	26.4	NA	NA

Source: Tobacco Institute, *The Tax Burden on Tobacco*, Vol. 24, 1989, p. 6 (cigarettes per capita), and for price per package and tax percentage—p. 83 (1970), p. 93 (1980); and U.S. Department of Commerce, *Statistical Abstract of the United States 1989* (Washington: U.S. Government Printing Office, 1989), p. 119 (smoking percentages).

past twenty years, but the absolute level of this tax is much higher than before because of the rapid increase in the price of cigarettes. As the final columns in Table 14-11 indicate, since the 1970s the percentage of the population smoking has been on the decline, and the percentage of former smokers has been on the rise.

Efforts by the Surgeon General to publicize the potential risks of secondhand smoke contributed to widespread restrictions on cigarette smoking throughout the country. These have included regulations limiting the smoking behavior on airline flights as well as a diverse set of local smoking standards, particularly for restaurants. Although the main effect of the antismoking efforts has been to accentuate an already declining smoking trend and to increase the prevalence of restrictions on smoking, the shift in the acceptability of this particular product risk has been dramatic.

Particularly surprising is the nature of the discussion of smoking by government economists.[49] In its extensive discussion of smoking, the 1987 *Economic Report of the President* did little to address any of the economics issues at stake. To what extent is there a market failure? Do individuals have knowledge of the risks that smoking may pose? How substantial are the costs of changing smoking, and what is the welfare loss from this "addiction" phenomenon? For all of these risks to individuals from their own decisions, do the discouraging effects of taxes eliminate any market failure? If current taxes do not eliminate the market failure, what level of taxes is needed? Finally, in the case of secondhand smoke, for which smoking restrictions do the benefits of regulation exceed the costs? Are we going to treat passive smoking risks as a trump card that dominates other concerns that might be present irrespective of their magnitude? What is most striking is not the fact that society has undertaken such initiatives, largely through the personal energy of the Surgeon General, but rather the fact that the oversight economists have offered virtually unqualified support of these efforts in the absence of any regulatory analysis.

Perhaps the main point that economists are making by highlighting these antismoking efforts is that risks are not always the responsibility of a corporation. Responsibility for risk taking must be shared by the individual as well. This theme pervaded much of the Reagan administration's efforts, and it provided a counterpoint to the view that controlling risk is simply a responsibility of government and industry. However, the government has not yet distinguished situations where it is appropriate to rely upon personal responsibility for making decisions and contexts in which we should interfere with this responsibility by establishing regulations to overrule these choices.

The Overall Record on New Regulations

The early 1980s were not a period of major activity in terms of new regulations, but this hiatus was short-lived. By the mid-1980s, the earlier pace of regulation had returned.

The chief new additions to the regulatory agenda marked a shift in the emphasis on taking advantage of individual safety-enhancing actions to promote safety. The OSHA hazard communication regulation and the increased emphasis on·mandatory seat belt usage were examples of this policy direction. The antismoking crusade also marked an emphasis on the role of individual risk behavior, as did the risk communication component of EPA's radon policy. The increases in states' penalties against drunken driving were in a similar vein. The 1970s era of risk regulation was characterized by an emphasis on engineering controls and technological solutions to safety, whereas the 1980s attempted to incorporate more recognition of individual actions.

The extent of new regulatory activity was not, however, great. The most prominent administrators of major risk-regulation agencies with a strong commitment to their agency's agenda were William Ruckelshaus and Lee Thomas. However, since these individuals succeeded Anne Gorsuch, their successful performance could do little more than reverse the damage that had already been done. Moreover, none of the appointees demonstrated a commitment to their agencies' objectives coupled with a sound economic agenda for regulatory reform.

14.7 STRATEGIES FOR REGULATORY ENFORCEMENT

In some contexts, regulatory enforcement is not a major concern. NHTSA can readily monitor whether firms are in compliance with automobile design standards, since cars are a mass-produced product. Even an agency with a very small staff such as the CPSC has little difficulty in ascertaining whether firms are in compliance with its narrowly prescribed standards, such as safety cap requirements.

In some cases, however, effective enforcement design and targeting is an integral part of ensuring an effective regulatory program. The early OSHA enforcement efforts were characterized by infrequent inspections and low levels of penalties for violations, thus providing little incentive for firms to invest in safety. In contrast, EPA targets major sources of air and water pollution with at least one inspection annually. Nevertheless, a GAO study in the early 1980s suggested that noncompliance rates for air and water pollution regulations might be as high as 80 percent.[50] Internal EPA studies indicate that enforcement for conventional pollutants is more effective than for unconventional pollutants. Enforcement problems for asbestos, toxic pollutants, and hazardous waste sites are much more difficult.

One widely espoused recommendation by economists is to replace the reliance on a fleet of inspectors by an injury tax or a pollution tax, such as a marketable pollution permit scheme. Environmentalists have never supported such market-oriented policies because they have the appearance of enabling firms to buy their way out of safety and environmental improvements. Industry has provided little support for such a penalty system, since creating effective incentives involves the imposition of nontrivial costs, thus increasing the stakes above the current regime.

Concern with effective enforcement presupposes, of course, that the agency's regulations are well designed. Unfortunately, standards for agencies such as OSHA and EPA are often excessively stringent. Lax enforcement is not necessarily the solution, since exempting firms from any safety or environmental requirements is also not the ideal. In many cases, however, there is an effort to strike an appropriate balance by establishing phased compliance schedules to accommodate the substantial economic costs that a firm may face. Because of the difficulties of adjusting for ill-designed regulations through diminished enforcement, I will use the effective enforcement reference point as the policy objective.

OSHA's Enforcement Efforts

Under the Carter administration, OSHA's emphasis was on increasing the degree to which inspections focused on consequential hazards. The number of inspections undertaken declined, but the emphasis on serious violations and the level of penalties increased. This strategy complemented the standards reform effort to eliminate the less consequential regulations. Unfortunately, OSHA's disappointing enforcement effort, which was documented in Chapters 11 and 12, was coupled with substantial opposition by firms subject to the regulations.

Thorne Auchter, Reagan's first head of OSHA, sought to decrease the confrontational role of OSHA by making inspections more of a consultative activity. This low-key inspection effort was coupled with a decrease in the inspection staff. To maintain any impact from inspections with a diminished number of full-scale inspections, one must increase their output.

The innovation Auchter made was to introduce what OSHA termed "records-check inspections."[51] Auchter introduced a new, more cursory type of inspection so that the total number of inspections rose, whereas the number of comprehensive inspections declined. Beginning in October 1981, OSHA inspectors at a firm examined the firm's lost workday accident rate for the past two years (or three years in the case of very small employers). Firms with injury rates below the national manufacturing average were exempted from inspections, and firms with injury rates in excess of the national average received a detailed inspection. This procedure established a mechanism for targeting inspections to enhance their productivity and contributed to Auchter's reputation as a "well-informed and effective manager."[52] By fiscal 1983, records-check inspections exceeded 10,000 per year, constituting more than one out of every six OSHA inspections.

One can view the records checks as being a mechanism for obtaining current information on firms' safety performance in a relatively low-cost manner, enabling OSHA to better target its efforts. One might, of course, modify the records-checks approach by making the inspection exemption threshold industry-specific.

The adoption of records-check inspections came under substantial fire by outside critics since the procedure completely exempted from an inspection firms that might violate OSHA standards.[53] Falsification of accident records to obtain the exemption also was a potential problem, but no studies have documented any change in injury-reporting practices.

If such inspections had been introduced as an additional component of the enforcement effort rather than as part of a general policy of reduced enforcement, it might have been better received. Since the total change in OSHA policies reflected a drop in the number of inspections coupled with a replacement of full-scale inspections by more cursory records-check inspections, the overall appearance was that of diminishing the enforcement effort.

The other component of OSHA's enforcement effort—penalties—had increased gradually under the Carter administration but were still at very low levels. To decrease OSHA's confrontational character, Auchter imposed a dramatic reduction in penalties and, in particular, required that any penalty in excess of $10,000 must be formally approved by the OSHA director. The chilling effect of this policy is reflected in an 80 percent reduction in the frequency of penalties above the $10,000 threshold.[54] Company appeals of inspection decisions also became viewed as a negative index of an inspector's job performance, as the emphasis was on negotiated solutions rather than confrontations.

The statistics in Table 14-12 indicate the character of these changes. The early years of the Reagan administration marked a decline in the number of inspections. The actual decline is even greater since a substantial portion of these inspections are records-check inspections. The average safety inspection time dropped from sixteen hours per inspection in 1980 to ten hours per inspection in 1983, and the average case hours per health inspection declined from forty-four hours per inspection in 1980 to thirty-three hours per inspection in 1983. The citations issued per hour of safety and health inspections increased, so that the productivity of these inspections per unit time rose over that period.

The dramatic shift in the financial incentives created by OSHA is indicated by the data in the final column of Table 14-12. The drop in penalties began in fiscal year 1981, for which the Carter and Reagan administrations overlapped. By fiscal year 1982, total OSHA penalties had dropped to $5.6 million, a figure that is far less than the $80 billion in wage compensation that workers received in that time period for job risks.[55]

Table 14-12. Summary of Federal OSHA
Inspection Activity

Fiscal year	Inspections (*thousands*)	Violations (*thousands*)	Proposed penalties (*$millions*)
1972	28.9	89.6	2.1
1973	47.6	153.2	4.2
1974	78.1	292.0	7.0
1975	80.9	318.8	8.2
1976	90.3	380.3	12.4
1977	59.9	181.9	11.6
1978	57.2	134.5	19.9
1979	57.9	128.5	23.0
1980	63.4	132.4	25.5
1981	57.0	111.4	10.8
1982	61.2	97.1	5.6
1983	68.9	111.7	6.4
1984	72.0	111.6	8.1
1985	71.3	119.7	9.2
1986	64.1	129.0	12.5
1987	61.5	137.0	24.5
1988	58.4	154.9	45.0

Source: OSHA computer printouts and data published in U.S. Department of Labor, Occupational Safety and Health Administration, *Report of the President to Congress on Occupational Safety and Health*, various years.

This period of deregulation subsequently gave way to a reversal in OSHA's emphasis. There was a resurgence in the penalty levels by 1987 and 1988, with considerably more penalties being levied in 1988 than in any year in OSHA's history. The extent of the change in enforcement stringency is borne out in the data presented in Table 14-13 on the number of OSHA penalties in excess of $1 million. Until 1986, OSHA had never penalized a firm by that great an amount based on a single set of citations. However, in the late 1980s, Secretary of Labor Brock introduced a severe penalty structure for egregious violations. A substantial and increasing number of such penalties were levied, ranging as high as the 1989 penalty of $7.3 million against USX. This single firm's penalty exceeded the total penalties levied for the entire country for 1982 or 1983. Moreover, the fines imposed by OSHA attracted widespread attention to the enforcement effort, altering the public's perception of its stringency.

The decade of the 1980s consequently was one of enforcement extremes. By most criteria the enforcement effort in the early 1980s was the most lax in OSHA history, whereas by the end of the decade OSHA had become more vigorous in its enforcement than ever before. The strategy of deregulation through regulatory neglect had been abandoned.

The EPA Enforcement Effort

The enforcement strategy at EPA bore some similarities to that at OSHA, with the principal exception being that Reagan's first appointee as head of EPA, Anne Gorsuch, was generally regarded as a poor manager.[56] Environmental critics charged that Anne Gorsuch had abandoned EPA's mission: "There is a massive regulatory resistance going on in this administration. . . . This administration is massively disobeying these laws because they don't like them. In this context, the only mechanism we have for enforcement is the courts."[57]

Anne Gorsuch had shifted substantial enforcement authority to the states, decreasing the federal technical support for the enforcement effort as well as the federal financing of it. Organizations such as the National Governors' Association expressed dismay at the shift in EPA policy: "The perception within the regulating community was that there would be no enforcement. . . . That made the states' job so much harder."[58]

For the politically prominent Superfund program, Gorsuch also erred by appointing personnel who had no apparent regulatory commitment or expertise.[59] Gorsuch was succeeded in March 1983 by William Ruckelshaus after Gorsuch's highly contentious and weak performance. Ruckelshaus had been the initial head of EPA in 1970, and his selection reflected the need to restore the credibility of the agency. The successor to Ruckelshaus, Lee Thomas, was a career administrator who continued the policies of Ruckelshaus. Bush's appointee, William Reilly, intensified the aggressiveness of EPA activity.

Table 14-14 provides a quantitative perspective on the enforcement effort by summarizing EPA's civil referrals to the U.S. Department of Justice—EPA's principal enforcement sanction. During the Gorsuch era, referrals to the Justice Department for violations of air and water regulation declined substantially, as did total

Table 14-13. Trends in Large OSHA
Penalty Levels

Year	Number of penalties above $1 million
1972–1985	0
1986	1
1987	4
1988	6
1989	9

Source: Based on data provided in the Occupational Safety
and Health Administration, U.S. Department of Labor,
"Penalties Proposed," internal OSHA computer printout,
July 16, 1990.

referrals. Perhaps most striking was the drop in referrals for hazardous-waste violations. Since these violations pertain to regulations that had been established only
recently and should have been the major growth area for new EPA initiatives, the
reversal in these referrals to less than half their level in 1980 is a substantial
departure. The hazards posed by toxins and pesticides, which would eventually
constitute an increasingly important part of the EPA's agenda of the 1980s, received
almost no attention whatsoever.

The data in Table 14-15 on administrative actions undertaken by EPA provide a

Table 14-14. EPA Civil Referrals to the Department of Justice

Fiscal year	Air	Water	Hazardous waste	Toxics, pesticides	Total
1972	0	1	0	0	1
1973	4	0	0	0	4
1974	3	0	0	0	3
1975	5	20	0	0	25
1976	15	67	0	0	82
1977	50	93	0	0	143
1978	123	137	2	0	262
1979	149	81	9	3	242
1980	100	56	53	1	210
1981	66	37	14	1	118
1982	36	45	29	2	112
1983	69	56	33	7	165
1984	82	95	60	14	251
1985	116	93	48	19	276
1986	115	119	84	24	342
1987	122	92	77	13	304
1988	86	123	143	20	372

Source: Based on Russell (1990), Table 7–6, using data from *Mealey's Litigation Reports:
Superfund*, Vol. 1, No. 18 (December 28, 1988), p. c-1.

Table 14-15. EPA Administrative Actions Initiated (by Act), Fiscal Years 1972 through 1988

	Clean Air Act (1970)	Clean Water and Safe Drinking Water Acts (1972/1974)	Resource Conservation and Recovery (1976)	Superfund (CERCLA) (1980)	FIFRA[a] (1947)	Toxic Substances Control Act (1976)	Totals
1972	0	0	0	0	860	0	860
1973	0	0	0	0	1,274	0	1,274
1974	0	0	0	0	1,387	0	1,387
1975	0	738	0	0	1,641	0	2,352
1976	210	915	0	0	2,488	0	3,613
1977	297	1,128	0	0	1,219	0	2,644
1978	129	730	0	0	762	1	1,622
1979	404	506	0	0	253	22	1,185
1980	86	569	0	0	176	70	901
1981	112	562	159	0	154	120	1,107
1982	21	329	237	0	176	101	864
1983	41	781	436	0	296	294	1,848
1984	141	1,644	554	137	272	376	3,124
1985	122	1,031	327	160	236	733	2,609
1986	143	990	235	139	338	781	2,626
1987	191	1,214	243	135	360	1,051	3,194
1988	224	1,345	309	224	376	607	3,085

[a]FIFRA = Federal Insecticide, Fungicide, and Rodenticide Act.
Source: Based on Russell (1990), Table 7–7, using data from *Mealey's Litigation Reports: Superfund*, Vol. 1, No. 18 (December 28, 1988) p. C-5.

similar perspective. The lowest number of administrative actions was in 1982, but by the late 1980s administrative enforcement actions had returned to the higher levels of the Carter administration.

The restoration of the enforcement effort in fiscal 1984 and 1985 marks the impact of the Ruckelshaus reforms on EPA's enforcement credibility. In a January speech at EPA, Ruckelshaus observed: "Unless they [the states] have a gorilla in the closet, they can't do the job. And the gorilla is EPA."[60]

The reality of the gorilla in the closet became reflected in the actions EPA undertook. Enforcement patterns for particular EPA programs often changed dramatically. Under the Superfund program established in 1980, EPA undertook no administrative actions whatsoever before the Ruckelshaus era. In fiscal year 1984, the number of administrative actions EPA initiated jumped to 137 per year, and it eventually climbed to 224 per year.[61]

The main contribution of the Gorsuch era at the EPA was to scale back the enforcement effort and slow down the implementation of the newly emerging programs for hazardous wastes and toxic substances. The contribution of the Ruckelshaus and Thomas era was twofold. First, they restored the enforcement capabilities of EPA to their levels at the start of the decade. Second, they fostered the development of enforcement efforts in the newly emerging areas of EPA's agenda.

14.8 THE IMPACT OF REGULATION ON HEALTH, SAFETY, AND ENVIRONMENTAL QUALITY

The ultimate objective of social regulation policies is to influence health, safety, and environmental outcomes. Assessing the impact of the regulatory activities of the 1980s is not straightforward. Some of the ultimate costs of these regulations have not been fully transmitted throughout the economy. This is particularly true for situations involving noncompliance, phased schedules for compliance to accommodate industries in economic hardship, and regulations promulgated in the 1980s but with increasingly stringent requirements being imposed over time. A second complicating factor is that regulation is not the only influence on safety and environmental outcomes. Safety risk levels of all kinds have been declining throughout the century.[62] As society has become wealthier, our preferences for safety are enhanced. Ideally, we would like to distinguish the effects of government regulation from the trends that otherwise would have taken place in the absence of regulation.

Table 14-16 provides a summary of several death risk trends. One can view 1970 as marking the beginning of the decade of safety and environmental regulation. All three sets of death rates in Table 14-16 have been in decline since the 1930s. The rate of decline for work accidents was somewhat greater in the 1980s than in previous decades, while the rate of decline in motor vehicle accidents is a bit higher than in the 1970s. The 1980s rate of decline in home accidents, which reflects the activities of the CPSC and the FDA, was almost identical to that in the 1970s. Overall, death rates continued to drop in the 1980s at roughly the same pace as in previous decades.

Job Risk Trends

Other job risk measures suggest somewhat different risk trends. Table 14-17 reports four different measures of workplace risk levels that capture injuries other than death risks. The bottom panel of Table 14-17 presents the percentage annual growth rates for these four different risk measures: the rates of decline for total injuries, lost workday injuries, nonfatal injuries without lost workdays, and the total rate of lost

Table 14-16. Principal Death Risk Trends

	Annual rate of increase in death rates		
	Work (*per 100,000 population*)	Home (*per 100,000 population*)	Motor vehicle (*per 100,000 population*)
1930–1940	−1.8	−0.2	−3.3
1940–1950	−2.3	−2.2	−4.0
1950–1960	−2.8	−2.1	−3.5
1960–1970	−1.2	−1.7	−0.8
1970–1980	−1.6	−2.7	−3.4
1980–1990	−3.2	−2.4	−4.3

Source: Calculations by the author using death-rate data from the National Safety Council (1988), pp. 14–15, 70–71.

Table 14-17. Occupational Injury and Illness Incidence Rates
per 100 Full-time Workers

| Year | Injuries and illnesses | | | |
	Total cases	Lost workday cases	Nonfatal cases without lost workdays	Lost workdays
1973	11.0	3.4	7.5	53.3
1974	10.4	3.5	6.9	54.6
1975	9.1	3.3	5.8	56.1
1976	9.2	3.5	5.7	60.5
1977	9.3	3.8	5.5	61.6
1978	9.4	4.1	5.3	63.5
1979	9.5	4.3	5.2	67.7
1980	8.7	4.0	4.7	65.2
1981	8.3	3.8	4.5	61.7
1982	7.7	3.5	4.2	58.7
1983	7.6	3.4	4.2	58.5
1984	8.0	3.7	4.3	63.4
1985	7.9	3.6	4.3	64.9
1986	7.9	3.6	4.3	65.8
1987	8.3	3.8	4.4	69.9
1988	8.6	4.0	4.6	76.1
Percentage annual rate of increase:				
1973–1980	−2.9	+2.3	−6.3	+2.9
1980–1990	−0.1	0.0	−0.3	+2.0

Note: Data for 1976–1988 exclude farms with fewer than eleven employees.

Source: Calculations by the author and data from the U.S. Bureau of Labor Statistics, "BLS Reports on Survey of Occupational Inuries and Illnesses in 1988," USDL-89-548, November 15, 1989, Table 6, and U.S. Bureau of Labor Statistics, *Occupational Injuries and Illness by Industry,* various years.

workdays. The patterns for these four measures indicate a slowing in the rate of decline or, in the case of total lost workdays, a lower rate of increase.

Since cyclical factors and other influences are at work, one needs a more detailed econometric analysis to isolate the independent influence of regulatory policy. The findings in Chapter 12 for 1973–1983 indicated that the effect of the previous year's OSHA inspections on injury rates in the current year ranges from a low value of 2.6 percent for total injury rates, to an intermediate value of 3.6 percent for lost workday case rates, and to a high value of 6.1 percent for the rate of total lost workdays. Moreover, there is no evidence of a drop-off in the impact of these inspections on injuries with the advent of the records check inspections. A more detailed examination of the performance of OSHA records check inspections by Ruser and Smith (1989) indicates that for plants potentially subject to the records check procedure that reported injury rates declined by 5 to 14 percent. There was, however, underreporting of job injuries during that period.[63] What we do not know is whether there was any change in the extent of underreporting. On balance, however, there is no evidence that the institution of records check inspections decreased the overall efficacy of the typical OSHA inspection.

Auto Safety Effects

Analysis of the impact of automobile safety regulation is also complicated by the role of competing influences that affect the safety trend, such as the character of highway construction and the age composition of the population. There is substantial controversy in the literature over the effect of automobile safety regulations on highway accident rates because of the possibly counterproductive effect of safety belt regulations on driver behavior.[64] Drivers wearing safety belts faced lower expected accident costs, and as a result will have a reduced incentive to exercise care.[65] The general consensus in the literature is that automobiles have become much safer for passengers, but there has been an apparent increase in the risk posed to pedestrians and bicyclists. The competing magnitudes of these effects has long been debated.

The performance of the other aspects of automobile regulation is mixed. Automobile emissions standards have lowered the pollution levels for new cars, but the penalty levels on the cars that fail to comply with the standards have led motorists to keep old, high-emission vehicles on the road.[66] Fuel-economy standards also are a binding constraint, but most economists would prefer market-based incentives, such as a gasoline tax, so that motorists can respond to the changing terms of trade rather than be constrained by specific fuel-economy standards on corporate fleets.

Pollution Trends

The net effect of automobile and other pollution regulations on environmental outcomes is summarized by the pollution trends in Table 14-18. The data in this table provide information on emissions, which are correlated with air quality but are not an exact measure of it. Moreover, the monitoring data involve substantial error, where the direction and magnitude of the error is unknown. Perhaps the most striking aspect of the table is that the wave of deregulation efforts and lax environmental enforcement that characterized the 1981–1982 period did not lead to a rapid deterioration of environmental quality. The improvements in environmental quality were at a slower pace than in earlier years, but there is no evidence of a worsening in air quality for the five different measures of pollution listed.

The first type of air pollution emission listed in Table 14-18 is that of particulates, which arise primarily from fuel combustion (e.g., coal combustion by railroads), forest fires, industrial processes, and highway motor vehicles. The rate of decline in particulate emissions in the 1980s was 2.6 percent annually. This rate is much less than during the 1970s, when tremendous progress was made against this class of emissions.

The second type of emissions, sulphur dioxide, arises from stationary fuel combustion and industrial processes. The principal contributor to this type of pollution is fuel combustion involving sulphur-bearing coal. After an increase in sulphur oxides in the 1960s, there was a decline in these emissions through both the 1970s and the 1980s at roughly comparable rates, primarily because of increased controls of emissions by nonferrous smelters and sulphuric acid plants.

Table 14-18. National Pollution Emissions Trends

Year	Particulates	Pollutant (*teragrams/year*)			
		Sulfur oxides	Nitrogen oxides	Carbon monoxide	Lead (*gigagrams*)
1960	21.6	19.7	13.0	89.7	NA
1970	18.5	28.3	18.5	101.4	203.8
1975	10.6	25.8	19.5	84.1	147.0
1980	8.5	23.4	20.9	79.6	70.6
1981	8.0	22.6	20.9	77.4	56.4
1982	7.1	21.4	20.0	72.4	54.4
1983	7.1	20.7	19.3	74.5	46.4
1984	7.4	21.5	19.8	71.8	40.1
1985	7.1	21.1	19.8	67.0	21.1
1986	6.8	20.9	19.0	63.1	8.6
1987	7.0	20.6	19.3	64.1	8.0
1988	6.9	20.7	19.8	61.2	7.6
Percentage annual growth rate:					
1960–1970	−1.5	+3.7	+3.6	+1.2	—
1970–1980	−7.5	−1.9	+1.2	−2.4	−10.1
1980–1988	−2.6	−1.5	−0.5	−3.2	−20.0

Source: U.S. Environmental Protection Agency, *National Air Pollutant Emission Estimate, 1940–1988*, Office of Air Quality, Research Triangle Park, N.C., EPA-450/4-90-001 (March 1990), p. 2.

The third class of emissions in Table 14-18, nitrogen oxides, arise from both highway motor vehicles as well as stationary sources, such as coal-fired electric utility boilers. After an increase in these emissions during the 1960s and 1970s, there was a slight decline in such emissions during the 1980s. Automobile emissions controls are among the policies that have contributed to this trend.

The fourth class of emissions included in Table 14-18 is that of carbon monoxide, for which highway motor vehicle emissions are the largest contributors. The rate of decline in carbon monoxide emissions increased in the 1980s.

Of the sets of statistics in Table 14-18, the lead statistics in the final column provide the strongest evidence of improvements in environmental quality. These gains can also be traced to specific regulatory policies. The primary sources of these lead emissions are motor vehicles and industrial processes. The impact of EPA's successive reductions in the allowable lead content of gasoline in 1985 and 1986 was dramatic. Lead emissions were cut almost in half between 1984 and 1985, and between 1985 and 1986 were reduced by more than half again. Within a two-year period, 80 percent of all lead emissions were eliminated. Moreover, based on the OMB review of the regulatory impact analysis, this environmental improvement also represents a situation in which the benefits to society of the improved environmental quality exceed the costs. This decrease in lead emissions is perhaps the major environmental success story of the 1980s.

For other EPA efforts that were central to the environmental policy in the 1980s, there are no comparable measures of environmental pollution levels, but there are some indices of policy achievements.

For the Superfund program established by legislation in 1980,[67] the 1980s marked a significant environmental cleanup effort. By 1989, EPA had identified over 30,000 Superfund sites and had inspected almost 10,000 of them. In over 12,000 cases, EPA concluded that no further action was warranted. In terms of actual cleanup activities, EPA had initiated removal actions in 1,347 cases, although it has completed only a small fraction of these removal efforts. These removal actions pertained to 274 of the 1,063 sites that EPA put on its national priority list. If one views this listing as being comprehensive, EPA had begun to address roughly one-fourth of its high-priority waste sites in the 1980s. The extent of the risk that was reduced and the extent that should have been reduced given the costs and benefits of cleanup are not known. Moreover, without any comparable efforts in the 1970s, there is no good reference point for assessing the pace of the cleanup.

14.9 THE REGULATORY RECORD OF THE 1980S

The 1980s record in terms of influencing the structure of safety and environmental policies is very mixed. The initial efforts of the Reagan administration emphasized deregulation and budgetary cutbacks rather than changes in the structure of regulation. This approach reflected an antiregulation approach rather than meaningful regulatory reform. This misplaced emphasis dissipated much of the political momentum for regulatory reform at the start of the Reagan administration. Because of the disappointing performance of prominent officials such as Reagan's first head of EPA, much of the 1980s was spent restoring the credibility of the agencies rather than making substantive advances. There were also some regulatory achievements —the phasedown of lead in gasoline, the introduction of the OSHA hazard communication policy proposed by Carter and enacted by Reagan, and expediting the approval of drugs for life-threatening diseases.

By the mid-1980s, the regulatory reform effort had ended. Vice-President Bush terminated his Task Force on Regulatory Relief. Regulatory agencies proposed regulations with greater costs than ever before. OMB became less influential in altering the structure of regulation, and regulatory enforcement became more vigorous than before the onset of deregulation.

The window of opportunity for regulatory reform was not great, and this opportunity had been squandered on a misguided deregulation agenda. There was no attempt whatsoever to address the fundamental long-term problems arising from agencies' restrictive legislative mandates. At a more modest level, there was not even a broad-based effort to adopt market-based approaches to controlling risk or to emphasize more performance-oriented regulations. By the mid-1980s regulatory policy returned to the same patterns as in earlier administrations, except that OMB appears to have had some limited influence in eliminating some of the most inefficient regulations.

In effect, there were two Reagan regulation agendas—the deregulation agenda that pertained from 1981 to 1983, and the return to the traditional regulatory agenda from 1984 to 1989. The Bush administration has continued the policies of the second Reagan agenda. In retrospect, the deregulation efforts will be viewed as a temporary policy aberration rather than as an effort with any lasting impact.

The extent to which this record should be viewed negatively depends in large part upon the reference point used for the assessment. Advocates of meaningful regulatory reform will be disappointed in this performance because of the foregone opportunity for fundamental change. The widespread consensus on the direction for reform reflected in the economics literature contrasts with the very mixed nature of the reform efforts. The impetus for meaningful regulatory reform and effective oversight appears to have been lost, as the task of undertaking the unfulfilled risk and environmental agenda of the 1980s had taken precedence.

NOTES

1. For a history of the development of these regulatory agencies, see the discussion in MacAvoy (1979) and Cornell, Noll, and Weingast (1976).

2. More specifically, Representative William Steiger predicted that injuries would be reduced by "50 percent or something like that." See his statement in the U.S. Congress, Committee on Education and Labor, Select Committee on Labor, *Occupational Safety and Health Act of 1970*, Oversight and Proposed Amendments, 1972, pp. 274–278.

3. For a description of the optimistic projections, see the discussion in Peltzman (1975).

4. Perhaps the most comprehensive statement of the general principles that should guide regulatory reform appears in the U.S. Office of Management and Budget (1988).

5. See Thaler and Rosen (1976), R. S. Smith (1976), and Viscusi (1979a).

6. In some instances, as in the case of EPA policy, the conservatism bias may be less scientifically based since there is an effort to ensure a "margin of safety" beyond the no-risk level. From an economic standpoint, the aversion of society to incurring risks should be reflected in the valuation of the payoffs rather than a misrepresentation of the probabilities that influence these payoffs. See Chapter 9 and Nichols and Zeckhauser (1986).

7. Lobbyists from the coal-producing areas likely to be most affected by a regulation permitting the choice of coal and focusing on the overall pollution level rather than on the means of attaining the pollution control exerted substantial influence in determining this policy. See Crandall (1983).

8. See, for example, the discussion in MacAvoy (1977) and Viscusi (1983).

9. For example, some economists such as Lave (1981) indicate a variety of decision criteria that can be applied other than simply benefit-cost analysis in its traditional form. However, even these modifications of the traditional benefit-cost framework provide for a greater degree of balancing than is achieved by the decisions of regulatory agencies.

10. EPA also introduced related efforts called netting and banking. The netting policy begun in 1976 enabled firms to achieve compliance even though one part of the plant was being modernized, thus avoiding the entire plant being held to the new source requirements. The banking policy enables firms to store their pollution rights if they are in compliance. See Crandall (1983), and for a recent discussion of such policies, Hahn and Noll (1990).

11. *Federal Register*, Vol. 44 (December 11, 1979), p. 71779.

12. Stockman's comments are based on his memorandum, "Avoiding a GOP Economic Dunkirk," December 1980, p. 15.

13. See the statement by Ronald Reagan in the U.S. Office of Management and Budget, *Regulatory Program of the United States Government*, April 1, 1988–March 31, 1989 (Washington: U.S. Government Printing Office, 1988), p. viii.

14. Executive Order 11821, November 24, 1974.

15. Executive Order 12044, March 24, 1978.

16. See Miller and Yandle (1979) for a selection of the regulatory analyses prepared by President Ford's oversight group.

17. Executive Order 12291, February 17, 1981.

18. See the U.S. Office of Management and Budget (1988), pp. 13–14.

19. This was undertaken under Executive Order 12498, January 4, 1985.

20. U.S. Office of Management and Budget (1988), p. 20.

21. For advocacy of this budget concept, see DeMuth (1980b) and Litan and Nordhaus (1983). In Viscusi (1983) I provide a detailed critique of the regulatory budget approach.

22. For review of these analyses, see the Office of Management and Budget (1988), especially pp. 16–17.

23. Statement by James C. Miller III, in "Deregulation HQ: An Interview on a New Executive Order with Murray L. Weidenbaum and James C. Miller III," *Regulation*, Vol. 5, No. 2 (1981) p. 19.

24. See Pete Earley, "What's a Life Worth?" *Washington Post Magazine*, June 9, 1985, p. 13.

25. Some of these statistics, drawn from Morrall (1986), were based on earlier estimates presented in Viscusi (1983).

26. See Thaler and Rosen (1976), R. S. Smith (1976), and Viscusi (1979a, 1983).

27. For a review of these calculations, see Viscusi (1983).

28. For a detailed recounting of the Carter administration experience, see Eads and Fix (1984), especially pp. 125–132.

29. One of the most expensive components is the high-altitude emissions standard that was adopted earlier as part of the Carter administration reforms but for which the estimated savings were $500 million as opposed to $1.3 billion. It should also be noted that the legitimacy of the "public" cost calculation and the "industry" cost calculation is questionable because of the complicated way in which costs affect prices. These calculations often assume, for example, that the safety measures are not valued by consumers but are simply a deadweight loss.

30. See Graham (1989), p. 145.

31. See Eads and Fix (1984), p. 132.

32. As Stockman (1986), p. 155 observed: "Lewis and the others had cooked up a theory that the auto industry had been so overregulated and crippled by air bags, pollution control devices, safety standards, and other government-imposed Ralph Naderite schemes that it was now up to the government to undo the damage. . . . This cover-up for protectionism really frosted me."

33. 29 C.F.R. § 1926.800 (1) (1985). Through this standards reform, OSHA attempted to bring its regulation into conformance with the National Electrical Code, which had undergone its last major revision in 1981—four years before the final OSHA standard was promulgated.

34. Presidential Task Force on Regulatory Relief, "Reagan Administration Regulatory Achievements," August 11, 1983, p. 68.

35. See the *Economic Report of the President*, February 1990 (Washington: U.S. Government Printing Office, 1990), pp. 193–197.

36. Office of Management and Budget (1988), p. 16.

37. Niskanen (1988) reports that David Stockman blocked the acid rain initiative developed by William Ruckelshaus.

38. These estimates are provided in Viscusi (1983), p. 143 (Table 8.2).

39. See Grabowski and Vernon (1983) for an extensive assessment of the FDA's drug-approval policies.

40. This comment was made to me by an FDA official in a training session on the use of economic analysis presented at the FDA in 1982.

41. See Stokinger (1984).

42. For the permissible exposure limits advocated by the ACGIH for which we have evidence on the benefit-cost tradeoffs, the cost per case of cancer prevented appears to be generally in the reasonable range. See Broder and Morrall (1983) and Mendeloff (1988).

43. A description of the activities and views of the oversight group is provided by the Office of Management and Budget, "OSHA's Proposed Standards for Grain Handling Facilities," 1984 (unpublished memorandum). Also see the letter from Christopher DeMuth, Administrator for Information and Regulatory Affairs, OMB, to the Solicitor of the U.S. Department of Labor, Francis X. Lilly.

44. *Ibid.* pp. 5–6.

45 See Viscusi (1983), pp. 143–144, for supporting data.

46 *Federal Register*, Vol. 49, No. 97 (May 17, 1984), pp. 20818ff.

47. For a review of the benefits and costs of seat belt use, see Arnould and Grabowski (1981).

48. Council of Economic Advisors (1987), p. 184.

49. *Ibid.* pp. 184–186.

50. See the discussion in Rochelle Stanfield, "Ruckelshaus Casts EPA as 'Gorilla' in States' Enforcement Closet," *National Journal*, May 26, 1984, p. 1034.

51. Assistant Secretary for Occupational Safety and Health, U.S. Department of Labor, *OSHA Revised Field Operations Manual* (1984), pp. II–III.

52. See Niskanen (1988), p. 130.

53. See Simon (1983).

54. See Simon (1983).

55. See Viscusi (1983).

56. See Niskanen (1988), p. 128.

57. This statement is by Jonathan Lash, senior staff attorney at the Natural Resources Defense Council, *National Journal*, December 19, 1981, p. 2233.

58. Statement by Edward A. Helme, Director of the National Governors' Association Natural Resources Group, Rochelle Stanfield, "Ruckelshaus Casts EPA as 'Gorilla' in States' Enforcement Closet," *National Journal*, May 26, 1984, p. 1035.

59. Rita Lavelle's management of the Superfund program attracted criticism for managerial incompetence and alleged sweetheart deals with industry.

60. *Ibid.* p. 1034.

61. Mealey's Litigation Report: *Superfund*, Vol. 1, No. 18, (December 28, 1988), p. C-5.

62. The only exception to this pattern is that of automobile fatalities, which are also in decline if one recognizes the changing age distribution and the change in the number of miles driven.

63. See Ruser and Smith (1989) for discussion of the underreporting problem.

64. The initial paper in this area is that of Peltzman (1975). For further discussion of these issues and the controversy over this line of research, see Blomquist (1988), Crandall et al. (1986), and Graham (1989).

65. To obtain a status report of this debate, see Crandall et al. (1986) for advocacy of the safety-enhancing viewpoint, and see Blomquist (1988) for the most recent perspective from the school of thought that places substantial weight on the counterproductive impacts of safety policies.

66. See Crandall et al. (1986).

67. The following statistics are based on the discussion in Acton (1989), particularly the material in Appendix A.

References

Acton, J. P. (1973). *Evaluating Public Programs to Save Lives: The Case of Heart Attacks*, Santa Monica: Rand Corporation.
—— (1976). "Measuring the Monetary Value of Lifesaving Programs," *Law and Contemporary Problems* 40(4): 46–72.
—— (1989). *Understanding Superfund*, Santa Monica: Rand Corporation Institute for Civil Justice.
Akerlof, G. (1970). "The Market for 'Lemons': Qualitative Uncertainty and the Market Mechanism," *Quarterly Journal of Economics* 84: 488–500.
Allais, M. (1953). "Le Comportement de l'Homme Rationnel Devant le Risque: Critique des Postulats et Axioms de l'Ecole Americane," *Econometrica* 21: 503–546.
Ames, B. N., Magaw, R., and Gold, L. S. (1987). "Ranking Possible Carcinogenic Hazards," *Science* 236: 271.
Arnould, R. and Grabowski, H. G. (1981). "Auto Safety Regulation: An Analysis of Market Failure," *Bell Journal of Economics* 12: 27–45.
Arnould, R. and Nichols, L. M. (1983). "Wage-Risk Premiums and Workers' Compensation: A Refinement of Estimates of Compensating Wage Differentials," *Journal of Political Economy* 91(2): 332–340.
Arrow, K. (1971). *Essays in the Theory of Risk-Bearing*, Chicago: Markham Publishing Co.
—— (1974). "Optimal Insurance and Generalized Deductibles," *Scandinavian Actuarial Journal* 1–42. Reprinted in *Collected Papers of Kenneth J. Arrow;* Vol. 3, *Individual Choice under Certainty and Uncertainty*, Cambridge: Harvard University Press (1984), 212–260.
—— (1982). "Risk Perception in Psychology and Economics," *Economic Inquiry* 20: 1–9. Reprinted in *Collected Papers of Kenneth J. Arrow;* Vol. 3, *Individual Choice under Certainty and Uncertainty*, Cambridge: Harvard University Press, (1984), 212–260.
Ashford, N. (1976). *Crisis in the Workplace: Occupational Disease and Injury*, Cambridge: MIT Press.
Atkinson, S. E. and Halvorsen, R. (1990). "The Valuation of Risks to Life: Evidence from the Market for Automobiles," *Review of Economics and Statistics* 72(1): 133–136.
Bacow, L. (1980). *Bargaining for Job Safety and Health*, Cambridge: MIT Press.
Bartel, A. and Thomas, L. G. (1985). "Direct and Indirect Effects of OSHA Regulation," *Journal of Law and Economics* 28: 1–26.
Baxter, R. and Allen, F. W. (1989). "Assessing Environmental Risks: The Public's Views Compared with Those of the Environmental Protection Agency," Annual Conference of the American Association for Public Opinion Research, *New York Times* May 22, 1989, B7.
Beck, G. J., et al. (1981). *Follow-up of Active and Retired Cotton Textile Workers*, Report prepared for Office of Assistant Secretary of Policy, Evaluation and Research, U.S. Department of Epidemiology and Public Health, Yale University.
Bell, D. (1982). "Regret in Decision Making under Uncertainty," *Operations Research* 30: 961–981.
Berger, M. C. et al. (1987). "Valuing Changes in Health Risks: A Comparison of Alternative Measures," *Southern Economic Journal* 53(4): 967–984.
Berkowitz, M. and Burton, J. (1987). *Permanent Disability Benefits in Workers' Compensation*, Kalamazoo: W. E. Upjohn Institute for Employment Research.
Berry, D. A. and Fristedt, B. (1985). *Bandit Problems: Sequential Allocation of Experiments*, London: Chapman and Hall.
Biddle, J. E. and Zarkin, G. (1988). "Worker Preferences and Market Compensation for Job Risk," *Review of Economics and Statistics* 70(4): 660–667.
Bird, L. (1989). *Drive*, New York: Doubleday.
Blomquist, G. (1979). "Value of Life Saving: Implications of Consumption Activity," *Journal of Political Economy* 96 (4): 675–700.
—— (1988). *The Regulation of Motor Vehicle and Traffic Safety*, Boston: Kluwer Academic Publishers.
Booth, W. (1988). "FDA Looks to Speed up Drug Approval Process," *Science* 241: 1426.

Bouhuys, A., et al., (1979). "Priorities in Prevention of Chronic Lung Diseases," *Lung* 156(2): 129–148.

Briys, E., Kahane, Y., and Kroll, Y. (1988). "Voluntary Insurance Coverage, Compulsory Insurance, and Risky-Riskless Portfolio Opportunities," *Journal of Risk and Insurance* 55: 713–722.

Broder, I. and J. F. Morrall, III (1984). "The Economic Basis for OSHA's and EPA's Generic Carcinogen Regulations," In R. J. Zeckhauser and D. Leebaert, eds., *What Does Government Do?* Durham, NC: Duke University Press.

Broome, J. (1978). "Trying to Value a Life," *Journal of Public Economics* 9:91–100.

Broussalian, V. K. (1976). "Risk Measurement and Safety Standards in Consumer Products," In N. Terleckyj, ed., *Household Production and Consumption*, NBER Studies in Income and Wealth no. 40, New York: Columbia University Press.

Brown, C. (1980). "Equalizing Differences in the Labor Market," *Quarterly Journal of Economics* 94(1): 113–134.

Butler, R. J. (1983). Wage and Injury Rate Responses to Shifting Levels of Workers' Compensation," In John D. Worrall, ed., *Safety and the Work Force*, Ithaca: Cornell University, ILR Press.

Butler, R.J. and Worrall, J. (1985). "Work Injury Compensation and the Duration of Nonwork Spells," *Economic Journal* 95: 714–724.

Centaur Associates (1979). *A Review and Analysis of the Effectiveness of Respirators*. Report prepared for the Occupational Safety and Health Administration.

——— (1983). *Technical and Economic Analysis of Regulating Exposure to Cotton Dust*, Vol. 1. Report prepared for the Occupational Safety and Health Administration.

——— (1984). *Preliminary Regulatory Impact Analysis of Alternative Respiratory Protection Standards*, Draft report prepared for the Occupational Safety and Health Administration.

Cheit, E. (1961). *Injury and Recovery in the Course of Employment*, New York: Wiley.

Cook, P. J. and Graham, D. A. (1977). "The Demand for Insurance and Protection: The Case of Irreplaceable Commodities," *Quarterly Journal of Economics* 91: 143–156.

Cooke, W. and Gautschi, F. (1981). "OSHA, Plant Safety Programs, and Injury Reduction," *Industrial Relations* 20: 245–257.

Cornell, N., Noll, R., and Weingast, B. (1976). "Safety Regulation," In H. Owen and C. Schultze, eds., *Setting National Priorities: The Next Ten Years*, Washington, Brookings Institution.

Council of Economic Advisors (1976). *Economic Report of the President*, Washington: U.S. Government Printing Office.

——— (1987). *Economic Report of the President*, Washington: U.S. Government Printing Office.

——— (1989). *Economic Report of the President*, Washington: U.S. Government Printing Office.

——— (1991). *Economic Report of the President, 1991*, Washington, U.S. Government Printing Office.

Cousineau, J., Lacroix, R., and Girard, A. (1988). "Occupational Hazard and Wage Compensating Differentials," University of Montreal Working Paper.

Crandall, R. W. (1983). *Controlling Industrial Pollution: The Economics and Politics of Clean Air*, Washington: Brookings Institution.

Crandall, R. W. and Graham, J. D. (1984). "Automobile Safety Regulation and Offsetting Behavior: Some New Empirical Estimates, *American Economics Review* 74: 328.

Crandall, R. W. et al. (1986) *Regulating the Automobile*, Washington: Brookings Institution.

Crandall, R. W. and Portney, P. (1984). "Environmental Policy," In P. Portney, ed., *Natural Resources and the Environment: The Reagan Approach*, Washington: Urban Institute 47–81.

Dardis, R. (1980). "The Value of Life: New Evidence from the Marketplace," *American Economic Review* 70(5): 1077–1082.

DeMuth, C. (1980a). "Constraining Regulatory Costs-Part I: The White House Review Programs," *Regulation* 4: 13–26.

——— (1980b). "The Regulatory Budget," *Regulation* 4: 29–43.

Dillingham, A. (1985). "The Influence of Risk Variable Definition on Value of Life Estimates," *Economic Inquiry* 24: 277–294.

Dorsey, S. and Walzer, N. (1983). "Workers' Compensation, Job Hazards, and Wages," *Industrial and Labor Relations Review* 36(4): 642–654.

Eads, G. and Fix, M. (1984). *Relief or Reform? Reagan's Regulatory Dilemma*, Washington: Urban Institute.

Egan, T. (1989). "Building Codes: Designs for Last Quake, Not Next," *New York Times*, October 22, 1989, p. A26.

Einhorn, H. and Hogarth, R. (1985). "Ambiguity and Uncertainty in Probabilistic Inference," *Psychological Review* 92: 433–461.

——— (1986). "Decision Making under Ambiguity," *Journal of Business* 59: S225-S250.

Eisner, R. and Strotz, R. H. (1961). "Flight Insurance and the Theory of Choice," *Journal of Political Economy* 69: 355–368.

Ellsberg, D. (1961). "Risk, Ambiguity, and the Savage Axioms," *Quarterly Journal of Economics* 75: 643–669.

Evans W. and Viscusi, W. K. (1991). "Estimation of State- Dependent Utility Functions Using Survey Data," *Review of Economics and Statistics*, 73: 94–104.

Fama, E. et al. (1969). "The Adjustment of Stock Prices to New Information," *International Economic Review* 10(1): 1–21.

Fischhoff, B. et al., (1981). *Acceptable Risk*, Cambridge: Cambridge University Press.

Fischhoff, B. and Beyth-Marom, R. (1983). "Hypothesis Evaluation from a Bayesian Perspective," *Psychological Review* 90: 239–260.

French, M. T. and Kendall, D. L. (1991). "The Value of Job Safety for Railroad Workers," Working Paper, Research Triangle Institute, forthcoming in *Journal of Risk and Uncertainty*, 5, in press.

Fuchs, V. (1974). *Who Shall Live? Health, Economics, and Social Choice*, New York: Basic Books.

Fuchs, V. and Zeckhauser, R. (1987). "Valuing Life—A Priceless Commodity," *American Economic Review Papers and Proceedings* 77(2): 263–268.

Gallup Organization (1989). *Air Travel Survey, 1989*, Produced for Air Transport Association of America (Princeton: Gallup Organization, 1989).

Garbacz, C. (1989). "Smoke Detector Effectiveness and the Value of Saving a Life," *Economics Letters* 31: 281–286.

Garen, J. (1988). "Compensating Wage Differentials and the Endogeneity of Job Riskiness," *The Review of Economics and Statistics* 70(1): 9–16.

Gerking, S., de Haan, M., and Schulze, W. (1988). "The Marginal Value of Job Safety: A Contingent Valuation Study," *Journal of Risk and Uncertainty* 1(2): 185–200.

Ghosh, D., Lees, D., and Seal, W. (1975). "Optimal Motorway Speed and Some Valuations of Time and Life," *Manchester School of Economic and Social Studies* 43: 134–143.

Grabowski, H. G. and Vernon, J. M. (1983). *The Regulation of Pharmaceuticals: Balancing the Benefits and Risks*, Washington: American Enterprise Institute.

Graham, J. D. (1989). *Auto Safety: Assessing America's Performance*, Dover: Auburn House Publishing.

Grether, D. (1980). "Bayes Rule as a Descriptive Model: The Representativeness Heuristic," *Quarterly Journal of Economics* 95: 537–557.

Griliches, Z. (1967). "Distributed Lags: A Survey," *Econometrica* 35(1): 16–49.

————, ed. (1971). *Price Indexes and Quality Change*, Cambridge: Harvard University Press.

Hahn, R. W. and Hester, G. L. (1989). "Where Did All the Markets Go?" *Yale Journal on Regulation* 6(1): 109–154.

Hahn, R. W. and Noll, R. (1990). "Environmental Markets in the Year 2000," *Journal of Risk and Uncertainty* 3(4): 351–360.

Hamermesh, D. S. and Wolfe, J. R. (1990). "Compensating Wage Differentials and the Duration of Wage Loss," *Journal of Labor Economics* 8(1): S175-S227.

Hammond, P. J. (1982). "Utilitarianism, uncertainty and information," In A. Sen and B. Williams, eds, *Utilitarianism and Beyond* Cambridge: Cambridge University Press, pp. 85–102.

Hartunian, N. S. (1981). *The Incidence and Economic Cost of Major Health Impairments: A Comparative Analysis of Cancer, Motor Vehicle Injuries, Coronary Heart Disease, and Stroke*. Lexington: Lexington Books.

Hausman, J. A. (1978). "Specification Tests in Econometrics," *Econometrica* 46: 1251–1271.

Hersch, J. and Viscusi, W. K. (1990). "Cigarette Smoking, Seatbelt Use, and Differences in Wage-Risk Tradeoffs," *Journal of Human Resources* 25: 202–227.

Herzog, H. W., Jr. and Schlottmann, A. M. (1987). "Valuing Risk in the Workplace: Market Price, Willingness to Pay, and the Optimal Provision of Safety." University of Tennessee Working Paper.

Hogarth, R. and Kunreuther, H. (1985). "Ambiguity and Insurance Decisions," *American Economic Review Papers and Proceedings* 75: 386–390.

Houthakker, H., Verleger, P. and Sheehan, D. (1974). "Dynamic Analysis for Gasoline and Residential Electricity Demand," *American Journal of Agricultural Economics* 59: 412–418.

Huber, P. (1983). "Exorcists vs. Gatekeepers in Risk Regulation," *Regulation* 7(6): 23–32.

Insurance Services Office (1977). *Product Liability Closed Claims Survey*, New York: Insurance Services Office.

Ippolito, P. M. and Ippolito, R. A. (1984). "Measuring the Value of Life Saving from Consumer Reactions to New Information," *Journal of Public Economics* 25: 53–81.

Iskrant, A. and Joliet, P. (1968). *Accidents and Homicide*, Cambridge: Harvard University Press.

Johnson, N. L. and Kotz, S. (1972). *Distributions in Statistics: Continuous Multivariate Distributions*, New York: Wiley.

Jones-Lee, M. W. (1976). *The Value of Life: An Economic Analysis*, Chicago: University of Chicago Press.

——— (1989). *The Economics of Safety and Physical Risk*, Oxford: Basil Blackwell.

Jury Verdict Research (1990) and (1991). *Current Award Trends in Personal Injury*. Solon, Ohio: Jury Verdict Research.

Kahneman, D., Slovic, P., and Tversky, A., eds., (1982). *Judgment under Uncertainty: Heuristics and Biases*, Cambridge: Cambridge University Press.

Kahneman, D. and Tversky, A. (1979). "Prospect Theory: An Analysis of Decision under Risk," *Econometrica* 47: 263–291.

——— (1982). "The Psychology of Preferences," *Scientific American* 246: 160–173.

Kakalik, J., et al. (1988). *Costs and Compensation Paid in Aviation Accident Litigation*, Rand Report R-3421-ICJ. Santa Monica: Rand Corporation.

Karni, E. (1985). *Decision Making under Uncertainty: The Case of State-Dependent Preferences*, Cambridge: Harvard University Press.

Keeney, R. L. and Raiffa, H. (1976). *Decisions with Multiple Objectives: Preferences and Value Trade-offs*. New York: Wiley.

Kerr, R. (1989). "1988 Ties for Warmest Year," *Science* 243 (4893): 891.

Kniesner, T. J. and Leeth, J. D. (1991). "Compensating Wage Differentials for Fatal Injury Risk in Australia, Japan, and the United States," *Journal of Risk and Uncertainty* 4(1): 75–90.

Krupnick, A. J. and Cropper, M. L. (1992). "The Effect of Information on Health Risk Valuations," *Journal of Risk and Uncertainty* 5(2): 29–40.

Kunreuther, H. et al. (1978). *Disaster Insurance Protection: Public Policy Lessons*, New York: Wiley.

Lave, L. B. (1981). *The Strategy of Social Regulation: Decision Frameworks for Policy*, Washington: Brookings Institution.

———, ed. (1982). *Quantitative Risk Assessment in Regulation*, Washington: Brookings Institution.

——— (1987). "Health and Safety Risk Analyses: Information for Better Decisions," *Science* 236: 291–295.

Leigh, J. P. (1987). "Gender, Firm Size, Industry and Estimates of the Value-of-Life," *Journal of Health Economics* 6: 255–273.

Leigh, J. P. and Folsom, R. N. (1984). "Estimates of the Value of Accident Avoidance at the Job Depend on Concavity of the Equalizing Differences Curve," *The Quarterly Review of Economics and Business* 24(1): 56–66.

Lichtenstein, S. et al., (1978). "Judged Frequency of Lethal Events," *Journal of Experimental Psychology* 4: 551–578.

Linneman, P. (1980). "The Effects of Consumer Safety Standards: The 1973 Mattress Flammability Standard," *Journal of Law and Economics* 23: 461–479.

Litan, R. E. and Nordhaus, W. D. (1983). *Reforming Federal Regulation*, New Haven: Yale University Press.

Luce, R. D. and Raiffa, H. (1957). *Games and Decisions*, New York: Wiley.

MacAvoy, P., ed., (1977). *OSHA Safety Regulation: Report of the Presidential Task Force*, Washington: American Enterprise Institute.

——— (1979). *The Regulated Industries and the Economy*, New York: Norton.

Machina, M. J. (1982). "Expected Utility Analysis without the Independence Axiom," *Econometrica* 50: 277–323.

——— (1987). "Perception of Risk," *Science*, 236: 537–543.

Magat, W. A., Viscusi, W. K., and Huber, J. (1991). "The Risk-Risk Metric for Valuing Chronic Health Risks: Application of the Contingent Valuation Method to Cancer and Nerve Disease," Report to U.S. EPA.

Marin, A. and Psacharopoulos, G. (1982). "The Reward for Risk in the Labor Market: Evidence from the United Kingdom and a Reconciliation with Other Studies," *Journal of Political Economy* 90(4): 827–853.

McCaffrey, D. (1983). "An Assessment of OSHA's Recent Effects on Injury Rates," *Journal of Human Resources* 18: 131–146.

Mendeloff, J. M. (1979). *Regulating Safety: An Economic and Political Analysis of Occupational Safety and Health Policy*, Cambridge: MIT Press.

——— (1988). *The Dilemma of Toxic Substance Regulation*, Cambridge: MIT Press.

Merchant, J., *et al.* (1973a). "An Industrial Study of the Biological Effects of Cotton Dust and Cigarette Smoke Exposure," *Journal of Occupational Medicine* 15(3): 212–221.

—— (1973b). "Dose-Response Studies on Cotton Textile Workers," *Journal of Occupational Medicine* 15(3).

Meyer, B., Viscusi, W. K. and Durbin, D. L. (1990). "Workers' Compensation and Injury Duration: Evidence from a Natural Experiment," National Bureau of Economic Research, Working Paper no. 3494.

Miller, J. C. and Yandle, B. (1979). *Benefit-Cost Analyses of Social Regulation*, Washington: American Enterprise Institute.

Miller, T. (1990). "The Plausible Range for the Value of Life: Red Herrings among the Mackerel," *Journal of Forensic Economics* 3(3): 17–39.

Miller, T. and Guria, J. (1991). "The Value of Statistical Life in New Zealand," Report to the New Zealand Ministry of Transport, Land Transport Division.

Mishan, E. J. (1971). "Evaluation of Life and Limb: A Theoretical Approach," *Journal of Political Economy* 79: 687–705.

Moore, M. J. and Viscusi, W. K., (1988a). "Doubling the Estimated Value of Life: Results Using New Occupational Fatality Data," *Journal of Policy Analysis and Management* 7(3): 476–490.

—— (1988b). "The Quantity-Adjusted Value of Life," *Economic Inquiry* 26(3): 369–388.

—— (1989). "Promoting Safety through Workers' Compensation," *Rand Journal of Economics*, 20(4): 499–515.

—— (1990a). *Compensating Mechanisms for Job Risks: Wages, Workers' Compensation, and Product Liability*, Princeton: Princeton University Press.

—— (1990b). "Discounting Environmental Health Risks: New Evidence and Policy Implications," *Journal of Environmental Economics and Management*, 18(2), pt. 2: S51-S62.

—— (1990c). "Models for Estimating Discount Rates for Long-Term Health Risks Using Labor Market Data," *Journal of Risk and Uncertainty*, 3(4): 381–402.

Morrall, J. F., III (1981a). "Cotton Dust: An Economist's View." In R. Crandall and L. Lave, eds., *The Strategic Basis of Health and Safety Regulation*, Washington: Brookings Institution, 93–108.

—— (1981b). "OSHA After a Decade," paper presented at American Enterprise Institute Conference.(1986).

—— (1986). "A Review of the Record," *Regulation*, 10(2): 13–24, 30–34.

National Center for Health Statistics, "Estimates of Selected Comparability Ratios Based on Dual Coding of 1976 Death Certificates by the Eighth and Ninth Revisions of the International Classification of Diseases," *Monthly Vital Statistics Reports* 28 (1980).

National Research Council Committee on Byssinosis (1982). *Byssinosis: Clinical and Research Issues*, Washington: National Academy of Sciences.

National Safety Council (1982). *Accident Facts*, Chicago: National Safety Council.

—— (1985). *Accident Facts*, Chicago: National Safety Council.

—— (1988). *Accident Facts*, Chicago: National Safety Council.

—— (1989). *Accident Facts*, Chicago: National Safety Council.

—— (1990). *Accident Facts*, Chicago: National Safety Council.

Nelson, J. P. and Neumann, G. (1975). "Labor Productivity and the Coal Mine Health and Safety Act of 1969," Working paper, Pennsylvania State University.

Nichols, A. and Zeckhauser, R. J. (1981). "OSHA after A Decade: A Time for Reason," In L. W. Weiss and M. W. Klass, eds., *Case Studies in Regulation: Revolution and Reform*, Boston: Little, Brown.

—— (1986). "The Perils of Prudence: How Conservative Risk Assessments Distort Regulation," *Regulation* 10(2): 13–24.

Niskanen, W. A. (1988). *Reaganomics: An Insider's Account of the Policies and the People*, New York: Oxford University Press.

O'Hare, M., Bacow, L., and Sanderson, D. (1983). *Facility Siting and Public Opposition*, New York: Van Nostrand Reinhold.

Oi, W. (1973). "An Essay on Workmen's Compensation and Industrial Safety," In *Supplemental Studies for the National Commission on State Workmen's Compensation Laws*, Washington: U.S. Government Printing Office, 41–106.

—— (1974). "On the Economics of Industrial Safety," *Law and Contemporary Problems*, 38(4): 538–555.

—— (1975). "On Evaluating the Effectiveness of the OSHA Inspections Program," Working paper, University of Rochester.

Olson, C. A. (1981). "An Analysis of Wage Differentials Received by Workers on Dangerous Jobs," *Journal of Human Resources* 16: 167–185.

Peltzman, S. (1975). "The Effects of Automobile Safety Regulation," *Journal of Political Economy* 83(4): 677–725.

Portney, P. R. (1981). "Housing Prices, Health Effects, and Valuing Reductions in Risk of Death," *Journal of Environmental Economics and Management* 8: 72–78.

———, ed. (1990). *Public Policies for Environmental Protection*, Washington: Resources for the Future.

Pratt, J., Raiffa, H., and Schlaifer, R. (1965). *Introduction to Statistical Decision Theory*, New York: McGraw-Hill.

Raiffa, H. (1961). "Risk, Ambiguity, and the Savage Axioms, Comment," *Quarterly Journal of Economics* 75: 690–694.

———, (1968). *Decision Analysis: Introductory Lectures on Choices under Uncertainty*, Reading: Addison-Wesley.

Research Triangle Institute (1976). *Cotton Dust: Technological Feasibility Assessment and Final Inflationary Impact Statement*, pt. 1. Report prepared for the Occupational Safety and Health Administration.

Rice, D. P. and Cooper, B. S. (1967). "The Economic Value of Human Life," *American Journal of Public Health*, 57: 1954–1966.

Roberts, L. (1988). "Is There Life after Climate Change?" *Science* 242(4881): 1010–1012.

——— (1989a). "A Corrosive Fight Over California's Toxics Law," *Science*, 243(4889): 306–309.

——— (1989b). "Ecologists Wary About Environmental Releases," *Science* 243(4895): 1134–1141.

——— (1989c). "Is Risk Assessment Conservative?" *Science* 243(4898): 1553.

Rosen, S. (1986). "The Theory of Equalizing Differences," In O. Ashenfelter and R. Layard, eds., *Handbook of Labor Economics*. Amsterdam: North-Holland, 641–692.

——— (1988). "The Value of Changes in Life Expectancy," *Journal of Risk and Uncertainty* 1(3): 285–304.

Ruser, J. W. and Smith, R. S. (1988). "The Effect of OSHA Records-Check Inspections on Reported Occupational Injuries in Manufacturing Establishments," *Journal of Risk and Uncertainty* 1(4): 415–435.

Russell, C. (1990). "Monitoring and Enforcement," In P. Portney, ed., *Public Policies for Environmental Protection*, Washington: Resources for the Future, 243–274.

Samuelson, W. and Zeckhauser, R.J. (1988). "Status Quo Bias in Decision Making," *Journal of Risk and Uncertainty* 1(1): 7–60.

Savage, L. J. (1972). *"The Foundations of Statistics*, 2nd rev. ed., New York: Dover Publications.

Schelling, T. (1968). "The Life You Save May Be Your Own," In S. Chase, ed., *Problems in Public Expenditure Analysis*, Washington: Brookings Institution, 127–162.

——— (1984a). *Choice and Consequence*, Cambridge: Harvard University Press.

——— (1984b). *Micromotives and Macrobehavior*, New York: Norton.

Schilling, R. S. F., et al. (1963). "A Report on a Conference on Byssinosis," In *Fifteenth International Congress of Occupational Health*, International Congress Series No. 62 2: 137–145.

Schneider, S. H. (1989). "The Greenhouse Effect: Science and Policy," *Science* 243(4892): 771–781.

Scholz, J. T. and Gray, W. B. (1990). "OSHA Enforcement and Workplace Injuries: A Behavioral Approach to Risk Assessment," *Journal of Risk and Uncertainty* 3(3): 283–305.

Schultze, C. L. (1982). "The Role and Responsibility of the Economist in Government," *American Economic Review* 72: 62–66.

Schwartz, A. (1988). "Proposals for Product Liability Reform: A Theoretical Synthesis," *Yale Law Journal* 97: 357–419.

———, (1989). "Views of Addiction and the Duty to Warn," *Virginia Law Review* 75: 509–560.

Shavell, S. M. (1987). *Economic Analysis of Accident Law*, Cambridge: Harvard University Press.

Simon, P. (1983). *Reagan in the Workplace: Unraveling the Health and Safety Net*, Washington: Center for Study of Responsive Law.

Slovic, P. (1987). "Perception of Risk," *Science* 236: 280–285.

Slovic, P., Fischhoff, B., and Lichtenstein, S. (1982). "Facts versus Fears: Understanding Perceived Risk," In D. Kahneman, P. Slovic, and A. Tversky, eds., *Judgment under Uncertainty: Heuristics and Biases*, Cambridge: Cambridge University Press, 462–492.

Smith, A. (1937). *The Wealth of Nations*, New York: Modern Library.

Smith, R. S. (1974). "The Feasibility of an 'Injury Tax' Approach to Occupational Safety," *Law and Contemporary Problems* 38(4): 730–744.

——— (1976). *The Occupational Safety and Health Act: Its Goals and Achievements*, Washington: American Enterprise Institute.

——— (1979a). "Compensating Differentials and Public Policy: A Review," *Industrial and Labor Relations Review* 32: 339–352.

——— (1979b). "The Impact of OSHA Inspections on Manufacturing Injury Rates," *Journal of Human Resources* 14: 145–170.

——— (1990). "Mostly on Monday: Is Workers' Compensation Covering Off-the-Job Injuries?" In D. Appel and P. Borba, eds., *Workers' Compensation Insurance Pricing*, Dordrecht: Kluwer Academic Publishers.

Smith, V. K. (1983). "The Role of Site and Job Characteristics in Hedonic Wage Models," *Journal of Urban Economics* 13: 296–321.

Smith, V. K. and Gilbert, C. (1984). "The Implicit Risks to Life: A Comparative Analysis," *Economics Letters*, 16: 393–399.

Spence, A. M. (1977). "Consumer Misperceptions, Product Failure, and Producer Liability," *Review of Economic Studies*, 44: 561–572.

Spencer, D. and Berk, K. (1981). "A Limited Information Specification Test," *Econometrica* 49: 1079–1085.

Stigler, G. J. (1975). *The Citizen and the State: Essays on Regulation*, Chicago: University of Chicago Press.

Stockman, D. A. (1986). *The Triumph of Politics: How the Reagan Revolution Failed*, New York: Harper & Row.

Stokey, E. and Zeckhauser, R. J. (1978). *A Primer for Policy Analysis*, New York: Norton.

Stokinger, H. (1984). "Modus Operandi of Threshold Limits Committee of ACGIH," *Annual American Conference of Individual Hygiene* 9: 133.

Thaler, R. and Rosen, S. (1976). "The Value of Saving a Life: Evidence from the Labor Market," In N. Terleckyz, ed., *Household Production and Consumption*, New York: Columbia University Press, 265–298.

Tietenberg, T. H. (1986). "Uncommon Sense: The Program to Reform Pollution Control Policy," In L. W. Weiss and M. K. Klass, eds., *Regulatory Reform: What Actually Happened*, Boston: Little, Brown, 269–303.

Torrance, G. W. (1986). "Measurement of Health State Utilities for Economic Analysis: A Review," *Journal of Health Economics* 5: 1–30.

Tversky, A. and Kahneman, D. (1974). "Judgement under Uncertainty: Heuristics and Biases," *Science* 185: 1124–31.

——— (1981). "The Framing of Decisions and the Psychology of Choice," *Science* 211: 453.

——— (1986). "Rational Choice and the Framing of Decisions," *Journal of Business* 59: S251-S278.

University of Michigan Institute for Social Research (1975). *Survey of Working Conditions*, SRC Study no. 45369, Ann Arbor: University of Michigan, Social Science Archives.

U.S. Bureau of the Census (1973). *Industrial Characteristics*, Subject Report PC(2)-7B, Washington: U.S. Government Printing Office.

U.S. Department of Commerce (1974). *County Business Patterns*, Washington: U.S. Government Printing Office.

——— (1984). *Statistical Abstract of the United States, 1982–1983*, Washington: U.S. Government Printing Office.

U.S. Department of Justice (1986). *Tort Policy Working Group Report*, Washington: U.S. Government Printing Office.

U.S. Department of Labor, Office of the Assistant Secretary for Policy Evaluation and Research (1971a). *Compendium on Workmen's Compensation*, Washington: U.S. Government Printing Office.

——— (1971b). "*Injury Rates by Industry*," BLS Report No. 389, Washington: U.S. Government Printing Office.

——— (1982). *Compliance with Standards, Abatement of Violations, and Effectiveness of OSHA Safety Inspections*. Technical Analysis Paper no. 62, Washington: U.S. Government Printing Office.

——— (various years). *Employment and Earnings*, Washington: U.S. Government Printing Office.

——— (various years). *The President's Report on Occupational Safety and Health*. Washington: U.S. Government Printing Office.

U.S. Environmental Protection Agency, Office of Air Quality, (1990). *National Air Pollutant Emission Estimates, 1940–1988*, Washington: EPA-450/4–90–001.

U.S. Office of Management and Budget (1988). *Regulatory Program of the United States Government, April 1, 1988-March 21, 1989* Washington: U.S. Government Printing Office.

——— (1990) *Regulatory Program of the United States Government, April 1, 1990 − March 31, 1991* Washington: U.S. Government Printing Office.

Viscusi, W. K. (1978a). "Labor Market Valuations of Life and Limb: Empirical Estimates and Policy Implications," *Public Policy* 26(3): 359–386.

——— (1978b). "Wealth Effects and Earnings Premiums for Job Hazards," *Review of Economics and Statistics* 60(3): 408–416.

———— (1979a). *Employment Hazards: An Investigation of Market Performance*, Cambridge: Harvard University Press.

———— (1979b). "Job Hazards and Worker Quit Rates: An Analysis of Adaptive Worker Behavior," *International Economic Review* 20(1): 29–58.

———— (1979c). "The Impact of Occupational Safety and Health Regulation," *Bell Journal of Economics* 10(1): 117–140.

———— (1980). "Imperfect Job Risk Information and Optimal Workmen's Compensation Benefits," *Journal of Public Economics* 14(3): 319–337.

———— (1981). "Occupational Safety and Health Regulation: Its Impact and Policy Alternatives," In J. Crecine, ed., *Research in Public Policy Analysis and Management*, vol. 2, Greenwich, Conn.: JAI Press, pp. 281–299.

———— (1983). *Risk by Choice: Regulating Health and Safety in the Workplace*, Cambridge: Harvard University Press.

———— (1984a). *Regulating Consumer Product Safety*, Washington: American Enterprise Institute.

———— (1984b). "Structuring an Effective Occupational Disease Policy: Victim Compensation and Risk Regulation," *Yale Journal on Regulation* 2(1): 53–81.

———— (1984c). "The Lulling Effect: The Impact of Child-Resistant Packaging on Aspirin and Analgesic Ingestions," *American Economic Review* 74: 324–327.

———— (1985a). "A Bayesian Perspective on Biases in Risk Perception," *Economic Letters* 17: 59–62.

———— (1985b). "Are Individuals Bayesian Decision Makers?" *American Economic Review* 75(2): 381–385.

———— (1985c). "Consumer Behavior and the Safety Effects of Product Safety Regulation," *Journal of Law and Economics* 28(2): 527–554.

———— (1985d). "Cotton Dust Regulation: An OSHA Success Story?" *Journal of Policy Analysis and Management* 4(3): 325–343.

———— (1986a). "Reforming OSHA Regulation of Workplace Risks," In L. Weiss and M. Klass, eds., *Regulatory Reform: What Actually Happened*, Boston: Little, Brown, 234–268.

———— (1986b). "The Impact of Occupational Safety and Health Regulation, 1973–1983," *Rand Journal of Economics* 17(4): 567–580.

———— (1986c). "The Structure and Enforcement of Job Safety Regulation," *Law and Contemporary Problems* 47(1): 601–624.

———— (1986d). "The Valuation of Risks to Life and Health: Guidelines for Policy Analysis," In Proceedings of 1984 NSF Conference, J. Bentkover, V. Covello, and J. Mumpower, eds., *Benefits Assessment: The State of the Art* Dordrecht, Holland: Reidel Publishers, 193–210.

———— (1988). "Pain and Suffering in Product Liability Cases: Systematic Compensation or Capricious Awards," *International Review of Law and Economics* 8: 203–220.

———— (1989). "Prospective Reference Theory: Toward an Explanation of the Paradoxes," *Journal of Risk and Uncertainty* 2(3): 235–264.

———— (1990). "Sources of Inconsistency in Societal Responses to Health Risks," *American Economic Review* 80(2): 257–261.

Viscusi, W. K. and Evans, W. (1990). "Utility Functions that Depend on Health Status: Estimates and Economic Implications," *American Economic Review*, 80(2): 353–374.

Viscusi, W. K., Magat, W. A. and Forrest, A. (1987). "Altruistic Consumer Valuations of Multiple Health Risks," *Journal of Policy Analysis and Management* 7(2): 227–245.

Viscusi, W. K. and Magat, W. A. (1987). *Learning about Risk: Consumer and Worker Responses to Hazard Warnings*, Cambridge: Harvard University Press.

Viscusi, W. K., Magat, W. A., and Huber, J. (1987). "An Investigation of the Rationality of Consumer Valuations of Multiple Health Risks," *Rand Journal of Economics* 18(4): 465–479.

———— (1991a). "Communication of Ambiguous Risk Information," *Theory and Decision* 31: 159–173.

———— (1991b). "Pricing Environmental Health Risks: Survey Assessments of Risk-Risk and Risk-Dollar Tradeoffs," *Journal of Environmental Economics and Management* 201: 32–57.

Viscusi, W. K. and Moore, M. J. (1987). "Workers' Compensation: Wage Effects, Benefit Inadequacies, and the Value of Health Losses," *Review of Economics and Statistics* 69: 249–261.

———— (1989). "Rates of Time Preference and Valuations of the Duration of Life," *Journal of Public Economics* 38: 297–317.

Viscusi, W. K. and O'Connor, C. (1984). "Adaptive Responses to Chemical Labeling: Are Workers Bayesian Decision Makers?" *American Economic Review* 74(5): 942–956.

Viscusi, W. K. and Zeckhauser, R. J. (1979). "Optimal Standards with Incomplete Enforcement," *Public Policy* 26(4): 437–456.

von Neumann, J. and Morgenstern, O. (1953). *Theory of Games and Economic Behavior*, 3rd ed., New York: Wiley.

Warren, M. and Chilton, K. (1990). "Regulation's Rebound: Bush Budget Gives Regulation a Boost," Center for Study of American Business, OP81.

Weidenbaum, M. L. (1980). "Reforming Government Regulation," *Regulation* 4(6): 15–18.

Weiler, P. (1986). "Legal Policy for Workplace Injuries," American Law Institute Working paper.

——— (1989). "Pain and Suffering Damages," Harvard University Law School, Report to the American Law Institute.

Weinstein, M., Shepard, D., and Pliskin, J. (1976). "The Economic Value of Changing Mortality Probabilities: A Decision Theoretic Approach." Discussion paper no. 46D, Public Policy Program, Kennedy School of Government.

White, L. J. (1982). *The Regulation of Air Pollutant Emissions from Motor Vehicles*, Washington: American Enterprise Institute.

Wildavsky, A. (1988). *Searching for Safety*, New Brunswick: Transaction Publishers.

Wilson, R. and Crouch, E. A. C. (1987). "Risk Assessment and Comparisons: An Introduction," *Science* 236: 267–270.

Zeckhauser, R. J. (1970). "Medical Insurance: A Case Study of the Tradeoff between Risk Spreading and Appropriate Incentives," *Journal of Economic Theory* 2: 10–26.

——— (1973). "Coverage for Catastrophic Illness," *Public Policy* 21: 149–172.

——— (1975). "Procedures for Valuing Lives," *Public Policy* 23(4): 419–464.

——— (1986). "Behavioral versus Rational Economics: What You See Is What You Conquer," *Journal of Business* 59: S435-S449.

Zeckhauser, R. J. and Nichols, A. (1979). "The Occupational Safety and Health Administration: Its Goals and Achievements" In *The Study of Federal Regulation of the Senate Committee on Governmental Operations*, 95th Congress, First Session. Washington: U.S. Government Printing Office, 163–248.

Zeckhauser, R. J. and Shepard, D. (1976). "Where Now for Saving Lives?" *Law and Contemporary Problems* 39: 5–45.

Zeckhauser, R. J. and Viscusi, W. K. (1990). "Risk Within Reason," *Science* 248(4955): 559–564.

Index

Printed in the United States
70772LV00006B/2